THE AUTOCRITIQUE OF ENLIGHTENMENT

THE AUTOCRITIQUE
OF ENLIGHTENMENT

Rousseau and the Philosophes

Mark Hulliung

HARVARD UNIVERSITY PRESS

Cambridge, Massachusetts
London, England
1994

Library of Congress Cataloging-in-Publication Data

Hulliung, Mark.
The autocritique of Enlightenment : Rousseau and the philosophes /
Mark Hulliung.
p.   cm.
Includes bibliographical references and index.
ISBN 0-674-05425-3
1. Rousseau, Jean-Jacques, 1712–1778.   2. Enlightenment—France.
3. Philosophy, French—18th century.   I. Title.
B2137.H85   1994
194—dc20   94-1857
                                                       CIP

To the memory of Judith N. Shklar

Contents

Preface

THE TIME has come, I believe, for us to move a step beyond current interpretations of the Enlightenment. Much of the richness and complexity of the Enlightenment, its moments of self-doubt and its boldest experiments in self-criticism, are lost when Rousseau is removed from his milieu by calling him a preromantic or a pre-Kantian; or, again, when *Rameau's Nephew* is interpreted, in Hegel's manner, as a portent of the impending breakdown of the old aristocratic order, instead of being read as a revelation of Diderot's doubts whether the philosophes would ever become the self-sustaining, independent agents of Enlightenment they professed to be.

It is one of the peculiarities of recent scholarship that it is so willing to see the seeds of radicalism in the low French Enlightenment, the hack writers of Grub Street; so unwilling to detect the growth of republican thought in the high Enlightenment, the writings of the philosophes. I hope to do something to restore the balance in this study. If along the way I manage to show that there is more to such figures as Holbach and Helvétius than one would think to read the secondary literature, so much the better.

Primarily, however, my concern shall be to demonstrate that the Enlightenment gains enormously in depth and creative intellectual tension when Rousseau is readmitted to his cultural habitat, the world of the encyclopedists. Had the philosophes labored as diligently to answer Rousseau as they did to discredit his person, there is no limit to what the Enlightenment might have accomplished.

∽

O v e r the years I have accumulated a number of debts to other scholars. I hope they will forgive me for relegating them to the notes, provided my purpose in doing so is to underscore my gratitude to a single person, Judith N. Shklar. Her formidable intellect, vibrant and challenging personality, openness of mind, disdain for fads, contempt for ideologues, and unshakable integrity made her a model worthy of admiration. We are all the poorer for her premature death, at the height of her powers, during a period of her life when she was producing her routinely brilliant studies at an ever more feverish pace.

For her the Enlightenment was "home," because she shared both the skepticism and the faith of d'Alembert, Rousseau, and Montesquieu. Saddened by her death but comforted to realize that I was once in the presence of greatness, I dedicate this book to Dita.

Cast of Supporting Characters

There may be potential readers unfamiliar with the lesser philosophes, yet keenly interested in Rousseau, Diderot, and critiques of the Enlightenment. Brief comments about a few of the less well known figures of the philosophical party may be helpful to such readers.

Jean Le Rond d'Alembert *(1717–1783)*

Outstanding mathematician, able and successful man of letters, d'Alembert was dedicated to the cause of "philosophy" and attentive to the conditions necessary to secure the independence of its spokespersons. He shared editorial responsibilities for the *Encyclopédie* with Diderot until the grave political troubles of the late 1750s, when, at the urging of his mentor, Voltaire, he decided that discretion was the better part of valor. After that, d'Alembert concentrated his efforts on stacking the academies with philosophes. As a member of the Academy of Sciences since 1741 and of the French Academy since 1754, where he would eventually serve as perpetual secretary, d'Alembert was ideally situated to win the academies for his *parti pris.*

Georges Louis Leclerc, comte de Buffon *(1707–1788)*

Buffon's ongoing *Natural History* was one of the most widely read works of the century. Some of Rousseau's most audacious thoughts in the *Discourse on Inequality* are adapted from an unwilling Buffon. In *Émile* Rousseau again made use of the *Natural History.*

Étienne Bonnot, abbé de Condillac *(1714–1780)*

The most proficient of the philosophes in formal philosophical inquiry, Condillac devoted his life to spelling out the full consequences of Locke's epistemology and psychology. Not only are there no innate ideas; neither are there innate mental faculties, insisted Condillac, who backed up his claim with a bold effort to derive all the faculties from sense experience. Some of the philosophes—Grimm most belligerently—rejected Condillac's writings; all were influenced in one way or another by the timid and withdrawn abbé. Both Rousseau's *Discourse on Inequality* and his *Essay on the Origin of Languages* draw upon the work of Condillac, his companion during his early years in Paris.

Charles-Pineau Duclos *(1704–1772)*

Elected perpetual secretary of the French Academy in 1755, Duclos labored to restore the integrity of that institution, which made him unwilling to give special consideration either to titled persons lacking proper intellectual credentials or to philosophes, whom he regarded as unduly partisan and sectarian. Not the least remarkable of his achievements is that he was the one writer who managed to stay on good terms with Rousseau. Author of the highly successful *Considerations on the Mores of This Century* (1750).

Friedrich-Melchior Grimm *(1723–1807)*

One of Rousseau's friends during the early Parisian years, Grimm shared with Jean-Jacques a love of music and a determination to champion Italian opera at the expense of its French counterpart. Eventually the two men were to be bitter enemies, Rousseau priding himself on his poverty and independence, Grimm devoting his life to serving the *grands*. Grimm wrote a newsletter, the *Correspondance littéraire, philosophique, et critique*, for the crowned heads and potentates of Europe; formed strong ties with Catherine the Great; and succeeded in acquiring the title of baron.

Claude-Adrien Helvétius *(1715–1771)*

Helvétius was the author of two books, *De l'Esprit* and *De l'Homme*, each something of a scandal because he espoused environmental determinism and reduced all motives to the search for physical pleasure. The stir caused by *De l'Esprit* (1758) figured in the events leading the authorities to revoke the "privilege" that had permitted open publication of the *Encyclopédie*.

Helvétius was the first among the philosophes to argue that a republic of letters can thrive only in a political republic. Before long, others would arrive at the same political conclusion, even as they continued to reject his philosophical assumptions.

Paul-Henri Thiry, baron d'Holbach *(1723–1789)*

Holbach contributed several hundred articles to the *Encyclopédie*, many on metallurgy, mineralogy, and geology, and a few on political topics, such as the essay "Representatives." He was the author, also, of anonymous works, well known for their atheism and materialism, insufficiently known, in my judgment, for their republican and constitutionalist politics. His Parisian home was a leading center of the Enlightenment, a place where philosophes of varying outlooks and nationalities could debate ideas over dinner and exchange views with administrators and other public figures, French and foreign.

Anne Robert Jacques Turgot, *baron de l'Aulne (1727–1781)*

Turgot was a philosophe and a distinguished public servant. As a philosophe he contributed to the *Encyclopédie*, propounded a theory of progress, and advocated physiocratic principles in economics. As a public servant he rose to the exalted post of controller-general of finances in 1774, at the beginning of the reign of Louis XVI, only to be dismissed in 1776.

THE AUTOCRITIQUE OF ENLIGHTENMENT

Introduction:
Rousseau and the Philosophes

Fᴇᴡ periods of intellectual and cultural history elicit such persistent
interest as the Enlightenment. Whether it is to reclaim or to reject our
heritage, we constantly find ourselves returning to the writers of the eighteenth century. Enlightenment-bashing, whether from the standpoint of
romanticism, existentialism, critical theory, structuralism, or deconstruc-
tion, continues to be a favorite activity of intellectuals, many of whom
wish to call the entire tradition of "humanism" into question. Those who
cherish the heritage of the Enlightenment, for their part, regard every such
challenge as another reason to appreciate the age of Diderot, Hume, and
Kant. With so much at stake it is not surprising that over the last several
decades scholarly studies of the Enlightenment in various national contexts, of specific authors and themes, of the diffusion of "philosophical"
ideas from capital to provinces, and of the fate of enlightened ideals in
revolutionary politics have flourished as never before.

Yet it is arguable that at least one topic of the utmost importance, the
relationship between Rousseau and the philosophes, has been relatively
neglected. Everyone knows that during the *siècle des lumières* all roads led
to Paris, that Galiani and Beccaria came from Italy, Hume and Adam
Smith from Scotland, Ben Franklin from America, Grimm and Holbach
from the German states, and that Kant who traveled not at all was nevertheless profoundly moved by Rousseau. It is also widely acknowledged
that when Rousseau originally arrived in Paris in the early 1740s he did
so as a would-be philosophe, whereas when he left it in the mid-1750s
his departure marked the beginning of his reputation as an ex- and anti-

philosophe. Less recognized is that the road from Paris to the Hermitage on Madame d'Épinay's estate was a trail not away from the French Enlightenment but to a better vantage point from which to launch an alternative Enlightenment, as a sequel to his earlier efforts to force the Enlightenment to question itself.

At first glance the claim that the exchanges between Rousseau and the philosophes have been insufficiently examined may seem odd. After all, there is no shortage of articles whose titles link Rousseau with one or another of the philosophes, and though books on the same topic are harder to come by, they too exist. Nor is the problem one of quality. No one can study the French Enlightenment without acknowledging a debt to, among others, Jean Morel, René Hubert, Jean Fabre, Jacques Proust, Henri Gouhier, and Robert Wokler, each of whom has enriched our understanding of Rousseau's relationship to one or more philosophes.[1] Yet no general study of the debate between Rousseau and the philosophes has been written. It is fair to say that the most noteworthy overviews of the Enlightenment have surprisingly little to say about Rousseau (those of Paul Hazard and Peter Gay, for example[2]), and that the most out-standing books on Rousseau have relatively little to say about the Enlightenment (for example, the works of Jean Starobinski, Roger Masters, and Judith Shklar[3]). Typical of the scholarly state of affairs is the preface of the distinguished historian J. H. Brumfitt's *The French Enlightenment*. After noting that Rousseau was both a philosophe and an antiphilosophe, Professor Brumfitt sidesteps his puzzlement by deciding "to exclude any detailed consideration of Rousseau."[4] In much the same vein Norman Hampson begins his fine study *The Enlightenment* with the statement, "It may be argued with equal plausibility that Rousseau was either one of the greatest writers of the Enlightenment or its most eloquent and effective opponent."[5] Despite many insightful subsequent comments on Rousseau's works, Hampson never attempts to decipher the riddle he has posed in such striking terms.

It may be useful for my purposes to distinguish between two broad trends in the interpretive literature dealing with Rousseau and the Enlightenment. One is a persistent effort to remove Rousseau from the Enlightenment by treating him as a preromantic, a maneuver first effected by literary critics and revived in more recent times by historians of science.[6] Such interpretations, as Peter Gay has noted of various applications of the notion of preromanticism to the philosophes, are exercises in "definition by larceny"; they are misdirected and unfortunate efforts "to strip the Enlightenment of its wealth and then to complain of its poverty."[7] We may add that Rousseau's immanent critique of the Enlightenment is automatically lost in an account of his significance that forgets he wrote for the *Encyclopédie,* personally introduced the most significant of the philosophes to one another, led the philosophes in the quarrel over French versus Italian music, shared their project of reconciling interest with virtue, and in his most vigorous indictments of the encyclopedists never ceased to deploy the Lockean empiricism, the philosophical account of history, the vocabulary of utility, rights, and a social contract, or the scientific modes of argumentation that constituted the common intellectual arsenal of the philosophes.

The second major interpretive trend, represented most ably by Ernst Cassirer and Peter Gay, places Rousseau within the eighteenth century but buries his powerful internal critique of the age of Enlightenment through the device of treating him as just one more philosophe. Thus Gay ends his massive two-volume study with a chapter on Rousseau and civic education. Neglected for a thousand pages, Rousseau is permitted to appear at the close of Gay's work for the purpose of showing that the philosophes were moving beyond their initial distrust of *le peuple.*[8] Fond of calling the philosophes a "family,"[9] Gay forgets that no strife is so bitter as that between enemy brothers;[10] he also forgets that once the personal side of Rousseau's fratricidal confrontation with the philosophes has been removed, what remains is nothing less than an all-out struggle over the route to enlightenment, Rousseau on one side, all the rest of the philosophes arrayed on the other, with no clear winner despite the numerical disproportionality of the combating parties.

Cassirer likewise absorbs Rousseau into the philosophical mainstream, but at the price of robbing Jean-Jacques of all that is most distinctive in his intellectual position. A Rousseau who is German, Kantian, and willing to renounce happiness as an end, a Rousseau whose "general will" is a warming-up exercise for the "categorical imperative," is the result.[11] Had Cassirer been willing to situate Rousseau in his proper French context, he sooner or later would have been forced to acknowledge that it was Diderot, not Rousseau, who spoke of a general will of mankind; he would have conceded, moreover, that Rousseau decisively destroyed Diderot's position in the first version of the *Social Contract.* Finally, he would have admitted that Rousseau always adhered to the typically French position that happiness is a very worthy moral ideal—the better to castigate society for making us so miserable.[12]

The theme of the following chapters is that all of Rousseau's writings, and even the manner in which he chose to live his life, should be regarded as the ultimate critique of the French Enlightenment, an autocritique complemented by a dazzling one-man alternative enlightenment that reached an exceptionally wide audience because Rousseau packaged his ideas in a best-selling novel, then in an educational treatise that read like a novel, and had the reading public eagerly and impatiently awaiting another story, that of his life. No wonder, then, that Grimm, Madame d'Épinay, and Diderot were tempted to write their own version of the *Confessions;* no wonder they felt compelled to destroy Rousseau before he discredited them and won the contest for control of the new and highly coveted prize, public opinion.

Rousseau threw both his contemporaries and us off the trail when he frequently stated that he belonged to no party,[13] neither the philosophical nor the clerical, or at other times that his aim was to reconcile the "party of humanity" with that of religion,[14] when in fact he added a third party to the picture, a party without a self-admitted head, but a party nonetheless and one with a very large following. On occasion he was more helpful in directing his readers to the polemical intent of his writings: "I avow in all good faith that when the works of my [philosophical] adversaries no longer subsist, mine will be perfectly useless."[15]

MY ACCOUNT of Rousseau's relationship to the philosophes inevitably suggests that some of the ways in which scholars have structured the eighteenth century are defective—for instance, the claim that the age began with reason but ended with tears and sentimentality.[16] On closer examination tears were plentiful throughout the century, early and late, as were exclamation marks, not to mention that sympathy, commiseration, and emotional identification with victims were constantly viewed as a primary training ground for the development of humanitarian convictions. The reverse is also true: around 1765 Diderot moved away from his earlier unbounded enthusiasm for the passions, preferring now those persons who knew how to assert the brain and control the diaphragm.[17] And Rousseau was never one—not even in his novel—to trust the passions after their radical distortion and denaturation by society. From beginning to end of the era, the philosophes championed both reason and sentiment.

Nor is there anything to be said in behalf of a second way in which the historical unfolding of the Enlightenment has been depicted: the frequently stated but poorly defended claim that the century began with natural law but increasingly moved to utilitarian morality.[18] Typical of the age, indeed, is Diderot's article "Natural Right," which makes its case for natural law by constantly invoking notions of self-interest and utility. Nothing is more foreign to the period, including to Rousseau, as we shall see, than to believe that utility and rights are foreign to each other. Hume's comment that natural law thinkers, whatever their original principles, ultimately base much of their argument on "the convenience and necessities of mankind"[19] has been read as a preparation for Bentham's savage dismissal of natural rights as "nonsense upon stilts";[20] it might be read, instead, as an appreciation of the genuine worth of treatises on natural right. Kant and Bentham forced a choice between natural rights and utility at the end of the eighteenth century that their predecessors had been careful to avoid.[21]

What then, if any, historical progression may one postulate that plausibly characterizes, in part at least, the age we are investigating? One approach is to chart an evolution from the first half of the century, in which two figures, Montesquieu and Voltaire, dominated the intellectual landscape, and the manuscripts of anonymous, relatively isolated lesser writers passed quietly from hand to hand through a clandestine network[22]—to the second half of the century, in which a self-conscious movement of philosophes coalesced, publicly asserted itself, and did battle with the Jesuits, the Paris Parlement, and traditionalist journalists, emerging victorious in the 1760s and taking over some of the most coveted institutions of the Old Regime, most notably the academies.

So far, admittedly, this account simply restates one of the standard scenarios, but it takes on a novel meaning once Rousseau is added to the picture. Beyond disrupting the philosophical movement during the critical decade of the 1750s, Rousseau publicly disclosed—I hope to show in the following chapters—the self-doubts of the party in which he once held membership. However much Diderot despised Rousseau's attacks on the philosophes, he himself questioned in *Rameau's Nephew* whether the new-fangled agent of Enlightenment, the supposedly autonomous philosophe, was a plausible ideal, and he did so in language that parallels and echoes Rousseau's. Holbach, too, had nothing good to say about Rousseau, and yet he would eventually paraphrase Rousseau's linkage of high culture with corruption and suggest that the integrity of the republic of letters could never be ensured unless Europe adopted the republican form of government.[23]

What Rousseau did to the philosophes is perhaps congenially expressed by borrowing and supplementing the words of personages in his milieu. If Madame du Deffand could wryly comment that Helvétius, the philosopher of self-interest, upset so very many persons because he divulged everyone's secret,[24] we may add that Rousseau upset the philosophes because he revealed those secretive thoughts they occasionally committed to paper but refused to publish. If to d'Alembert the philosophes were about to capture Troy,[25] then Rousseau was the Trojan horse in the camp of the philosophes. Finally, if *Le Christianisme dévoilé*[26] is a title typical of the philosophes, always out to unveil the priests, then Rousseau was the man who threatened to unmask the philosophes.

My objectives here are twofold: first, to place Rousseau's thought in its proper context, which is overwhelmingly the intellectual and social world of the philosophes. Even Geneva, of which Rousseau made so much at opportune moments, was largely a battlefield on which he fought the philosophes, rather than a significant influence on his thought.[27] Second, it is my intention to argue that a study of Rousseau's relationship to the philosophes can alter our general understanding of the French Enlightenment, not by discrediting all other readings but by viewing the age from a hitherto largely ignored but extremely important perspective.

It may also be argued that whatever refashions our image of the French Enlightenment does so as well for our understanding of the Enlightenment in general. Even allowing for the way different national contexts gave birth to different enlightenments,[28] there are good reasons for refusing to relinquish entirely the old-fashioned view that the French Enlightenment was the Enlightenment of enlightenments. We have already seen that virtually all of the outstanding intellectual figures of the age visited Paris. Once there, Grimm and Holbach stayed, and Galiani viewed his forcible recall to Italy as the tragedy of his life. For Beccaria the capstone of his career was that Morellet translated *On Crimes and Punishments* from Italian into French, the language of all educated persons; and that the philosophes did him the additional honor, equally treasured, of inviting him to Paris. For that matter Rousseau too, no matter how ostentatious his departure, was careful to move only to the outskirts of the city almost everyone regarded as the capital not just of France but of the Western world.[29]

While England might match France coffee house for coffee house, the

French salon was in a class by itself;[30] long a center for refining taste, polishing manners, displaying wit, and cultivating the art of conversation, the salon in the second half of the eighteenth century also became the caucus at which the elections of philosophes to the academies were arranged. At the residence of the Baron d'Holbach on the rue Royale the philosophes enjoyed a salon dedicated to and governed by themselves, the one salon where there was no hostess imposing a rule of constraint, where in consequence any topic could be debated, and through which passed the philosophical lights of all Europe, along with foreign diplomats and political figures as well as some members of the French administrative elite. Always ready with an apt phrase, Galiani proclaimed Holbach's home "le café de l'Europe."

The commanding position of the French Enlightenment may also be measured by the influence of its writers in other countries, for instance the well-known impact of Montesquieu in America or the direct indebtedness of Adam Smith to d'Alembert on the topic of the relationship between writer and public.[31] No less striking is Frederick the Great's eagerness to immerse himself in the writings of the philosophes, or his efforts to entice Voltaire to his court and keep him there (until it became evident that no palace was large enough for two such egos) and to found Prussian academies on the model of the French, staffing them, whenever possible, with such French luminaries as Maupertuis.

Furthermore, it was the French intellectuals, Buffon, Maupertuis, and Diderot among others, who realized the enormous significance of the fledgling life sciences. It was also they, including Rousseau, who boldly explored the possible social and political implications of the new sciences, even as the Dutch and the English, for all their virtuosity in experimental science, feared and resisted the new scientific developments. But what perhaps matters most of all, certainly by way of indicating that the French entry even today constitutes the Enlightenment of enlightenments, is that other than Kant no eighteenth-century thinkers continue to loom so large in our thoughts as Diderot and Rousseau.

If at its most modest mine is an effort to place Rousseau's texts in context, at its most expansive it is an attempt to recapture what amounts to the autocritique of Enlightenment. Not the least significant, albeit the most ignored, of all the many critiques of the Enlightenment that have been articulated during the last two centuries is the one the "age of criticism"[32] made of itself, largely through the instigation of Rousseau.

Compared with this the romantic critique, despite its incessant repetition by one or another self-proclaimed avant-garde, is irrelevant; it speaks past the Enlightenment, not to it.

Ours may not be an enlightened age, but it is one shaped by the Age of the Enlightenment. To the undeniable extent that we remain the children of the Enlightenment, both accepting and contesting its heritage, Rousseau's debate with the philosophes is inevitably a matter pertaining to the present no less than to the past.

The Virtue of Selfishness

NOTHING was more important to Bentham than that we should take our utilitarianism pure, simple, undiluted, without a trace of sentimentality or embarrassment; nothing was more important to the French philosophes than to avoid all-out utilitarianism, despite their constant and enthusiastic recourse to the notions of interest, self-love, and usefulness. Bentham for all intents and purposes would expurgate "virtue" from our moral vocabulary; the consistent refusal of the philosophes to do the same was self-conscious, adamant, and central to their shared intellectual project, that of reconciling interest with virtue, inclination with duty.[1] To many if not all of them an ethic of unalloyed self-interest was morally unworthy; to every one of them such an ethic was exactly what their religious and conservative enemies attributed to them, the better to dispose of the Enlightenment.

Not the least of Rousseau's many achievements was his brilliant demolition of the treaty between interest and virtue so carefully worked out by the philosophes. That he did so as a true son of the French Enlightenment, not as a pre-Kantian or a preromantic, that he was sympathetic to the concept of self-love and used it constructively as well as destructively, made his critique all the more decisive. After he finished, the most discerning of the philosophes had reason to believe that the reconciliation of interest with virtue was possible only through a much more radical Enlightenment than anything they had foreseen, or through a return to religion—the ultimate avowal of failure.

The Misanthrope Silenced

Kant's motto for the Enlightenment was Dare to Know; Holbach's might be stated as Dare to Love Thyself.[2] Although much of the baron's work appealed to only one camp within the philosophical movement, his warm endorsement of self-love, of *amour de soi* or *amour-propre*, was typical of the philosophes. Their championing of self-love and justification of self-interest were natural outgrowths of a larger campaign to reclaim human nature after centuries of Christian messages of self-abnegation. Saint Augustine had spoken of two cities formed by two loves, "the earthly by the love of self, even to the contempt of God; the heavenly by the love of God, even to the contempt of self."[3] Against Augustine and his disciples at Port Royal, the philosophes wrote to vindicate the city of man, including in their remarks a sustained justification of the propensity of each of the members of the earthly city to express love of self through the pursuit of self-interest. Only by accepting and relishing our nature can we be at home, whole and complete, here and now, in what may be the only city we shall ever inhabit.

Any discussion by a philosophe of self-interest and self-love was almost invariably part of a larger effort to challenge the Church's presentation of the human condition. So it was with Voltaire's attempt to refute Pascal's *Pensées* at the end of the *Lettres philosophiques* (1734); the respective orientations of the two authors to self-love was only one facet of a grand quarrel over human nature and human possibilities, a fight in which the representative of the Enlightenment tested himself against a figure of the previous century who remained the most formidable, tenacious, and worthy of opponents.

Ironically, the philosophes were in large measure responsible for rescuing the *Pensées* from the oblivion to which the religious authorities had consigned it.[4] Bossuet and Malebranche had ignored Pascal, and Arnauld did his best to offer the world an expurgated and bland edition of the *Pensées*.[5] Hence the philosophes remained unaware of, among other things, the biting political jottings in Pascal's masterpiece. Yet for all the Jansenist revisionism, the philosophes understood quite well that the *Pensées* were a significant challenge to their account of *la condition humaine;* they understood because Voltaire focused their attention on the relevant passages that survived the scissors and paste of Port Royal.[6]

"I dare," wrote Voltaire, "to take the side of humanity against this sublime misanthrope."[7] Why Voltaire and all the philosophes should return incessantly to Pascal[8] is clear: he could so easily have been their precursor rather than their nemesis. An experimental scientist, Pascal ridiculed Descartes' a priori dismissal of the possibility of a vacuum; Pascal also understood both the promise and the limitations of *l'esprit de géométrie,* pursued pioneering studies in the mathematics of probability, and was a leader in applied science, all of which might make him seem the author of an early version of various planks in the program of the philosophes.[9] What is more, he spoke not as a member of those cloistered at Port Royal but as someone familiar with the *mondain,* the libertine, and the *honnête homme,* willing to grant them that happiness is our inevitable and legitimate desire[10] and quite capable of addressing them in their worldly language. In his intended audience as in his scientific method, Pascal's position is largely indistinguishable from that of the philosophes, which made his assertion that happiness can be found only in capitulation to the "hidden God" especially menacing.

Pascal's gambit was to end rather than to begin with the doctrine of original sin; without the mystery of original sin, a doctrine incomprehensible and repugnant to reason, we can never understand ourselves[11] or find shelter from the storm of human existence. Or so he hoped to prove by alluding to our agitated, divided, perpetually empty and unhappy selves. A hodgepodge of the highest and the lowest, the human self, however abject and debased, is haunted by memories of the wholeness and happiness that characterized it before the Fall.[12] In Christianity, and only in Christianity, we discover "the cause of our weaknesses, the treatment that can cure them, and the means of obtaining such treatment."[13]

Among the foremost symptoms of our illness are that we can never sit still,[14] cannot find satisfaction in ourselves, and seek to flee from our nothingness, to fill the void within by endlessly chasing after desires which, once fulfilled, immediately yield to successor desires[15] rather than providing the inner peace for which we yearn. Our human condition is one of inconstancy, boredom, and anxiety[16] and is marked by relentless efforts to escape from self-knowledge[17] by means of an implicit strategy of living outside ourselves, passing the time in an unbroken sequence of meaningless diversions. "Nothing could be more wretched than to be . . . reduced to introspection with no means of diversion."[18] Absorbed in past or future, never living in the present, our lives end before we have begun to live. "We never actually live, but only hope to live, and since we are always planning how to be happy, it is inevitable that we should never be so."[19]

Should we turn to our fellow humans in the hope that what we are with them will compensate for how little we are alone? To do so is to forget that "Jesus tore himself away from his disciples to enter upon his agony; we must tear ourselves away from those who are nearest and dearest to us in order to imitate him."[20] It is also to forget that we shall die alone; no one else can do it for us.[21] Besides, even our most intimate relationships are shallow: the woman a man lives with is no longer the woman he once loved,[22] and friendship is based upon not knowing what our friends say about us after we have left the room.[23]

How utterly disgusting, then, if such are our intimate ties, must our ordinary social relations be. It is only by mutual deception that the social world of our making, one composed of restless egos, each out for self, can be made bearable.

> The nature of self-love and of this human self is to love only self and consider only self ... He wants to be the object of men's love and esteem and sees that his faults deserve only their dislike and contempt ... He takes every care to hide his faults both from himself and from others ... Anyone who has an interest in winning our affection avoids rendering us a service he knows to be unwelcome; ... we hate the truth and it is kept from us; ... we like being deceived and we are deceived.

There is no place for charity in a world where "man is nothing but disguise, falsehood, and hypocrisy, both in himself and in regard to others."[24]

Exceptionally well versed in science, Pascal chose in the *Pensées* to underscore its limits. Science is incapable, he notes, of telling us right from wrong,[25] nor—he tells us in a passage deleted by Port Royal—can it give us reason to feel at home in the infinite, dreadful spaces it depicts as constituting physical reality.[26] Both where we have come from and where we are going, genetic and final causes, are outside the reach of physics.[27] Even efficient causes come down to a matter of blind, unreasoned conviction or plain habit: "When we see the same effect always recur, we conclude that it is necessarily so by nature, as that there will be a tomorrow, but nature often gives us the lie and does not obey its own rules."[28]

Because they think, humans are the glory no less than the refuse of the universe;[29] yet scientific reason lets us down in time of need and our everyday reason also fails, defeated in the interminable civil war between reason and the passions.[30] "All our reasoning amounts to surrendering to passion,"[31] and we are left at odds with, and divided against, ourselves. When the skeptic, the *mondain*, and the libertine have exhausted the alternatives, they will realize that there is no place to go but back to the Church; if they behave long enough as believers, attending mass, genuflecting, sprinkling themselves with holy water, they will believe.[32]

Much of Voltaire's response hinged on showing that what Pascal had portrayed as dire was perfectly harmless and insignificant if placed within the philosophy of John Locke, already treated in an earlier chapter of the *Lettres philosophiques*, or *Letters Concerning the English Nation*. Of course, we live outside ourselves since, according to Locke, "ideas can only come from outside . . . Hence man is either outside himself or an imbecile."[33] Similarly, from the viewpoint of sensationalism, "enjoyment can only come from outside. We cannot receive sensations or ideas except through external objects, as we can only feed our bodies by bringing into them foreign substances which turn into our own bodies."[34] Such Locke had taught the English and, with Voltaire's help, would henceforth teach the French.

In general, we must stop trying to escape from our bodies because mind and body cannot be separated; the Christian dualism of Pascal divides us against ourselves and then blames us for the divided self with which it has afflicted us. The same is true of the religious uses of Cartesianism, whether in the Jansenist thought of Arnauld or the less harsh Oratorian philosophy of Malebranche.[35] No one can withdraw his soul from the world, for our body anchors us there and where our body is, so too is our mind. It follows that when Pascal, Arnauld, and Malebranche chastised humans for not turning inward, for failing to divorce themselves from the world, they uttered nonsense. "Our condition is precisely to think about outside things, with which we have a necessary connection . . . To think about oneself, apart from all natural things, is to think about nothing at all."[36] The *vita contemplativa* is an incoherent ideal because the person it lauds cannot possibly exist,[37] assuming Locke's history of the human soul is more reliable than the novel on the same topic written by Cartesians and religious enthusiasts.[38]

Against Pascal's complaint that humans are incomprehensible, Voltaire could say Locke had shown that, knowing neither body nor mind,[39] unable to ascend from sense-experience to metaphysical wisdom, our human understanding is indeed quite limited. Still, we can know as much as we need to know; reason, including scientific reason, is probabilistic and instrumental, permitting us to cope with concrete problems, to muddle through and pursue our happiness, whatever guise it takes. As for our restlessness, Locke, whose *tabula rasa* disinvited belief in original sin, had made it a central proposition of his psychology that a certain feeling of uneasiness, of unquenchable desire, keeps us going;[40] without our habit of sinking into boredom, we should vegetate and be useless.[41] Born to act, for us inactivity is death.[42] Thus is human nature vindicated when Pascalian propositions are relocated in a Lockean framework.

The cure for our supposedly divided selves, Voltaire suggested, may be found in the very *amour-propre* that Christian thought diagnosed as a deadly malady. A morality of self-love does not divide us in two, a higher and a lower self, nor does it ask that we repress our wants, needs, and desires; all it asks is that we accept the inevitable, that in all our actions we never forget ourselves. To embrace self-love instead of condemning it is to be whole and entire, at one with ourselves and on good terms with others.

> It is as impossible for a society to be formed and be durable without self-interest as it would be to produce children without carnal desire . . . It is love of self that encourages love of others, it is through our mutual needs that we are useful to the human race. That is the foundation of all commerce, the eternal link between men. Without it not a single art would have been invented, no society of ten people formed.[43]

Pascal is precisely and exactly wrong to assert that the general good must come first, that "the bias toward self is the beginning of all disorder . . . in politics and economics."[44] In point of fact a proper penal code rests on self-interest, as does trade.

To demand selflessness of our fellows, as Pascal does, is to damn ourselves to find nothing but disappointment in the midst of the very social and collective existence that permits each individual to seek his or her happiness through interacting with others. To demand selflessness is to make inhuman demands, to lose one's own humanity, to become the monster one has claimed to discover in the human creature.[45] Finally, it is to denature oneself and then to cry with anguish about not fitting into the scheme of nature. From a misfit such as Pascal was by his own choice, one is not surprised to hear a description of the human condition as "a number of men in chains, all under sentence of death, some of whom are each day butchered in the sight of others."[46]

For a refutation of such an account of our lot, Voltaire believes he need do no more than remind the reader of the joy of life in Paris, where the social art has been perfected and happiness is plentiful.[47] Two years later he ended *Le Mondain* with the line "Paris to me's a paradise." No wager is necessary to take up residence in paradise, no renunciation or self-abnegation; a Parisian address suffices. This is true even if the greatest of cities is the realm of none for all, all for one, that one being oneself.

Self-Love Vindicated

Implicit in Voltaire's response to Pascal, explicit elsewhere in his work, and endlessly repeated by all the philosophes except Rousseau, is the time-honored notion of natural sociability. Far from outcasts, we thrive as integral elements of the natural order of things insofar as we are social beings. We have every reason to love rather than hate ourselves, because our self-love links us to others in a mutual exchange of benefits and services. Each philosophe regarded it as his task to continue Voltaire's dual project of eulogizing social existence and attacking the antisocial lives of the clergy.

Arguments against celibacy and seclusion are so much the common currency of the French Enlightenment that one blow delivered against the monastic life blends into another. Nevertheless Diderot's *The Nun* and *Supplement to Bougainville's "Voyage"* do stand out. Self-exiled from society, alienated from their very bodies, monks and nuns become inhuman to others because they are so to themselves. When he observes the life of a nun Diderot soon finds himself enumerating "all the symptoms of wasting and self-consuming nature."

> Do all these lugubrious ceremonies played out at the taking of the habit . . . suspend the animal functions? On the contrary, do not these instincts awaken in silence, constraint, and idleness with a violence unknown to the people in the world who are busy with countless other things?[48]

It is not only monks and nuns who suffer the ill effects of the repressive moral code of Christianity; so do we all. A decade after *The Nun* Diderot used Bougainville's Tahitians to denounce the misery common in European countries, where the inhabitants are cajoled by priests to violate the "law of nature," which among other things is a call to sexual enjoyment. The mores of Tahiti, by sanctioning considerable sexual freedom, are conducive to the "general welfare and individual utility"; unknown to Tahitians are those worries about underpopulation that vex the French. As opposed to the "hypocritical parade of virtue" that reigns in the old world, the inhabitants of the new world place their confidence in something "more universal, powerful, and lasting—self-interest." Loving themselves and one another, Tahitians need only do what comes naturally to serve the common good.[49]

From what has already been said, it is not difficult to infer how the philosophes handled Pascal's lament that our most sophisticated reasoning amounts to little more than a guise under which we indulge our passions. So be it, they said in effect, since passion is what imbues our human nature with its capacity for greatness. "It is passions alone, and strong passions, that can elevate the soul to great things,"[50] wrote a youthful Diderot in the *Pensées philosophiques* (1746), a book whose title recalls Pascal's. "Deadened passions degrade men of extraordinary quality. Constraint annihilates the grandeur and energy of nature."[51] What might Pascal have accomplished, inquired Diderot, had he not wasted his time in useless and harmful religious disputes?[52] In *De l'Esprit* (1758) Helvétius embellished at great length the theme that all human achievement, whether in public affairs, science, or letters, depends upon how our social arrangements foster or block the development of persons driven by strong passions. Properly channeled, ambition is nothing to be ashamed of, because all members of society can benefit from the passion for distinction that animates some individuals.

Why worry that reason is feeble compared with passion if the latter is the more reliable guide to individual happiness and the social good? Bayle, whom all the philosophes regarded as one of their forerunners, had long ago remarked that the reasoning animal rarely acts on the basis of reason;[53] it is possible that Hume, while in Paris, expressed his view of reason as the "slave of the passions."[54] Yet neither thinker regarded the weakness of reason as a counsel of despair. Nor did Diderot, who in his *Introduction to the Great Principles* (c. 1764) spied another opportunity to extol the passions: "It is wrong to attribute our crimes to the passions ... The passions always inspire us well, because they inspire us only with the desire for happiness; it is intelligence [*esprit*] that leads us badly and makes us take the wrong road ... It is reason and not nature that misleads us."[55] Worried that Diderot sometimes went too far, Duclos nevertheless insisted more than a decade earlier that intelligence *(esprit)* only makes us honest, whereas sensibility makes us virtuous.[56] If utilitarianism had to depend on rational self-interest it would fail; fortunately, we can dispense with a calculus of felicity because our passions are better than our interests— better at making us care about those for whom we feel sympathy, those nearest us, but also, potentially, anyone who shares our human condition. Through pity or commiseration we identify with and are naturally concerned for others. Where interest sometimes withers and separates, self-love overflows and combines.[57]

Beyond the *tabula rasa,* beyond our innocence at birth, we are not only free of original sin but naturally good. The belief in *bonté,* in natural goodness, is by no means peculiar to Rousseau. Time and again one encounters it, as when Diderot writes, "Human nature is good? Yes, and very good ... It is our miserable conventions that pervert man; human nature should not be blamed."[58] No Jansenist could agree with such a statement, nor could a Jesuit unless reason were viewed as the centerpiece of human nature,[59] a belief the philosophes usually rejected. In the psychology common to almost all the philosophes—one gleaned as much, perhaps, from Montaigne as from Locke—humanitarianism is and must be anchored in sentiment. "I am wonderfully lax in the direction of mercy and gentleness," wrote Montaigne. "Yet to the Stoics pity is a vicious passion; they want us to succor the afflicted, but not to unbend and sympathize with them." Not because of anything revealed by philosophical reason "but because it is really my feeling, and perhaps excessively so, I consider all men my compatriots, and embrace a Pole as I do a Frenchman, setting this national bond after the universal and common one."[60] Most of the philosophes agreed with Montaigne that the sentiment of commiseration for specific afflicted persons is the origin and sustenance of a more general or even universal humanitarian concern. Reason comes later and must never be the Stoic reason that repudiates the passions. Rather, it is a reason that seconds the sentiments and finds arguments in their behalf: reason and sentiment, not reason versus sentiment.

In their efforts to vindicate self-love the philosophes could turn the writings of the moralists of the Grand Siècle, even the Jansenist contributors, to their own ends. "Although nothing is so opposed to charity ... as *amour-propre*," wrote the Jansenist Pierre Nicole, "yet there is nothing so akin to charity in its effects."[61] From such a starting point, Nicole went on to depict a self-regulating society, functioning smoothly, efficiently, effectively, no matter that each individual component of this social whole lived in estrangement from himself, his fellows, and his true religious calling. Given our sinful selves, such a world of reciprocal, interlocking selfishness is better than the alternative of all-out conflict.

To Helvétius the message of hope waiting to be salvaged from the pessimism of Nicole is that good intentions are unnecessary. In Nicole's words, "an enlightened self-love, which knows its true interests,"[62] is all any society needs to thrive in this material and temporal world. Consequences are everything, then, intentions nothing, concluded the author of *De l'Esprit*.[63] No wonder Bentham would cite Helvétius as his intellectual progenitor; both writers, it appears, expounded the full-bodied utilitarianism that replaced the higher self–lower self dualism with the moral dictate that pleasure not only is but ought to be the end of our actions.

Sometimes the philosophes were too partisan to savor the irony that Nicole or the Jansenist fellow traveler La Rochefoucauld prepared the way for "enlightened" reflections on self-love and interest.[64] Thus the seventeenth-century moralists receive no credit but do come in for considerable abuse in the *Encyclopédie* article "Interest," probably written by Saint-Lambert. Proper distinctions among such words as self-love, pride, and interest are wanting in the pages of Nicole and La Rochefoucauld, charges the encyclopedist,[65] whose own vocabulary is no more precise. More generous than Saint-Lambert, or more eager for a worthy pedigree, Helvétius defended La Rochefoucauld from the charge he painted too sinister a portrait of us. The *Maxims* show us as we are,[66] and as such their pithy wisdom provides an early step toward that psychological and social science Helvétius was setting forth in his writings.[67]

So much Helvétius explicitly argues. Implicitly, his writings also suggest that the more La Rochefoucauld succeeded in deflating our most grand and glorious deeds through unveiling their self-regarding roots, the more the *Maxims* thereby inadvertently advanced the later program of "enlightenment." La Rochefoucauld would humble us by exposing the selfishness of virtue; in fact, however, he had demonstrated the virtue of selfishness: which is to say, he had proved how readily self-interest endorses virtuous actions. The time for rejoicing is at hand, for with no shameful lower self to overcome, we can safely dispense with all moralities demanding submission to a higher self.

In asserting that the scattered but brilliant insights of the moralists could be incorporated into a scientific morality modeled on the success of experimental physics, in assuming, furthermore, that a new social science could underwrite and guarantee a morality no longer based on self-sacrifice, Helvétius expressed aspirations that in modified form were common to the philosophes. Both the old wisdom and the new teach us to love ourselves.

Both Interest and Virtue

The distinctiveness of French utilitarianism is best underscored by comparing it with the English variant. In his *Fable of the Bees* Mandeville held that "neither the friendly qualities and kind affections that are natural to man nor the real *virtues* he is capable of acquiring by reason and self-denial are the foundation of society; but that what we call *Evil* in this world, *moral* as well as natural, is the grand principle that makes us sociable creatures."[68] Godwin, Malthus, and Bentham agreed with Hume's verdict that it is a "contradiction in terms," an unnecessary and misleading paradox, to speak of vice when discussing that which is generally beneficial to society.[69] By the time one arrives at Bentham the English utilitarians are ready to drop the word "virtue" from the moral vocabulary and to embrace wholeheartedly, without reservation or apology, a purely hedonistic and egoistic concept of "interest."

In eighteenth-century France the situation was altogether different. Setting foot on French soil, one finds utilitarian arguments everywhere, utilitarianism nowhere. Although consequences matter as much to Diderot as to any utilitarian, intentions are even more his concern in his early writings.[70] As for Helvétius, he speaks so incessantly, favorably, and passionately of virtue that Bentham should have had reservations about finding himself in *De l'Esprit* or *De l'Homme*. For his part Holbach is one of various philosophes who preceded John Stuart Mill in introducing into discussions of "interest" a distinction between higher intellectual pleasures and lower physical ones[71] that flatly contradicts Bentham's "pushpin is as good as poetry." Thirty years after criticizing Pascal's condemnation of self-love, Voltaire still felt the need to resort to irony when defending it: "*Amour-propre* is the instrument of our preservation; it resembles the instrument for the perpetuation of the species; we need it, we cherish it, it gives us pleasure, and we must hide it."[72] Saint-Lambert may sound initially like Bentham in his call for a clarification of the moral language of self-love and interest; but the major concern of his article "Interest" is less to cleanse the moral vocabulary than to express the view that Helvétius spoke too frankly and approvingly of self-interest in *De l'Esprit,* the book the reactionaries used as a welcome excuse to shut down the *Encyclopédie.*

How different was the intellectual landscape on the two sides of the English Channel. In France the daring Diderot and Holbach, it seems, were sympathetic not to the innovative *Fable of the Bees* but to the *Essay on Man,* Pope's restatement of the traditionalist themes of cosmic order and social hierarchy. Frequently leaders, Diderot and Holbach here were followers of the general Gallic predilection for Pope over Mandeville.[73] Much to French liking was Pope's dilution of "interest" through the declaration that God and Nature "bade Self-Love and Social be the same."[74] Champion of aristocratic humanism, enemy of the new monied world of Robert Walpole, Pope in good Tory fashion admired "the amazing Whole"[75] and feared that the new egoism might destroy the social order. One of his predecessors was Shaftesbury, who may well have directly inspired Pope's statement that "the whole Universe [is] one system of society," and society a microcosmic copy of the universe.[76] That Diderot's first important work, the *Essay on Merit and Virtue* (1745), is a sympathetic commentary on Shaftesbury indicates that the philosophes were as anti-utilitarian as utilitarian. Those English thinkers who redeployed the word "interest" in such a way that its meaning was swallowed, digested, and absorbed into traditional moral philosophies were Diderot's early heroes.

Yet utility was forever on Diderot's lips, even if pure utilitarianism was never in his heart. For as long as the Church continued to hold huge tracts of land, effectively removing them and their clerical residents from productivity, utility would remain a meaningful word in France—or at least a useful one. Philosophically anemic compared with its full-blooded English cousin, utilitarianism in France was nevertheless fervently determined to carry out its social mission.

The entanglements of the French moral vocabulary were inevitable because the philosophes had to go no less than halfway with utility to attack the Church, but could not afford to go all the way if they were to defend themselves against counterattack. Time and again conservative journalists and churchmen treated the philosophes as if they advocated a doctrine of straightforward egoism, and claimed that what followed was profligacy, the breakdown of authority, the rejection of duty and obligation. Theater was viewed by the philosophes as it had long been characterized in France, as the highest of the arts and the one of greatest educational value; so it came as a stunning blow for them to see their likenesses lampooned on stage by Palissot in *Les Philosophes*. In the first scene of the second act a valet picks the pocket of his philosophical master, who is busy speechifying about self-interest as the inevitable and proper source of all human behavior.[77] Hence it is that "virtue," not "interest," figures as the primary word in the moral diction of the philosophes. Personified, apostrophized, accompanied by exclamation points, the word virtue cannot be uttered too often or spoken with too much solemnity in their writings.

To prevent the Church from having a monopoly on virtue is a primary objective of the party of humanity; a concern of equal importance is to take the sting out of virtue by making it downright easy. "Either/or" is deleted from the moral constructions of the philosophes, replaced by "both/and": virtue and happiness, virtue and pleasure, virtue and interest, virtue and self-love. What nature has joined together let no religion rend asunder. A return to virtue without a return to the dual self, higher and lower, was the objective of the encyclopedists.

"Let no one tell us again that virtue demands doleful sacrifices,"[78] wrote Holbach in a sentence that summarizes the moral philosophy of the French Enlightenment. Rather than floating above our natures, always slightly beyond our grasp, virtue depends simply on the recognition that we are naturally sociable beings, need one another, seek happiness, and that "no one can be happy alone."[79] To be virtuous it is enough that we act in accordance with our natures, each pursuing his individual happiness through giving to others, so that he may receive in return.[80]

Usually the skeptic, d'Alembert was convinced that "morality is perhaps the most complete of all the sciences," because "properly understood interest" is a certain truth and an excellent foundation for resolving questions of mutual duties and obligations.[81] Holbach adds that for people to be virtuous only one thing is necessary, that they have an interest in being so.[82] Lest someone think "interest" too cold a word Holbach is ready, following the advice set forth by Saint-Lambert in the article "Interest," to substitute the term "self-love" after distinguishing it from egoism.[83] No one can be indifferent to his or her own happiness, nor can anyone fail to realize that his or her satisfaction is intimately connected to that of friends, family, and country. Self-love is necessarily an expansive emotion, one that renders the distinction between selfishness and selflessness meaningless.

Expressed in the language of interest, this means that individual and collective interest are not in conflict. Expressed in the language of virtue, it means that virtue is what is useful to the species;[84] it is the good of the human collectivity ensured through mutual services and exchanges: "reciprocal utility constitutes virtue."[85] Whether reading Holbach, d'Alembert, Diderot, or any other philosophe, the strategy is always the same. Virtue is translated into happiness, pleasure, interest; then happiness, pleasure, interest are translated into virtue.

How far one can advance in the direction of hedonism after beginning with obligation may be seen in Diderot's answer to the question "What are the Duties of Man?" "To make himself happy. Whence follows the necessity of contributing to the happiness of others, or, in other terms, of being virtuous."[86] In one and the same quotation we observe how easily Diderot could pass either from virtue to hedonism or from hedonism to virtue. The expressions duty, happiness, virtue move in a circle, such that to start with any one of them is necessarily to revolve to the other two. By his own account Diderot dedicated his life to proving that virtue and happiness are inseparable.[87] On any other terms it would be inhumane to request people to lead virtuous lives.

From what has been said it is obvious that virtue in the writings of the philosophes is frequently just a connecting link, a switch station, ensuring the compatibility of individual and public interest. Sometimes, however, they wanted it to be considerably more: the striving for greatness that Bentham associated with his aristocratic enemies never disappears from the ideals of the philosophes. Helvétius is forever calling for great men and great deeds; his educational plans aim to make their occurrence the rule rather than the exception. Diderot's *Salons* condemn those painters who flatter "frivolous natures," *les natures légères,* and warmly commend those who favor the reign of "strong natures," *les natures fortes;* he will settle for nothing less than an art that serves a "grand taste" *(grand goût).*[88] Despite his predilection for all that savors of sexual titillation, Diderot complained that Boucher's paintings feature naked "breasts and buttocks" that are never anything more than provocations of the senses.[89] Along the same lines, he welcomed the youthful Jacques-Louis David's contribution to the Salon of 1781.

On the face of it, Diderot is in agreement with Helvétius; yet it was his disagreements with *De l'Esprit* and *De l'Homme* that spurred him to a more demanding virtue. In insisting on reducing our most noble acts to efforts to satisfy purely physical drives Helvétius had, thought Diderot, fallen into an absurd and demeaning disjunction between motive and performance. Diderot saw materialism gone mad in the insistence of Helvétius on reducing the projects of a genius to "a fuck in the morning and a shit in the evening."[90] How, within his narrowly articulated morality of interest, Diderot inquires, can Helvétius explain that he has spent many years working on *De l'Homme,* a book which will not appear until after his death? It is all very well for Helvétius to recommend that authors strive for "eternal" as opposed to "momentary utility" in their writings—that they write for all times rather than to please the puny and immediate tastes of their age. But why should writers follow the advice of Helvétius unless they first reject his moral premises?[91]

Before reading Helvétius but even more afterwards, Diderot sensed that a virtue tied too closely to narrowly defined self-interest must be repudiated. A virtue that is grand, sublime, that raises humans to new heights without asking them to rise above themselves, was Diderot's objective. Enlightenment is impoverished if it settles for reversing the Church in the small; not hatred of *l'infâme,* Diderot noted in a letter, but love of virtue is what unites the philosophes.[92]

It is not surprising, therefore, to hear Diderot or some other philosophe occasionally define virtue as self-sacrifice.[93] From the viewpoint of the philosophes the trick was to have one's renunciation and enjoy it too— to earn glory for sacrificing our desires to some great cause, yet to come out ahead by the time the final curtain drops on our noble deed. Starting from the notion that it is through interacting with others that one's self is constituted and enriched, Holbach has no trouble concluding that "it is always to our own interest . . . that we sacrifice ourselves."[94] Similarly, d'Alembert held that "the enlightened love of ourselves is the principle of all moral sacrifice."[95] What Holbach and d'Alembert put into a formula was placed on stage in Diderot's *Le Fils naturel.* For the sake of friendship Dorval feels compelled to renounce his love of Rosalie. Heartbroken he may be, speechless he is not: "Dear and barbarous duties! Friendship which enchains me . . . , you shall be obeyed. Oh virtue, what are you if you demand no sacrifice?"[96] All's well when Dorval and Rosalie discover they are brother and sister, but even without so convenient a dénouement Dorval would be both a better and a happier man for having done such a fine deed. "My sadness ceased from the moment I began to be just . . . I have been restored to my character."[97]

How comforting to realize that virtue heals rather than divides the self. And how satisfying after a noble act, how unsettling after an ignoble, to see ourselves through the eyes of others.[98] Nothing was more common than for the Church to argue that in the absence of God's eyes to watch their private deeds, unbelievers will not be virtuous; nothing more predictable than the philosophical response that we see ourselves through the eyes of others even when they are not looking. Both remorse and self-esteem are largely, if not entirely, a matter of internalizing the regards of our fellows.

A favorite strategy of the philosophes was to unite inclination with obligation through a morality of what much later would be called "my station and its duties." For all their commitment to natural rights, the philosophes, by taking Pufendorf as their model for reasoning in the social contract tradition, avoided the all-out individualism that might have ensued.[99] Pufendorf wrote *On the Duty of Man and Citizen;* Holbach wrote on "the duties of man founded on his nature."[100] Chapter by chapter Holbach followed Pufendorf's lead in enumerating the duties of the rich and the poor, nobles and peasants, merchants, artisans, men of letters, military officers, magistrates, lawyers, husbands, wives, children, and friends. D'Alembert thought that historians should glean from the materials of the past a list of the duties inhering in each social rank so that children could be educated accordingly.[101]

What better way to have a morality in which "ought" flows effortlessly from "is," a morality that is "natural" and goes down easily, than to endorse the very old but forever renewable morality of social roles? To describe the role of father is to prescribe the actions of a good father; it is to enumerate the duties that are fulfillments rather than denials of sentiment. Had Burke bothered to read the philosophes he so bitterly denounced, he would have found that they preceded him in singing the praises of "the little platoon we belong to in society, . . . the first link in the series by which we proceed toward a love to our country and to mankind."[102] Burke's words sound, ironically, like Holbach in English translation.

Much the same moral program was fostered in Diderot's writings on the theater and in his dramas, *Le Fils naturel* and *Le Père de famille.* What the priest tries unsuccessfully to do from the pulpit, the playwright could more entertainingly and hence more effectively do on the stage.[103] The theater can be a school for morals if plays focus not on character but on different social conditions, on the duties, difficulties, and rewards that attend each social role. Rather than this or that person, it is the intendant, the philosophe, the grand seigneur, the member of a family who should appear on stage.[104] It must be remembered that "the duties of men are as rich a resource for the dramatic poet as their vices and ridiculous affectations; upright productions will succeed everywhere, but more surely among a corrupt people than elsewhere. It's in going to the theater that they will save themselves from the evil persons surrounding them."[105] "Enthusiasm," given its religious connotations, was usually a pejorative word in the philosophical vocabulary; yet an enthusiasm for virtue was not out of place in circles frequented by the philosophes. And why not be enthusiastic about a virtue so enjoyable, costing so little? Doing our duty turns out to be no different from what we have yearned to do all along.

Voltaire's case is particularly illustrative because, anything but a moral enthusiast, he nevertheless resisted the temptation to drop virtue from his moral discourse. In 1736 he penned *Le Mondain*, a eulogy of luxury, pleasure, enjoyment, a work in which Christian/Stoic virtue, possibly virtue as such, was denounced as a relic of a past age of barbarism and incivility. That same year Madame du Châtelet, his lover, was busy translating *The Fable of the Bees*, the poem lauding the results of the "vice" of selfishness. Mandeville's irony is echoed years later in Voltaire's remark that self-love is, like the organ of generation, our indispensable but hidden source of pleasure.

On the verge, it seems, of substituting a morality of interest for one of virtue, Voltaire had second thoughts about continuing down such a dangerous road. Polemically, he was much better off to write a play such as *The Orphan of China*, in which he used the stage to condemn the bloody military virtue embodied by Genghis while applauding the virtues of civility represented by the mandarins. Another safe and effective strategy was to define virtue, following the lead of the abbé de Saint-Pierre, as *bienfaisance*, benevolence, charity without Christianity. Thus did the relatively late (1764) *Philosophical Dictionary* save the word virtue,[106] reshaping it to serve the movement against *l'infâme*. In the relatively early (1734) *Treatise on Metaphysics*, Voltaire hedged his bets by defining virtue as what is useful to society.[107]

Needing influential allies if they were to lead society in a more human-itarian direction, the philosophes espoused a virtue fit for worldlings, never too demanding, compatible with and even grounded in self-interest, capable of occasional elevation to the heights of enthusiasm, suitable for a nobility better educated than its ancestors, more concerned to be up to date, looking for moral outlets to replace the warlike and anarchical feudal virtues that fit so poorly in an increasingly centralized state. Surely *bien-faisance*, Voltaire's choice, was appropriate for this eighteenth-century audience, which ever since the death of Louis XIV had turned from Ver-sailles to Paris and, in time, to the philosophes to learn what to think.

Bienfaisance could emerge almost unnoticed from *noblesse oblige* and pass over just as readily into humanitarianism. All the philosophes there-fore agreed with Voltaire in fostering an explicitly *mondain* virtue. But where he, a man of the earlier generation, still remembered the *esprit*, the *libertinage*, the impeccable but antitheoretical taste of a worldling such as Saint-Evremond, they were determined to anchor the worldling ethic in a virtue based on the application of the methods of science to the study of human nature and society.[108]

This new science of society would, of course, be cold comfort if it revealed that our social relations were hopelessly contaminated. What it demonstrated, happily, was precisely the opposite. Remove the *Contagion sacrée*[109] from our daily lives and what remains is a society where interest and virtue are one, and the world is safe for worldlings. With the deity pulled down from the skies, society becomes the deity: Dumarsais "looks on civil society as a divinity on earth";[110] for Holbach "social life is a religious act."[111]

Citizens and Believers

Rousseau agreed with his fellow philosophes in denying original sin, in replacing it with a belief in natural goodness, and in asserting the convic-tion that love of self is inevitable, proper, conducive to the love of some others, and potentially conducive to pity for the suffering of all others, even strangers.[112] Rousseau also agreed that virtue must be embedded in interest so that obligation and inclination will coincide, and the self will not be embroiled in unending internal conflict. But if he and the philo-sophes share the same initial premises, how drastically divergent their conclusions. Only by abandoning Paris for the hinterlands or, better yet, by never setting foot in the capital in the first place, can innocence and goodness possibly survive—and even then only for the few. For the many, interest and virtue can be united only if the polity is changed, not incrementally, not through reform, but through the advent of a radically new republican order, totally incompatible with the Old Regime.

It was as a contributor to the *Encyclopédie,* in his article "Political Economy," that Rousseau first turned the Enlightenment against itself in such a way that he became an overt threat to the philosophes. Earlier in that same volume five Diderot, in the entry "Natural Right [*Droit naturel*]," repeatedly called upon a concept of the "general will" to evade the snares laid by a hypothetical "violent reasoner" who justified his destructive actions with appeals to self-interest. Good encyclopedist that he was, Rousseau dutifully listed a cross-reference to "Natural Right." Diderot, it seems, was not deluded by Rousseau's gesture; for he commissioned the faithful Boulanger to write a second article on political economy,[113] with no other rationale than one of spelling: Rousseau's article, being entitled "Économie politique," appeared under the letter *E,* excuse enough for Boulanger to publish "Œconomie politique" under *O.* Where Rousseau's article was republican and hopelessly at odds with existing society, Boulanger's was monarchical by default and traced the origins of our mitigated social woes to religious fanaticism.[114] In short, Boulanger's essay was that of an orthodox philosophe, Rousseau's that of a philosophe transmuting into an antiphilosophe.

About a year after the appearance of the fifth volume of the *Encyclopédie* in 1755, Rousseau composed another essay, this one even more damaging to the author of "Natural Right" because it was a succinct and brilliant critique of Diderot's article.[115] Given that Rousseau did not publish this piece, Diderot was spared a direct confrontation with the man who was soon to be his "enemy brother." But as we shall see in Chapters 3 and 4, Diderot and some of the other philosophes would later share Rousseau's doubts whether the "violent reasoner," arch-advocate of self-interest, could be silenced, barring a reconstruction of the French polity far more fundamental than anything they originally envisioned.

Author of the *Encyclopedia*'s article "Hobbism,"[116] Diderot probably had the natural man of the famous and infamous English philosopher in mind when he postulated a reasoner "tormented by violent passions." However far beyond the pale, this hypothetical person, out to serve his interest at the expense of everyone else's, can be restored to morality if an appeal is issued to what is most distinctive in his makeup: his reason and his membership in the *genre humain*. Both these traits may be put to moral use, Diderot suggested, through placing the question of right and wrong "before the entire human race . . . , since the good of all is the only passion it has. Particular wills are suspect . . . but the general will is always good." For each individual the general will is "a pure act of understanding in the silence of the passions"; for the collectivity it is "the general will of the species." Whatever wants and needs characterize humanity, and are therefore in the interests of every human, should be deposited under the rubric of "natural right."[117]

"On the General Society of the Human Race," Rousseau's rebuttal of Diderot, immediately places a novel twist on the familiar theme that society is constituted to attend to our wants and needs: "Our needs bring us together in proportion as our passions divide us, and the more we become enemies of our fellow men, the less we can do without them . . . Rather than all striving toward the general good, men only come together because all are moving away from it."[118] Why social reciprocity should take so perverse a form is not mysterious. Though our natural needs are limited, our social needs are unlimited; hence Pascal was correct to say we are insatiable, but wrong to blame our sinful nature when it is society, having altered our nature, that is at fault. Locke's *tabula rasa,* at the same time that it clears us of the charge of original sin, traces our misdeeds to the social environment that shapes and molds us. Forced to prove ourselves to others, we stop being ourselves and are only what we are for others. The innocent love of self *(amour de soi)* and capacity for commiseration that once characterized us yield to socially induced selfishness *(amour-propre)* and to satisfactions derived from witnessing the miserable plight of other persons.

Shall we repair to the "inner voice"? That strategy is doomed because what we take for "nature's gentle voice" has long been the voice of society, which "stifles humanity in men's hearts by awakening personal interest."[119] Even the tears shed for suffering humanity are a social performance, meant to impress others with the sensitivity of our souls.[120] Shall we appeal, as Pufendorf did,[121] to what we share with all humans? That too is a mistake, for as any reader of Hobbes should know, what is common to all is—in Rousseau's words—"as much a subject of quarrel as of union." Whatever is desired by all is in limited supply for each one, not to mention that it is our differences from other persons that our vain, weak selves wish to assert. Hobbes made only one mistake, a confusion of cause and effect: he blamed our incessantly competitive and aggressive social behavior on human nature, when it is society that should be held accountable.[122] Religion may denature us, as all the philosophes contended, but society does so even more. We have come far, indeed, from the deification of society by the likes of Dumarsais and Holbach.

As for Diderot's request that each individual consult his or her reason in the silence of the passions, Rousseau reminded the philosophes what they, Diderot more vehemently than most, had always known, that our passions come first, reason later and as little more than, in the words of Hobbes, the "scouts and spies" of the passions.[123] It turns out that Pascal scored heavily, after all, when he wrote that all our reasoning amounts to little more than giving in to passion. Diderot's violent reasoner is driven by "violent passions"; his being is possessed by deeply harmful emotions that are the result, not of the "wretchedness of man without God," but of the wretchedness of man in society. Naturally good, we have become socially bad; the natural passions that were admirable have yielded to vicious social passions.

In any case a rational understanding of the good of the species matters not at all if my personal good remains in doubt. "It is not a matter of teaching me what justice is, but of showing me what interest I have in being just," writes Rousseau in the name of the "independent man," his expression for Diderot's "violent reasoner." The rationally self-interested actor, if he exists, will understand that he had better do the vile deeds to others that they will do to him, should he fail to strike the first blow. What is the rational course, if not to ally with the strong so as to share the spoils they extract from the weak? "The proof that this is how the enlightened and independent man would have reasoned is that this is how every sovereign society accountable for its behavior only to itself does reason."[124]

Domestic politics, Rousseau notes in "Political Economy," may be cited to prove the same point:

> Aren't all the advantages of society for the powerful and rich? . . . Aren't all the exemptions reserved for them? And isn't public authority entirely in their favor? When an esteemed man steals from his creditors or cheats in other ways, isn't he always sure of impunity? . . . If this same man is robbed, the forces of law and order go into action immediately, and woe to the innocents he suspects . . . How different is the picture of the poor man! The more humanity owes him, the more society refuses him.[125]

Anyone foolish enough to do unto others as he would have them do unto him is, inevitably, a victim.

Against Diderot, Rousseau noted that "the term *human race* suggests only a purely collective idea which assumes no real union among the inhabitants who constitute it." So much, then, for Diderot's general will of the species (and so much, too, for the Kantian "regulative idea" of a general will). The only way for the general will to be more than a meaningless abstraction is to give it political embodiment in a republic. Likewise, the only way to encourage virtue, which is the "conformity of the private will to the general,"[126] is for the republic to foster civic virtue: "It is certain that the greatest miracles of virtue have been produced by patriotism. By combining the force of egoism with all the beauty of virtue, this sweet and ardent sentiment gains an energy which, without disfiguring it, makes it the most heroic of all the passions."[127] Inside the sentiment of patriotism lies a concealed syllogism, only the major premise of which is ever uttered: My country is great and admirable. Unstated are both the minor premise of my membership and the conclusion that I, too, am admirable. Yet however fueled by *amour-propre,* patriotism is responsible for what Hobbes could never explain except as insanity, that we are willing to sacrifice our very lives for something larger than ourselves.

All the foregoing comments on virtue were stated by Rousseau in his *Encyclopédie* article on political economy. In that same essay he sketched a civic way of life, a plan for the political education of the many, that would make the renewal of the general will our daily task. Rousseau portrayed a society dedicated to public affairs, a world in which social activities were, as in the ancient polis, fundamentally political in nature. We must be citizens first and foremost, cradle to grave: "The instant of our birth should be the beginning of the performance of our duties." In such a setting the family is charged with a public mission: "The Romans' virtue ... turned all their homes into as many schools of citizens."[128] Our reward for devotion to the common good is that we love our duty and ourselves; obligation and inclination are united, and the divided self created by society meets with a political cure.

Strong medicine, indeed, and not easily swallowed by the philosophes, always willing to compromise, and readily convinced that no difficult choices have to be made. No matter how much the partisans of humanity hated the Jesuits, a strange alliance of philosophe and Jesuit may be observed in the encyclopedia article "Society," large portions of which are borrowed from Father Buffier's *Treatise on Civil Society*.[129] What the *mondain* Jesuits shared with the *mondain* philosophes was the conviction that the exchange of services in civil society is proof that virtue could be made easy. Even Helvétius, the one philosophe in the 1750s who shared Rousseau's republicanism and admiration of Sparta, thought virtue can be made painless. Did not Plutarch's life of Lycurgus, with its account of naked women dancing in honor of heroic soldiers, more than hint that supposedly austere Spartan virtue was actually ensured by sexual abundance?[130] And is not the public interest simply the adding together, through legal sanctions, of private interests? Is not the "general will" just another expression for the "will of all"?

Would that it were so. But the truth is that civic virtue's healing powers are not without their unpleasant side effects. Montesquieu expressed the matter well when he pointed to an affinity between civic and monastic virtue:

> The love of our country is conducive to a purity of morals, and the latter is again conducive to the former . . . How comes it that monks are so fond of their order? It is owing to the very cause that renders the order insupportable. Their rule debars them from all those things by which the ordinary passions are fed; there remains only this passion for the very rule that torments them. The more austere it is, . . . the more force it gives to the only passion left them.[131]

Rousseau underscored the simultaneous magnificence and horror of civic virtue by relating the story of a Spartan mother, unmoved by the news that her five sons had perished in combat, but deeply gratified to learn Sparta had won the battle.[132] Both the monk and the citizen have been "denatured," the monk because of the mistaken belief in original sin, the citizen because of the correct belief that our socially acquired nature must be redirected to find its satisfaction in identification with the public good.

"Happy are the peoples among whom one can be good without effort and just without virtue," Rousseau sighed.[133] Alas, such peoples, save for a few Swiss mountain-dwellers and the downtrodden inhabitants of tiny Corsica, no longer exist.[134] Nonrepressive virtue is impossible, now that *amour-propre* has exiled the natural goodness of *amour de soi* to the outermost limits of the psyche. Under present circumstances the "will of all" would signify the exaltation of the reign of *amour-propre*, rather than the triumph of the "general will." Reluctantly but necessarily Rousseau was driven to reintroduce the morality of the higher self. For us to enjoy doing the right thing, we must constantly be pulled out of our selves in an incessant whirl of civic rituals. *Laissez-faire, laissez-passer,* are the slogans of the historically acquired lower self. True freedom, freedom from base passions, freedom of self-mastery, comes solely to citizens who consent to be "forced to be free."

Not coercion but subtle psychological pressure is what Rousseau has in mind; in a well-regulated republic, he repeatedly advises, "every citizen shall feel the eyes of his compatriots upon him every moment of the day."[135] The philosophes counted on the internalized eyes of others to hold us morally accountable, forgetting that living to please the members of a corrupt society was what got us into trouble in the first place. Only when the eyes always watching us are those of fellow citizens are we likely to overrule the lower self.[136]

What are we to do if, as is almost always the case, the public assemblies of a republic have nothing to do with our daily existence? Julie knows how to state the arguments of "dangerous reasoners" with perfect lucidity. She grants the "common utility" of virtue, but asks,

> what does that matter compared with my particular interest, and which in the end concerns me more, that I should attain happiness at the expense of others or they should attain theirs at my expense? If fear of shame or punishment prevents me from acting badly for personal benefit, I have only to do wrong in secret and virtue will no longer have anything to say to me.

In the eyes of God she finds a substitute for the eyes of citizens.

> Adore the Eternal Being ... It is he who never ceases to cry to the guilty that their secret crimes have been seen, and who says to the forgotten just person, Your virtues have a witness ... Supposing this immense being does not exist, it still would be good to occupy ourselves constantly with him, in order to be more master of ourselves and happier.[137]

Does Pascal say it any better in his notorious "wager"?

One can well imagine how frustrated Diderot must have felt when he read Julie's words. Originally the *Encyclopédie* article on natural right had been assigned to Boucher d'Argis; Diderot wrote his version because the essay submitted by his colleague copied Burlamaqui in founding natural law on God and "internal sentiment." It was undoubtedly with great satisfaction that Diderot replaced God with reason, and internal sentiment with a pure act of understanding.[138] How troubling it must have been to discover that Rousseau had raised compelling doubts about our ability to silence the violent reasoner within each of us, short of returning to faith.

We can reconcile interest and virtue by re-creating Sparta in the modern world, as Rousseau proposed in the case of Poland; or reconciliation can be effected through appeals to eternity. Most assuredly, however, we cannot merge interest and virtue, as Voltaire and the philosophes would, through glorifying *la vie mondaine.*

Utility for Citizens and Children

How much a philosophe Rousseau remained even after controverting all the most significant recommendations of the philosophical party may be seen in his enduring concern to justify his proposals in the language of self-interest and utility. At the outset of the *Social Contract* he announced his intention "to reconcile in this research what right permits with what interest prescribes." That the interest in question was at least as much personal as it was collective is made clear in Rousseau's discussion of what, supposedly, is the most collectivistic of his concepts, the "general will."

> Why do all constantly want the happiness of each, if not because there is no one who does not apply this word *each* to himself, and does not think of himself as he votes for all? Which proves that the equality of right, and the concept of justice it produces, are derived from each man's preference for himself.[139]

Elsewhere in the same work Rousseau tries to formulate the general will by canceling out the differences of the various private wills—evidence that he was constantly on the lookout for ways, whenever possible, to sidestep the "higher self."[140] Kant, Hegel, and T. H. Green, fervent devotees of the "higher self," may have believed that they were the children of Rousseau; if so, they must be added to the list of his unwanted and illegitimate offspring.[141]

"How can one find a real and this-worldly advantage in being good among the many wicked—there is the philosopher's stone which is still to be found,"[142] Rousseau wrote to Dom Deschamps in August 1761. A year later in *Emile* he is still skeptical that such a discovery can be made, unless the highly unlikely occurs, that we find ourselves living in the social and political order prescribed in the *Social Contract.* Under present conditions arguments based on self-interest have their limits, for "as soon as an interest causes a promise, a greater interest can cause the violation of the promise."[143] Nevertheless Rousseau does all he can in *Emile* to enlist interest, whenever possible, in his cause. Education goes wrong when it speaks of duty too early; the genetic order is one in which "the first sentiment of justice does not come to us from the justice we owe but from that which is owed us."[144] It is Emile's concern for *mine* that prepares him to appreciate what is *thine*. One day he will be ready for questions of duty, but only after prolonged preparatory work within the realm of interest; so wrote Rousseau in words sounding like those of many another philosophe.

To make Emile an independent, autonomous person, able to go his own way rather than yield to society, is a difficult task. One of the few weapons at the disposal of the educator who would help his pupil fend off social pressures is "immediate and palpable interest." Anytime Emile can see that to learn something is to serve his "present interest," he is acting for himself, not for the sake of opinion.[145] As long as he thinks only of himself, he is not yet seeing himself through the eyes of others. Unworried about others, he is neither their slave nor—a second way of losing independence—their master.

Weak, the child tries to compensate by dominating others; cries that were originally for help degenerate into tears shed to order others to serve his whims.[146] Again utility comes to the rescue. Many questions asked by children have no other purpose than to compel adults to respond. "In what way is what you ask me useful to know?"[147] asks the tutor, who has never requested anything of Emile unless its utility was immediately obvious. Because the child cannot answer the tutor's query their conversation is over, and it will not be renewed until the youngster addresses the interests of his *amour de soi* rather than those of his budding *amour-propre*.

Utility also has its uses in teaching the child to appreciate those members of society who do the most vital work and receive the least in return. A reader of *Robinson Crusoe*, Emile knows how to evaluate the social contributions of his fellows. "He will want to know all that is useful, and he will want to know only that." Artists are worth little, artisans a great deal more; farmers, and after them ironworkers and carpenters, are the most valuable.[148] Born to the aristocracy, Emile thinks as a democrat without knowing what the word means, simply because utility is his constant concern.

When Rousseau refuses to follow utilitarianism, it is for the noteworthy reason of protecting the individual human being.

> If someone tells us it is good that a single man should perish for all, I shall admire this adage from the lips of a . . . virtuous patriot who consecrates himself willingly . . . to die for the safety of his country. But if this means that the government is allowed to sacrifice an innocent man for the safety of the multitude, I hold this maxim to be one of the most execrable that tyranny ever invented . . . Rather than that one ought to perish for all, all have engaged their goods and their lives for the defense of each one.[149]

Some three years after Rousseau wrote these words Helvétius coined a formula that Bentham saw as a direct forerunner of his own, "the greatest good of the greatest number."[150] Rousseau was all for this utilitarianism, but insisted upon the qualifications necessary to prevent it from being used to abrogate individual rights; which is to say, his qualification of utilitarianism is such as to offer further evidence of his entire agreement with the goals of the Enlightenment.[151]

The Misanthrope Avenged

To the philosophes Rousseau was the author who transformed the comfortable conceptual universe they inhabited into the worst of all possible intellectual worlds. He was the writer who journeyed both back to religion and onward to the uncharted waters of radical republicanism—this after setting sail from the philosophical port of sympathy for *amour de soi*, for self-interest, and for the project of grounding virtue in interest. With a friend like Rousseau, the philosophes did not need traditionalist and Catholic enemies.

Rousseau was also the man who offered a mirror image of Pascal from within the philosophy of the Enlightenment. Pascal had recited the litany of human woes: the divided self; the self that, lost in past or future, is never present to itself; the social relations that revolve around never telling the truth either to others or to ourselves; the supposedly august human reason that, in fact, is the captive of despicable passions. After denying original sin in good philosophical fashion, Rousseau proceeded to restate systematically the functional equivalent of Pascal's negative account of the human condition. Our social existence does, indeed, make us live in regret of lost opportunities or in anticipation of future successes; as a result, we never live in the present or, more poignantly, we die before we have lived.[152] Moreover, society constantly does battle with the remnants of our natural pity, thus dividing us into partially social, partially natural selves. Reason develops after the rise of noxious, socially induced passions, and as their slave. Finally, it is true, painfully so, that social exchanges are a matter of seeming instead of being, of *paraître* rather than *être*.[153] Society, for the philosophes our savior, is in every regard the reason why we need salvation, whether under the auspices of religion or of a civic republic.

Add that Rousseau's general will, besides contradicting Diderot's, was another mirror image of Pascal. In the *Pensées* we learn that to "tend toward the general" through absorption in the body of Christ is to witness the transfiguration of *amour-propre*.

> To be a member is to have no life . . . except through the spirit of the body . . . We love ourselves because we are members of Christ. We love Christ because he is the body of which we are members. All are one.

How very different, remarks Pascal, this Christian self-love is from the worldly variety:

> The separated member believes itself to be a whole, . . . and tries to make itself its own center and body. But it only wanders about and becomes bewildered at the uncertainty of its existence.[154]

Compare, nuance for nuance, Rousseau's later vision of civic membership, expressed in words startlingly reminiscent of Pascal's religious phraseology:

> Your true republican is a man who imbibed love of the fatherland . . . with his mother's milk. That love makes up his entire existence: . . . the moment he is alone, he is nothing.[155]

Down to the details of its rhetorical embellishments Rousseau's thought recaptures the "feel" of the *Pensées,* even as Jean-Jacques continues to press the agenda of the Enlightenment.[156]

Holbach in the early 1770s still found it necessary to take on Pascal; Voltaire throughout his life, and even in his last year, continued to search for a proper refutation of the sublime misanthrope; Condorcet, especially when editing Voltaire's works, sensed the need to rejoin the battle.[157] Clearly the philosophes could never be done with Pascal.

All the less, then, could they ever be done with Rousseau, who posed an even greater threat. After reading him it was difficult to share Voltaire's complacent conclusion that Paris refuted Pascal. Could it be that Pascal had been correct all along, albeit for the wrong reasons, and that the correct reasons would come to light when one faced up to what was revealed by "the philosophy of the Enlightenment"?[158]

CHAPTER TWO

Philosophical History

UPON entering the French Academy in 1787 the historian Ruhlière delivered a speech in which he singled out 1749 as the turning point of the eighteenth century, the moment when the capital supplanted Versailles as the arbiter of taste, and the Parisian philosophes gained an invaluable opportunity to mold what was called "public opinion."[1] He might have added that 1749 was also the year when Rousseau read in the *Mercure de France* that the Academy of Dijon had called for papers on the question "Has the progress of the arts and sciences done more to corrupt or to purify morals?" The resulting *Discourse on the Sciences and Arts* was only one of several works at mid-century that were exercises in the new history, *l'histoire de l'esprit humain*, as its practitioners called it, or simply *l'histoire philosophique*. In 1750 Turgot read two lectures before the Sorbonne on the progress of the human mind through the ages; a year later Voltaire's *Century of Louis XIV* appeared, as did another important contribution to philosophical history, d'Alembert's *Preliminary Discourse* to the *Encyclopédie*.

The advent of philosophical history was not a sudden event, of course. Most of the first two chapters of the *Century of Louis XIV* had already appeared in 1739,[2] and in 1745 Voltaire sketched a *Nouveau plan d'une histoire de l'esprit humain* in the *Mercure*. Even before the dawn of the eighteenth century, moreover, Fontenelle had written essays on the mind in early societies, as revealed by fables and oracles, and on the claims of the Moderns against the Ancients—essays suggesting those twin themes of a primitive mentality and the possibility of progress that were central to later contributions to the genre of philosophical history.

Long in the making, philosophical history was also a long-lasting intellectual enterprise, its final statement, Condorcet's *Esquisse d'un tableau historique des progrès de l'esprit humain,* written during the Revolution and in the shadow of the guillotine. Between the precise midpoint of the century and Condorcet's sketch near the end, the most significant experiments in the new history, arguably, were Voltaire's *Essai sur les moeurs et l'esprit des nations* and two works by Rousseau, the *Discourse on the Origin of Inequality* and the (unpublished until 1781) *Essay on the Origin of Languages.*

Why write history, if it is a story of political intrigue, military slaughter, and persecution, a tale full of sound and fury, signifying nothing? The aim of philosophical history was to substitute intellectual and cultural history for political and military history, the record of the triumphs of the mind for the bloody and vainglorious triumphs of the sword.[3] Keeping the nobles and king at bay was one objective, fending off the Church the other of philosophical history. When the philosophes wrote that the purpose of the new history was to rid us of error by detecting the origin of false beliefs, they usually meant superstition. Tracing the birth of the gods to the fears of primitive peoples, who were totally at a loss for scientific explanations of threatening natural phenomena, was a means of freeing moderns from religious enthusiasm.[4] A more subtle and deeply embedded source of error lay in language; consequently, from Locke on, the philosophes repeatedly attempted to undo our linguistic befuddlement, to eliminate meaningless words or to recover the meanings that predated linguistic corruption. Before long it became clear that linguistic analysis required study of the history of language. Not the least of the anticipated results was the destruction of those Cartesian innate ideas that threatened to become an impregnable fortress of religious belief in the modern and "enlightened" world.

Rousseau's *First and Second Discourses* and *Essay on the Origin of Languages* were major contributions to a program of research that was common to the entire philosophical movement. As always, however, Rousseau was with the philosophes only to turn their thought against them. In his hands philosophical history taught that the attempted separation of political from cultural history had pernicious political consequences; that the philosophes, moreover, harbored many "innate" and pernicious ideas in their fundamental assumptions; that one had merely to rearrange the statements of the philosophes in the appropriate order to draw the conclusion that civilized society was a greater threat than religion to the integrity of human nature; and that the proposed clarifications of the French language were the crushing finale to what the philosophes themselves implied was historical "progress" in the regrettable form of destroying what may well have been the finest expressions of *l'esprit humain*.

Ruhlière was correct in citing the middle of the century as the coming of age of the philosophes. But he should have added that it was also the coming of age of philosophical history and of Rousseau's use of that history to launch his attack on the position staked out by the philosophes. After completing his destructive agenda, Rousseau turned to philosophical history once more to assist him in outlining his alternative Enlightenment (see Chapter 5).

Cultural versus Political History

Have there been only kings on the face of the earth?[5] So asked Voltaire when he outlined his *Nouveau plan d'une histoire de l'esprit humain*. The point of the *Century of Louis XIV* was "to depict for posterity, not the actions of a single man, but the spirit of men in the most enlightened age the world has ever seen."[6] In these pages the reader was told to expect "not a bare record of campaigns, but rather a history of the manners of men."[7] It may be questioned, however, whether Voltaire's performance matches his rhetoric; for if the sections on the new cultural history highlight the novelty of the *Century of Louis XIV*, the old history of battles and courtly intrigue constitutes its overwhelming bulk.

On history, as in many other matters, d'Alembert was happy to follow Voltaire's lead and to pursue the philosophical agenda more rigorously than his master. The *Encyclopédie*, he noted, deliberately ignores "the conquerors who have desolated the earth [and concentrates] on the immortal geniuses who have enlightened it"; the editors and contributors hold that "the very names of princes and nobles have no claim to be found in the *Encyclopédie* except for whatever good they have done the sciences, because the *Encyclopédie* owes everything to talents, nothing to titles, and is the history of *l'esprit humain*, and not of human vanity."[8]

Both in the *Century of Louis XIV* and in the *Essay on the Mores and Spirit of Nations* Voltaire took great comfort in finding in the historical record evidence of four earlier enlightenments, four centuries dear to a philosophe seeking relief from the tale of the past as one of unending crimes and follies, four periods of hope proving that the ongoing eighteenth-century Enlightenment was not without illustrious historical antecedents. So welcome was Voltaire's formulation that one finds it again, in whole or in part, in d'Alembert, Turgot, and other philosophes.

"The man of taste," wrote Voltaire, "numbers only four ages in the history of the world; four happy ages when the arts were brought to perfection and which, marking an era of the greatness of the human mind, are an example to posterity." The first of these ages was that of Philip and Alexander or, rather, of all those writers and artists associated with the Greek enlightenment, Aristotle, Plato, Phidias, and Praxiteles, among others. Then came Caesar and Augustus, and the Roman enlightenment—the age of Lucretius, Cicero, Livy, Virgil, Horace, Ovid. Next, after many centuries of darkness, the voyager through history reaches the time of the Medici and the Renaissance in Italy. Finally, we set foot in the age of Louis XIV, which is also the period of classical French literature. "All ages resemble one another in respect of the criminal folly of mankind, but I know only of these four ages so distinguished by great attainments."[9]

In the second half of the *Preliminary Discourse* d'Alembert took up Voltaire's scheme of enlightenment gained, lost, and reborn, beginning with the Renaissance. Of the three faculties of the human mind, memory, imagination, and reason, it was memory that was the first to revive after twelve bleak centuries. Awed by antiquity, given to worship the Greek and Roman past, the Italian humanists cluttered their minds with ancient documents. For d'Alembert no greater measure of the shortcomings of this earliest of modern enlightenments was thinkable than the esteem in which erudition—the knowledge coming from books rather than nature—was held. With the wisdom of hindsight it was clear, thought d'Alembert, that the "progress of the mind" since the Renaissance followed a path from memory to imagination to reason, from history to belles-lettres to philosophy. His being the age of philosophy, d'Alembert was convinced that there was no further use for erudition—an opinion shocking to the visiting Gibbon but typical of the philosophes. What could be more damning than for Turgot to interrupt his epic of the progressive evolution of the human mind when he came to the subject of erudition, a form of knowledge "which does not move forward at all."[10] Ever the perfect hostess, Madame Geoffrin arranged for the erudites and the philosophes to attend her salon on different evenings.

That humanist historiography had been a matter of mere memory was only one of d'Alembert's complaints about the likes of Livy, Bruni, and Guicciardini. In his *Reflections on History* d'Alembert expressed displeasure with the rhetorical splendor that compromised the commitment to truth of ancient historians and their Renaissance imitators.[11] All such humanist historical writings, moreover, were overburdened with endless descriptions of military battles, the very subject matter most deserving of neglect. D'Alembert is far from unsympathetic to a hypothetical critic of historical writing who favors reading the history of an insect or a plant to all the annals of Greece and Rome.[12] History is the lowest form of knowledge except when written by philosophers.[13]

All in all, d'Alembert's comments on the Renaissance are anything but a ringing endorsement. The "first century of Enlightenment"[14] it may have been, but what set the Renaissance apart from the "age of philosophy"[15] was as remarkable as what tied it to that later age. To be so hard on the Renaissance and yet to save the day for the theme of pre-Enlightenment was possible because d'Alembert could suggest that as the imagination (the second faculty of the mind) asserted itself, the result was a great outpouring of literature, beginning in the Renaissance and culminating in the age of Louis XIV, the period that Voltaire immortalized in one of his best historical works. Even the Jansenists, Voltaire and d'Alembert agreed,[16] contributed to the grandeur of the seventeenth century by purifying French prose.

What an age it was, remarked Voltaire, when "a Duc de la Rochefoucauld, author of the *Maxims,* after discoursing with a Pascal and an Arnauld, goes to the theater to witness a play of Corneille."[17] Turgot's lectures on philosophical history, in keeping with the judgment advanced by Voltaire, feature sentences that substitute exclamation points for periods whenever the march of progress reaches the era of the Sun King: "O Louis, what majesty surrounds thee! What splendor thy beneficent hand has spread over all the arts! Thine happy people has become the center of refinement! Rivals of Sophocles, of Meander, and of Horace, gather around thine throne! Arise, learned academies, and unite your efforts for the glory of his reign!"[18]

Grand it was, this century of Louis XIV, so magnificent that it overshadowed its successor century. At one and the same time the classical era of French letters was a testimonial to the grandeur of the human spirit and to the inevitable inferiority of what followed, no matter how enlightened. To the end of his days Voltaire believed his was an age of cultural decline, that Augustan Rome and the France of Louis XIV marked limits beyond which the human mind could not pass and perhaps would never again equal. Fontenelle sometimes believed the same, as did Turgot and various other philosophes.[19]

By no means did the absence of an eighteenth-century Corneille, Racine, or Molière imply that the world was moving backwards. On the contrary Voltaire, who was so much more skeptical than Turgot about the ultimate triumph of progress,[20] nevertheless proclaimed that "the intellect of Europe has made greater progress in the last one hundred years than the whole world has made since the days of Brahma, Fohi, Zoroaster, and Thaut of the Egyptians."[21] Much had already been accomplished by the philosophes and more was certain to follow, provided that Louis XV or his successor learned to support arts and letters with the munificence that had characterized the reign of Louis XIV. "All these great men were known and protected by Louis XIV,"[22] asserted Voltaire, who accentuated and exaggerated the generosity of the Sun King so as to chide Louis XV for his stinginess.[23] "Louis XIV . . . gave greater encouragement to the arts than all his fellow-kings together."[24]

Possibly of more lasting importance than all his many other undertakings, definitely of greater significance than his many foolish wars, was the Sun King's record of presiding over the inauguration of academies, the Académie Royale des Beaux-Arts (1648), the Académie des Inscriptions et Belles-Lettres (1663), the Académie d'Architecture (1671), and the Académie des Jeux Floraux (1694). Generally speaking, the status of intellectuals in England, as depicted in Voltaire's *Lettres philosophiques,* was one their French counterparts were certain to envy—with a single but most notable exception: the Royal Society of London fares poorly when compared to the Académie des Sciences (1666). "In Paris membership of the Academy means a guaranteed small fortune for a mathematician or chemist; on the contrary, it costs money to belong to the Royal Society."[25]

It may be that royal patronage cannot restore French letters to their seventeenth-century heights; it may be that there is a deeper, more "philosophical" explanation of literary malaise than the shortfall of pensions. Even so, progress need not disappear from human affairs. Turgot both gives reasons for the failure of art to progress and points to the consolation awaiting anyone who examines the chronicle of continuing scientific advance: "Knowledge of nature and of truth is as infinite as they are: the arts . . . are as limited as we are. Time constantly brings to light new discoveries in the sciences; but poetry, painting, and music have a fixed limit ... The great men of the Augustan age reached it, and are still our models."[26] D'Alembert, too, in the *Preliminary Discourse* and whenever he devotes his energies to philosophical history, stresses the history of science, the one realm in which progress is undeniable.[27]

Whenever he can discuss Galileo, Harvey, Huyghens, Pascal the scientist, or Leibniz the mathematician, d'Alembert is at ease, untroubled for the moment by his conviction that barbarism is "our natural element, reason and good taste only passing."[28] The revival of learning begins with memory and its intellectual offspring, historiography; moves on to imagination and the magnificence of letters in the Grand Siècle; and reaches its zenith with the maturation of science, proof that the faculty of reason has finally come into its own. What makes this progression even more enticing is that science can, to some degree, use imagination rather than sacrificing it on the altar of reason. It was a worthy achievement on the part of Fontenelle, duly praised by d'Alembert,[29] that he had been able to write about science with the literary grace of a man of letters. Many an aristocratic lady, who otherwise would have been scientifically illiterate, learned at least the rudiments of the new physics through reading the dialogues of Fontenelle. For his part d'Alembert, by writing the *Preliminary Discourse,* expanded his own reputation from that of a formidable mathematician to that of a man who henceforth held joint membership in the ranks of the scientists and the *gens de lettres.*[30] Thus d'Alembert joined Fontenelle in using belles-lettres, the realm of imagination, to further the scientific cause.

Able to enlist imagination in the service of science, the philosophes were equally adept in showing how the faculty of reason can avail itself of the uses of memory. Philosophical history was precisely the merger of reason with memory that called for an end to the long-standing animus against history common to such otherwise divergent philosophers as Locke and Descartes. It was not exclusively high culture and high enlightenment that fell within the purview of this new history written by philosophes. Turgot also paid attention to the history of the mechanical arts because it proved that the Middle Ages were not blank pages in the history of progress. All the more likely, then, that the forward march was irreversible, since it had withstood the famine of Gothic ignorance, drawing more than enough nourishment from the everyday intelligence of the most simple and uncultured persons. The needs of life sustain the mechanical arts in the worst of times, and these arts are "a succession of physical experiments which progressively unveil nature."[31] Science never disappears from the face of the earth, and its persistence guarantees that the chain of progressive historical continuity remains unbroken.

Many of the philosophes did not share Turgot's conviction that progress is irreversible.[32] D'Alembert's comment that barbarism is our natural element, Voltaire's vision of history as alternating periods of light and darkness, of catastrophic rather than evolutionary change,[33] Fontenelle's apparent belief that, despite progress, the primitive mentality still lies dormant just beneath the surface of the most sophisticated nations,[34] were far more typical of the philosophes. All the more important, argue Diderot and d'Alembert, that the *Encyclopédie* should be a collective effort in philosophical history,[35] all the more essential that its contributors address their topics historically as well as systematically[36] and that the editors keep uppermost in mind their daunting task of recapitulating the usable past so that future generations can build on the firm foundations laid by the encyclopedists. No generation should ever again find itself compelled by the neglect of its ancestors to collect and reassemble all human knowledge.[37] Updating being so much easier than starting over, it is the surest way of perpetuating progress.

The knowledge the encyclopedists intended to pass on to the future included an exhaustive account of the mechanical arts, past and present. It was not enough to record the list of inventions through the ages, as Turgot had done; Diderot wanted to supplement such knowledge with an explanation, whenever possible, of how new techniques and machines came into existence. Usually he found insufficient evidence to re-create the history of invention, and so resorted to conjecture; that which was lost in historical narrative by such a procedure could be gained in philosophical insight—in the suggestion, that is, of an orderly and logical sequence leading from the first intimations to the fully developed machine or procedure.[38]

Whatever was missing in our knowledge of past mechanical arts would be compensated for by a thoroughgoing *Description des arts* in the eighteenth century. Discoveries, inventions, techniques, methods of organizing production in Diderot's day—all this was to be documented in the *Encyclopédie.* D'Alembert had opened the *Preliminary Discourse* by saying that the *Encyclopédie* was to be "the work of a society of men of letters." Four years later Diderot emended the official posture of the editors on the composition of the contributors: "This is a work that cannot be completed except by a society of men of letters and skilled workmen."[39] A partnership (between unequals) was needed to spread enlightenment in the form of material progress; the philosophe would visit the workshops, and a few of the skilled workmen would become ever so slightly philosophical.

In addition to descriptions and illustrations of productive techniques, the encyclopedists set out to clarify the language of the artisans, whose nomenclature was marred by excessive synonyms and by such imprecision as using the generic name "machine" or "engine" when referring to different tools.[40] Previously intellectuals had studied the language of workers as a form of dialect and without reference to practices; Diderot insisted on referring words to things and on admitting technical terminology to the linguistic stock of the *gens de lettres*.[41]

In writing the history of production the philosophes added another chapter to *l'histoire de l'esprit humain,* an installment stressing the interrelationship of theory and practice that Bacon, their acknowledged forerunner, had placed on the agenda of modern philosophers, whom he urged to break with the classical prejudice against the mechanical arts. Quite in keeping with Bacon's injunctions was Diderot's remark to the effect that there is as much intelligence in a machine for making stockings as in a system of physics or metaphysics.[42] Not the least of the goals of the *Description des arts* was to popularize so effectively the standard of utility as to remove the social stigma attached to the status of worker, and to entice—or cajole—the *grands* into abandoning their useless lives.[43]

Philosophical history had a social point but it did not offer its readers much in the way of social history. Beyond commentary on popular superstition and an occasional remark on mores, Voltaire's *Essai sur les moeurs et l'esprit des nations* did not live up to its title; satirical wit and an everready yardstick for measuring how closely various ages resembled the Enlightenment are not likely to yield insightful social history. D'Alembert's article "Character" contains some remarks on national character, but his claim that the *Germania* of Tacitus may be consulted for insight into the Germans of his age underscores his shortcomings as a historian of social mores.[44] Diderot's "philosophic suppositions" about the origins and development of the mechanical arts are by his own account not "true history"; the logic of analysis and composition is the method of his philosophical history of productive techniques, ordinary minds its intended audience, clarity of exposition its objective.[45] Diderot was not writing history of any kind, so he could not possibly contribute to what we now term social history.

Not that the philosophes tried to write social history and failed; such an intellectual endeavor was never their intent, notwithstanding the efforts of some students of the Enlightenment to read the concerns of our age into an earlier period.[46] What the philosophes wanted was to link together past, present, and future, ensuring by their own efforts the progressive unfolding of history, since history left to itself was utterly devoid of direction and bereft of meaning. To many of them belles-lettres were so unprogressive that simply to regain the prowess of the age of Louis XIV was an uphill struggle. Hence they counted heavily on science, pure and applied, to pull the weight of mankind from one era to another in a noncyclical, unilinear, and possibly progressive temporal movement.

"What's it good for?" is the question the uncultured many always ask of the activities of the cultured few, noted Diderot,[47] whose pronouncements on the ingenuity of the artisans are characteristically accompanied by declarations that the people will never learn to think for themselves.[48] For all his care to make the cultured elites discern the theory hidden in the practice of workmen, Diderot was just as eager to make the workmen respect theory, which they would never do unless its utility were demonstrated. Diderot's was not a narrow utilitarianism, disdainful of pure science and philosophical speculation; it was a utilitarianism, instead, that sought to protect the theorizing of the few from the surrounding masses by giving the people ample reasons to believe that abstract theory might one day improve their lives. Only when the theory implicit in practice was displayed to the *grands* and the practice implicit in theory displayed to the populace could the hope of continuing progress be safeguarded.[49]

Of all historical outlooks, perhaps none is further removed from social history than that which in its more modest form is biography and in its more enthusiastic incarnation is the "great man" approach. If so, philosophical history may well be deemed the very opposite of social history, for the writings of d'Alembert and company were largely chronologies of great thinkers, each praised for those of his contributions still serviceable to the men and women of the eighteenth century. The *éloges* delivered by Fontenelle as perpetual secretary of the Academy of Sciences, and later by d'Alembert as secretary of the French Academy, prepared the way for the new history. Fontenelle early in the century, d'Alembert in the middle, Condorcet toward the end, had much the same goal in mind when delivering eulogies of academicians. Where once there had been the funeral orations of Bossuet and the "lives of the saints," where the old historians had recorded the heroic butchery of nobles and king, there would now be the new hero of history, the philosophe whose deeds enriched lives instead of causing deaths. For the glory of fighting, the philosophes substituted the grandeur of scientific discovery and literary achievement—accomplishments beneficial to humanity and therefore worthy of remembrance.[50]

Forging a bond of intellectual inheritance and continuity among past, present, and future, philosophical historians manufactured progress rather than recording it. What history left to itself would never do, the philosophes would do to history by mentally intervening in the past, tying it to ongoing efforts in the present, for the sake of making possible a better future. All would gain from what the philosophes were doing, the philosophes most of all from the history by and largely about philosophers.

Cultural as Political History

Rousseau's *Discourse on the Sciences and Arts* argues, in effect, that the separation of cultural from political history was itself a political act. Specifically, it amounted to a glorification of monarchies and a denigration of republics; for when philosophes wrote history they praised the eras during which previous philosophes had flourished, which were times of declining republics and ascendant principalities.

The great age of Athenian philosophy, art, and letters was marked politically by the waning of the republic and the rise, as Voltaire had indicated, of Philip and Alexander. The story of the Roman enlightenment duplicated that of the Greek: Cicero, Livy, Virgil, and Horace obtained their fame during the death agony of the republic and the triumph of Caesar and Augustus. In modern times Florence had enjoyed a great intellectual rebirth, a renaissance, but it was not only ancient Roman literary genres that were reinvigorated; also reborn was the pattern of princely power supplanting a civic way of governing and living. The Medici never for a moment assumed that their patronage of the arts was politically neutral; only an historian as determined as Voltaire to write the politics out of the relationship between politics and the arts could so radically distort the historical record.

How very political Voltaire's supposedly nonpolitical history is may be seen in his comments on the seventeenth century. For Voltaire it was not enough to offer the aesthetic judgment that "the age of Louis XIV is of the four great periods perhaps the one which most nearly approaches perfection." Besides the quality of French letters in the era of the *grand monarque,* Voltaire took special pride in pointing out that "Europe has owed both her manners and social spirit to the court of Louis XIV."[51] Each of his readers was invited to share Voltaire's admiration of the triumph of absolute monarchy in France and of the dissemination of the French example across Europe. Call this history if your name is Voltaire; call it monarchical ideology if you answer to "Jean-Jacques."

"It is not the history of revolutions of states or of wars ... that must be studied," wrote Fontenelle in his essay *On History.*[52] Rousseau was quite willing to agree that the old political and military history was worthless but adamant that philosophical historians were, in fact, anything but silent about revolutions and wars. Voltaire was conspicuously recording revolutions—revolutions that were far more than coups d'état; he was actively endorsing the downfall of republics and the rise of monarchical successor states. Omitted from Voltaire's account, however, was an explanation of these dramatic changes. Rousseau was ready to supply the missing pages of Voltaire's history in the *Discourse on the Sciences and Arts.* The decline of the citizens' militia in Italy and in antiquity was what made the Florentine, Roman, and Athenian polities ripe for overthrow, and this waning of military virtue was itself directly linked to the enervation of the civic life that always accompanies, or is accompanied by, the flowering of the arts. No more than his fellow philosophes did Rousseau recite the history of battles, but he did place the military ethos under the magnifying glass and found that it waxed and waned in direct proportion to the absence or presence of the arts. Simplicity of mores was historically associated with military virtue; polished mores with armies no longer composed of citizens.

Lest Voltaire somehow miss the point, Rousseau drove it home by extending his findings to the Chinese, the Spartans, and the Scythians. Crude, primitive, even barbaric, the Scythians were "the most miserable of peoples, yet they successfully resisted the world's most powerful kings."[53] Athens was "the abode of civility and good taste, the country of orators and philosophers"; Sparta, by contrast, "chased the arts and artists, the sciences and scientists from its walls." Nevertheless, it was Athens that fell to Sparta.[54] China is "an immense country where honors for learning lead to the highest offices of state," wrote Rousseau, sounding for all the world like Voltaire, who saw the mandarins as philosophes for whom knowledge was indeed power.[55] Very un-Voltairian, however, was the question Rousseau then proceeded to pose: "If neither the enlightenment of government officials, nor the supposed wisdom of laws . . . of that vast empire were able to save it from the yoke of the ignorant and coarse Tartar, what purpose did all its learned men serve?"[56]

Beyond its specific argument, Rousseau's critique of philosophical history was noteworthy for its considerable rhetorical power. "Citizen" was a word dear to the philosophes, one that appeared with regularity in the pages of the *Encyclopédie*[57] and in the other writings of the members of the philosophical party. Not all the philosophes agreed with d'Alembert's estimate that the expulsion of the Jesuits in the 1760s would improve the lot of the party of humanity; all were as one, however, in saying he had done well to address from the civic point of view the issues presented by a religious order's owing allegiance to a foreign power.[58] Even more important than "citizen" in the discourse of the philosophes was "virtue," the dominant word in their moral vocabulary. Rousseau's masterstroke was to argue that we can have neither citizens nor virtuous persons unless the two are merged in civic virtue. Because philosophical history had divorced politics from mores, it had also separated citizenship from virtue, effectively undermining both.

Much later, in *Emile,* Rousseau complained bitterly that "the French, having judged it suitable to usurp the respectable name of citizens, . . . have denatured the idea of citizenship to the point where one no longer has any conception of it." Under such circumstances it would be better, he thought, to efface *patrie* and *citoyen* from the modern French language.[59] This conclusion is already suggested by his very early *Discourse on the Sciences and Arts:* "We have physicists, geometers, chemists, astronomers, poets, musicians, painters; we no longer have citizens."[60]

Subjects, not citizens, "happy slaves," not free men, the French are the willing servants of monarchy, the intellectuals the most eager of all to aid and abet the social and political order that makes modern men as small as they were great in the republics of old. What do our modern arts, letters, and sciences do, other than "spread garlands of flowers over the iron chains with which men are burdened, and stifle in them the sense of that original liberty for which they seemed to have been born?"[61] What do the Parisian and provincial academies do, other than defeat the agrarian ideal central to republican thought, as stated by Aristotle and the Roman authors? After noting the "many establishments created for the benefit of the learned," Rousseau drew a perverse conclusion: "It seems there are too many farmers and that a lack of philosophers is feared."[62]

Under a well-regulated republic a plain man who serves his country receives the recognition that is his due; this same person in a monarchical regime is ignored or derided, his honors usurped by those who practice the "pleasing" rather than the "useful" arts. *Gens de lettres* live to please—and at the expense of those who furnish the means of subsistence.[63]

How can anyone speak, as the philosophes did, about the unity of theory and practice in a society where "there are a thousand prizes for noble discourses, none for noble actions?"[64] Monarchy is all theory and no practice, all seeming and no being. In Sparta, where the practice of civic life was everything, theory was unnecessary; as for the Romans, all was well as long as they were content to practice virtue; "all was lost when they began to study it."[65]

While still relatively young Rousseau observed with disappointment the corruption of the much-vaunted and supposedly immortal Venetian commonwealth: "Since then, my views had become greatly enlarged by the historical study of morals. I had come to see that everything was radically connected with politics, and that . . . no people will ever be other than what the nature of its government makes it."[66] The *First Discourse* was his initial effort to pass on this political insight to the philosophes. Sometimes inadvertently, sometimes deliberately, philosophical history before Rousseau had been a celebration of monarchy; in his hands its republican uses became evident, as he showed how monarchy defaced everything it touched.

If modernity paled when contrasted with the civic virtue of antiquity, it fared no better when measured against the standard of an original, natural, unspoiled simplicity and decency. A rich example was furnished by the American Indians, used by philosophes to argue that progress had occurred, used by Rousseau to demonstrate just the opposite. Fontenelle among others had underscored the similarity of the myths of the Indians and the Homeric Greeks, proof that the vaunted Greeks were primitives and that the Moderns were infinitely more sophisticated than the Ancients.[67] How amused and pleased with themselves the philosophes must have been to make this particular argument for progress by drawing upon the Jesuit Father Lafitau's researches on the "mores of the savage

Americans compared with those of the earliest times."[68] How annoyed and displeased they must have been with Rousseau, who when praising the Indians at the expense of the civilized Europeans was careful to cite Montaigne as his source,[69] the same Montaigne all the philosophes regarded as one of their own but ahead of his time. Whatever the misdeeds of the Indians, the savages were the very picture of unspoiled goodness compared with the Spaniards who raped the Americas.

Other peoples appearing in the *First Discourse* just long enough to take a quick bow include the Germanic tribesmen, the Swiss who fought the Hapsburgs, and the "herring fishers" of the Netherlands who braved Philip II of Spain. Each of these combined, in some measure, the republican spirit with the original simplicity of nature so dissimilar to Spartan denaturation. The point of mentioning these once exemplary peoples is to show that our historical "progress" may equally well be regarded as regress. "Our souls have been corrupted in proportion to the advancement of our sciences and arts toward perfection."[70]

Rousseau's essay begins with an endorsement of enlightenment and ends with a plea for deliverance from the same: "It is a grand and beautiful sight to see man emerge from obscurity somehow by his own efforts; dissipate, by the light of his reason, the darkness in which nature had enveloped him."[71] Such are Rousseau's words at the outset, but after surveying the historical record he prays that God "deliver us from the enlightenment and fatal arts of our forefathers."[72]

Diderot devoted many years to the single most visible monument of the Enlightenment, the *Encyclopédie,* so that "the labors of past ages may be useful to the ages to come, that our grandsons, as they become better educated, may at the same time become more virtuous."[73] So much labor lost, then, Rousseau insisted, because placed within the conceptual universe of classical thought, the modern world was as corrupt as the ancient had been virtuous. Radically deficient in civic virtue, the moderns were also devoid of that natural goodness[74] found sometimes in an older, now defunct world, occasionally still found in the most unpolished of the souls dwelling in the land of the living.

Conjectural History

Rousseau's *Discourse on the Origin of Inequality* and *Essay on the Origin of Languages* belong to another version of philosophical history, one initiated by Fontenelle in his early conjectural essays on the origins of fables and oracles, then refurbished in 1746 by Condillac in his *Essai sur l'origine des connaissances humaines,* which had an enormous impact on how the philosophes viewed the legacy passed on to them by Locke's *Essay Concerning Human Understanding.* The *Histoire naturelle* of Buffon, the first volumes of which appeared in 1749, and part of d'Alembert's essay of 1751 introducing the *Encyclopédie* added further installments to the repertoire of conjectural histories immediately preceding Rousseau's work. Roughly the first half of the *Preliminary Discourse* was devoted to sketching a hypothetical development of *l'esprit humain* from the most remote times, an intellectual exercise that should be distinguished from the cultural history, from the Renaissance to the Enlightenment, that d'Alembert outlined in the second half of his essay. Within the pages of the first volumes of the *Encyclopédie,* moreover, Marmontel's article "Critique," Diderot's distinction between true and philosophical histories of inventions, and his assertion that "each city has two origins, one philosophical, the other historical," constituted significant contributions to the theory and application of hypothetical or conjectural history, the second form of philosophical history.[75]

Because Condillac was the chief intellectual inspiration of philosophical history in its guise as hypothetical or conjectural history, it may be said that Rousseau was present at its birth as well as the sponsor, years later, of some of its most remarkable intellectual adventures. First of the philosophes to know and esteem Condillac, Rousseau introduced him to Diderot, who helped the shy and withdrawn author of the *Essai sur l'origine des connaissances humaines* secure a publisher.[76] From its inception Rousseau was fully informed about the new way of thinking, and had ample time to ruminate on its possibilities before the Academy of Dijon called for essays on the question of the origins and legitimacy of inequality.

Lockeans all, the philosophes split on the question whether conjectural history was the fulfillment or the repudiation of their godfather's sensationalism. Voltaire, who had imported Locke in the *Lettres philosophiques,* resisted hypothetical history. Reared during the years of the debate on early Roman history that split the Académie des Inscriptions and ended in the victory of *le Pyrrhonisme de l'histoire,* Voltaire was not about to squander on conjectural fantasies the hard-fought respectability that historical studies had slowly attained over the succeeding decades. Probable truths are within our reach if we study modern history, where evidence is readily available and the record unencumbered by the fables that fill the records of antiquity. All is lost, however, if metaphysical speculation finds the home in historical studies denied it in philosophy by Locke.[77]

So spoke Voltaire, but the philosophes who refused to follow his lead also regarded themselves as the children of Locke. D'Alembert's statement that philosophical history addressed the "origins of our ideas"[78] reveals the Lockean inspiration of the new form of inquiry, as does the constant occurrence of the word "origins" in the titles of works devoted to conjectural history. It was Locke's contention, repeated by the philosophes, that failure to remember having acquired an idea was what misled us into believing it innate.[79] Consequently philosophical historians devoted themselves to the task of helping us overcome our amnesia, the forgetfulness that afflicts both individuals and the entire species. To recover the past we must resort to a conjectural account because it is impossible to recall our earliest years or those of the human race. "Back to origins," the most Lockean of injunctions, was obeyed with special rigor by those who went beyond sense-experience to conjectural history.

Ultimately what the philosophes wanted to unearth was the origin of religion, buried under the ignorance and fear of natural forces so characteristic of primitives and children. Hence the philosophes translated the works of English deists who had explained the psychopathology of fanatical belief; and for similarly antireligious reasons they reissued the writings of Protestants unmasking pagan superstition. To recollect the source of religious convictions is to gain freedom from the demons of our imagination. Such exercises in reconstituting an unrecorded past were all the more necessary because the Church had learned to save its teachings from criticism by having recourse, whenever possible, to the Cartesian notion of innate ideas. After waging a bitter rear-guard campaign against Descartes, the Church sometimes turned to him for salvation.

Every pretender to the title of an innate idea had to be exposed by showing its coming to be, otherwise we shall never unlearn the mental habits that foster superstition. The research program of the philosophes was to trace the roots of all ideas set forth as innate; any conception in their thought that so much as hinted of the innate was a scandal. Nothing, therefore, was more characteristic of the French philosophes than their denial of the "moral sense" spoken of in enlightened English and Scottish thought. Diderot, Helvétius, Holbach, Condorcet, the philosophes one and all, rejected the notion of a moral sense or a moral instinct that they found in Hutcheson or Smith.[80]

Diderot answered with the voice of all philosophes when he responded to the question whether in ethics and aesthetics legitimate appeal might be made to a "sixth sense."

> I replied that this sixth sense, which a few metaphysicians have brought into fashion in England, is a figment of the imagination; that all our ideas come from experience; . . . that when we are conscious of the motives of our actions, judgments, and proofs, we are said to have knowledge of them; that when we cannot remember them we are said to possess taste, instinct, or flair.[81]

Similarly, in the *Encyclopedia* article "Beau," Diderot replaced Hutcheson's "internal sense" of beauty with an account of the beautiful based on relationships of objects to persons, objects to objects, or of one aspect of an object to another. As he saw it, the sense of beauty was a slowly acquired capacity for perceptual virtuosity that required a historical explanation.[82]

For all his admiration of the creative powers of exceptional persons, Diderot always insisted that genius was not above rational comprehension. Having discovered that the dome of St. Peter's in Rome was not only elegant but the strongest of designs, Diderot rejected the claim that Michelangelo's achievement was inexplicable. Instead he sketched a hypothetical biography of young Michelangelo wrestling with classmates and piling up books, unknowingly learning "the curve of greatest resistance."[83]

Insistent on understanding the workings of Michelangelo's genius, Diderot was even more determined that the virtuosity of experimental scientists should not remain mysterious. Socrates' personal "demon," Michelangelo's so-called "instinct," and the "spirit of divination" that enabled great scientific practitioners to "smell out" the way to conduct a difficult experiment were all based on years of accumulated wisdom whose ways and means have never been conceptualized by their proud possessors. All such extraordinary persons are obliged, he argued, to look inside themselves, "to substitute for their familiar demon clear and intelligible notions, and to pass these on to others."[84] If it was intolerable that artisans should refuse to reveal their trade secrets,[85] it was no more acceptable for artists and scientists to pretend that their accomplishments were the result of innate, ineffable characteristics.

Following in the footsteps of Condillac, the philosophes not only laid claim to Locke's heritage; they also set out to prove themselves more Lockean than Locke. The "historical, plain method"[86] of the *Essay* was descriptive rather than genetic. Locke took for granted an autonomous power to reflect on sense data; explained the origin of ideas entering the mind but not the origin of our mental faculties; and never addressed the genesis of language. Convinced language, far from merely expressing our thoughts, is what makes thinking possible; recognizing, furthermore, that language is a collective inheritance, Condillac boldly inserted a hypothetical history of language into his *Essai*. It was as vital for Condillac, the empiricist, to write the history of language as it had been for the rationalists of Port Royal to delineate its structure—the grammar believed by Cartesians to be the expression of innate laws of thought.[87]

Down, then, with innate language; down also, adds Condillac, with innate mental faculties. Memory, imagination, judgment, will—all the faculties—were derived from, if not reduced to, sensation in his *Treatise on the Sensations* (1754). Step by hypothetical step, Condillac brought a statue-man to mental life through pure sensation, in fulfillment of the empiricist program of research. From the historical, plain method to hypothetical history the distance was great indeed; nevertheless, if Newtonians could legitimately invoke abstractions such as force and mass, Condillac could with similar warrant conjure up the abstraction of a statue not yet exposed to external stimuli. How else can we imaginatively reenact the birth of the faculties?

It is tempting to suggest that philosophical history in its guise as conjectural history is the study of the development of mind, whereas in its incarnation as cultural history it is the study of the products of the mind, the arts and sciences: tempting and perhaps useful, but not entirely correct, for Condillac's hypothetical history of language has much to say about the arts as they once were but will never be again. Rousseau's *Essay on the Origin of Languages in Which Something Is Said about Melody and Musical Imitation* takes up where Condillac left off. Reworked by Jean-Jacques, Condillac's *Essai* becomes the last thing its author intended, a searing indictment of the culture and politics of modernity.

To the philosophes, cultural history was the story of what had gone right, conjectural history largely but not exclusively the tale of what had gone wrong over the centuries. By conjecturally delving into the distant and hidden past, the philosophes hoped to locate the moments when error entered the human mind. Churchmen turned to "sin," philosophes to "error," to explain why so many backward steps prevented humanity from marching progressively forward across the ages. Projection of human traits onto natural objects was one way the primitive and childish mind had gone astray, argued the philosophes; improper use of language was another. From Locke on, a hue and cry against scholasticism as a systematic abuse of language characterized the works of the philosophes, Rousseau's included.[88] Eventually the clarification of language the philosophes sought was added to the tasks of conjectural history: every abstract word had to be decomposed, the experience leading to its formulation reconstructed, so as to recapture its meaning or to purge it as meaningless.

Conjectural history shares with cultural history the objective of making progress possible. Bacon had championed the moderns by declaring them the true ancients; Fontenelle did the same by comparing mankind to a single person who matures but does not die. With the help of Locke, all the philosophes sought to give new significance to this well-worn comparison of the species to an individual; the child psychology and educational program of Locke, so impressive when applied to the particular person, spell progress when applied to mankind,[89] or so the philosophes believed. How shocking, then, to hear Rousseau conclude that our progress has been "so many steps toward the perfection of the individual and toward the decrepitude of the species."[90]

Conjectural History Radicalized

Repeatedly Rousseau informs us that his *Discourse on Inequality* is a "conjectural"[91] history of "the development of our faculties and the progress of *l'esprit humain*."[92] As if to make certain the reader appreciates both his affinities with the philosophes and his distance from them, he coins the word "perfectibility" for use in this essay,[93] then goes on to raise the possibility that this, the most special of all faculties, the one that (along with freedom) makes us different from the animals, may be the source of all our miseries. In words almost identical to those uttered in the *First Discourse,* he laments "the fatal enlightenment of civilized man."[94] Philosophical history had been the praise of the enlightened present and the hope for an even more enlightened future; then came Rousseau who wrote the *Second Discourse* so that his contemporaries could learn "to judge our present state correctly." Recast by Rousseau, philosophical history was "the eulogy of your first ancestors, the criticism of your contemporaries, and the dread of those who will have the unhappiness to live after you."[95]

Whether it was a matter of looking for earlier enlightenments or of presupposing a rational actor in the state of nature, the philosophes always read themselves back into the past, after which they projected themselves into a future that was a fulfillment of their present strivings. Unlike his predecessors, Rousseau believed the philosophical historian should take change seriously, should realize how different the past was from the present, how barbaric the future that awaits the very societies that pride themselves on their civility.

Marmontel's article "Critique" bears directly on the project of philosophical history. Read one way, Marmontel yields the standard position of the philosophes; read another, his methodological injunctions yield Rousseau's astonishing challenge to his comrades. "There are truths," wrote Marmontel, "that the distance of places and times render inaccessible to experience, and being for us only in the order of possibles, cannot be observed except with the eyes of the mind." The problem of seeing with our mind what our eyes cannot view may be resolved if we recognize the "chain of facts" that binds together past, present, and future. Setting out from the present, the critic must trace the chain back to its beginnings and forward to its eventual consequences. "To reduce the investigation of physical truths to rules, the critic must hold the middle and the end points of the chain."[96]

Argument by analogy, sanctioned by Locke himself,[97] was the method by which Marmontel expected to move from the observed present to the unobserved past and future. When a primitive mind interprets the unknown on the basis of the known, the consequence—noted Fontenelle—is the expansion of ignorance through the investment of nature with human traits.[98] By contrast, when a philosophe armed with mature reason does the same, the result is a lighting up of dark, obscure times and places.

Such was the standard argument, yet there are ample indications that as the philosophes strove to see the unseeable, they did so with "eyes of the mind" suffering from severe myopia. Voltaire's frequent repetition of the mistake of the English deists who posited the existence of an original, natural religion preceding the corruptions of later ages,[99] his portrayal of Julian the Apostate and Confucius, of mandarins and Brahmans as early philosophes, exemplify his failure to divest himself of the "enlightened" present as he traveled across time. Even Hume, great philosopher though he was, applied his empiricism to history in a manner that canceled out the significance of time: "Would you know the sentiments, inclinations, and course of life of the Greeks and Romans? Study well the temper and actions of the French and English."[100] How different, in the end, were the philosophes from the priests they despised, who defended the contemporary relevance of Church traditions by charging the living clergy with the task of reading the present into the past and the past into the present?[101]

In terms of the "chain" spoken of by Marmontel, the philosophes started from the middle, that is, from the present, and then moved backward and forward in time, carrying their present with them. Holbach, for instance, held that to discuss rights and duties "it suffices to consider man such as he presents himself to our view, such as he constantly acts before our eyes."[102] Against such a backdrop one can well appreciate Rousseau's frequently quoted words: "The philosophers who have examined the foundations of society have all felt the necessity of going back to the state of nature, but none of them has reached it . . . All of them . . . have carried over to the state of nature ideas they have acquired in society: they spoke about savage man and they described civil man."[103] Not the least absurd result is that natural man is portrayed, in total abandonment of Locke's developmental psychology, as a kind of philosophe,[104] so adept is he in the exercise of abstract reasoning.

Alone among his contemporaries, Rousseau understood how difficult it is for a person living in society to think his way back to the state of nature. Our pitiful plight is that the more we understand nature, the less we comprehend human nature: "As all the progress of the human species continually moves it farther away from its primitive state, the more new knowledge we accumulate, the more we deprive ourselves of the means of acquiring the most important knowledge of all; so that it is, in a sense, by dint of studying man that we have made ourselves incapable of knowing him."[105] In consequence all discussions of natural right, premised as they are on failed concepts of human nature, are worthless.

Rousseau appreciated "the surprising power of very trivial causes when they act without interruption;"[106] he understood that to follow the chain through endless centuries would be to see not more of the same but endless transformations, so great that "the human soul, altered in the bosom of society by a thousand continually renewed causes, . . . has changed its appearance to the point of being nearly unrecognizable."[107]

How may the philosophical historian formulate a conjectural but defensible notion of prehistorical humans? By a series of negations. What social man is, natural man was not. In society we have infinite desires and needs, chase after the illusion of the perfect love, are tormented by our imagination with thoughts of what we might have been or perhaps will be; as social beings we make use of language, are bound together in a multiplicity of relationships, must work and toil, are nevertheless dependent on others and see ourselves through their eyes. After deleting the foregoing social constructions from our experience, we are left with an independent animal living in an eternal present, who copulates but knows nothing of romance, grunts rather than speaks, does have sensations, but for whom imagination, memory, and reason do not exist—an animal whose only needs are something to eat when hungry and water from a nearby stream when thirsty. Like the newborn baby in society, the species in its earliest infancy was a *tabula rasa*.

It was not only Locke but the French Lockeans Rousseau was thinking of when he wrote his description of the original human being. In volume three (1749) of the *Histoire naturelle* Buffon set forth a disquisition on the senses, including a section discussing a "first man," just come to life, who encounters the world and himself through the exercise of his five senses.[108] Shortly thereafter Diderot, in his *Letter on the Deaf and Dumb* (1751), issued a somewhat similar call for exercises in "metaphysical anatomy."[109] Several years later, while Rousseau was writing the *Second Discourse*, his friend Condillac was composing the *Treatise on the Sensations* in which a statue-man, starting from bare sensation, is progressively brought to possession of all the mental faculties. Rousseau's original human parallels the result of Condillac's thought experiment, both in his original emptiness and in the subsequent tale of the experiences that lead humankind from its original purely sensate existence to one that includes memory, imagination, and all the powers of the mind now taken for granted. What makes Rousseau unique is that he transposed the statue-man from epistemological debates to the theory of natural rights, specifically to discussions of the "state of nature."

Having set forth a depiction of an animal-man, Rousseau was now in possession of the middle and one end of Marmontel's chain. The state of nature was the first link in the chain, Paris the middle link. What Rousseau saw when he looked at the humans of his day was the civility noted by all the philosophes and, what none of them was willing to see, a brutal inequality, words divorced from actions, actions that contradicted words, and an unhappiness engulfing all social ranks, masters as well as servants.

Diderot had undertaken the educational labors of the *Encyclopédie* so that his countrymen would become "more virtuous and more happy."[110] Rousseau in the *Second Discourse* continued to observe in polished France that which he had pointed to in the *First Discourse,* "the semblance of all the virtues without the possession of any."[111] As for happiness, there was laughter aplenty amid the glitter of Parisian society, but no genuine joy where ridicule was the source of humor. Maupertuis was correct to find that the evils of life outweigh the goods, his only mistake being his failure to realize that such is the condition of social man, not man as such. "It is not without difficulty that we have succeeded in making ourselves so unhappy."[112]

With first and middle links defined, Rousseau turned his attention to the missing connections between these two established points: "When two facts given as real are to be connected by a series of intermediate facts which are unknown or considered as such, it is up to history, when it exists, to present the facts that connect them; while it is up to philosophy, when history is lacking, to determine similar facts that might connect them."[113] Diderot had gone so far as to say that a philosophical history can be more illuminating than a true history;[114] Rousseau appears to agree, and to hold that nothing is more effective than philosophical history at dissolving the petrified beliefs of the philosophes. When Rousseau wrote conjectural history, one after another of the unquestioned assumptions of the philosophes—each the functional equivalent of an innate idea— melted into a pliable historical acquisition.

Foremost among the axiomatic and therefore unquestioned assumptions of Rousseau's peers was their belief in natural sociability. As advocates of natural rights, they had all read their Grotius who posited sociability as a given; as foes of Pascal, they were anxious to wrap mankind in the warm blankets of nature and society, sewing the two together so tightly that the seams did not show. Contrary to their advocacy of empiricism, they regarded social relationships as the expression of a herdlike human essence, never examining the possibility that it is society that turns humans into a conformist herd.[115] Ironically it was the philosophes, for all their rhetoric about natural sociability, who failed to explain how deeply socialized we have become; it was Rousseau who, having denied the congruence of nature and society, set out to trace the social origins and development of almost everything that now characterizes humanity. None of the philosophes could even begin to compare with Rousseau, the theorist of natural man, when it came to explaining the power of society to shape and mold our every thought and desire.

An instinct for Voltaire,[116] a law of physical nature for Helvétius and Holbach,[117] *amour-propre* was another item on the list of what supposedly has to be simply because it is. All the philosophes were guilty of repeating the mistake of Hobbes, who attributed to man in the state of nature a striving to get ahead of everyone else that obviously assumes a social context. Left to ourselves in the natural state, we no more have a fully developed sense of self than does a newborn in society. Placed in a social setting, we both gain a sense of self and lose ourselves in the eyes of others: "The savage lives within himself; the sociable man, always outside of himself, knows how to live only in the opinion of others; and it is, so to speak, from their judgment alone that he draws the sentiment of his own existence."[118] Originally ours was a harmless love of self, the natural desire of any creature to remain alive; later, through social interaction, love of self became transmuted into selfishness. The shape *amour-propre* takes, the extent to which it overrides *amour de soi*—these matters remain open because they depend on the type of education a person receives.

Again in defiance of Locke, the philosophes frequently separated reason from the passions and treated reason as timeless or fixed. Voltaire's insistence upon applying the standards of his France to all times and places, Diderot's appeal in "Natural Right" to a reason that speaks in the silence of the passions, are striking examples. Rousseau, by contrast, identified the socially generated passions of humans moving away from nature as the parents of human reason. In empiricism it is the comparison of perceptions that yields reason; to which Rousseau added that the comparative perceptions in question are less of natural objects than of oneself with others.[119] Reason, then, is a power that comes to be; born after and of *amour-propre*, it is both temporal and tainted, less a tribute to human greatness than to pettiness. All of Rousseau's works may be read as efforts to disentangle reason from its disreputable social origins. But as matters now stand, "one no longer finds anything except the ugly contrast of passion which presumes to reason and understanding in delirium."[120]

Above all, the philosophes regarded property as an unquestionable right, sanctioned by nature and "right reason." To listen to theorists of natural right and their eighteenth-century progeny, one would think that property rights have always existed, when within the expansive temporal framework of conjectural history they belong to the "last stage" of our loss of nature. Rousseau opens the second part of the *Discourse on Inequality* with the statement that the first man to fence off a plot of land and declare "this is mine" was the architect of civil society and thus of injustice and misery. He continues: "This idea of property, depending on many prior ideas, . . . was not conceived all at once in the human mind. It was necessary to make much *progress,* to acquire much industry and *enlightenment* . . . before arriving at this last stage of the state of nature" (emphasis added).[121] It is necessary to write the history of inequality and of progress, with emphasis on the latter term if one is a philosophe, on the former if one is Rousseau.

Inequality begins when humans have settled together in juxtaposed huts, such that each person, in daily contact with his kind, begins to see himself through the eyes of others and is anxious to be seen in a favorable light. From the moment we care what our neighbors think of us, our concern is to find a standard of rank-ordering in which we score higher than our fellows: "People grew accustomed to assembling in front of the huts . . . Each one began to look at the others and to want to be looked at himself . . . The one who sang or danced the best, the handsomest, the strongest, the most adroit, or the most eloquent became the most highly considered; and that was the first step toward inequality and, at the same time, toward vice."[122] Nothing more characterizes our selfishness than how it feeds on the insecurities of our socially acquired selves. The less we belong to ourselves, the more we demand that others reassure us, even to the point of preferring us to themselves, which can never be.[123]

The entire fate of socialized humanity is present in embryo at the first dance, both the shared joy of spontaneous interaction and the development of a comparative, calculating rationality, driven by *amour-propre.* Once ensconced in the bosom of society, our varying and unequally distributed attributes, so irrelevant in the state of nature, begin to make all the difference. Those who are more cunning take the lion's share of all things desirable, most of which are longed for only insofar as other persons are deprived of the same.[124]

In the meantime the growth of infinite desires, having nothing to do with natural needs, gives humans a reason to seek together what they cannot achieve separately. Increasing economic interdependence, praised by Turgot in his lectures on progress, entails the loss of independence and freedom.[125] It also provides new opportunities for the more clever and able to take advantage of their simpler comrades. "Personal qualities are the origin of all inequalities, wealth is the last term to which they are reduced—an observation which can permit a rather exact judgment of the extent to which each people is removed from its primitive institution."[126] No longer do great holdings of inherited wealth have anything to do with merit, and never did riches bear any relationship to justice: "for we are born with our talents, only our virtues belong to ourselves."[127]

Rousseau was familiar with Locke's argument that, in mixing our labor with the land, we come to view property as an extension of our persons. But his familiarity with the *Second Treatise of Government* was the kind that breeds contempt. Maliciously, Rousseau comments that because the rich spread their selves over their vast properties, they are far more subject to injury than the persons in the state of nature, who carry their entire being with them wherever they go.[128]

Locke's masterstroke against Filmer's attack on the idea of a natural right to property was to suggest that lands originally prepared by God for mankind as a whole were later legitimately carved through labor into individual parcels. When was unanimous consent to individual ownership voted? asked Filmer.[129] No vote was needed, replied Locke: it was enough that, one by one, and without formal consultation or explicit agreement, tracts of land were appropriated by the sweat and toil of industrious persons. Whenever fences surround and divide all that was once the commons, unpropertied historical newcomers can sail to America or sell their labor to landowners in Europe.[130]

Filmer raised the question of consent for reactionary purposes; Rousseau did so to press a radical critique of all notions of a natural right to property, not excepting Locke's version based on labor.

> In vain the rich might say: I earned this field by my labor . . . They might be answered, by virtue of what do you presume to be paid at our expense for work we did not impose on you? Do you not know that a multitude of your brethren die or suffer from need of what you have in excess, and that you needed express and unanimous consent of the human race to appropriate to yourself anything from common subsistence that exceeded your own?[131]

The rich man spreads his personality too far; the poor man cannot afford the luxury of personality—such are the effects of property.

Nothing is more unnatural than the so-called natural right to property. It is only after nature has been driven out of us by society that human reason, the loyal servant of *amour-propre,* comes to formulate the concept of property rights granted by mother nature. Dead is the earth goddess who supposedly sanctions property rights, her body long ago hacked into pieces and devoured by her greedy, insatiable, denatured offspring. Having removed ourselves from nature, we then begin to do to fellow humans what animals refrain from doing to their own kind: kill one another to satisfy passions of greed and vanity.[132] So destructive are "the usurpations of the rich and the brigandage of the poor . . . that nascent society gives way to the most horrible state of war."[133] Wrong about nature, Hobbes is in every respect right about society.

Property is a means by which the privileged seek to codify radical and ever worsening inequality. Yet in the absence of external support it is an institution that, giving rise to civil wars, is bound to undermine its own foundations. Therefore the rich hit upon the invention of government, ostensibly to bring security to everyone, in fact to enable the wealthy to hold on to their already disproportionate possessions and to place themselves in a position to take from the poor, at a later date, the little they now have—all in the name of law and justice.

"All ran to meet their chains thinking they secured their freedom."[134] Little eloquence was necessary to dupe the crude humans of that early age when the first and, to date, only social contract was written and signed. But not even the simplest of men would have accepted the agreement if expressed in its true light: "Let us summarize in a few words the social compact of the two estates. You need me for I am rich and you are poor, so let us come to an agreement between ourselves. I shall permit you to have the honor of serving me on condition that you give me what little you have for the trouble I shall take to command you."[135] Nearly all the philosophes asserted, at one time or another, the theory of a social contract in which the protection of property arrangements was the foremost concern; none was willing to admit that he was expressing approval of everything that had gone wrong with human history.

After bemoaning the historical record as one of butchery, the philosophes turned around and grounded their social contract in tradition, partly to give concrete embodiment to philosophical abstractions, but also to present their reforms as unthreatening. Diderot opened his article "Autorité politique" with the challenging words "No man has received from nature the right to command others," an obvious denial of divine right; yet he ended the essay with praise of France, ruled in accordance with fundamental laws, and condemnation of Turkish despotism—a position hardly distinguishable from Bossuet's contrast of absolute with arbitrary monarchy.[136] In "Droit naturel" Diderot again appealed to historical example, no longer to specific countries but, rather, to "the principles of law written by all civilized nations."[137] Where else, he asked, can one expect to find a suitable depository of the general will?

To appeal to the legal principles of civilized nations, as Diderot did, was to remember one's reading of Grotius and to forget one's Montesquieu. The author of *The Spirit of the Laws* had noted that because modern writings on public law draw their examples from ancient histories, the result was "the erection of injustice into a system."[138] Rather than tame Leviathan, the classically educated Grotius, forever citing the bloody histories of the Jews and Romans, set it free to do whatever it wished and inadvertently encouraged modern states to proclaim a right to enslave and exterminate that exceeded current injustices.[139] Rousseau, too, would have none of Grotius: "His most persistent mode of reasoning is always to establish right by fact. One could use a more rational method, but not one more favorable to tyrants."[140] By implication Diderot and all the many philosophes who admired *The Law of War and Peace* merit condemnation along with their master for extolling a version of natural rights that fosters political absolutism and is an apology for whatever exists. Willing to admit a difference of method between the much praised Grotius and the frequently decried Hobbes, Rousseau nevertheless asserts that "their principles are exactly alike."[141]

Reversing Grotius who established right by fact, Rousseau wrote the *Second Discourse* "to test the facts by right."[142] Few facts, thus considered, passed inspection, least of all the historical social contract. Why tolerate an agreement conjured up by the rich man "to make his adversaries his defenders, . . . and to give them different institutions, as favorable to himself as natural right was contrary to him?"[143] Ostensibly the protector of natural rights, the social contract has been written to consummate their destruction.

Just as Rousseau criticized enlightenment in general from a standpoint sympathetic to enlightenment, so likewise did he attack theories of natural right as an advocate of natural right. It was not the notion of natural right per se but the use of that notion to legitimate absolute monarchy that aroused his wrath. Grotius held that rights are alienable, can be bought and sold, and have in fact been forfeited by many peoples, each of whom has chosen to purchase temporary security by capitulating to an arbitrary governmental authority. Rousseau countered by asserting that freedom, no less than "perfectibility," distinguishes humans from the other animals;[144] whence it follows that rights are inalienable: "To renounce one's freedom is to renounce one's status as a man, the rights of humanity and even its duties . . . Such a renunciation is incompatible with the nature of man."[145] Why Grotius should have gone so wrong is, then, not to be explained solely by noting the dedication of his book to Louis XIII;[146] his other fault was conceptual and lay in his failure to understand human nature.

"It is this ignorance of the nature of man that throws so much uncertainty and obscurity on the true definition of natural right."[147] Is there, however, anything left to "human nature" after peeling off all the socially acquired layers? Several years after the *Second Discourse* Helvétius would answer "no," and was consequently obliged to drop the doctrine of natural right, replacing it with utilitarianism. Rousseau answered in the affirmative, as he was entitled to by virtue of his refusal to accept Condillac's diminution of mind to a passive receptacle. In this regard Rousseau's position remained closer to Locke's than to that of the leading French Lockean philosopher, it being one thing to borrow Condillac's program of research when exposing the self-evident truths of the philosophes as sheer dogmatism, but quite another to treat mind in a way that invited determinism.

Before society begins to write its messages on the mostly blank slate of the mind there exist, Rousseau argues, "two principles anterior to reason, of which one interests us ardently in our well-being and our self-preservation, and the other inspires in us a natural repugnance to see any sensitive being perish or suffer, principally our fellow-men. It is from the conjunction of these two principles, without the necessity of introducing that of sociability, that all the rules of natural right appear to me to flow."[148] Rightly understood, generosity, benevolence, clemency, friendship, and humanity are all "the products of a constant pity." Commiseration is a natural sentiment which "carries us without reflection to the aid of those whom we see suffer; in the state of nature, it takes the place of laws, morals, and virtue."[149]

Prepared so well by nature to respect the rights of others, we lose our capacity for empathic identification with the suffering of fellow humans in direct proportion to our absorption into a world of social relations.[150]

Ambition, rivalry, class divisions are the more marked the further we travel from our original nature. It is too late for there to be any *natural* rights, too late to ground a new social contract on pity or any other natural sentiment, so little do our passions any longer have a basis in nature.

Long ago, when the foundations of natural right were still intact, the prerational occupants of the state of nature understood nothing of rights. Later, when reason is in play, nature is gone or is unreliable. As an extension of *amour-propre*, as the purveyor of oppressive doctrines of natural right, reason has been part of the problem rather than the source of a solution. Yet both in the preface to the *Second Discourse* and in the essay written in refutation of Diderot's "Natural Right," Rousseau insists that reason rise above its social origins, that it strive to "re-establish [the rules of right] when, by its successive developments it has succeeded in stifling nature."[151] Someone must come forward and announce those "principles of political right"[152] which, as conjectural history intimates, are the only possible substitute for natural right. And so it is that Rousseau's *Social Contract*, an ahistorical treatise, concludes the philosophical history of the *Discourse on Inequality*.

In the first version of the *Social Contract* Rousseau attempted to lay the "true foundations ... of natural right" and to articulate "the rules of reasoned natural right,"[153] expressions deleted from the final version, perhaps for fear they were misleading. After all, the rights guaranteed by signing Rousseau's ideal social contract are not natural rights but the functional equivalent of the same. Procedure is now more important than substance, convention more important than nature. That we freely consent to the new order, that all shall be dependent on the law and hence no one dependent on another person, that the laws we obey are laws we as citizens give ourselves, that laws must always be general and therefore incapable of overriding the rights of any individual or group—such are the political principles that underwrite our non-natural rights. Only in the event that government exceeds its authority may anyone utter words about natural right.[154]

Rights, consent, contract, obligation—Rousseau realized his vocabulary, so typical of modernity, would never amount to more than words unless reinforced by a rebirth of the civic virtue of antiquity. All our rights must be provisionally ceded to the community, lest individuals use them against one another in a high-sounding battle of wills—a self-righteous assertion of thinly veiled *amour-propre*[155]—that destroys the general will.

If no general will, then no community, and no rights that are upright. Until now, the effect of law has been to "contain men without changing them."[156] Existing legal arrangements, besides codifying the domination of the rich,[157] leave intact the impulses that culminated in the reign of inequality and injustice. Consequently, "one who dares to undertake the founding of a people should feel that he is capable of changing human nature."[158] Locke's stand on property is in every way objectionable, but his environmental psychology suggests that a return to the civic education of old could create moderns who have internalized the laws of a just republic. "The true constitution," proclaims Rousseau, "is not engraved on marble or bronze, but in the hearts of the citizens."[159]

Nature is "always the same," wrote Turgot, who contrasted it with human history, which "affords from age to age an ever-changing spectacle."[160] In thus setting history against nature, Turgot's intent was to extol the progress of the human species. Rousseau parted company with the champions of progress insofar as he lamented the loss of nature and of ourselves that progress has entailed. Still, the "perfectibility" that sets us apart from the animals, source though it is of our undoing, holds out the possibility that the person before our eyes is not the final word, that in a civic republic of the future the most common sight may be a different person, at one with himself and with his comrades.

"Let us consider what can be done on the basis of what has been done,"[161] wrote Rousseau, whose rejection of the past did not encompass antiquity. Romans did not need to use conjectural "eyes of the mind" to see what humans could be at their best; they had only to look out the window. Moderns should not worry, as Voltaire and d'Alembert did, over the accuracy of ancient historians, since whatever was lost in factual truth was gained in political inspiration. "The ancient historians are filled with views which one could use even if the facts which present them are false."[162]

The World We Have Lost

In the *Second Discourse* Rousseau attempted to discover and follow the "forgotten and lost routes that must have led man from the natural state to the civil state";[163] he did so to offset the amnesia that had resulted in proclamations of self-evident truths on the part of the very thinkers who denounced innate ideas. After designating Paris and the state of nature as the middle and beginning of Marmontel's chain, he wrote the mournful history of inequality that connected those two links. And he did one thing more: he recalled an enviable period during which the progress of the species was such that nature and society were one. Once upon a time the golden age spoken of by poets was more than a myth. That era was a reminder of what humans can be, and a new reason to condemn modern society. The world we have lost must be revisited, if only to learn how much we have lost.

Sometime after leaving the original, animal-like state of nature and long before the coming of society, there was a mean between those two periods far better than either. Rousseau counted the family among the many unwarranted givens postulated by the philosophes, but was quite willing to agree that once man and woman settled down in huts, the familial unit became natural. Nature offers us new opportunities at different moments in time, and truly outdid herself in giving birth to the first families.[164]

During the era of "nascent society" the family was a social unit that was natural, a natural unit that was social.

> Although natural pity had already undergone some alteration, this period of the development of human faculties, maintaining a golden mean between the indolence of the primitive state and the petulant activity of our vanity, must have been the happiest and most durable epoch ... All subsequent progress has been in appearance so many steps toward the perfection of the individual, and in fact toward the decrepitude of the species.[165]

Love of self and of others were one and the same in these early families, wherein *amour-propre* was absent, *amour de soi* present and expansive. Man and woman loved and found themselves in each other and in their children.

Something of this may still be seen in civilized societies, especially when the mother breast-feeds her child. In general, however, once the family became absorbed into a larger society, the relationships between husband and wife, parents and children, were corrupted; society penetrated the family, which henceforth served as an early training ground in *amour-propre*. To the extent that anything of the original family remains intact, it serves now only to pass on to children mixed messages that divide the self; precisely because the mother loves her child, she teaches him to push everyone aside in his race to the top. As it has come to be, the family also contradicts civic values in that it encourages us to sacrifice the public good to private interests.

Rousseau tells us more about the world we have lost in the *Essay on the Origin of Languages*. The family is not the only social institution missing from the original state of nature that later appears in the age of gold as an outgrowth of nature; language follows the same pattern. Animals do not speak, nor, presumably, did the first animal-humans. But when the first huts were constructed and the first society born, words whose source was the heart were sung by eager lips. This language, poetic and musical, the first of all languages, was natural because it expressed the unspoiled passions, particularly those of love. The purely natural being has no passions; the social being before our eyes has artificial passions. In between, Rousseau spied the creatures of the golden age, social and natural, whose passions are blessed by nature herself. Both Rousseau and the philosophes were champions of the passions, they of the passions as they are, he of the passions as they were. For the debased humans of his own day, Rousseau advised the repression and transformation of the passions into civic virtue. Nostalgia for the lost age when virtue was unnecessary fills the pages of the *Essay on the Origin of Languages*.

Were our needs merely physical, our language might never have exceeded communication through gestures: pantomime and other visible signs might well have sufficed to satisfy all our wants.[166] It was to express their passions that the men and women of old learned to speak. Not "aidez-moi" but "aimez-moi" was the meaning of the first words.[167] When in a dry southern clime men and women met at a watering hole, the sight of one another aroused long dormant passions. "Imperceptibly, water became more necessary. The livestock were thirsty more frequently."[168] Gesture being no longer adequate, the time was ripe for the social institution of speech.

Born before the maturation of reason,[169] born of passion, desire, and imagination, the first language was as emotionally expressive as it was referentially inexact.[170] A profusion of synonyms, a dearth of adverbs and abstract names, use of onomatopoeia, are some of the characteristics of language in its infancy.[171] Figurative, poetic, and unwritten, sung rather than spoken, this early language was one of inflections, intonations, accents.

"It is a mistake to think that accent marks can make up for oral intonation. One invents accent signs [*accens*] only when intonation [*l'accent*] has already been lost."[172] In short, French is a language which is the opposite of the original language; bare, monotonous, unmusical, and unpoetic, the language of the French people, in common with their entire culture, has lost contact with the sustenance nature and passion alone can supply. The superiority of light, melodic Italian opera to the artificial instrumental harmonies of Rameau that drown out the human voice, the unmusical quality of the French voice when permitted to sing, provide ample contemporary evidence for Rousseau's position.

All of which is to say that the *Essay on the Origin of Languages* is the culmination of Rousseau's musical articles in the *Encyclopédie* and of his leadership of the philosophes in the *querelle des Bouffons*. To a man, the philosophes who participated in the dispute sided with Rousseau in their praise of the *opera buffa* and ridicule of the singsong of Lulli.[173] None of them, however, was prepared for Rousseau's vehement assertion in the *Letter on French Music* (1753) that the French neither had nor would ever have music, because true music was sung but was unsingable in French.[174]

Yet they should have understood that Rousseau's *Letter* was merely their own position pursued to its conclusion. They, too, held that music is, or should be, spoken expression and evocation of passion; and they were thoroughly embarrassed by Rameau's anti-empiricist theories of harmony as a law of nature.[175] Rousseau was years ahead of their eventual rejection of Rameau's philosophical claims, and his repudiation was more comprehensive. Only modern Europeans, noted Jean-Jacques, enjoy harmony, an acquired taste of an overly developed civilization. Although music and language are always conventional, some of these conventions bear the imprimatur of nature; others, like Rameau's music which muffles the human voice, are the denial of nature.[176]

Our preference for instrumental harmonies over the melodies of the human voice is one measure of how far we have removed ourselves from nature. In the beginning music, poetry, and language were one;[177] later, as civilization was built on the grave of nature, there was a parting of the ways. More and more, music was one thing, speech another. More and more, language declined from poetry to prose. Once written down, language was not so much stabilized as radically altered,[178] its emotive power lost forever or only momentarily remembered, perhaps, when attending a performance of an Italian opera or Rousseau's *Le Devin du village*.[179] The moment over, we return to our denuded, self-congratulatory civilization. At an exquisite opera, we sometimes smile when a performer dies singing, a sure sign of how much we, in our pride and shallow pursuit of wit, have relinquished.[180]

Rousseau was not the first philosophe to place the debate on music, poetry, and language in the large, theory-building framework of philosophical history. As early as 1746, years before the battle between the corners of queen and king, Condillac devoted Part 2, Section 1, of the *Essay on the Origin of Human Knowledge* to a conjectural history of language. Hardly an argument of the *Essay on the Origin of Languages* is missing, whether in outline or in total, from Condillac's earlier work.[181] The major difference between Rousseau and Condillac concerns the question when to assign the word "natural," when the word "conventional."

Sometimes it is the senses, in Condillac's account, that lead to complex ideas, and then language is of secondary importance in explaining the development of the human mind; at other times thought so much presupposes linguistic signs that the more or less mechanical association of ideas is relatively discounted.[182] In the first version language is straightforwardly a natural acquisition pertaining to animals and humans; in the second it is mediately natural, because to Condillac society was present from the beginning, providing a basis in nature for linguistic rules.

Never a pure empiricist, Rousseau rejected the notion that sensations by themselves could develop the human mind: "The more one meditates on this subject, the more the distance from pure sensations to the simplest knowledge increases in our eyes."[183] Language and thought are inseparable, society impossible without language, language impossible without society. From which Rousseau concluded, first, that because society, the progenitor of language, is in truth a historical acquisition, we cannot assume that language always existed; and second, that once words were spoken, social and linguistic convention were responsible. Here as always Rousseau stressed how powerful society is as an entity in its own right, rather than as an expression of nature. Where Condillac cited *nature,* Rousseau cited *convention.*

Of even greater significance, Condillac made the opposite mistake of citing convention when nature was the appropriate category. It was Condillac's conjectural argument, amplified by Rousseau, that when the barbarians from the North spread across the Roman Empire, they confounded the Latin tongue with their own language, as cold as the climate of the countries from which the invading tribes hailed.[184] "Help me" was the primary cry of peoples who knew nothing of abundance, peace, repose, or of what accompanies these, the passions. As a result, the want of accents so characteristic of northern languages was imported to southern regions, such that even Italian is not a genuinely musical language, Rousseau contended, but merely one less resistant to music than French.[185]

Applying his conjectural findings to the France of his own day, Condillac nonetheless managed to conclude on a cheerful note. Italian music is admirable, but so too is French, each appropriate for its cultural (conventional) context.[186] The French language has smothered imagination and destroyed poetry and therefore can never hope to compete with the artistic wonders of ancient Greek culture; in compensation the simplicity of French lends itself to the clarity of expression that has so much to do with the European intellectual hegemony of Paris.[187] Different cultures, different conventions, and France the beneficiary of the historical changes that have moved Europe progressively away from music, poetry, and all the gifts of imagination—such was Condillac's stand.[188]

All Rousseau had to add was that the clarity of French can never offer anything approaching adequate compensation for what we have lost, which is nothing less than the splendors of nature, those elevated natural passions of the golden age, crushed by society and history. Where Condillac lauded a progressive evolution of *convention,* Rousseau lamented an irreparable demise of *nature.* At most, in Rousseau's view, the precision of French expression can make us understand the devastation that has proceeded apace with our notorious "progress." Such is the meaning of the beauty and sadness of the French language as written by Rousseau, especially in the *Essay on the Origin of Languages.* In elegant and lucid French, he challenged his readers to comprehend how anemic and impoverished all modern languages are, especially French. Rousseau wrote prose; Voltaire, long the cultural leader of France, penned emaciated poetry that illustrated Rousseau's point. Jean-Jacques did not have to be a preromantic to press his conclusion; it sufficed for him to be a faithful reader of Condillac, known to his contemporaries as the most philosophically sophisticated philosophe and to us as someone whose name is absent from every list of preromantics.

PHILOSOPHICAL HISTORY, both as cultural and as conjectural history, had aimed not so much to record as to promote progress. Along came Rousseau, who boldly embraced this genre of writing, so typical of the Enlightenment, and asked what was progressive about the obliteration of the golden age or the history of ever-increasing inequality. Enlightenment would have to be re-thought if it was to be more than a celebration of both injustice and the fatal divorce of culture and nature.

Rousseau was still not done. Marmontel had spoken of the middle and two ends of the chain, the present, past, and future; Rousseau took Paris for the middle, natural man as the commencement, and closed the *Second Discourse* with a conjectural finale to all that history has been and continues to be: "Here is the ultimate stage of inequality, and the extreme point which closes the circle and touches the point from which we started. Here all individuals become equals again because they are nothing."[189] The writings of Rousseau are sprinkled with apocalyptic asides, such as this footnote in *Emile:* "I hold it to be impossible that the great monarchies of Europe still have long to last."[190] By no means is he calling for the French Revolution; his statement is rather one of despair. The vision of equality as common enslavement to a despot, sketched in the last pages of the *Discourse on the Origin of Inequality,* continues to haunt his dreams.

We now know that the *Second Discourse* was originally meant to include a section denouncing the priesthood and superstition.[191] Whatever Rousseau's reasons for deleting that part of the planned text, it is singularly appropriate that he did so. Second to none of the philosophes in his ability to write tirades against the Church, Rousseau would have detracted from his own message had he included the section in question. Philosophical history had always taken "error," usually a code word for religious belief, as its target. Rousseau's contributions to philosophical history were written to show that the greatest "error" of all—the idol that had to be thrown down—was not God, the idol of the priests, but rather society, the idol of the philosophes.

CHAPTER THREE

From Criticism to Self-Criticism

"I T was on the 9th of April, 1756," Rousseau recalled years later, "that I left Paris, never again to live in a city."[1] Upon his departure the "Holbachian clique," he adds, openly predicted his return within three months and showered ridicule on him for deciding to forsake the capital. Why his comings and goings should matter so much to one of the leading centers of the French Enlightenment—the philosophical salon of the Baron d'Holbach—is not explained in the *Confessions*. The meaning of Rousseau's ride to the Hermitage on that fateful day is, however, anything but mysterious. All who frequented Holbach's residence on the rue Royale understood perfectly well the symbolic significance of Rousseau's move to the countryside.

In France a disgraced minister, forced to retire from Versailles and Paris, was said to be living in "exile," so unthinkable was it that anyone of worth would freely choose to live in the hinterlands. Rousseau's self-exile, therefore, was dramatic proof he was in earnest in the *First and Second Discourses* and the *Preface to Narcisse,* and had decided that the most effective way to refute the convenient dismissal of his writings as mere paradoxes was to conform his practice to his theory. Voltaire had cited Paris to deny Pascal's account of the human condition; in leaving Paris, Rousseau indicated that the solution of the philosophes was itself part of the problem. By implication all who stayed in Paris were obstacles to enlightenment properly understood.

What made Rousseau's withdrawal all the more disturbing was that it placed him in the position of appearing to be the only writer willing to make the sacrifices the philosophes themselves indicated might be necessary if the new intellectuals were to serve as agents of enlightenment.

"Liberty, Truth, Poverty" should be the motto of the philosophe, wrote d'Alembert.[2] It is a measure of how powerfully Rousseau captivated public opinion that the Marquis d'Argenson, in his notebook, mistakenly attributed d'Alembert's motto to Rousseau.[3]

Without saying a word, Rousseau spoke most eloquently the day he rode out of Paris. By gestures and symbols he contributed to an ongoing discussion that, perhaps more than any other, defines the French Enlightenment. As never before, the writers of the eighteenth century wrote about themselves, their circumstances, their social role, their need to attain group identity and to carve out for themselves a respected niche in the social order. For every page written on the "human condition," the philosophes penned another on their condition, on the arrangements necessary to support a new kind of intellectual, above patronage, independent, self-supporting even if born outside the ranks of the privileged, and thus qualified to be a spokesperson for humanity.

Looking back from 1787, Ruhlière noted it was in the pivotal year 1749 that "the dignity of men of letters" became a common expression.[4] The question remains, however, whether anyone other than the philosophes spoke about the grandeur of the writer's calling. Certainly the philosophes attempted through philosophical history to portray their predecessors as the heroes of times past; still, even they recognized that their self-serving version of history was based upon a highly selective reading of events that omitted the political and social context.

Well educated in Locke's environmental psychology, the philosophes knew they could no more float above their milieu than could other members of society. Sometimes, it is true, they spoke as if the social preconditions of their triumph were already in place, but rarely, if ever, were the most able in their ranks deceived by their own propaganda. The account of the social context that is conspicuously absent from the historical writings of the philosophes is brilliantly present in their appraisal of their own prospects. For they realized that it is one thing to take from the past what one wants by imaginative recollection but quite another to have one's way in the present. Arguably, the best studies we possess today on the "sociology of intellectuals" in the eighteenth century are the works written not on but by the philosophes.

The great many essays of the encyclopedists on the special role and mission of the philosophe as the agent of enlightenment begin with high-sounding rhetoric—idealistic, effusive, optimistic. A few years later the tone has already changed and what was a language that aimed to foster a glowing self-image has undergone a metamorphosis into a troubled expression of self-doubt. Criticism was the specialty of the philosophes, a skill learned from Bayle and expanded into a vision of "the age of philosophy" as one of metaphysical reason displaced by a critical reason that could elucidate any subject, from the sciences to the arts to social conduct.[5] When the philosophes began to speak of themselves, it was only a matter of time before criticism became self-criticism.

From the 1760s onward the philosophes had largely won their bid for respectability, as measured by their increasing numbers in the academies and the success of their most mediocre representatives, Morellet, Suard, and Marmontel, among others, in obtaining sinecures and pensions.[6] The trouble was that each such victory for a philosophe might very well signal less the progress of reform than the capitulation of a reformer to the Old Regime.[7] Rousseau's self-advertised independence, ensured by copying music at so much per page, was a constant goad to his erstwhile companions.

But the more the philosophes despised Rousseau, the more the most able and daring of their numbers slowly evolved to a position that paralleled his on society and politics. Rousseau was not the only one to point out that under existing conditions the "violent reasoner" cannot be answered, nor was he isolated in ruminating on a republican solution. Ever so slowly it began to dawn upon some of the philosophes that the phrase "republic of letters" would never be a meaningful expression unless the word "republic" were taken more seriously.

How some of the philosophes came increasingly to resemble the Jean-Jacques they more and more hated is the subject of this chapter. Ours shall be a story fundamentally of convergence and only secondarily of influence; hence Rousseau will remain in the background while the philosophes carry the action.

Into the World

On many questions the philosophes were divided into different camps, but they were united in siding with the *vita activa* as opposed to the *vita contemplativa*. Were they not heirs of the likes of Socrates, Cicero, and Guicciardini, those illustrious predecessors who had been so deeply involved in the public issues of their respective days; was it not the claim of all the philosophes that the lamp that drove the darkness out of their dens was worth precious little unless carried from the study into the world?

Given their Lockean starting point, the philosophes could not possibly be attracted to the contemplative ideal. Voltaire set the pattern early in the century of declaring that to live is to act, to think is to enhance our actions.[8] Sensation comes first, followed by reason, which is an instrument for serving our needs, not for revealing the ultimate nature of things.[9] All metaphysics is illicit and literally non-sensical because it exceeds the reach of the senses that inform human reason. Condillac spoke for the entire French Enlightenment when he said that "whether we soar into the highest heavens or descend into the greatest depths, we cannot go outside our-selves."[10] Ontology and cosmology are therefore nothing more than psychology in disguise, and discussions of the divinity are merely enumerations of human traits unwittingly projected upon an abstraction.[11]

Frequently the philosophes dismissed the history of speculative philosophy as one of linguistic abuse or damned metaphysical writings with the faint praise of classifying them alongside the great works of literature. Reification of nouns and other generic words into essences, noted one philosophe after another, was the basic fallacy underlying all the great philosophical systems.[12] An equally serviceable maneuver on the part of the encyclopedists was their comparison of metaphysical works to novels, or Montesquieu's comment that Plato and Malebranche belong on any list of the great poets.[13] Always the conclusion was the same: because no meta-worlds are waiting to be explored, the philosopher who withdraws into a contemplative existence has chosen a useless and self-deluded life.

In any case there were battles the philosophes had to fight or be unworthy of their self-description as the party of humanity. Involvement, commitment, struggle were the order of the day because there was an oppressive criminal law to attack, an educational system to reform, and a crusade against slavery to be launched. The Lockean reason that dwelled entirely in the world, the modest reason that substituted probability and tolerance for certitude and fanaticism, was made to order for the purposes of the philosophes.

On Locke's premises the light Plato sought outside the cave cannot be experienced and may not exist. It is not only our fate but our calling to remain in the cave of the temporal and material world, where our challenging task is to dispel the shadows from every nook and cranny, despite

the many threatening pitfalls. As for Plato's belief that death is the eman-
cipation of the soul from its bodily tomb, a disciple of Locke can only
shake his head in dismay. In the absence of the body, there can be no
meaningful discussion of the soul. No wonder the Church Fathers
regarded Plato as an unbaptized Christian.

The self-image of the worldly new intellectuals is nowhere better articulated than in the essay "Le Philosophe," possibly the handiwork of
Dumarsais and definitely the darling of the entire philosophical movement. First published in 1743, reissued by Diderot for the *Encyclopédie*,
this essay made yet another showing in 1773 under the auspices of Voltaire.[14] Point by point, the author calls upon the themes of the Enlightenment and shows their special relevance to the person of the philosophe.

In "Le Philosophe" Dumarsais condemned Stoic withdrawal as sternly
as Voltaire had denounced Pascal's Christian abdication of the world.
Fleeing and avoiding his fellows, unmoved and unfeeling, the sage of
Stoicism is inhuman in his indifference to humanity. "Our philosopher
[in contrast] does not think he lives in exile in this world; he does not
believe himself to be in enemy territory."[15] Hostile to philosophies of
isolation and self-denial, Dumarsais notes that his philosophe "wishes to
find pleasure in the company of others, and to find pleasure he has to
give pleasure." As author of the lyrical article "Enjoyment"[16] and of
another written in defense of "Epicureanism,"[17] Diderot was bound to
love "Le Philosophe," and it is understandable that he should have been
mistakenly identified as its author for so long.

On even the most cursory reading of "Le Philosophe" it is evident that
the author has no use for otherworldly religion. Yet the this-worldly philosophe is not without religious sentiments. "One might say that he looks
on civil society as a divinity on earth: he offers it incense and honors it
with probity." While other men do their duty from mindless habit, the
philosophe does so because he understands that his pleasure, his interest,
his sense of self-worth commend the loyal discharge of one's social obligations. Sentiment and reason concurring in their approval of morality,
the religious sanctions that may be necessary for some persons are irrelevant in the case of the philosophe: "Do not fear that he will engage in
acts contrary to probity, when no eyes are watching him. No! . . . He is
filled with concern for the good of civil society and . . . knows its principles
far better than other men."

For Dumarsais as for all the philosophes there was much more than a philosophical point at stake in the argument that ethics may be safely divorced from religion. Their pressing concern was to answer churchmen who charged that free thinkers were subversives sapping the moral foundations of society. Dumarsais is at pains, therefore, to stress that the philosophe is "not a troublesome member of society," much as Voltaire almost a decade earlier had insisted that philosophers are so "devoid of emotional fire," and the number of reflective persons so "exceedingly small," that the thought of upsetting the social order never so much as enters their heads.[18] After defending themselves the philosophes, for whom turnabout was always fair play, went on the offensive against their religious critics. Who is responsible for the devastating civil wars of modern times, they inquired, if not the clergy?

The philosophe is concerned, according to Dumarsais, "with directing all his efforts toward achieving the ideal of the *honnête homme.*" If the French already were, as Montesquieu and Duclos held, the most sociable of peoples;[19] if the philosophe, furthermore, were to be the most sociable of Frenchmen, as Dumarsais wished, and the most adept at exercising the *art de plaire,* then he would find himself in the ranks of the one category of gentlemen sufficiently ill defined to remain open to those born outside the nobility. Not a hereditary title but a sufficient supply of what Aristotle referred to as "external goods" was what a philosophe needed to be an *honnête homme:* "He requires, over and above the bare necessities, the modest superfluity which is essential for an *honnête homme . . .* Only counterfeit philosophers, with their dazzling maxims, have propagated the false notion that the barest necessities suffice for a philosopher." The sweet fruit of the gardens of Epicurus beckon; the harsh diet of the Cynics, apparently, is fit only for dogs.[20]

That he personally was the very embodiment of this philosophical *honnête homme* was a point almost certainly not lost on "M. de Voltaire, seigneur de Ferney et autres lieux." In calling himself by the aristocratic term *de* Voltaire, in playing the grand seigneur on an appropriately massive scale at Ferney, Voltaire, the most famous of living French writers, a commoner by birth, had made himself the ultimate fulfillment of the social aspirations of the philosophes. "Do you know, sir [Madame du Deffand wrote to Voltaire], what proves the superiority of your mind and convinces me that you are a great philosopher? It's that you have become rich. All those who say one can be happy and free while living in poverty are liars, mad men, and fools."[21] To win the approval of the cynical

Madame du Deffand was difficult. Voltaire did so by amassing a fortune through financial dealings fair and foul, at the same time turning out one highly polished literary gem after another.

D'Alembert may well have been thinking of Voltaire when he suggested that a philosophe willing to spend some time as a trader or financier could readily enrich himself, perhaps in a single year.[22] Diderot, however, refused to generalize from Voltaire's example; so opposite is the life of the merchant to that of the man of letters, he remarked, that rarely do the respective attributes of the two professions meet in one person.[23] With his usual good sense, doubtless seconded by a willingness to concede his incomparability, Voltaire shied away from suggesting that others follow his example. Instead, he urged the younger generation of philosophes to find their way into the academies: "Those who are born without a fortune easily find in the institutions of Louis XIV the wherewithal to strengthen their independence. We no longer see, as in the past, those dedicatory epistles that self-interest and baseness offered to vanity."[24] So Voltaire wrote, jubilantly, in his article "Gens de lettres," published in the *Encyclopédie.*

Before a writer could win a seat in an academy he had first to make his way in society, preferably as a regular guest in the salons, where the most influential persons mingled with intellectuals under the watchful eyes of socially astute hostesses. During the years preceding his admission to the salons, a person blessed with the gift of *esprit* might frequent the cafés, but once he entered what by the eighteenth century had come to be called *le monde*,[25] it was natural for an author to discover that the best coffee was not to be found in cafés. When *Le Mondain* appeared in print in the 1730s, the man of letters who doubled as a *mondain* was still a rarity; by the time Voltaire published "Gens de lettres" in the 1750s, nothing was more common than the author who was also a man of the world. "The spirit of the century," Voltaire noted, "has made the men of letters as fit for society as for the study; and it is in this that they are superior to those of past centuries. They were separated from society until the time of Balzac and Voiture. Since then they have become a necessary part of it."[26] What Voltaire means, stated more forthrightly, is not so much that writers have become part of society as that they form part of the part that dictates to the social whole.

Writing at mid-century Duclos devoted a significant amount of his influential *Considerations on the Mores of This Century* to the social situation of *gens de lettres*. One of his principal points, repeated endlessly by other philosophes after 1750, was this: now that writers were as much included in the circles of high society as formerly they had been excluded, both the *gens du monde* and the *gens de lettres* were beneficiaries. "The *gens du monde* have cultivated their minds, informed their taste, and acquired new pleasures. The *gens de lettres* . . . have gained consideration, perfected their taste, polished their wit, sweetened their mores, and acquired insights . . . they could never have drawn from books."[27] Each author had read his Horace, knew that *plaire et instruire* were the writer's objectives, and recognized that there was no better way to learn the *art de plaire* than to circulate in select society, where mastery of the social graces was constantly on display.[28] Conversational ease, badinage, gallantry filled the pages of Fontenelle's highly instructive writings because he had successfully taken up a position in *le monde;* his example in the first half of the eighteenth century was remembered by the philosophes in the second half.

By mid-century, however, gallantry sounded decidedly quaint in serious writings. Fontenelle, it is important to remember, was a man formed by the seventeenth-century salon, in which the language of love was in demand;[29] the ladies of the succeeding century appreciated gallant words but no longer permitted such usage to set the conversational tone of their salons.[30] Although authors of the second half of the eighteenth century were still obliged both to please and to instruct, the emphasis fell somewhat more on *instruire,* somewhat less on *plaire.* Voltaire in 1752 mocked Fontenelle's gallant metaphors and similes, and had one of his fictional characters complaiñ that so much effort to please was an obstacle to instruction.[31] In general, the attitude of the philosophes was that they had completed their course in "le commerce du monde";[32] the aristocracy, in turn, had been substantially reeducated, thanks largely to the attention Louis XIV paid to the arts and letters.[33] The time was right for the philosophes to take not just themselves but their program of enlightenment into *le monde.*

Either noble birth or wealth could lead to membership in the ranks of the *grands.* Most philosophes and men of letters, lacking both those qualifications, needed to constitute themselves into an acknowledged social group—one that had ties to the socially influential and politically powerful and yet retained the collective strength to prevent its individual members from falling back into the pattern of *domesticité,* whether as tutors, secretaries, or any of the usual positions of servility in the houses of the great lords. Not just financial independence but survival against attacks by clerical enemies and hostile journalists dictated an alliance of philosophes if not of writers in general. "It is absolutely necessary that the wise defend themselves," Voltaire told Helvétius. "They can form a respectable corps, instead of being disunited members cut to pieces by fanatics and fools."[34]

Duclos shared Voltaire's concern for the corporate identity of *gens de lettres* in a corporate society: "Letters do not exactly constitute an estate [*un état*], but they take the place of one for those who have no other, and win for writers distinctions that the men who are their superiors in rank do not always obtain."[35] However marked the differences of rank in the hierarchical order of the Old Regime, men of letters will fare reasonably well if they have their own rung on the social ladder. This is all the more true because a taste for letters has become a social mania, and the privileged orders, accordingly, have issued a standing invitation to the writers to move back and forth, to and fro, between the higher social stations and their own.[36]

Hierarchy itself, Duclos was quick to note, is not an insuperable problem. Proverbial wisdom has long held that love equalizes by elevating the inferior, games of chance equalize by lowering the superior, "and I am persuaded that *esprit* would have been added, had the proverb been formed after *esprit* became a passion."[37] Intelligence and wit allow the baseborn to have their day because the highborn are so conspicuously superior in French society that the *grands* have nothing to gain and something to lose in denigrating persons of talent.[38]

As perpetual secretary of the French Academy, Duclos demonstrated his determination both to accommodate persons of noble blood and to win back that institution for the men of letters. Under his regime those with titles were welcome in the Academy if they deposited their privileges at the door upon entering and reclaimed them when leaving. Always deferential, Duclos nevertheless rebuffed the attempt of the comte de Clermont to carry his titles with him into the assembly: "If you confirm by your example an equality which is only imaginary, [Duclos argued,] you will grant the Academy the greatest honor it has ever received; you will lose nothing of your rank, and I even dare say you will add to your glory in elevating ours."[39] Upholding the rule of academic equality, Duclos championed the welfare of the republic of letters at the same time that he served a royal institution and conceded the worth of aristocratic titles.

Diplomacy, tact, and unshakable commitment to the cause of letters were the hallmarks of Duclos' direction of the Academy.

The philosophes could not help but feel both gratitude that Duclos had done so much for *gens de lettres* and disappointment he did not do even more, especially for them. Clearly he belonged to the philosophical sub-group that prided itself, understandably, on being the avant-garde of the literati. Duclos dined with the philosophes at the home of the Baron d'Holbach; his writings made the familiar points about the constructive interplay of interest with virtue, and featured typical philosophical pro-nouncements on the moral betterment that accompanies enlightenment and on the need for educational reform, and called for a rebirth of civic and patriotic sentiments.[40] Yet Duclos, who was as much at ease at Ver-sailles as in the philosophical salon of Holbach, refused to be a dues-paying member of the emerging *parti philosophique*. Repelled by anything that smacked of fanaticism, protective of his independence, whether threatened by nobles or philosophes, Duclos struggled to restore the French Academy to writers after a long period of institutional capitulation to *gens de condition* and *gens en place*. But he was no ally to those who would turn the Academy into the bastion of ideologues, and nothing is more characteristic of Duclos than that he should be the one man of letters never to fall out with Rousseau, who similarly advocated enlightenment while repudiating party membership.

D'Alembert as academician gave the philosophes all that Duclos with-held. Member of the Academy of Sciences since 1741, then admitted in 1754 to the French Academy where he would eventually succeed Duclos as perpetual secretary, d'Alembert was both the academician par excel-lence and an ardent philosophe. The residence of his companion, Made-moiselle de Lespinasse, was a sparkling culmination of the evolution of the salon, that peculiarly French institution, from its original incarnation as a rarefied setting in which the stress was on taste, manners, and topics such as the psychology of sentiments to the later salon, where the guests were sometimes permitted to discuss the education of citizens and other themes typical of the Enlightenment.[41] With d'Alembert in attendance, the salon of Mademoiselle de Lespinasse served, moreover, as a hotbed of academic politics; it was there that elections to the French Academy were decided well in advance of the formal vote by the forty immortals. For both d'Alembert and de Lespinasse no qualification for election was more essential than advocacy of the philosophical cause.[42]

Overall, the philosophes pursued two strategies in their efforts to form what Voltaire called a corporate body and Duclos the functional equivalent of a social "station" or "estate." The first strategy was traditionalist and as much imposed upon them as their own invention. Once invited to the salons, the philosophes were molded into a cohesive group and subjected to discipline by the women in charge. Formed in this manner into the beginnings of a corps, the philosophes attained the additional benefit of a dignified social status through interacting with the privileged and influential orders. What Ruhlière termed "the dignity of men of letters" was in the first instance a trickle-down dignity, conferred on writers by their social superiors. Only in the second instance, after initiation into the royal academies, did authors possess the corporate identity and prestige that came with membership in one of the institutional pillars of the ancien régime.

The second strategy, represented by Diderot, marked a break with tradition and a recognition that books were commodities bought and sold at the marketplace. As editor of the *Encyclopédie*, Diderot wanted to believe that the growth of the reading public in the eighteenth century might prove adequate for writers to be self-supporting, even if, as in his own case, they were disinvited to salons because of their frank speech and never admitted to the academies because their youthful writings were too indiscreet, their mature works too challenging and unconventional. Usually the enemy of the monopolies of guilds, he was willing in the *Letter on the Book Trade* to plead the case of the guild of publishers. Freedom of different publishers to issue their own pirated edition of marketable books was not *laissez-faire* but theft. Unlike other philosophes who had nothing good to say about booksellers, Diderot saw new possibilities for the independence of writers in the contractual relation between authors and publishers.

When it came to fostering a sense of collective identity, Diderot stressed the claim of the encyclopedists that theirs was the undertaking of a "society of men of letters," the principles of whose association stood in marked contrast to the corporate structure of the Old Regime. As he saw matters, the *Encyclopédie* was the work of a group brought into being by the decision of a number of individuals to engage in a collective enterprise in publication, each author acting alone as he contributed to the joint product. "I wish the members of this society to work separately because ... if one wanted the work to be perpetually in the making, but never finished, the best way to secure that result would be to form a permanent society." Very likely Diderot was referring to the Academy of Sciences, because its *Description et perfection des arts et métiers* had been commissioned by Colbert in 1675 but did not begin to appear in print until 1761, a decade after the commencement of the *Encyclopédie* and its *Description des arts.*[43]

Instead of salons and academies, in place of intimate encounters in smoke-filled rooms or pompous ceremonies in official chambers, the "society of men of letters" should exist by means of individual communications with an editor, himself the employee of publishers eager to make a profit selling their wares at the marketplace. "Literary projects which great noblemen conceive," Diderot wrote, "are like the leaves that appear in the spring, grow dry in the autumn and fall in a heap in the depths of the forest." Whence it follows that writers who look to the *grands* both forfeit their freedom and see their literary projects flounder. Not only the nobles but ministers, too, lead men of letters into futile undertakings, for governmental leaders come and go and "a new minister does not as a rule adopt the projects of his predecessor." Away from the court, then, away from the salons and academies; let us turn, rather, to merchants and traders. "Private individuals are eager to harvest the fruits of what they have sown; the government has none of this economic zeal."[44]

When the *Encyclopédie* ran afoul the Sorbonne in 1752, its ensuing suspension was soon lifted, less from sympathy with its message than out of respect for the property rights and economic investments involved in a major economic enterprise.[45] Diderot wasted no time in discerning what this striking experience meant to writers. As opposed to seeking aristocratic protection, they should remind the monarchy that what's good for the traders is good for the country.[46]

Whether they pursued the old strategy or the new of achieving group solidarity and social standing, the philosophes agreed that the best way for their kind to exercise influence in France was to make themselves the arbiters of the new phenomenon of public opinion. Toward the end of the century Ruhlière traced the expression, "the empire of public opinion," back to its middle years. Probably he was thinking of the words of Duclos, published in 1750: "The powerful command [but] the *gens d'esprit* govern, because over time they form public opinion."[47]

The rapidity of scientific discovery, Diderot observed, made it inevitable that a "revolution will occur in the minds of men"; the only question was who will have "the power to change men's common way of thinking." As envisioned by Diderot, the contributors to the *Encyclopédie* had as their task nothing less than the "general education of mankind."[48] He and his colleagues were fully prepared to accept so honorable a calling.

The Stoic in Spite of Himself

"Le Philosophe," be it recalled, is as much a denunciation of the old model of the Stoic sage as an idealized depiction of the new man of letters. No philosophical figure fares worse in the writings of the philosophes than the Stoic, no philosophy comes under attack more often than Stoicism. It was the strategy of the encyclopedists to expose the Stoic ideal as impossible, inhuman, and as less the vision of the wise man than the fool. Using the lessons learned from Locke's bodily, this-worldly philosophy, and adding some arguments extracted from the classics of the Grand Siècle, the philosophes launched an all-out assault on one of the most venerable ideals of the philosophical tradition. How embarrassing, then, that after such sustained exercises in destruction they were driven back, willy-nilly, to the same Stoic ideal as the only way to cope with what their researches indicated was the actual, rather than the idealized, social situation of the philosophe.

All the philosophes were sympathetic to Montaigne, who had originally sounded the Stoic theme "that to philosophize is to learn to die" but later reversed himself, deciding in retrospect that "death is indeed the end but not therefore the goal of life."[49] They could also cherish the *Maxims* of La Rochefoucauld, even though its strategy of deflating vanity did not omit assaults upon the pretensions of philosophers. "The scorn for riches displayed by philosophers," charged La Rochefoucauld, "was a secret desire to recompense their own merit for the injustice of Fortune by scorning those very benefits she had denied them; it was a private way of remaining unsullied by poverty, a devious path toward the respect they could not command by wealth."[50] Just as the philosophes had welcomed his many maxims that reduced virtue to hidden interest, since each such exposé was another proof we have an interest in being virtuous, so now they gratefully accepted La Rochefoucauld's stand that the philosophe was no different from other men in desiring riches, reputation, and pleasures—all those goods to which the Stoics professed to be indifferent. Instead of feigning indifference to whatever is beyond our reach, said the new philosophers, let us reach out and claim our just deserts. Worldly and successful philosophers practice virtue in *le monde,* unlike the Stoics who made a virtue out of their social isolation and insignificance.

At the time he wrote his *Essai sur la société des gens de lettres et des grands* (1753–54) d'Alembert was already a respected scientist, a member of the Academy of Sciences, and on the verge of admission to the French Academy. His *Preliminary Discourse* to the *Encyclopédie* had established his credentials as a writer, made him the talk of Europe, and gave Frederick the Great reason to display public interest in a figure so formidable and so well established at the very center of European culture. For the sake of those who would follow in his footsteps d'Alembert decided to place on record what he had learned about the social situation and prospects of *gens d'esprit.*[51] D'Alembert's *Essai* is a guidebook offering advice to intellectuals on how to be *in* society but not *of* it. Its tone is as sober and chilling as that of "Le Philosophe" is warm and indulgent.

Neither d'Alembert nor any of his philosophical comrades objected to the maxims of La Rochefoucauld that assumed philosophers were as much under the sway of self-love as the next man. It was perfectly true, as La Rochefoucauld suggested, that "philosophy easily triumphs over past ills and ills to come, but present ills triumph over philosophy."[52] What are the writer's circumstances here and now? was therefore the question that must be answered. Dumarsais had stated what ought to be; d'Alembert addressed what is. Voltaire in his polemic against Pascal had cited the human body to place us in the world, all of us, even the monk and the contemplative sage; d'Alembert stressed that the world of which we inescapably form a part includes the social surroundings called *le monde.* Whether the philosophe possesses *le monde* or *le monde* possesses the philosophe is a question that must be answered by setting aside idealistic programs and ruthlessly facing up to social realities, come what may. D'Alembert was determined to accept so thankless and so vital a task.

Rather than revisiting the abstract debate over the active versus the contemplative life, d'Alembert focuses the discussion on the more concrete question of the subject matter studied by different types of intellectuals. Some devote their energies to the *sciences exactes,* others the *sciences agréables.* To succeed in mathematics, d'Alembert notes, requires no recourse to anyone other than another expert in that purified intellectual realm. Living in relative seclusion comes naturally to geometers; neither seeking out nor sought by *le monde,* mathematicians quietly pursue their intellectual programs all the better for being unknown to all but their own kind. The case of the *beaux esprits*—the creative artists, whether writers, composers, or painters—is altogether different, because they seek an audience that extends well beyond fellow professionals. Even the most talented writers are far from self-contained because "the more one has ability, the more one is dissatisfied with what one has."[53] In principle one artist could consult another artist or one writer a second of his kind, but typically *beaux esprits* are ill at ease with their rivals. Besides, it is in the very nature of the calling of the literary intellectual to write about and for the inhabitants of *le monde.*

D'Alembert's vision of the mission of the intellectuals, "to give the law to the rest of the nation in matters of taste and philosophy,"[54] could not be more elevated. But he knew that the would-be opinion makers were themselves constantly bound by the opinion of others. If erudites were an exception,[55] that was because they might as well be living in another century; their insignificance was marked by the position of the Académie des Inscriptions at the bottom of the academic hierarchy. Granted, those who dedicate their intellectual careers to belles-lettres need to enter society to learn their trade; yet the consequent submission of authors to opinion was enough to make d'Alembert speak approvingly of Diogenes.[56]

When looking for persons to judge his work, the man of letters has three criteria in mind: that his judges shall be free of the bias that stems from rivalry; that they shall know something; finally, that they shall not know or care enough to be harsh critics.[57] Without question the *grands* fit all the foregoing requirements, most of all because their taste for letters is indeed a taste, sometimes an affectation, as Duclos had written.[58] Although it is true that Louis XIV made ignorance unfashionable, neither he nor his successor did anything to alter the fundamental miseducation of the nobility. Limited to externals, the training of the *grands* was better suited to help them lord it over the people than to prepare them to exercise astute judgment.[59] Not surprisingly, "the man of letters who flatters them most, however mediocre he may be, is for them the first in his genre."[60]

From the standpoint of the writer, even the best of the *grands* leave a great deal to be desired: "Among the most affable great seigneurs, there are few who with men of letters divest themselves of their grandeur to the point of forgetting it completely. This is clear in conversations when one is not of their opinion."[61] However objectionable these wealthy or titled but half-educated connoisseurs, there are not enough of them to go around. Consequently writers hungry for applause settle for second best or less, and are willing to ally themselves with anyone who has at his disposal many hired echoes of his voice.[62]

Frequently rich persons surround themselves with literary hacks who amuse their patron and themselves at the expense of talented writers. D'Alembert speaks with loathing and contempt of "the crowd of little societies and tribunals where the great geniuses are *ripped apart* by persons unworthy to read them."[63] Earlier Duclos and later Voltaire made the same point with explicit use of the animal imagery that is hinted at by d'Alembert's verb. When he rewrote his essay "Gens de lettres" for his *Philosophical Dictionary,* Voltaire withdrew the optimistic language of the version that had appeared in the *Encyclopédie.* The revised version ends on this note: "The man of letters is without recourse; he resembles the flying fish: if he raises himself up a little, birds devour him; if he dives, fish eat him."[64] Duclos wanted to see the hope but was too intelligent to miss the despair of writers surrounded by enemies and frequently at odds with one another in their quest for recognition. He ends his chapter "Sur les Gens de lettres" with an analogy drawn from the human pastime of cheering on one animal as it destroys another. Nowadays, he suggests, it is writers who occupy the pit, clawing at their own kind while the crowd revels in the bloodletting.[65]

So much then for the notion that the literati, at long last, have attained a fixed social rank or station. It is the special burden of writers, d'Alembert observes, that they spend their lives "between arrogance and servility,"[66] sometimes rising in the morning with the intention of being free, only to revert by evening to their slavery.[67] "It is not in an antechamber that one learns to say, think, and do great things,"[68] but that is the room awaiting many of the writers who crave wealth. Those who never make it to the antechambers of the *grands* will use any and all means to extricate themselves from their plight; their sole consolation is that it is easier the second time round to sell pen, self, and self-respect.[69]

Despite the customary disdain of the philosophes for Plato, the author of "Le Philosophe" endorsed the saying that peoples will be happy "when kings are philosophers, or philosophers kings!"[70] D'Alembert, by contrast, categorically rejects such high-sounding declarations as the rhetorical equivalent of whistling in the dark. "Philosophy flees the court; it would be misanthropic, ill at ease, and out of place there."[71] Unshakable in his conviction that, after skill in governing, "the art of instructing and enlightening men is the most noble prerogative of the human condition,"[72] d'Alembert was equally insistent on acknowledging the enormous gap between the actual worth of writers and the recognition of their merit at court: "In countries where the press is not free, the license to insult men of letters with satires proves how little genuine respect they enjoy . . . Why is it more permissible to outrage a writer who honors his nation than to ridicule a placeman who dishonors his?"[73] Several years later d'Alembert witnessed a glaring illustration of his point when Palissot, under the protection of the Princesse de Robecq, mistress of the Duc de Choiseul, was permitted to stage performances of *Les Philosophes,* a heavy-handed satire on Diderot, Duclos, Rousseau, and Helvétius.

Having succeeded Voltaire as *historiographe de France,* Duclos knew something about court life, enough to recommend that writers might benefit from living at Versailles, but only because the superiority of the *grands* was so unmistakable in such extravagant surroundings that the man of letters could count on their benign neglect.[74] It has been said that d'Alembert's *Essay* was a reversal of Duclos' comments on writers in his *Considerations.*[75] A more accurate account should note the many subtle disclaimers and diplomatic evasions with which Duclos spices his upbeat portrayal of the situation of *gens de lettres.*

D'Alembert, Duclos, Voltaire—all the philosophes—agreed that there was safety in numbers, and repeatedly called upon the *gens de lettres,* minimally, to form an alliance; maximally, to live in the company of one another. Doubtless, commented Duclos, one writer will sometimes quarrel with another writer, this author will be tempted to attack that rival, but soon "the fools will reconcile [the squabbling writers]." "They will sense that their disunion goes directly against their general and individual interest."[76]

Though d'Alembert, too, sees self-interest as a motive for the union of philosophes, he believes their society within society can be more than just a defensive alliance: "the society of men of letters is the most useful and noble that any man who thinks can desire."[77] As much as possible the *gens de lettres* should live in a self-enclosed space,[78] permitting *grands* to enter only if they possess credentials as distinguished writers. Who better to appreciate a work of art, to judge the degree of difficulty conquered, than the men of letters?[79] Each author should, while addressing the public, write for fellow professionals. Any writer who can avoid *le monde* should do so; those who cannot, the *beaux esprits* who must frequent society to write about it, should simply be spectators forced to attend a comedy that does not bear a second viewing; they should witness social performances "as [does] the audience which judges the actors, and whom the actors dare not insult."[80]

D'Alembert's essay might well have borne "the revenge of Stoicism" as its subtitle. The Stoic sage, having been booted out the front door in "Le Philosophe," is reluctantly readmitted by d'Alembert through the servants' entrance. In their eulogy of worldly existence the philosophes had set forth an ebullient morality of social roles; now d'Alembert once again uses the imagery of the actor on stage, but this time with all the familiar Stoic nuances of disdain for those who, playing their socially assigned parts, have lost themselves along the way. Were it true that the philosophe could safely discard Stoicism, d'Alembert would be the first to rejoice. Sadly, the autonomy of the new intellectual, the self-proclaimed agent of Enlightenment, can in practice only be affirmed by an ethic of self-denial.

All the world's a stage, and the philosophe must be the one person who refuses to step foot on it. Surrounded by *le monde*, he must live on a social island with fellow philosophes, making day trips when necessary to the surrounding world of wealth and glitter, always returning in the evening to his own bed. Unable, within the terms of the philosophy of the Enlightenment, to ask writers to scorn honors, d'Alembert offers them this advice: "Write as if you loved glory; conduct yourself as if indifferent to it."[81] Unable to ask writers to despise riches, d'Alembert no sooner invokes the words "Liberty, Truth, Poverty" than he modifies his position. "When I say that poverty ought to be one of the words in the motto of men of letters, I do not claim that they are obliged to be indigent . . . ; I only say they must not dread it."[82] Never has the Stoic message been delivered with less enthusiasm or more equivocation.

External conformity, internal freedom—such had been the slogan of Stoics, and d'Alembert felt obliged to revive it for the philosophes. In his case the road to a philosophy of resignation passed through the familiar Enlightenment notions of respect for the natural rights of all persons and for the exceptional merit of some individuals, before arriving at its final, unhappy destination. Equal in natural right, we are unequal in ability, he begins. Talents mark "the real differences among men" and are the source of the favorable reputation the French nation enjoys with foreigners. Yet in "exterior consideration" social rank and title are everything, talent nothing, and the *gens de lettres* must settle for whatever scraps of esteem are tossed at their feet. Seemingly on the verge of sketching a treatise on (in)justice, d'Alembert opts to argue instead that the established hierarchy of wealth and hereditary status is as it must be, because in the absence of unmistakable external signs of rank, however arbitrary and absurd they may be, society would crumble.[83] There is not now, nor will there ever be, agreement outside the mathematical sciences as to which persons are meritorious.

Fortunately the editors of Port Royal had censored the passages of the *Pensées* in which Pascal made a similar argument about how, in our pitiful world, there is no alternative to pretending that might makes right or to feigning the conviction that inherited titles deserve respect.[84] What d'Alembert did not know could not torment him.

D'Alembert's final word is that intellectuals should give only their external selves to the existing arrangements and tactfully sidestep direct confrontation with the prejudice that underpins the social order.[85] What he does not say is that his philosophe, unlike Dumarsais', will likely spend his life in a garret somewhere in the Faubourg Saint-Germain, trying without success to save his family from misery.[86]

The Self-Doubt of a Philosophe

What a strange creature he was, this new intellectual, a Stoic who wanted to be an Epicurean, a caustic critic of the ethics of self-abnegation who lived in constant denial of his desires, a man condemned constantly to act against his beliefs in order to uphold them. In society but not of it, forever forcing himself to rise above his social setting despite a Lockean psychology that denied the possibility of sustaining such a tight-rope act, he was the most unnatural of beings and the one who spoke the most frequently in praise of nature. Were we to discover an unguarded entrance to the mind of the philosophe, we would find that inside his self-possessed exterior there is a divided self engaged in a dialogue of self-doubt. The *Essay on the Society of Men of Letters* by d'Alembert leads directly to *Rameau's Nephew* by Diderot.

The conversation of "Lui," the fictionalized nephew, with "Moi," ostensibly Diderot, takes place on at least three different levels. In the first instance Lui is one of those bought-and-paid-for intellectual hacks who make a living entertaining their masters by defaming the philosophes. Second, Lui is as Diderot himself might have been, had he not landed the job of editor of the *Encyclopédie*. A bohemian in his early Parisian years,[87] a teacher of mathematics who did not learn his subject until after accepting a position as teacher,[88] an unbeliever who occasionally wrote sermons,[89] the author of a mildly pornographic novel,[90] Diderot realized that he barely escaped being a Lui. Most of all, however, Lui *is* Diderot, the suppressed side of his person secretly at war with the official side, the Moi who is the encyclopedist and philosophe.

Rameau's Nephew begins with a citation to a satire by Horace on the Stoic theme that only the wise man is free. Davus the slave knows his master Horace is anything but free: "You, who lord it over me, are the wretched slave of another master, and you are moved like a wooden puppet by wires that others pull."[91] Lui agrees but adds, in effect, that no one is free, so the wise man is the one who makes the most of his slavery, who plays his servile part with gusto and is accordingly rewarded with money, fine food, and beautiful women. The jester at court and the fool of *le monde* are always in demand,[92] whereas neither *la cour* nor *la ville* has any use for the wise man.

Diderot, the better to challenge himself, makes Moi an infinitely more formidable figure than the actual nephew of the great composer. Is it rational for someone to pursue a program of reform dictated by reason in an age that is unwilling to listen to reason? How enlightened is an agent of enlightenment who wastes his life pursuing goals society is certain to frustrate or pervert? Such questions Diderot puts to himself through the mouth of Lui, the interlocutor who frequently silences Moi but is himself never silenced by *monsieur le philosophe*. Forever "unmasking" or "unveiling" their opponents, the philosophes occasionally turned their critical skills against themselves, nowhere so brilliantly, forcefully, and uncompromisingly as in *Rameau's Nephew*.

In the *Salon of 1765* Diderot repealed Duclos' declaration of 1750 that intellectuals finally have an estate of their own. Young artists are "without an estate, without resources, and [consequently] without mores."[93] Characterized by what he is not ("without"), defined by withdrawing one social trait after another, the man of letters as depicted in the writings of both Diderot and d'Alembert is a social being who has never found his way out of the state of nature. Usually skeptical about arguments positing a presocial condition, d'Alembert in 1760 could think of no better way to capture the life of a writer than to liken it to existence in a Hobbesian state of war.[94] Diderot in 1776 began a brief discussion of men of letters by comparing human nakedness in the state of nature to our decorative titles worn in society. Whereas the robes and insignia of most ranks confer consideration upon their least deserving members, there is one profession, that of letters, whose members cannot parade their dignity without suffering ridicule. "It is with men of letters as with the tight-rope walker: they are between baseness and arrogance."[95] Like other *beaux esprits,* only more so and with greater self-awareness, Lui is "a mixture of arrogance and baseness."[96] A confounded Moi can only marvel to witness "so much sagacity and vileness" combined in one person.[97]

There is one thing even more important than the protection afforded by an estate. "What difference," asks the nephew, "does it make whether you have an estate, provided you are rich, since a station is only wanted to make money?"[98] Years earlier Rousseau, in the *Second Discourse,* had commented that in the end all social distinctions come down to money;[99] earlier still, the relatively staid Duclos queried, "Why be astonished by the consideration that wealth brings? It is certain that riches are not merit, but they are the means of all the commodities, pleasures, and sometimes even of merit."[100] Obviously French soil was well prepared for the nephew's eulogy of sparkling coins: "Gold, gold is everything; and everything, without gold, is nothing."[101]

Unproductive, untalented, and untitled, tax-farmers and financiers occupy the pages of *Rameau's Nephew* much more than aristocrats. Such unsavory but pretentious characters deserve nothing but are granted everything because they have money. The lion's share of the protection nobles formerly dispensed is now doled out by these ignorant louts, who offer sustenance and comfortable cages to the lowlife specimens of the literati. Seemingly Lui cannot speak too frequently of his growling intestines, nor of mealtime when he and his kind come out of their "lairs."[102] "We are all grumpy and fiercely hungry. Wolves are not more voracious nor tigers more cruel."[103] After shredding their meat, they do the same to the good names of the philosophes. Poor in a society wherein "you can't bring dishonor upon yourself if you are rich";[104] estate-less in a world composed of estates, the philosophes are disgraced, exposed, vulnerable— easy prey for the "menagerie"[105] of the financier.

Suppose we put aside the predatory language of d'Alembert, Duclos, Voltaire, and Diderot, the verbs of tearing and rending, the images of cock fights, flying fish attacked from above and below, beasts in the jungle stalking their prey. Suppose the security problem of the new, free-standing intellectual were satisfactorily resolved. The purport of Diderot's dialogue is that, were the external threat removed, the philosophe would have that much more time to reflect on his woefully divided internal self. Having asserted the ready compatibility of virtue with all the worldly goods—with interest, happiness, pleasure, and enjoyment—the philosophes found that their own situation stood in flat contradiction to their general social theory; their unenviable choice was whether to compromise themselves or be miserable. What's more, deep down they feared that the "age of philosophy" was only a passing phase during which philosophy was *à la mode,* soon to be displaced by another fashion. To forfeit everything and yet to fail—the worst of all possible worlds—could readily be the finale to the struggle of the philosophes to make enlightenment popular.

For whom shall the philosophe write? Ideally for the public, so much spoken of, so fervently hoped for, yet still far too small to make the author of successful books financially self-supporting.[106] To make matters worse, remarks Moi, the usual reader "is like a child and prefers being amused to being instructed."[107] Very receptive to *plaire,* invariably bored by *instruire,* the French audience has so expurgated Horace that his message about writing has become an anticipation of Juvenal's "bread and circus." Voltaire in *Micromégas* had made fun of authors who spend more time amusing than instructing their readers; yet when Lui, the fool, makes fun of the foolishness of writers who would educate the public, Moi sides with Lui. No one who has read Diderot's letter to Voltaire of February 19, 1758, should be surprised by this turn of events: *"Be useful to men?* Is it certain one does anything but amuse them, and that there is much of a difference between the philosophe and the flute-player? They listen to one and the other with pleasure or disdain, and remain what they are."[108]

Duclos had struggled valiantly to save the French from the consequences of their reputation as a "frivolous" people. Childhood, he noted, is an age of innocence; it is a time when misadventures and pranks do not compromise our underlying natural goodness. Now the Frenchman, he adds, is the "infant of Europe"; from youth to old age, his character is that of a child—a misfortune in some respects, but with the compensation that deliberate, calculating evil remains foreign to his character.[109]

Ingenious the argument of Duclos may be, but whatever it saves with one hand is thrown away by the other. To concede that the French are permanently infantile is to deny that enlightenment stands a fighting chance in France. One philosophe after another preceded Kant in declaring that "Enlightenment is man's emergence from his self-caused immaturity."[110] It is telling, therefore, that Moi is convinced the public craves literature that satisfies its desire for childish amusements. The public for which the philosophe wished to write barely exists and is as hungry for entertainment as it is indifferent to enlightenment.

For every failure of an intellectual to raise the tone of discussion in society, there is a corresponding instance of an author, the level of whose written discourse is lowered by the audience he addresses. After mimicking the prattle that is his daily fare in some of the highest circles of Parisian society, the nephew asks:

> *Lui:* Do you suppose that things like these, repeated over and over every day, kindle the mind and lead to great ideas?
>
> *Moi:* No, of course not. It would be better to shut oneself up in a garret, eat a dry crust, drink plain water, and try to find oneself.[111]

"What use to a philosophe," asks d'Alembert, "are our frivolous conversations, other than to diminish the human spirit?" It was not in a salon that Descartes learned to apply algebra to geometry; it was not at court that Newton discovered universal gravitation; nor did living in retreat prevent Malebranche from writing prose that remains the model for all philosophers. As a counselor of writers, d'Alembert advocated that anyone wishing to paint the age while remaining aloof should not borrow its degrading language. As an unyielding critic of his own kind he observed that writers, who should legislate for the *grands* in matters of language and taste, have in fact "tacitly agreed" to borrow the usages of their social superiors.[112]

Lui also speaks of a "tacit agreement," expanding it to encompass all of society. Not entirely ignorant, it appears, of theories of a "social contract," the nephew regrets he has been denied the opportunity to articulate a full-blown defense of those who hoodwink, dupe, or lie in order to claim their victuals and other goods. "How I wish I could defend under the terms of this universal and sacred compact the people who are accused of wickedness when one should rather accuse oneself of stupidity!"[113] Self-interest is the rule of rules, the one fixed, unalterable, eternal human truth that no one, not even Lui, can dispute. Just prior to his speech in behalf of the tacit agreement Lui remarks that "in a subject as variable as manners and morals nothing is absolutely, essentially, universally true or false—unless it be that one must be whatever self-interest requires . . . If virtue by chance led to fortune, I should have been as virtuous . . . as the next man."[114] It is definitely the law of society, and possibly the law of nature, that one being lives at the expense of another.[115] Do unto others before they can do unto you is therefore the maxim of enlightened self-interest. "No one but the idiot or the loafer is taken advantage of without levying tribute on anybody else . . . The only thing that matters is to see straight."[116] The nephew does not have an interest in being virtuous; nor does anyone else.

A loser from the standpoint of interest, virtue fares no better when measured against the standard of happiness.

> *Lui:* Then according to you people should be decent?
> *Moi:* To be happy?—Certainly.
> *Lui:* Yet I see a quantity of decent people unhappy and a quantity of people happy without being decent.[117]

By his own account Diderot wanted all his life to write a book proving that "even in a society as poorly ordered as ours, where successful vice is often applauded and virtue that fails is almost always ridiculed, . . . there is no better path to happiness than to be a good man."

> It is the work the most to my liking, the most important and interesting to undertake, the one I would recall with the most satisfaction in my last moments. It is a question I have meditated a hundred times. [But] I have not dared pick up the pen to write the first line. I say to myself: "If I do not emerge victorious in this effort, I shall be the apologist of evil."[118]

Recalling the article "Natural Right," we may say that by the 1760s Diderot was no longer certain he could silence the "violent reasoner." Endowed with a face and a personality, the violent reasoner is Lui, who pleads his case so convincingly that Moi must frequently request a new topic of conversation.

At best the violent reasoner has been domesticated. For all his willingness to dismiss country, friends, and duty,[119] Lui cannot help but love his son.[120] Similarly, the practitioners of the trades, family men all, have "idioms" by which they gouge the public day in and day out for the sake of the family fortune.[121] The difference between Lui and ordinary persons is that he, a virtuoso of vice, a connoisseur of wrongdoing,[122] is less likely to leave his calculating evil at the workplace at the end of a day's labor.

Ordinary evil is of no interest to someone who has dedicated his life to studying the extraordinarily vicious ways of the rich.

The implications of Lui's findings for programs of educational reform, so dear to the philosophes, are deliciously perverse. Lui takes pride that he has learned, as any enlightened person should, to discard his prejudices: "Bad company is as instructive as debauchery: one is indemnified for the loss of innocence by the loss of prejudice. In a society of bad men, they stand undisguised and one learns to see them as they are."[123] Other than learning from the company he keeps, the nephew has done some reading and finds particularly helpful Molière and La Bruyère. Naturally Moi, who is addicted to moralizing, anticipates that it is lessons in duty, love of virtue, and hatred of vice that Lui distills from the French classics. He is stunned when Lui praises the moralists because selections from their writings, well chosen and edited, would form a thoughtful how-to manual for con artists: "When I read *Tartuffe*, I say: Be a hypocrite if you choose, but don't talk like one. Keep any useful vices, but don't acquire the tone and air which would make you ridiculous. Now to avoid these one must know what they are, and the authors mentioned have given us excellent portraits." Without benefit of reading a page of Machiavelli, the nephew understands that the semblance of virtue is occasionally useful, the reality of virtue harmful, and that the reputation of chronically consorting with vice is a liability, even in a vice-ridden age.[124] An education that is all exterior, all show, the very kind of education d'Alembert found so regrettable in noble circles, is the one—Lui recognizes—that ensures social success.

When Moi states his intention to teach his daughter grammar, mythology, history, geography, a bit of drawing, and a great deal of ethics, Lui suggests it would be much better to encourage her to be a coquette.[125] Later in the dialogue, the nephew discusses the education of his son: "One must not, like most fathers, stupidly give children who are destined to live in Paris the education of ancient Sparta ... I want my child happy, or what amounts to the same thing, honored, rich, and powerful ... If you wise men blame me, the majority (and success itself) will absolve me. He will have gold ... and if he has a great deal, he will lack nothing, not even your admiration and respect." Lui struts before his son, a gold coin in plain sight, to let the youngster appreciate that self-respect and wealth are one and the same. The schooling he gives his child is in the vices and foolish traits that will guarantee his offspring free entry to the tables and purses of the *grands*. Moi concedes that a son "reared on a system so exactly framed on our actual behavior will go far."[126]

What use is an education, asks the nephew, unless it "leads to all the enjoyments without trouble or danger?" Author of a passionate article in the *Encyclopédie* on enjoyment, Moi is at a loss: "I am almost with you there, but let's not go into it."[127] Stoicism without conviction, Stoicism despite one's convictions, is the philosophy of Diderot and all the philosophes who remained uncompromisingly loyal to the cause.

The implications of Lui's arguments for writers are devastating. The market for treatises on virtue is all but nonexistent, and the authors of such works will surely be dismissed by the well-heeled, who see in writings of that ilk so many satires against themselves. Besides, virtue is not entertaining. Lui must give bored people an excuse to smile derisively; "now what is laughable is absurdity and folly. I must consequently be absurd and a fool." Vice comes easily to the nephew, is amusing to the fat cats, and does not threaten their smug sense of superiority. So Lui gives free reign to his vices, "vices congenial to the habits of my countrymen, agreeable to the tastes of my protectors, and closer to their little needs than any virtues could be."[128] This is not to say that Lui lacks respect for Moi's literary prowess, his ability to turn a fine phrase, or his skill at persuading with well-chosen words. These talents the nephew admits he envies, because they could be very beneficial to him in his part-time career as a pimp hired by sophisticates.[129]

Now and then Moi disdains Lui, never for very long, rarely with full conviction, always with an ambivalence completely missing from the nephew's contempt for "all the little Catos like you who despise us from sour grapes, whose modesty is the prop of pride, and whose good conduct springs from lack of means."[130] La Rochefoucauld could not, and did not, say it any better. Belatedly, thanks to the nephew, the author of the *Maxims* has his revenge on the philosophes who had turned his meaning inside out and upside down.

Shall a philosophe sacrifice now to be remembered later? Plausibly it is in the long-term interest of a writer to relinquish worldly goods if immortality will be his eventual reward. More than anyone else in the Enlightenment, Diderot repeatedly apostrophized posterity. In the *Prospectus* to the *Encyclopédie* he appealed "To Posterity, and to the Being who does not Die." When writing the article "Encyclopedia," he beseeched future generations to honor the memory of their enlightened predecessors.[131] To the sculptor Falconet he wrote, "posterity for the philosophe is what the other world is for the religious man."[132]

There are moments when Lui is tempted to seek out, at whatever cost, his latent creative genius. On his quest for the gifted man within he knocks on the door of his being, only to find that either nobody's home or he's not answering. "Sacrifice one's well-being for a chancy success!" Safer and better, he concludes, to return to his role as the clown of high society: "It isn't glory but it's soup."[133] The fame conferred by contemporaries is worth desiring, but to sacrifice one's life for it is to make an exceptionally poor wager.

As for the fame that comes after death, the glory and immortality dispensed by posterity, what difference does it make to someone who is in no condition to hear the applause? "To rot under marble or to rot in bare earth is still to rot."[134] Appeals to long-range self-interest, however eloquent, cannot persuade because in the long run we are all dead.

"Project your vision into centuries to come . . . Think of the welfare of our species," Moi exhorts Lui. But the nephew is unmoved by this future-oriented rewrite of the article "Natural Right." "The best order, for me, is that in which I had to exist—and a fig for the most perfect world if I am not of it."[135] My welfare, here and now, is what counts, and must be sought even when it conflicts with the interests of present and future generations. A life of self-sacrifice, to Lui, is much the same as committing suicide one day at a time.

Rameau's Nephew moves to its breathless and memorable finale when Lui, master of the art of pantomime, acts out the "positions" and "postures" assumed by persons of different social ranks, each well versed in the gestures suitable to his role in society. Without any philosophical training, calling solely upon his keen observations and uncanny ability to mimic all he sees, the nephew restates in his own fashion the initial premises of the philosophes and then draws conclusions the opposite of theirs.

"I am in *this* world and here I stay"—the words are Lui's but could just as easily be from the mouth of a philosophe doing his best to discredit Christian writings *De contemptu mundi*. No less than the advocates of enlightenment, the nephew sees futility and lost opportunity in efforts to escape from our social and natural surroundings. Where he and the philosophes part company is on the question whether to stand erect in *le monde* until knocked down by the *grands*, or to escape from blows directed against the unprotected by crawling from mansion to mansion. Either way, walking in danger or crawling in safety, one is the plaything of *le monde.*

Hostile to metaphysics, the philosophes denied that we can climb above the world and view it from the outside; so too, the nephew—borrowing Montaigne's phrase—denies that he sits "perched on the epicycle of Mercury," looking down from a privileged vantage point on "the different pantomimes of the human species."[136] Montaigne's words were immediately followed in the *Essays* by a denunciation of those presumptuous thinkers who would answer the ultimate questions, far beyond human ken, when they failed to understand their own kind, "ever present before their eyes."[137] Lui watches the human spectacle without ever pretending to transcend it; he moves up and down the social scale, is whatever he must be at the moment, sees all, remembers all, mimics all. Knowledge of the human condition, knowledge gained from participation rather than contemplation of society, is his.

It is also the case that Lui's unconceptualized philosophy is as fully attentive to the human body as either Locke's book on the senses or Montaigne's insistence upon describing his body as an integral part of his being. True to his manner, the nephew declares defecation one of life's joys; his special interest, however, is in the eating that precedes his triumphal visits to the toilet.[138] Or more precisely, his constant concern is to ensure that he shall never stop eating: "I always come back to hunger." In words that paraphrase Montaigne he laments that "some men are replete with everything while others, whose stomachs are no less importunate, ... have nothing to bite on."[139] Never for a moment does Lui forget he has a body, nor does he fail to notice how we transform bodily needs into social performances. "The needy man ... skips, twists, cringes, crawls. He spends his life choosing and performing positions."

Thereupon the nephew assumes the bearing, visage, and movements of every imaginable social type—courtier, priest, footman, judge, magistrate. Effortlessly, he takes off one mask and dons another, each time leaving the old self behind at a moment's notice, while instantaneously transforming himself into another person. Lui has become Vertumnus, the Roman god mentioned at the beginning of the dialogue, who could will himself another person whenever he wished. The suppliant man, the compliant man, the man enthralled—these roles and more Lui plays so effectively as to call for the conclusion that in society appearances are the only reality.

The longer Lui dances his pantomime, the more the moral preaching of the philosophes sounds as hollow and vapid as the drivel that emanates from pulpits. Though anything but a Stoic, the nephew has shown Moi that the world is indeed a stage, and that the morality of social roles, so dear to the moral philosophy of the philosophes, Diderot most of all, is a sham. Repeatedly the philosophes stressed that, even when alone, we feel the eyes of others and therefore do not transgress the moral code. Now, as Lui performs and Moi watches in speechless amazement, it becomes clear that we are never anything except what others would have us be. The homilies delivered by the *parti philosophique* are so many incantations rationalizing the forfeiture of our integrity and our very selves to an unworthy social order. Once again the philosophes were establishing right by fact, deciding what ought to be by citing what is.

Early in the dialogue Moi and Lui denounce the morality of social roles as it pertains to the lesser ranks of society—the traders, who employ "idioms" for exploiting the public, and a second group, the *"espèces,"* who are libellers and informants by profession, persons whose role is to do wrong but who are too role-bound, the nephew complains, to bring any originality or flair to their escapades.[140] Immediately following Lui's pantomime, near the end of the dialogue, the nephew and Moi turn to the peak of society, the king and court. Surprisingly the normally relentless Lui is willing to believe that royalty walks while everyone else takes up positions. Moi, now fully committed to Lui's viewpoint, refuses to tolerate such prematurely abandoned cynicism: "Whoever stands in need of another is indigent and takes a position. The king takes a position before his mistress and before God: he dances his pantomime steps. The minister executes the movements of courtier, flatterer, footman, and beggar before the king. The crowd of place-seekers dance all your positions in a hundred ways, each viler than the next, in front of the minister."[141] There is only one person who sits out the dance, Moi concludes: "the philosopher who has nothing and asks for nothing."[142]

In exempting the philosophe from the pantomime, Moi has restated d'Alembert's imperative in the *Essay on the Society of Men of Letters* calling for intellectuals to watch the social dance without becoming participants. "Diogenes made fun of his wants," remarks Moi, again duplicating d'Alembert, who had expressed admiration of the Cynic's independence, acquired through uncompromising dedication to "Liberty, Truth, Poverty." But if Moi's appreciation of Diogenes is truly Diderot, so is Lui's dismissal of the Cynic. Much of Diderot's article "Cynique" speaks favorably about the man who answered to no other man, not even Alexander; the essay in the *Encyclopédie* ends, however, with disdain for "enthusiasts of virtue," whether or not they wear clerical robes.[143] How could the author of *The Nun* possibly regard a life of self-abnegation as anything but a sin against human nature? It is a sign of fatal weakness that Moi, in his eulogy of Diogenes, draws a comparison with the monastic life: "The Cynics were the Carmelites and Cordeliers of Athens."[144] Moi's argument is entirely unconvincing because Diderot himself remained unconvinced.

Stoicism as a positive doctrine was regarded as unlivable by the philosophes, because they were certain that an Epicurean existence was their rightful due and the only outlook permitting humans to be human. Stoicism as an admonition against self-destructive forms of behavior was, however, taken seriously by Diderot and his kind. To be all things to all persons, to forfeit one's autonomy, is to become a "man without character" or a man divided against himself; so the Stoics had warned, and one philosophe after another repeated their warnings.[145] Lui, who "has no greater opposite than himself," who cannot say whether he is as he is by birth or by (mis)education, is a dramatic embodiment of all the Stoics and philosophes found despicable.[146]

Nevertheless there are good reasons to believe that Lui's chances of emerging in one piece from the dialogue are better than those of its author. Diderot, who is Moi and Lui at the same time, suffers from a self so divided that Pascal might well shout with glee. As for Lui, he fulfills every criterion for a great actor that Diderot specified in the *Paradoxe sur le comédien*—that the actor is everyone and hence no one, that his lack of character enables him to assume any character, that he movingly expresses the external signs communicating passions while himself remaining unmoved.[147] Unfortunately Lui never performed on a stage where his gestures and pantomimes, in a play written by Diderot or Voltaire, would have taught the audience their duties or the need to end the crimes perpetrated in the name of religion. But in front of Moi and in the mind of Diderot he staged a performance instructing *monsieur le philosophe* in the meaning of self-doubt.

Diderot felt empathy for the many struggling men of letters, those "poor devils" as they were frequently called and as Lui calls himself, who foolishly gambled their lives on somehow making a living with their pens;[148] but the best Diderot could do to even the score was to suggest—

in a private letter—that all social ranks, royalty included, are composed of "poor devils."[149] Surely the nephew would have approved, and then walked off, saying, "he laughs best who laughs last."[150] The trouble is, *le monde* laughs both first and last at the *gens de lettres.*

Many reasons may be suggested for Diderot's refusal to publish *Rameau's Nephew,* not the least being that it revealed too much. Enough of the powers that be were already controverting the philosophes without the party of humanity publicly interrogating itself or placing on display the profound misgivings and doubts of some of its most prominent members. Great work though it is, Diderot's dialogue between Moi and Lui was best left to the perusal and edification of the mice. In the meantime Diderot would steadfastly continue to pull the heavy load of the *Encyclopédie,* not always knowing why, yet remaining convinced, somehow, that such was his destiny, calling, and inescapable duty.

The Father Despoils the Philosophe

It was all very well for d'Alembert, ever the bachelor, to carry on about the nobility of poverty and to refuse, persistently and conspicuously, most offers of pensions and sinecures. Diderot, unlike his erstwhile co-editor of the *Encyclopédie,* had a daughter who with each passing year approached the day when she either would have a dowry and could afford a good marriage or would lack the means by which respectability was purchased.[151] If even Lui loved his son, how could the author of *Le Père de famille* bear to fall short of the full discharge of his fatherly duties? However fundamental Diderot's second thoughts about the morality of social roles, he never questioned the sanctity of fatherhood.

Unwilling to sell himself for personal gain, Diderot was sorely tempted to do whatever proved necessary to meet his obligations to his only child. In 1758 he did as so many other authors had done: he dedicated a dramatic work to a sovereign, Her Serene Highness the Princess of Nassau-Saarbrück. How fitting that the play in question was none other than *Le Père de famille.* Four years later, in 1762, Diderot actively sought a pension,[152] and in 1765 he successfully sold his library to Catherine the Great. Thereafter his finances were solvent, and he had the leisure to ponder the question how best to salvage his integrity after permitting a despot to buy it. Thinking he would have to bid adieu to his books, Diderot remarked that the father in him had despoiled the man of letters.[153] Although

Catherine graciously permitted him to hold on to his books for the rest of his life, he continued to sense that the philosophe in his being was not entirely pleased with the father.

It was Friedrich Melchior Grimm who submitted the dedication of *Le Père de famille* to the minor princess, and Grimm again who arranged for Catherine the Great to purchase Diderot's library: Grimm the diplomat and courtier, editor of the *Correspondance Littéraire,* a private newsletter written not for the public but for the crowned heads and potentates of Europe. With Rousseau out of the picture, Diderot became ever more closely allied with Grimm, in whose newsletter he published his art criticism, beginning with the *Salon de 1759.* By 1770 Diderot felt so strongly tied to Grimm that he could say, "I have never separated your actions, good or bad, from mine . . . For twenty years I have believed myself to be one man in two persons."[154] About the same time Diderot commented in passing that Grimm "is almost my only friend."[155]

Diderot adhered rigorously to the advice of d'Alembert, among others, that the philosophe should submit his writings to his fellow authors for criticism rather than awaiting the judgment of a public consisting of *grands* who were anything but great. As always, however, Diderot personalized an admonition others stated impersonally. The writings he decided not to publish, the very works for which he is now famous, the ones so different in tone from the hortatory and self-assured rhetoric of his entries in the *Encyclopédie,* were for the eyes of a select few, especially Sophie Volland and Grimm.[156] To Sophie he could reveal anything, including his misgivings about what the man of letters sacrifices to satisfy the father,[157] and in her he could confide his sometime belief in arguments set forth by Lui against Moi in *Rameau's Nephew.*[158] From Grimm, the critic, he expected professional comments on his works, uncompromised by envy or fear of offending the author.

Courtly manners were not the style of Diderot, whose love of uninhibited exchange made him *persona non grata* in the salons of Madame Geoffrin and Madame du Deffand. Forever frequenting the cafés other philosophes gladly abandoned the moment they "arrived" in society, Diderot could not possibly adorn his visage with the face powder for which Grimm was known. Although unable to answer Lui, Diderot was not tempted to follow the model of Parisian existence the nephew exemplified. Neither could Diderot live as Grimm did, a self-made and fabulously successful courtier. But he could learn from Grimm how to make one's way in *le monde,* or better yet, he could permit Grimm to do for Diderot what Diderot was unable or unwilling to do for himself. It was Grimm's diplomatic triumph that he arranged for Diderot to follow his own example while seeing to it that his friend could continue, outwardly, to look and act the same as he had before forming an alliance with Catherine.

Under Grimm's aegis it was fatally tempting for Diderot to become a courtier and yet continue to think himself merely one step removed from the status of an incorruptible "poor devil." For the rest of his life Diderot tugged periodically at the chain that he, with Grimm's assistance, had placed around his own neck. Perhaps he occasionally remembered the words Moi spoke to Lui: "You dance, you have danced, and you will keep on dancing the vilest pantomime."[159]

Birth of a Republican

It is startling to note how far the Diderot of *Rameau's Nephew* has evolved in the direction Rousseau had charted a good decade or more earlier. Rousseau had argued that society divides rather than unites the self, and now Diderot says the same. Rousseau had insisted that in society as it is, the voice of the violent reasoner cannot be silenced; Diderot gives that voice, through the good offices of Lui, permission to yell at the top of its lungs. Society as a pattern of mutual exploitation rather than mutual aid was another of Rousseau's themes taken up with a new vigor by the nephew. Finally, the "tacit agreement" discussed by Lui runs parallel to the social contract codifying established abuse that figures so prominently in the *Second Discourse* and *Political Economy.* Lui even manages, in his splendidly perverse way, to turn his thievery into a contractual act by calling it "restitution."[160] Whatever he takes from the rich he restores to the poor, namely himself.

The possibility that Diderot was indebted to Rousseau for his radically revised social philosophy can neither be ruled out nor definitively confirmed. In all likelihood Rousseau did not send his onetime comrade, soon to be his "enemy brother," a copy of his penetrating critique of "Natural Right." Nevertheless Diderot presumably encountered much the same criticism when he read Julie's comments on "dangerous reasoners" in *La Nouvelle Héloïse;* by inference, moreover, Diderot could have gleaned from the *Second Discourse,* a work he relished, many of Rousseau's arguments against the original, standard version of Enlightenment thought. Alternatively, it is quite conceivable that Diderot's thought would have evolved as it did even in the absence of Rousseau. Our findings in this chapter suggest that *Rameau's Nephew* was a contribution to an ongoing discussion in philosophical circles, a debate over the social prospects of philosophes that readily passed over to an expression of deep dissatisfaction and outright disgust with the existing social order.

Whether by direct influence or by accidental convergence, Diderot arrived at an understanding of the underlying social problem similar to Rousseau's. Arguably there was a corresponding convergence in the realm of proposed solutions. For Rousseau a republic was needed; for Diderot, too, republics began to look enticing. In the cover letter to Grimm accompanying his *Salon de 1763* Diderot asked why the ancient republics produced so many great artists.

> It's because rewards and honors awakened talents, and the people . . . were a redoubtable judge. Why such great musicians? Because music was part of a general education . . . Why such great poets? Because there were combats of poetry and crowns for the winners. Institute among us the same battles, make it possible to hope for the same honors and rewards, and soon we shall see the fine arts rapidly advance to perfection.[161]

Diderot wrote the foregoing words, significantly, not long after sketching the first draft of *Rameau's Nephew*. Great satire tears away the masks behind which society hides, but leaves everything as it is; politics can change what is. Historically, it is republics that have provided writers and artists with the enlightened public they crave, the audience that inspires the *beaux esprits* and spurs them to the heights of creative accomplishment.

By no means did the sale of his library to Catherine, two years later, mark the end of Diderot's budding republicanism. On the contrary, for him the integrity-saving complement to his courtier-like praise of Catherine was growing political awareness and constantly increasing hostility to the absolutism of the French and Prussian monarchies. Nowhere, perhaps, is the extent to which he had caught up to Rousseau more evident than in Diderot's vigorous attack on Grimm in 1781. Grimm had given Raynal, editor of the anticolonial *Histoire des deux Indes,* the choice of being a coward or a fool. Diderot, who contributed impassioned attacks on despots to Raynal's enlightened enterprise, seized the offensive against the man he had previously described as his other self. "You no longer understand, my friend, how inspired, courageous, virtuous men . . . write their works." Grimm's soul, Diderot continued, had "dwindled at Petersberg, at Potsdam, . . . in the antechambers of the great." "Oh, how useful and beneficial [your] doctrine for oppressors!" Old man that he now was, Diderot had not yet finished his youthful, republican tirade: "The book I love and that kings and courtiers detest, is the one that gives birth to Brutuses."[162]

That Diderot, a thinker of the highest stature, should so warmly endorse republican sentiments is well worth noting. What makes his growing republicanism all the more significant, as we shall see, is that it was part of a larger transformation in the outlook of a major segment of the philosophical party. Now that the political gap between Rousseau and the philosophes was closing, and some of the latter were becoming politically educated and open to republican thought, the time had arrived for Jean-Jacques to renew his debate with those he left behind the day he rode out of Paris.

CHAPTER FOUR

Three Enemies in One Person

THE closer the philosophes moved to the ground long held by Rousseau, the more sharply drawn were the lines of battle; the less feasible
was a reconciliation; the more public and celebrated was their conflict;
and the higher the stakes rose in the struggle between Jean-Jacques and
his estranged colleagues over the leadership and definition of the Enlightenment.

Occasionally, it is true, Rousseau did play the peacemaker, as when he
elected himself in *La Nouvelle Héloïse* to write the terms of a proposed
armistice between the philosophes and the fervently religious, by which
he accomplished nothing beyond proving that hatred of himself was the
sole article of faith common to believers and unbelievers. Perhaps inevitably, Rousseau convinced the philosophes not that they shared anything
with churchmen, but that he had carried his betrayal of their aspirations
so far as to aid and abet the enemy.

Blessed are the peacemakers, but Rousseau was a troublemaker even
when playing the conciliator, and the troubles he stirred up were, from
the viewpoint of the philosophes, completely at their expense. Beyond
returning to faith, Rousseau announced in the *Letter to d'Alembert* that
morals cannot stand on their own feet but must be propped up by
religion.[1] In a footnote, as if innocently, Rousseau denied the autonomy
of morals, one of the tenets the philosophes regarded as central to their
outlook, a belief they gladly inherited from Bayle, their godfather, to
whose pioneering efforts based on skepticism some added their own
efforts to lay a positive foundation for ethics in applications of the new
science of nature to human nature. No one, the philosophes believed,
could restore morals to religion without being their enemy, and yet Rousseau, their fellow philosophe and encyclopedist, had done precisely that.[2]

Preoccupied with their campaign against the Church, the last thing the philosophes needed was war on a second front. Such a war, however, was what they faced as Rousseau published one work after another, each seemingly more shrill in its denunciation of the philosophes. The *Letter to d'Alembert* (1758) signaled a public break with Diderot, an explicit disagreement with d'Alembert, and an implicit but unmistakable assault on Voltaire. What could be worse than for Rousseau to rail, rightly, against superstition and error, while suggesting, perversely, that philosophy was one source of our prejudices? In the *Letter to d'Alembert* he denounced "this age when prejudices reign so proudly and error gives itself the name of philosophy."[3] Rousseau thereby announced to the world that his was not a personal quarrel with Diderot or Voltaire; it was with the entire philosophic movement because its members were destroying one set of prejudices only to replace them with another.

Before long the philosophes learned that Rousseau's critique of d'Alembert's article "Geneva" in the *Encyclopédie* was only the opening shot in an all-out offensive Jean-Jacques had launched against them and their version of enlightenment. Soon his most systematic works were to appear, *La Nouvelle Héloïse, Emile,* and the *Social Contract.* In the first two of this trilogy of masterpieces Rousseau spiced his pages with incessant attacks on the philosophes, and in all three he complemented the critical works of his earlier years, most notably the *First and Second Discourses,* with the constructive projects of the late 1750s and early 1760s. By 1762 he had completed both his anti-Enlightenment and his alternative or counter-Enlightenment.

With the passing of time Rousseau's status in the ranks of the philosophes changed from that of a manageable nuisance to that of an uncontrollable and deadly adversary, the enemy within who knew all and turned all he knew against his former comrades. He was no Palissot, the protégé of Voltaire who sold his soul to the established powers when he elected to make a career of mocking the philosophes; Rousseau's conspicuous poverty made it very difficult to dismiss him as someone whose sole concern was pensions and patronage. Born of the Enlightenment and loyal to its ideals, himself a favorite butt of Palissot's satires, Rousseau nevertheless sounded increasingly like the traditionalist journalists and churchmen who accused the philosophes of undermining the family. As if that were not enough, Rousseau's tirade against actors and the theater was reminiscent of the polemics of Bossuet or Nicole; his insistence, moreover, on outfitting morals with a religious anchor smacked of reactionary hostility to the party of humanity.

"More conservative than thou" was, then, one of Rousseau's favorite themes; his other incessant motif was "more radical than thou." The republicanism he championed was a weapon aimed at the philosophes, whose success in gaining admission to the academies signified their incorporation in the monarchy. As for those who stayed out of the academies and adopted an ever more republican political theory, Rousseau was insistent that theirs was a timid and inferior version of republican thought, completely unequal to the tasks at hand.

Rousseau was not just another enemy; he was three enemies in one person. To borrow the language the Revolution bequeathed to subsequent ages, he was the enemy on the left, the enemy on the right, and the enemy within.

The Hidden Republic

Tocqueville complained that the philosophes cared about the condition of writers but were indifferent to forms of government.[4] It would be more accurate to argue that because of their keen interest in the situation of intellectuals, the philosophes became very concerned about forms of government, some of them—as was hinted in Chapter 3—concluding that only a republic could solve the problems that plagued the republic of letters. We must now draw a sketch of this incipient republicanism, so as to provide the backdrop for our subsequent examination of how Rousseau outflanked the philosophes to the "left" even during their most politically bold moments.

It was England to which the philosophes looked for an image of a social order in which writers received their due; England was the road they traveled when searching for an answer to their dilemma, some of them calling an early halt to their intellectual voyage, others staying the course to the republican end. "Such is the respect the English nation has for talent that a man of parts always makes his fortune there," Voltaire wrote in the *Lettres philosophiques.*[5] Decades later, as the final volumes of the *Encyclopédie* appeared despite the obstacles the Old Regime placed in the way, Grimm noted that in England those who shouldered the burden of this enormous enterprise would have made their fortune. Having published this great monument to enlightenment in France, Grimm continues, the editors and authors met with a different outcome; one of the publishers, Le Breton, used his profits to buy the Parisian house that de Jaucourt, a major contributor, was forced to sell in order to pay his secretaries.[6]

Fair pay for services rendered was one objective of the philosophes; respect was another. In the letter "On the Consideration Due to Men of Letters," Voltaire's emphasis is at least as much on respect as on money; he points with pride to the public offices held by Addison, Newton, and Congreve. Three decades later we spy Diderot writing sentences that might as well be purloined from Voltaire's *Lettres philosophiques:* "In England, philosophers are honored, respected, rise to public offices, are buried with kings . . . In France, warrants are issued against them; they are banished, persecuted, overwhelmed by pastoral letters, satires, libels. Am I not right to say the French are children who throw rocks at their teachers?"[7] Both Voltaire and Diderot indicated that intellectuals should be granted public office as a mark of social esteem; the question that remains to be answered is whether they cared what kind of regime their kind would serve.

In Voltaire's *Lettres philosophiques,* lamented Tocqueville, "Parliament is hardly mentioned; the truth was that he envied the English above all for their freedom to write as they liked, while their political freedom left him indifferent, and he quite failed to realize that the former could not have survived without the latter."[8] It is not difficult to understand Tocqueville's view, given the seeming willingness of Voltaire to endorse any government in which philosophes were noteworthy figures. The historical works of Voltaire overflow with praise of China, where classically trained intellectuals, the non-Western counterparts to the French philosophes, staffed the officialdom.[9] Willing to laud the Chinese political order Montesquieu had placed under the heading of despotism, Voltaire also insisted with pride in "Gens de lettres" that in cleansing society of prejudice "men of letters have in effect served the [French] state." He himself served briefly as royal historian and on several occasions wrote in behalf of the policies of ministers, sometimes at their invitation. To all appearances any state would do, whether despotic in the Chinese manner, absolute in the French, or constitutional in English fashion. What was good for the philosophes was good for the country.

Yet appearances can be deceiving, because the *Lettres philosophiques,* Tocqueville notwithstanding, does contain a letter on Parliament and another on government, these two immediately followed by one on commerce that has a direct bearing on the two concerned with political matters. However cursorily, Voltaire sketches the outline of a commercial people, free from its feudal past, powerful through its navy and trade; an England in which aristocrats do not disdain agriculture or commerce and are not exempt from taxes; where seigneurial dues are a thing of the past, and the House of Commons, "though only second in rank, is first in prestige." At the outset of these letters Voltaire listed the reasons why the members of Parliament are mistaken to compare themselves to ancient Romans. But before he has finished the chapter on commerce, Voltaire notes approvingly that English merchants liken themselves to Roman citizens.[10] Without placing a label on the English regime, Voltaire invited the French to admire a commercial republic. Among other things, the *Lettres philosophiques* may be said to have initiated, in the most understated fashion imaginable, a tradition of political thought in France that was republican in all but name.[11]

That the English were republicans despite their monarch was Montesquieu's point as well in *The Spirit of the Laws* (1748). Though never saying so in the most direct manner, Montesquieu made of England a model in its own right,[12] a lesson in what may await a nation that has bid adieu to its "intermediary bodies" and must, in consequence, either become a despotic or a popular and free state.[13] For the time being, at least, the English were the most free of peoples. Call England a constitutional monarchy and Montesquieu will not object, for like Voltaire, he prefers using noninflammatory labels; yet his reference to a country that is a "republic hidden under the form of a monarchy"[14] can only be to England. The second most free people, in Montesquieu's estimation, are the Dutch[15] who as commercial republicans share something with the English, unlike the French who, living in a society that revolves around the aristocratic "principle" of honor, have little in common with the islanders. Perhaps it was from Bolingbroke that Montesquieu and Voltaire learned to think of England as a republic; but whatever they borrowed from the Commonwealthmen was supplemented by their own conclusion, quite foreign to Bolingbroke, that modern republics would do well to place relatively more emphasis on commerce than on civic virtue.[16]

Helvétius was well acquainted with both Voltaire and Montesquieu, and it is in the pages of his frequently maligned *De l'Esprit* (1758) that French readers encountered a fully elaborated argument, sustained by numerous references to England, linking the triumph of the republic of letters with the presence of a political republic. None of the philosophes could accept or even take seriously Helvétius' attempt to reduce everything to physical sensibility; all were upset by the scandal his book stirred and the difficulties it created for the *Encyclopédie*. But we must never forget that Diderot rated it, if inferior to Montesquieu or Buffon, yet "among the great books of the century."[17]

Both *De l'Esprit* and the posthumous *De l'Homme* are major contributions to the philosophical examination of the situation of the intellectual. Where d'Alembert, Duclos, and others had been, Helvétius was certain to follow: their warnings against internal bickering, against the temptation to flatter the *grands*, and against hopes of gaining acceptance of challenging writings in one's lifetime, except by the young, were repeated by Helvétius.[18] Much, however, was new in *De l'Esprit*; the predecessors of Helvétius had ended their researches with findings that took them to the edge of despair or the verge of politics. It was Helvétius who dared to transform the thoughts of the philosophes on the plight of intellectuals into a systematic treatise on politics and the arts.

Voltaire in the *Lettres philosophiques* comments on English government and then on English letters, without drawing a strong connection between the two.[19] Montesquieu offers the tantalizing remark that "the character of the [English] nation is especially evident in their literary works."[20] By and large, however, Montesquieu's insight was left undeveloped for ten years, until Helvétius made it a mainstay of his notorious book on the human mind. In *De l'Esprit* we learn that the form of the government, in every country, both shapes the style of its literature and accounts for the prevalent social image of the writer's calling.

English authors, Helvétius held, fare so well because they live in a republic: "If celebrated writers, as the example of Locke and Addison proves, up to the present have been more honored in England than anywhere else, that is because it's impossible not to make a fuss over merit in a country where each citizen has a part in the management of general affairs—where every man of intelligence can enlighten the public as to its true interests."[21] The words may sound familiar, but the intensely political accent is new. Helvétius marks a republican turning point in the French Enlightenment.

Intimate with Voltaire, Helvétius nevertheless ignored his mentor's effort to reduce Montesquieu to an apologist for the nobility of the robe.[22] Remove the chapters on climate from *The Spirit of the Laws*, keep the scheme for the classification of regimes, and one has the conceptual apparatus of *De l'Esprit:* the typology of Oriental despotisms, feudal monarchies, and republics ancient and modern, Sparta being the most significant of past republics, England the crucial modern republic. All the arguments of Helvétius derive from the intellectual framework he borrowed from Montesquieu.

In *De l'Esprit* all the old complaints about the fate of writers take on a new, political meaning. If the French are the "most frivolous people of Europe," that is because "citizens have, by the form of our government, less need of instruction than of amusement." If mean-spirited intrigue takes the place rightfully held by great ambition, that is because "the route of ambition is, by the form of our government, closed to the larger part of our citizens."[23] What public can an author address in a monarchical nation where "everyone treats public affairs with indifference?"[24] By the very nature of monarchy, public office is only sought to promote the private interests of one's family,[25] and the most successful of politicians is merely a courtier who never so much as thinks of the general interest.[26] Passions unstirred by great affairs, lukewarm personalities, pettiness that trickles down from bored and idle *grands* to the lower orders, pettiness carried from court to *ville* and *province*—such are the deleterious effects of monarchy.[27]

Whenever Helvétius compared republican England to monarchical France, it was to the detriment of his own country. "In London it is a merit to be instructed; in Paris it is ridiculous."[28] England is "a country where the people are respected," France a "monarchical state wherein the people receive no consideration."[29] If English writers are superior to French, "it is less to their language than to their government that they owe this advantage."

> In a free state a man conceives the highest thoughts and can express them as vividly as they enter his mind. Such is not the case in monarchical states: in these countries the interest of certain corporations, that of various powerful individuals, and most of all a false and small politics, thwart the *élans* of genius.[30]

The breach between politics and the arts opened by philosophical history was closed by Helvétius, who unlike Diderot or d'Alembert was from the beginning a political thinker. Each regime, he observed, impresses its image on literary style. Under despotism, for instance, allegory holds sway because "truth can be presented only in coded form."[31] Oratory is absent from arbitrary regimes, flourishes in healthy republics, but withers—as Roman history attests—when freedom wanes.[32] As for theater, so dear to the tastes of the French, the pattern is clear: successful tragedies pertain to republican peoples, whereas comedies are the dramatic substance on which monarchical audiences feed their impoverished tastes. "It is a certain feebleness of character, the necessary result of luxury and changes in our mores depriving us of all force and elevation of soul, that makes us prefer comedies to tragedies."[33]

On the French stage love is everything, politics nothing because in a monarchical polity and aristocratic society public matters are far removed from everyday life: "I say that in every country where the inhabitants have no part in the management of public affairs, where the words *patrie* and *citoyen* are rarely cited, one does not please the public except in representing on the stage passions agreeable to individuals, such as those of love."[34] Corneille's vigorous dramas were immediately successful for the reason that his age was one of ambition, sedition, passion, and greatness; his style of drama still fills the theater in England, but in France the triumph of the overly delicate Racine coincides with the rise of absolutism and the decline of the French spirit.[35] The bored French are in love with love because they have nothing better to love.

Eager to forget the hedonistic reductionism of Helvétius, the philosophes remembered his claim that republics provide the writer with the worthy audience that spurs the author to greatness. Some fifteen years after the publication of *De l'Esprit* we still hear what sounds like the voice of Helvétius in Holbach's *Système social,* especially the chapter "On the Influence of Government on National Character, Talents of Mind, and Letters." Without a *patrie,* argues Holbach as had Helvétius, there can be no eloquence; under such conditions "the oratorical art is exclusively reserved for the ministers of religion." A frivolous, vapid people, which is all any people can be that lives under a monarchical regime, resents and ridicules its teachers, particularly those who have something substantial to say. "Philosophy . . . is, above all, the science most exposed to scorn in a flippant and dissipated nation."

Holbach lamented as much as Helvétius the preoccupation of the French with the theme of romantic love, an obsessive motif that leads them away from public affairs. "Perpetual childhood" is bound to be the fate of the French since their society, whether at court or the salon, revolves around women. "For beings that everything conspires to keep in infancy, all that is necessary are fictional writings, novels, voluptuous paintings, dramas full of amorous intrigues, and gallant verses." Whatever harm the women fail to do is certain to be inflicted by young aristocrats, vain and stupid, who live only for the chance to die in a foolish war, and regard the best writers as the most useless of men.[36]

By 1760 Diderot had learned what Helvétius (and Rousseau) had always known, that "politics and morals go hand in hand."[37] Three years later Diderot wrote of oratory as Helvétius had previously and as Holbach would afterwards: "To speak well," he asserted in the *Salon de 1763*, "one must be a tribune of the people."[38] Diderot had come a long way indeed since 1751 when he published "Political Authority," which said no to divine right but yes to political absolutism justified by vague appeals to a historical contract. From 1763 to the end of his life Diderot seemingly could not decry too frequently the absence of a platform from which the orator could address his audience, nor could he search more earnestly for the political materials from which to construct a setting in which political speech could be projected to a national audience. As Cicero had spoken to the Romans, Diderot would the French. Only a republic was missing, without which oratory was declamation and nothing more.[39]

It is not surprising that Diderot's political thought evolved so dramatically. His republicanism can be read as the natural outcome of the dilemma of the philosophe stated in *Rameau's Nephew*, combined with the political solution offered by Helvétius. Add to this that nothing in Diderot's personal history blocked the way to the implantation of republican convictions. Along with Helvétius and his friend Holbach, he was not a member of the French Academy, nor did he aspire to such an honor.[40] Throughout his life, from his earliest writings on, he stated that a position in a royal academy was the surest way to stifle one's genius and embalm it in mediocrity.[41] Nor did he ever show the slightest desire to ingratiate himself with the ladies who ruled the antechambers to the academies; admission to Holbach's free-spirited salon—so singularly devoid of a reigning hostess—more than atoned for exclusion from the rest. Only one woman mattered to Diderot's career and that was Catherine, for whom he felt obliged to offer excuses and then to repent of his apologetics by writing essays ever more constitutional, republican, and insistent that the one fate worse for a people than governance by an enlightened despot was a succession of such reigns, because the ruled would inevitably lose all capacity to govern themselves.[42]

Even some of the leading members of the academies began to flirt with republican language. "It seems that what touches the public good is a stranger to us," Duclos commented, adding a few pages later that if conversation is more perfected at court than elsewhere, "this is because one is destined to speak there without saying anything."[43] With characteristic discretion Duclos avoided drawing a political conclusion to his thoughts on speech, perhaps wisely, given that his enemies accused him of being "too republican."[44]

Both Diderot and Rousseau spent time mastering Tacitus. Is it insignificant that d'Alembert, a highly successful yet fiercely independent academician, did the same? When d'Alembert found himself "in a country of persecution and servitude, in the midst of a slavish and sheeplike people,"[45] he may have remembered that Tacitus was recommended by Guicciardini to all those who would learn how to cope with life under a despotic regime.[46] Certainly d'Alembert shared with other philosophes an appreciation of the profound ambivalence of Tacitus' *Dialogue on Oratory*. Augustus had healed the wounds of civil war but not without silencing public speech;[47] was he, then, a savior or a despot?

For reasons of political strategy and tactics d'Alembert shied away from republican language, just as Diderot and Holbach, having opted for the opposite strategy, were naturally driven toward the vocabulary of Cicero. Allied with Voltaire, d'Alembert had elected to use the crown, insofar as possible, to control if not crush the infamous; the hope was that Frederick would impose toleration from above and that the French monarch might be induced to do the same, if only from motives of *raison d'état*. By contrast, Diderot and Holbach were ever more convinced not only that throne and altar were inseparable but that altar would inevitably master throne.[48] Spanish history was a decisive commentary on the tendency of monarchy to capitulate to Catholicism. More recently, Maupeou's dismissal of the parlements in 1770, arguably the move of a modernizing minister, had been defended through invocations of divine right,[49] which was by default the doctrine to which the French state unthinkingly turned for justification. To the likes of Diderot and Holbach the time had come to be on the lookout for ways to turn France into a republic hiding under the form of a monarchy.

Eloquence, oratory, and republics—these were the words on the lips and flowing from the pens of many philosophes.[50] To give them force and power two things more were needed: a pillar of respectability had to repeat the words of the philosophes publicly, and someone had to suggest an institutional setting for the advent of political oratory in monarchical France. One fine day in 1775 both these needs were filled at the same moment when Malesherbes rose to deliver his speech accepting admission to the French Academy: "In a century in which every citizen can speak to the entire nation by means of print, those who have the talent for instructing men or the gift of moving them—in a word, men of letters— are, in the midst of a dispersed people, what the orators of Rome and Athens were in the midst of a people assembled."[51]

Malesherbes was all the philosophes could possibly have desired: hailing from a prominent family in the nobility of the robe, himself the presiding judge of the Cour des Aides, he was a universally respected public servant. At the time of his remarkable speech of admission to the academy he was fresh from his able defense of the parlements during the four years of the Maupeou coup. No matter how often the parlements had acted as reactionary bodies, no matter how guilty they were of attempts to suppress enlightened works,[52] the philosophes overwhelmingly—with the notable exception of Voltaire—rose to their defense in the battle against "despotism."[53] For the time being, until a better institutional bastion of freedom could be found, the parlements would suffice. In the meantime Malesherbes had, in effect, invited the philosophes to continue doing in the future what they had just done to save the freedom of the French. Diderot wished in 1763 for the philosophes to become tribunes of the people; in 1775 he had reason to believe reality was catching up to his dreams.

It may well be that the strongest effort to construe France as a republic hiding under the form of a monarchy came from within the French state itself, especially from the Marquis d'Argenson and Turgot, each something of a *ministre-philosophe,* each convinced, in d'Argenson's words, that "everything good for republics augments monarchical authority."[54] Both men agreed with Bodin, their intellectual ancestor, that an absolutist France governed democratically would boast the most effective administration the monarchy had ever known.[55] It is an open question, however, whether the French state they proposed was a monarchy assisted by republican devices or, especially in Turgot's case, a republic assisted by a monarch.

In common with Montesquieu, d'Argenson avoids abstract discussions of political right, preferring to derive his generalizations from comparative and historical examinations of different societies. It so happens that d'Argenson's findings, no less than his method, have much in common with

The Spirit of the Laws. Turkey is a pitiful despotism, a state displaying "all the evils monarchical government can cause when it refuses the admission of any democracy."[56] Spain represents the woes of the Western variety of despotism, less total than the Oriental but quite devastating: plagued by superstition and massive inequality of possessions, in a state of economic decay, all its provinces overrun by royal officials such that the people are nothing, France's neighbor to the south was a warning of what other monarchies must avoid.[57] Holland is an entirely different story, small but a hundred times more powerful than its size would lead one to expect, thanks to the absence of a feudal nobility and the presence in the Netherlands of provincial governments allowing a degree of self-rule.[58] Visit the border territories where a monarchical people stands juxtaposed to a republican neighbor, advises d'Argenson, and you will always know on which side of the border you stand: the ample public works and signs of economic activity mark the republican side.[59]

D'Argenson's scheme is to rebuild monarchy by borrowing from republics the principle of participation. It is necessary "to admit the public more in the government of the Public,"[60] so that France may be transformed into a "true democracy residing in the midst of a monarchy."[61] Historically democracy has always been the ally of monarchy; aristocracy its foe.[62] Whether we speak of the old feudalism or the new one based on venality of offices,[63] aristocracy is an obstructive force, unlike democracy—the Third Estate, the cities, the people—which has traditionally supported the king's efforts.

All the workaday administrative affairs of each village should be entrusted to officials chosen from the locality, even from the ranks of the peasants.[64] How can the officialdom be popular if not drawn from and then returned to the populace? Richelieu, Colbert, and Louis XIV had attempted to run the country from the top down,[65] when it should be governed from the bottom up, by Officiers du Peuple rather than Officiers Royaux. France is to be ruled by a "popular administration"[66] which must be distinguished from rule by the Estates General or the parlements, those aristocratic bodies that detract from royal power.[67] "It will be said that the principles of the present treatise, favorable to democracy, lead to the destruction of the nobility, and that is not mistaken; nor is it an objection. It is a confirmation of our findings."[68] For the well-being of the state, French society must be restructured to respond in the future to talent as much as it has answered in the past to hereditary titles.[69]

D'Argenson hastens to add that however popular, democratic, and republican his proposed administration, the French state will remain adamantly monarchical; indeed, what will emerge is an enhanced monarchy, far superior to its predecessors. Better informed than he has ever been, the king will be ideally prepared to aggregate the interests of the French people, canceling out their differences, adding together their similarities, until the public interest emerges.[70] Let the people assemble for administrative purposes as frequently as they will, the king will continue in full possession of the legislative power.[71] Though their numbers shall diminish, the surviving Officiers Royaux can take comfort in knowing that "the laws constitutive of the state" are theirs alone to administer, for the Officiers populaires will deal solely with lesser matters.[72] Not even England[73] would be a match for the new France championed by the Marquis d'Argenson, the minister to whom the first volume of the *Encyclopédie* was dedicated.

An encyclopedist, a staunch advocate of rights and reforms, Turgot was more than a minister who sympathized with the philosophes. He was a full-fledged member of the party of humanity, so that when he assumed the post of controller general, a philosophe had finally come to power. On his order Dupont de Nemours drafted a *Mémoire sur les municipalités* (1775) that was another effort to graft a republican administration onto the ailing French monarchy. So bold is its language that the republic in question is no longer "hidden" under the form of a monarchy; it has daringly shown itself in plain view.[74]

In its broad outlines the *Mémoire* is initially strongly reminiscent of d'Argenson's earlier book. Local inhabitants will attend to local affairs, and an ever-widening series of representative assemblies, at the levels of villages, cities, and provinces, will meet to consider tax assessments and public works. Much as d'Argenson had envisioned, the purpose of these decentralized institutions would not be to pass laws but merely to furnish the king with the information needed for efficient administration. Again like d'Argenson, a demoted nobility "will retain only honorable distinctions rather than fiscal exemptions."[75] No longer would France be a crazy quilt of corporations living sometimes in conflict, at other times in mutual indifference. Under the new dispensation the nation would be "a single body perpetually animated by one sole objective, the public good and the preservation of the rights of each individual."[76]

"The English do not have the exclusive right of being citizens,"[77] the encyclopedist Turgot had written in 1757; the *Mémoire*, in fulfillment of his earlier comment, sets forth an ambitious plan for transforming French subjects into citizens. For many years the philosophes had denounced the woeful inadequacy of what passed for education in the colleges.[78] They typically called for reform, but Turgot wanted far more: a civic education that "would bring patriotism to that high degree of enthusiasm only seen before in some of the nations of the ancient world."[79] Education as understood by Turgot obviously had something in common with Rousseau's views. Indeed, some of Turgot's words are direct borrowings from writings previously published by Rousseau. "There are methods and institutions for training grammarians, mathematicians, doctors, painters. There are none for training citizens," Turgot wrote in words that paraphrased Rousseau's in the *First Discourse*: "We have physicists, geometers, chemists, astronomers, poets, musicians, painters; we no longer have citizens."[80]

Rather than turning out more wits, argued Turgot's mouthpiece, the academies should oversee the drafting of enlightened, civic textbooks that the schoolmasters will carry to each parish, even the most remote. "The study of the duties of the citizen, as member of a family and of the state, would be the basis for all other studies."[81] Only after they have learned to attend to the public interest and to discover their personal good in the public good will the citizens devote themselves to studies dealing with the more private aspects of their existence. As Rameau's nephew might put it, there will be fewer "trade idioms" in a civic France.

At times the echoes of Rousseau in Turgot's formulations are so inescapable that d'Argenson's treatise seems less to the point than the *Social Contract* in tracing the intellectual lineage of the *Mémoire sur les municipalités*. Before stating his definitive political formulation of the "general will," Rousseau expounded the contrast between "generality" and "particularity" in his *Letter to Voltaire on Providence* (1756). Following the lead Malebranche had set in his *Treatise on Nature and Grace*, Rousseau suggested that God governed the world not through constant intervention but by willing general laws.[82] In one and the same passage Turgot reformulates both Rousseau's divine and his civic invocation of the "general will." Addressing the monarch, Turgot points out that, owing to the shortcomings of the present political order, "You are forced to decree on everything, in most cases by particular acts of will, whereas you could govern like God by general laws."[83]

It is true that Turgot had no use for bicameralism, countervailing forces, or the civil wars that filled too many pages of republican history.[84] But he was hostile to the "legal despotism" of his fellow physiocrats and would eventually prove to be very appreciative of the unicameral legislature of Pennsylvania, praised by his friend Ben Franklin.[85] When Turgot objected to the separation of powers and to two legislative chambers, he was reasserting positions previously argued by both d'Argenson and Rousseau. It seems, however, that he found more to admire in Rousseau's *Social Contract* than in d'Argenson's *Considérations sur le Gouvernement ancien et présent de la France*. To Hume in 1767 Turgot remarked that Rousseau's book "amounts to a precise distinction between the sovereign and the government, but that distinction presents a very illuminating truth, and it seems to me to establish forever the idea of the inalienable sovereignty of the people, whatever the form of the government."[86] One is left to ponder whether Turgot preferred to have general laws emanate from the king, who is to the political world what the deity is to nature; or from the people, whose voice—in republican thought—is the voice of God.[87]

If Rousseau's "very illuminating truth" cannot be denied, then the king must merely be the trustee of the people and the executor of the general laws voted by a popular assembly. To place the people in charge of the administration of taxes, as Turgot proposed, was to invite a creeping constitutionalism, one reinforced in his case by such vigorous civic education that it all smelled of Rousseau. Reform of the monarchy, as conducted by Turgot, would have borne an amazing likeness to founding a republic.

Burning the Vanities

From the *First Discourse* to his final political writings, Rousseau's theme was consistently the same: both ancient history and the principles of enlightenment, properly employed, prove that republics can only be sustained through resisting or removing the high culture of the eighteenth century, along with its high priests, the philosophes. "My adversaries' discomfiture is evident whenever they have to speak about Sparta," remarked Rousseau. How embarrassing for the philosophes that the most virtuous and durable of Greek republics should have been the one "where there were no philosophers."[88]

With the assistance of Plutarch, Rousseau was able to use the ancients to expose the apologists of the moderns, the philosophes. "The Athenians," wrote Plutarch, "know what is decent, but the Spartans practice it";

to which Rousseau adds, "There are modern philosophy and ancient mores."[89] Not only do the moderns know; they talk incessantly about what they know, as did the Athenians, and with each speech or essay they widen the chasm between knowing and doing.

What did the philosophes' yearning for oratory signify if not their vanity, narrow self-interest, and the corruption that leads us to "make fine speeches on liberty in the depths of slavery?"[90] Echoing Montaigne, Rousseau reminded modern readers that Tacitus and other Roman historians had keenly observed the intimate connection between the arrival of oratory in Rome and the departure of civic virtue.[91] And who, precisely, is the Cicero so admired by modern men of letters? Is he the republican statesman or the early philosophe?

> I am sure there is not, at present, a single scholar who does not hold Cicero's eloquence in much higher esteem than he does his civic-mindedness, and who would not infinitely prefer to have written the Catilinarians than to have saved his country.[92]

Other than the Spartans, Rousseau had little use for "the babbling"[93] Greeks, least of all for the Athenians so admired by Voltaire. Supposedly a government of, by, and for the people, Athens in truth was far from a democracy, Rousseau proclaimed in the pages of the *Encyclopédie;* it might better be termed "a highly tyrannical aristocracy, governed by learned men and orators."[94] As for the moderns, "decency is no longer found save in words, and the more our souls are corrupted, the more we affect purity in discourses."[95]

Beautiful, moving speeches can actually harm a republic, especially when delivered by an actor on the stage. No sooner did d'Alembert, at Voltaire's urging, call for the Genevans to build a theater than Rousseau took up his pen in defense of his native republic. D'Alembert had publicly congratulated the Genevans on being so enlightened, so receptive to everything imported from Paris, on wanting only a theater to enjoy all the glories of French culture while avoiding the miseries France suffered at the hands of the Catholic Church. In the most immediate sense d'Alembert's concern was to provide Voltaire, now residing in the environs of Geneva, with a stage for the performance of his plays. In a larger sense the aim of the philosophes was to induce Geneva to break with its Calvinist past by embracing the theater, long accused of exciting the most sinful passions. Voltaire and d'Alembert had laid their plans with care except for one detail; they forgot that Rousseau signed his works "Citizen of Geneva."

Attentive to an immediate agenda, Voltaire and d'Alembert neglected the far greater question of the relationship between politics and the arts. Rousseau wasted no time locating the proper framework for dealing with the specific question raised in d'Alembert's article "Geneva." The theater is appropriate "in a big city, where mores and honor are nothing because each, easily hiding his conduct from the public eye, . . . is esteemed only for his riches."[96] When a people is bad the theater is good, since it diverts them for a few hours from wrongdoing;[97] which is to say, the theater is a perfect match for monarchies but out of place in a republic not yet corrupted by luxury and the arts born of leisure, excess, and inequality.[98] What Voltaire and d'Alembert had proposed, unknowingly, was to further their interests by undermining the civic ethos of the Genevans.[99]

That the theater should be used for the dissemination of philosophical messages, and the stage should supplant the pulpit, had been common refrains in the writings of the philosophes. Rousseau, however, insisted that the theater was a threat to the republican way of life. "People think they come together in the theater, and it is there that they are isolated. It is there that they go to forget their friends, neighbors, and relations."[100] One of the worst consequences of the theater is that it leads us to regard virtue as naturally given, already there, so much our birthright as to make deeds unnecessary; thus we mistake our vanity for virtue. When a man applauds a worthy action on the stage, "he applauds his fine soul. Has he not acquitted himself of all that he owes to virtue by the homage which he has just rendered it? What more could one want of him? That he practice it himself? He has no role to play; he is no actor."[101]

By their own account many of the philosophes enjoyed shedding tears, Rousseau perhaps more notoriously than the rest. Yet it was he, above all, who warned that tears are frequently nothing more than a social show. How Rousseau disdained those "weeping ladies in the boxes at the theater, so proud of their tears." Crying should signify a rediscovery of our capacity for pity, which is one of the very few traits present in the original makeup of man in the state of nature. Within society pity is the psychological foundation, the motive behind the most admirable humanitarian acts. Hence the theater is inexcusable; for it arouses our emotions of pity only to exhaust and stifle them. "In giving our tears to these fictions, we have satisfied all the rights of humanity without having to give anything more of ourselves; whereas unfortunate people in person would require attention from us."[102]

Foolishly, the philosophes have convinced themselves that they can utilize the stage to lead, when the fate of the playwright is always to follow. The mores and character of a country come first and are merely embellished on the stage.[103] When those *moeurs* are healthy, as in ancient Greece, where the theater was a celebration of the civic life, plays are part of the public treasure of the republic.[104] When both public and private life are empty, their substance having been drained off by *le monde,* the author of plays celebrates what merits contempt.

The first law of the artist is to succeed,[105] which he will do only if he masters the *art de plaire.* Now, what pleases *le monde* is ridicule of anything and everything, but especially of what can never be forgiven, the man who would be virtuous in a corrupt, sophisticated society. Molière's *Misanthrope* is his masterpiece and the most perfect statement of all that is despicable in French comedy. Not the good man, Alceste, but the man of *le monde,* Philinte, wins the admiration of the audience. Three times Alceste responds to Oronte with the words "I don't say that"; three times Rousseau responds to Molière's portrayal of the misanthrope as an inconsistent, feeble, and presumptuous man with the words "he had to make the audience laugh."[106] After attending a performance of the *Misanthrope* the audience could rest assured that anyone who challenged "worldly morality" could be laughed off the stage and out of society.

Both the *Letter to d'Alembert* and *De l'Esprit* were published in 1758, each a republican treatise on the topic of drama and politics. Love, the authors agreed, compromises our dedication to public affairs; but where Helvétius saw pettiness in romance, Rousseau discerned something far more insidious: "Love clothes itself with the enthusiasm of virtue; it usurps its force."[107] Supposedly Racine's *Bérénice,* in which the emperor Titus suppresses his passion and remains loyal to his office, teaches the priority of duty over love. In reality it does nothing of the sort: "Titus can remain a Roman; all the spectators have married Bérénice."[108] Yet the philosophes commonly resorted to amorous themes in their plays—even Voltaire, who despite his disdain for such nonsense was not about to lose his audience.[109]

Helvétius (and Holbach, later[110]) wanted a resurgence in his age of what Greek tragedy had been in its time: a civic drama dwelling on public themes, to the virtual exclusion of love. Rousseau denies that such a theater could succeed in the modern world, so lacking is our history in the necessary traditions and mores.[111] Besides, what do the heroes of antiquity have to do with us? Better that contemporary authors should address the woes of "simple, suffering humanity" than to overwhelm us with classical examples. In the modern world it is less heroic gestures than "simple and modest virtues which make the good citizen."[112] Genevans are not Spartans,[113] Rousseau admits; later he adds that they are not even Athenians.[114] The only suitable theater for Geneva is the one they can pride themselves on having refused to build. Would not Tacitus, whom d'Alembert translates, meditates, and imitates, agree?[115]

Will Geneva, if Rousseau wins the battle to keep French influence at bay, be a colorless, somber city, a constant reminder of Calvin? Not at all, but the *spectacles* within its walls will not be theatrical performances. Rather, they will be events held in the open air or in large, well-lighted rooms, and the performers will not be professional actors but the entire citizenry, acting according to a script they have collectively written. "Let the spectators become a *spectacle* to themselves; make them actors themselves."[116] Public festivals, dances, drinking bouts, contests in which some win but no one loses, are entertainments in which citizens "seek to communicate their joy and their pleasures." In France plays are aristocratic and exclusionary, even when written by commoners; Genevan festivals are popular, democratic, authored by the *peuple.* "The only pure joy is public joy, and the true sentiments of nature reign only over the people."[117] Why, then, do the philosophes malign the people? Perhaps it is because "the *peuple* do not confer chairs or pensions or places in academies."[118]

Rousseau was still defending a republic from the attacks of Voltaire and company in his last political work, the *Government of Poland* (1772). When the philosophes glanced at Poland, they saw feudal anarchy and Catholicism. When they looked at Catherine the Great, the enemy of the Poles, they saw the sovereign who purchased Diderot's library, assisted the family of Calas, asked d'Alembert to tutor her son, and offered the *Encyclopédie* a safe haven from persecution. Catherine needed propagandists to cover the trail of blood she had spilled on the way to the throne; and she was concerned to gain a foothold in France against Louis XV, whose foreign policy aimed to block her expansive ambitions. Grimm, Diderot, d'Alembert, and especially Voltaire gave her all she sought. To divide and rule in Poland, Catherine upheld the claims of religious minorities, excuse enough for Voltaire to announce to the world that Russia had fought a crusade in behalf of enlightenment. Even Helvétius, arch-republican that he was, dedicated *De l'Homme* to the despotic leaders of Russia and Prussia because French politics—the Maupeou coup in particular—had driven him to despair.[119]

A Russian victory over the Poles, as envisaged by the philosophes, was to be much the same as the triumph of modern France over its own feudal past—a morality play proving the worth of enlightenment under a centralized monarchy. In the sharpest possible contrast, the defeat of the Poles became, at Rousseau's instigation, the tragedy of a republic fallen victim to intervention by a despotic power. On the stage of Rousseau, Catherine shared the role of villain with the most enlightened French thinkers of the age.

Voltaire thought nothing finer than Catherine's importation of all things French—manners, mores, tastes, whether in dress, language, the arts, or positions offered to philosophes. Rousseau's first injunction to the Poles is "see to it that . . . everyone in public life never wears anything but distinctively Polish clothing, and that no Pole shall dare present himself at court dressed like a Frenchman." Rousseau's plan was to make the Poles so Polish they could never become Russians: everything the Poles were so ashamed of in the face of French cultural hegemony, everything distinctively Polish, was to be rehabilitated; everything French rejected, especially "the amusements one ordinarily finds in courts, gambling, the theater, comedies, operas."[120] Just as the Jews, though defeated and dispersed, never lost their Jewish identity, so the Poles would be swallowed by the Russians but never digested, not if they came to know and love their national heritage.[121]

Moeurs, the collective inheritance of the Poles, will gain a renewed energy if consecrated by patriotic passions. A citizens' militia, public festivals, national holidays, competitions directed toward honoring those who do most to honor their country—such is the constitution Rousseau offers the Poles, one written in their hearts, a way of life unlike any other save that of the ancient Spartans. From cradle to grave the Poles will be citizens: children will play together, never alone; adults will ever be in the public eye.[122] Backward countries are ill advised by philosophes to seek remedies through monarchical centralization, a cure far worse than the disease. Poland will thrive only on the condition that it is transformed into a "confederation of thirty-three tiny states, combining the strength of a great monarchy with the freedom of a small republic."[123]

Wary of anything too disruptive of customs and mores, which to Rousseau's mind are the "morality of the people,"[124] he would phase out serfdom rather than abolish it overnight, much as in France he recommended shame instead of legal sanctions as the means to desiccate the institution of dueling.[125] In matters of superstition he would so absorb the people in civic duties and national festivals that citizens would slowly lose interest in ecclesiastical ceremonies.[126]

The philosophes had far less patience with mores. Diderot, Holbach, and Voltaire generally took the position that law could and should dictate *moeurs,* and were especially adamant in this regard whenever speaking to or about Catherine.[127] As depicted by Voltaire in the *History of Russia under Peter the Great,* the prince need only will the new civilized Russia, and what had been barbarism would henceforth be civility. Peter laid the foundations of a Western, tolerant, progressive nation in one reign, upon which Catherine was now erecting, with the assistance of the philosophes, a Russian Enlightenment that would soon surpass the French original.[128] Rousseau predicted nothing good would come from Peter's refusal to permit Russians to be Russians.[129] He who does not respect *moeurs* and yet would govern will ultimately pay dearly for holding the people in disdain.

That a great legislator may be necessary Rousseau was the first to admit, but such a figure must follow the example of Lycurgus in abdicating the throne the moment he has transmitted his code of laws to the people.[130] Abdication was the last item on Catherine's agenda; second last was to compromise her absolute power through taking her legal code seriously. Voltaire might call her a Numa and a Solon;[131] Diderot, by contrast, increasingly knew Catherine for what she was and struggled, unsuccessfully, to disentangle himself from her web.[132] Rousseau virtually alone among the philosophes could pride himself on having rejected both Catherine's attack on the Poles and on the mores of her own people.

Only fundamental change, Rousseau was convinced, can save us from our socially mutilated selves; the task of the great legislator is therefore nothing less than that of changing human nature.[133] Yet it is wrong for anyone to rob the people of their *moeurs,* those customs, traditions, and folkways that make us who we are. Finding himself in an all but irresolvable dilemma, Rousseau was grateful to discover one country close to nature, where mores had not yet taken root: the tiny island of Corsica. This was the sole place in Europe truly fit for legislation;[134] in humble Corsica, not in proud Russia, it was fitting that laws should dictate mores.

For decades pillaged and denuded by Genoa, the Corsicans had risen up in patriotic rebellion against their despotic masters. The exploiters from the mainland had carried off everything from the island, its commerce, its trade, its nobility, its history and traditions. Corsica, it seems, was at that moment where Holland and Switzerland had been after expelling their tyrants, "when horror of the past is equivalent to amnesia, and when the state, set afire by civil wars, is reborn . . . and resumes the vigor of youth."[135]

Their history obliterated, the Corsicans had been restored to nature; all possibilities were open to them, and their legislator could be more like Emile's tutor than like Lycurgus. Rather than rising above nature, as had the Spartans, the Corsicans could be virtuous and just without knowing those words,[136] by simply continuing to be their natural selves.[137] Rousseau's message to them was "stay as you are";[138] similarly, Emile's tutor controls the environment, struggling with all his art to maintain the original, innocent nature of his pupil.[139]

Reduced by Genoa to an agrarian people, devoid of the slightest hint of a modern economy, the Corsicans should thank fate that their oppressors, thinking they were denying the islanders everything, unwittingly granted Corsica the means to be a democratic republic. With the nobility destroyed, lands can be more or less equally distributed,[140] each parcel farmed by an independent, free-standing family. Trade with the mainland will be forbidden, internal trade phased out,[141] until the whole island, each of its sections, and every family is self-sufficient and self-enclosed.[142] Citizens will cultivate their own gardens, except when serving in the militia or contributing their fair share to public works.

Carpenters will be esteemed, goldsmiths forbidden; "in the case of internal conflict, it is in the nature of our new constitution that the farmer should be the one to lay down the law to the worker."[143] Everything that suggests luxury, such as academies, carriages, and cities larger than villages, will be banned.[144] Pride must be rechanneled so that it will support rather than undermine equality: "Enact sumptuary laws, therefore, but make them always more severe for the leaders of the state, and more lenient for the lower orders; make simplicity a point of vanity."[145]

Corsica is the last place the philosophes looked to lay the foundations of a republic. To Rousseau it was the first place, France the last. It was the "prejudices" of the Corsicans, more than French foreign policy, Jean-Jacques feared, that might destroy the republican prospects of the beleaguered but proud island—prejudices defined *à la Jean-Jacques* not as religious superstition but as the burning desire to be like other, more civilized and enlightened peoples. "The sentiments of the Corsicans are upright, but their *fausses lumières* deceive them."[146] Never should the islanders forget that the republic of Genoa, "looking for a way to subjugate the Corsicans more fully, found none more effective than to establish an Academy among them."[147]

Rousseau and the philosophes agreed that the new society accompanying a republican polity should be one in which hereditary nobility counts for little or nothing. But Rousseau rejected their yearnings for a social order dedicated to fostering the development of individual talents, which to him would amount to nothing better than the triumph of *amour-propre* in its most virulent form. This longing for a competitive social order that would stimulate and reward talents was constantly expressed in Diderot's ever more political and republican writings, at first with only the intellectuals in mind, later the whole society.[148] How vehemently Rousseau disagreed may be discerned in his comment that "great talents are but the supplement of patriotic zeal; they are necessary only when a people does not love its country."[149]

After postulating natural equality, the philosophes quickly stipulated its social irrelevance, replacing it—in the language of a later day—with equality of opportunity and the "career open to talents." Turgot employed the majesty of philosophical history to write, against Madame de Graffigny's *Lettres d'une péruvienne* (1747), a natural history of inequality intended to combat all such sentimental appeals to a primitive uniformity of conditions. Talents, abilities, and differing natural endowments of mind make inequality both inevitable and desirable, argued Turgot, as did other men of letters. The more society rewards specialized talents, and the more advanced the division of labor, the better in consequence will the different parts of the social order interlock into one productive whole, governed less by political leaders than by the interests of the governed.[150]

This much vaunted interdependence, replies Rousseau, is more accurately described as the loss of independence, the forfeiture of personal autonomy to the "progress" which is the scourge of human history. Nothing is more fitting for the Corsicans than that they, like the Swiss living on the mountaintops, snowed in half the year, should be jacks of all trades and masters of none. Isolation thwarts the "progress" of the division of labor, permitting these honest folk to avoid parceling out and losing their souls. To Rousseau the worth of any product is inversely proportional to the number of hands through which it passes.[151] Best of its kind is anything produced by a single person.

By the same principles, when judging any trade we should

> put in the first rank the most independent and in the last those which depend on a great number of others . . . [Whatever art] is the most general and the most indispensable is incontestably the one which merits the most esteem . . . These are the true rules of appraising the arts and manufactures. Anything else is arbitrary and depends on opinion.

With perfect consistency Rousseau concludes that agriculture is the "first and most respectable of all the arts."[152] Although he never designates a trade to fit the last place, his works from the *First Discourse* and the *Preface to Narcisse* onward readily lead to the conclusion that this dubious distinction rightfully belongs to the men of letters. Striving to distinguish themselves from the people, offering the many nothing in compensation, intellectuals are the creations of luxury, that is, of inequality of riches, and do their best to add an inequality of talents.

It was always Rousseau's contention that talent is as arbitrary an apology for inequality as are noble titles, both coming down to accidents of birth, neither having anything to do with virtuous deeds.[153] Moreover, as seen in Rousseau's philosophical history—the reverse of Turgot's—a meritocratic society is the problem, the disease, and consequently cannot be the solution or cure. Hereditary status takes up but one chapter in the narrative of our downfall, explained primarily by the story line of our socially acquired need to find or feign a talent permitting us to convince others and ourselves of our superiority. Precisely because we are seduced so easily by the lure of inequality, the legislator must use every resource available to forestall our inevitable decline from the original condition in which our differences did not matter.[154] Opportunities for inequality to arise are few when, as with the Swiss mountain dwellers or the Corsicans, families live in blissful isolation from all but a few neighbors. Reaffirmations of equality are best attended to by civic rituals stressing our common national identity. "There must be no other permanent estate on the island than that of citizen, which ought to comprehend all the others."[155]

Competition, emulation, striving to outdo one's fellows should occur strictly within the civic framework that ties individual achievement to collective well-being. If the rivalry of intellectuals is at the expense of the public good, so is the mania for making money that dominates modern society and politics. "Ancient politicians incessantly talked about *moeurs* and virtue, those of our time talk only of business and money."[156] Inevitably, in such an atmosphere, all social attachments are reduced to the monetary currency, such that "in this age of enlightenment, everyone knows how to calculate to the penny the worth of his honor and his life."[157] The physiocratic element of the Enlightenment found no friend in Rousseau; nor, for that matter, did any other school of thought that put economics first.[158]

"No people will ever be other than what the nature of its government makes it";[159] such Rousseau had known from the beginning, such the philosophes would learn well before the end. The philosophes also agreed with Rousseau that the rulers should be merely the agents of the sovereign people; and though at first they permitted the people to alienate many of its rights to the monarch through contractual agreement, as Diderot had in "Political Authority," their thought evolved in a decidedly more constitutionalist direction as the years passed. Likewise the expression "general will" was constantly pronounced by Diderot and Holbach who, at the same time they continued to apply it to the human race, increasingly stressed the need to embody it concretely in particular political societies.

Yet here again we encounter the familiar pattern: each step in Rousseau's direction merely serves to reveal the depths of the chasm separating him from his erstwhile philosophical brethren. The philosophes called for representatives, who in Holbach's words were to be "elected citizens charged by society to speak in its name."[160] Shockingly, Rousseau took it upon himself to chastise this notion of representative government almost as vigorously as he rejected royal absolutism. From the inalienability of popular sovereignty it follows, he protested, that the people cannot have representatives but only deputies. Ancient cities did not have representatives; neither will Poles, despite the size of their nation. Rather, each of the thirty-three republics will send delegates to the occasional national gatherings held to coordinate military efforts. Bound by an imperative mandate, these delegates will do nothing more than relay messages from their locality.[161]

How vigorously Rousseau differs with the philosophes may be seen in their respective criticisms of England: they fear the corruption that has crept into representative government across the Channel; Rousseau believes that, corrupt or reformed, the Parliament necessarily violates the freedom of the English. "The English people thinks it is free. It greatly deceives itself; it is free only during the election of members of Parliament. As soon as they are elected, it is slave, it is nothing."[162]

"From the moment someone says *what do I care?* about the affairs of the State, it should be considered lost," declared Rousseau.[163] Especially in modern times, economic concerns threaten to absorb our attention, and we are easily convinced that the public good takes too many evenings. Wanting to alienate our freedom, we find in the executive authority an ally who can be counted on to help us banish ourselves from the public realm. The trustees we have named sooner or later put their corporate general will above that of the community, and strive to render themselves irreplaceable.[164]

Usually the philosophes held to the classical view of democracy as mob rule, the last stop in the cycle of degeneration. Rousseau's claim that democracy naturally yields to ever more restricted government[165] was also familiar to them as another reason why a democratic polity is unthinkable. Not surprisingly, they were totally unprepared for his argument that in the absence of democracy no government is legitimate. Unless popular sovereignty means the people are the legislators, it means nothing, Rousseau argued; and on the assumption that the people assembled truly are the sovereign, he continued, no fundamental law can restrain them. Whatever they will, so long as it does not violate the rule of generality protecting rights, is incontestably law. What's more, nothing holds because it *was* willed but only if it *is* willed, so that the people are free to override today their will of yesterday.[166] At the end of every year the people shall decide whether to keep their governors and their form of government.[167] The social contract itself is an agreement they are at liberty to vote out of existence.[168]

Not collectivism but anarchism was the charge lodged against Rousseau in the eighteenth century.[169] For the most part the philosophes initially preferred to back up their constitutionalist views with appeals to history of the Germanist sort; then, finding history intractable, they reluctantly set forth their "fundamental laws" as dictates of reason.[170] But while the absence of a satisfactory French constitutionalist tradition could push them in Rousseau's direction, they scrupulously avoided his basic conclusions. Rousseau's constitution ever in the making was far too radical for them, far too dangerous for the good of their cause, and the same can be said of his insistence on taking so literally the sovereignty of the people. They responded to the *Social Contract* with incomprehension, disdain, and not a little fear.

In Rousseau's view it is the *moeurs* of the people that prevent their abusing freedom. Books on *moeurs* were largely absent from Voltaire's library,[171] much as the subject of mores was barely touched upon in his *Essay on the Moeurs.* The legislator of Corsica, working with a blank slate, will direct his greatest efforts to instilling mores proper to a republican people. Where mores already exist, as in Poland, they will be carefully pruned and nurtured. Genevan mores are precious but highly vulnerable because the patricians are as determined to import all things French and aristocratic as the burghers are to keep the theater from entering the gates.

Less a predilection for monarchy, Rousseau believed, than an unthinking bias in favor of the aristocratic culture emanating from Paris shut the eyes of the philosophes to what could be done with the help of mores. "Blind we are amidst so much enlightenment!"[172]

From Politics to the Family

Eventually some of the philosophes experimented with the thought that the place for enlightenment to begin was the family, possibly a family located outside Paris, hidden away from *le monde* somewhere in those provinces previously regarded as places of exile. Diderot and Holbach, ever more disturbed by worldly corruption, found themselves attracted to a revitalized family that would provide a retreat in which enlightenment would be safe, and from which it might be carried to receptive areas of the surrounding society. Unfortunately here, too, they came up against Rousseau, whose Emile and Sophie, Wolmar and Julie, spoke to an exceptionally large audience, the readers of novels. Each such reader learned that the host and hostess of Clarens, normally so gracious, did not extend hospitality to philosophes, unwelcome because their free-thinking Parisian views undermined family life. In *Emile* and *La Nouvelle Héloïse* Rousseau sounded alarmingly like a churchman or a conservative journalist even as he pressed a program typical of the Enlightenment.

Just before the definitive rupture caused by the *Letter to d'Alembert,* Rousseau and Diderot had ample opportunity to discuss their parallel literary projects on the family, Jean-Jacques' novel and Diderot's plays. Later Holbach staked out a position on politics and the family that reads as a noteworthy variation on the themes articulated by his dear friend Diderot and bitter enemy Rousseau.

If *Rameau's Nephew* was a work Diderot could not publish, the exact opposite was true of *Le Fils naturel* (1757) and *Le Père de famille* (1758), both of which were to be sold as books as well as performed, to reach the largest possible audience. Whenever the philosophes made their point that virtue and interest can be reconciled, they turned to familial roles, especially that of the father; so it was with a sense of excitement that Diderot placed fathers, sons, and prospective wives on stage. In creating a new theatrical genre, the *drame*, Diderot insisted that private life should not be confined to comedy; he held that the topic of family life, even when the family does not boast a noble title, is inherently uplifting and thus merits noble treatment.

Without publicly saying so, Diderot intended his plays to protect himself and his kind from the constant charge that the philosophes, having substituted "interest" for religion and tradition, were out to destroy the family. Part of lacking an *état*, Diderot knew full well, was the inability of the philosophes to marry well; many were bachelors or married to the type of the laundress, which served to confirm claims they were rootless and irresponsible. No better answer to these damaging charges than Diderot's plays, with their edifying speeches about familial duty, incantations to virtue, and eulogies of domestic *moeurs*, frequently consummated by exclamation points. Starving for respectability, the philosophes sound positively maudlin whenever making public pronouncements on the family. As Diderot commented in a private letter, his comrades had to be on constant guard in their personal lives, avoiding all suspicion of impropriety, lest they hear "So that's how philosophes carry on."[173]

It says much about the philosophes that Diderot's Father of the Family rejects his son's request to marry Sophie—on the grounds that her poverty would reduce Saint-Albin to a social no man's land where he would be "sans état, sans fortune, sans considération."[174] No father can agree to a marriage that will rule out in advance his son's capacity to discharge the duties of fatherhood. Sophie herself accepts the father's judgment,[175] which is reversed only after it is learned that she is of suitable birth. In Diderot's earlier play, *Le Fils naturel*, the well-born Clairville decides to support his beloved by engaging in trade; not for him the prejudice that prevents a man from being useful.[176] Aristocrats, in Diderot's dramas, may risk derogation of status; middle-class persons have no such luxury.

Less "the rise of the bourgeoisie" than the assurance it will not fall is Diderot's concern. "Birth is given us, our virtues are our own,"[177] says Constance; but she is not urging the end of nobility. On Diderot's stage the message is that the nobles should be more like the middle class when it comes to productivity; the middle class more like the best nobles in their handling of wealth, that is, less preoccupied with profits than with living well and assisting the unfortunate. The Father of the Family gives alms to the poor, defers collecting a debt from a man struggling to stay afloat, but pays his own debts immediately, no matter what the state of his finances.[178] An acquisitive ethic, Constance cautions, gives one everything except the only goods that are valuable: "Real needs are limited, those of fantasy unlimited. Whatever fortune you would accumulate, Dorval, if your children lack virtue, they will ever be poor."[179]

Far from the least important feature of the *Fils naturel* is the role assigned to women. "We should leave preaching to the ladies," Diderot suggested to his mistress Sophie Volland.[180] In keeping with this view, Constance is a preacher of enlightenment. Many of the lines representing the beliefs of the philosophes are delivered by her, notably a harangue on the growing forces of light in an age also marked by fanaticism and prejudice. Children, she urges, should indeed be brought into a world where writings "inspiring men to universal benevolence are practically the only ones read. These are the lessons filling our theaters."[181] She addresses these words to Dorval, who exclaims in response, "Oh reason! Who can resist you when you take the enchanting accent and voice of woman?"[182]

More than a spokesperson of enlightenment, Diderot's woman inspires a passion that elevates her lover to new heights. "Anyone who approaches Sophie either becomes honorable or withdraws from her," Saint-Albin tells his father. "You do not know what I owe her. She has changed me."[183] The woman on Diderot's stage both pronounces the ideals of the Enlightenment and gives men the emotional resolution to turn theory into practice. Of course, not every woman is a Constance, a Rosalie, or a Sophie; but the *moeurs* Saint-Albin sees shining through the tattered clothing of Sophie, those *moeurs* that attest to her former membership in a higher estate,[184] are available to many women, each a potential contributor to the familial bliss that is an island of enlightenment from which the mainland may eventually be seized.

That the *moeurs* holding the family together are being progressively undermined in France was a theme Holbach drove home at length in his writings, perhaps most forcefully in the third part of his *Système social* (1773), entitled "On the Influence of Government on *Moeurs*." Here d'Holbach places the decline of the family in the context of a comprehensive discussion of society and politics. Rousseau is never named, but the arguments set forth by the baron read as glosses to the *First Discourse* and to several other works from the pen of Jean-Jacques. After delivering a scathing republican indictment of the cultural consequences of monarchy, Holbach proposes withdrawal to "domestic felicity, to happiness in private life."[185] As he waxed poetic over his proposed haven in a heartless world, Holbach must have recalled, now and then, Rousseau's extensive treatment of the same topic in his best-selling novel.

Paraphrasing Rousseau, Holbach dismissed the great ages lauded in Voltaire's cultural history. Alexander's century, despite its literary brilliance, witnessed the "annihilation of liberty in Greece"; the reign of Augustus, though that of Virgil and Horace, was also the "epoch of the total enslavement of the Romans." Louis XIV did much for the arts but even more for himself in making the French people so base as to raise him to the level of the gods.[186] The cultural refinement and good taste of past eras, Holbach generalized, were part of a pattern that featured the fall of republics and the rise of despotisms.

So much for bygone ages. As for his own monarchical time, Holbach found nothing to praise in the "bad taste of a frivolous and corrupt century."[187] Supposedly a "school of *moeurs*," the theater teaches us to commit adultery and to scoff at virtue. "Is not healthy morality forced to join with religion in condemning plays, where all conspires to seduce . . . and corrupt the heart and mind?"[188] It was not only with the priests that Holbach was in rare agreement; it was with Rousseau.

Corruption, Holbach continues, is a contagious disease, an infection endemic to the court, from which it spreads to the rest of the country.[189] Inevitably the *grands* set the tone of the nation,[190] to the detriment of all because boredom, lethargy, empty conversations, and foolish games are the daily fare of the rich and vapid. Waiting for them to lead is so much time wasted, since they throw away their lives on frivolous amusements, in utter disregard for the *moeurs* without which a nation is nothing. In place of matters of substance the *grands* devote their energies to keeping up appearances; always on stage, "one only lives in the opinion of others; each plays very poorly a role not made for him; no one wants to be himself, because no one is content with what nature has made him."[191] Restlessness and striving to fill the void within by meaningless diversions is indeed our condition,[192] much as Pascal had observed, but its explanation is social and best articulated by pilfering a few lines from Rousseau.

Luxury, a vice Holbach deemed "indigenous to monarchies,"[193] is the cause underlying all that ails France. Two of the most republican of the philosophes, Holbach and Helvétius,[194] rejected Voltaire's apology for luxury, while Diderot and Saint-Lambert searched for a compromise between Rousseau and Voltaire, or as Saint-Lambert wrote, between "the prejudices of Sparta and those of Sybaris."[195] To all these thinkers it was obvious that luxury based on a radically unequal distribution of lands, on the gluttony of the few and the poverty of the many, was a formula for the destruction of France. Holbach added the disturbing reflection that England was not that much better, with its citizens overburdened by a huge national debt, and its frenetic commerce casting social stability and civic commitment to the winds.[196] No longer could anyone conclude, he mused, that republics are as conducive to equality of possessions as monarchies to inequality. Helvétius, too, was not completely at ease with the consequences of commerce and finance in England; and it is clear that the thirty federated republics into which he proposed to divide France would have a decidedly agrarian economy.[197]

What to do? Abolish primogeniture, redistribute lands held by the church, do away with the tax exemptions of the First and Second Estates—on such measures there could be substantial agreement among philosophes. There was less consensus on the question of the ideal size of landholdings: the physiocrats called for large tracts in imitation of England; Holbach and Helvétius wanted many small plots in fulfillment of the republican formula dating back to Aristotle, while Diderot again took a position between the extremes.[198] What stands out is the willingness of many philosophes, especially those of republican convictions, to sacrifice a measure of economic "progress" for the sake of securing civic well-being.

At a deeper level the republican philosophes found themselves calling into question the very notion of progress that had characterized the genre of philosophical history. "Corruption," the correlate of "virtue" understood as civic virtue, entered their vocabulary the moment they converted to republicanism; so it is not surprising that the works of Helvétius and all the later writings of Diderot and Holbach are filled with discussions of the decay that follows the period when a society has become overripe.

Nor should we be caught unprepared for their expressions of nostalgia for a world we have lost. Helvétius hearkened back to an age when savagery and civility, nature and civilization, were in equilibrium; he longed for a return to the era preceding the "progress" that was a record of inequality and refined oppression. What Diderot, Helvétius, and Holbach admired was the bygone age "between the savage state and our marvelous civilized state, when there was a middle ground that retarded the progress of the child of Prometheus, . . . and held civilized man in a fixed position between the childhood of the savage and our decrepitude."[199] It may well be, Diderot sighed, that society reaches a stage of "deadly perfection" as naturally as hair grays in old age.[200]

Facing the future, the republican philosophes had difficulty avoiding pessimism. The fall of Maupeou or the rise of Turgot might temporarily rejuvenate flagging spirits, but their long-term doubts refused to dissipate. Wistfully they looked back to an epoch they designated as that of "nascent society," never bothering to note that Rousseau had used this very expression many years earlier in the *Second Discourse* to laud the happiest age of mankind, when halfway between society and nature, our condition was infinitely superior both to that of the purely natural and to the highly civilized man.[201]

In an earlier age people had *moeurs* and knew who they were, which is enough to set them apart from the residents of eighteenth-century France. As experienced by d'Alembert, Diderot, and Holbach, nothing and no one was secure in French society, despite its hierarchy and corporations. Rameau's nephew conjures up the picture of society common to many philosophes: a world in which tax farmers and financiers typify the chronic disarray of what passes for a social order, and in which predators hold the high ground because there is nothing money cannot buy. Presumably d'Alembert's justification of nobility, that titles are incontrovertible unlike claims to merit,[202] was sincere; for any order is better than none, especially in a nation marked by such awesome poverty that social chaos threatens to break out. How can a philosopher, d'Alembert asks, have the audacity to write a book on obligation?

> Can those who have nothing, who give everything to society and to whom society refuses everything, . . . can such people have any other moral principle than the law, and how can we persuade them that their true interest is to be virtuous when they might cease to be so with impunity? If I had found a satisfactory solution to this problem, I should have come forth with my moral catechism long ago.[203]

Not trusting the ground under their feet, the philosophes grasped any pillar of social stability within reach; arguably, the most radical of their ranks were the ones enticed by the most conservative solutions, especially in matters concerning the family.

The change in the intellectual climate can be gauged by contrasting the words of Turgot in 1757 with those of Holbach in 1773. Graveyards are not sacred to Turgot who, were land needed, would not hesitate "to turn over the ashes of the dead to nourish the living."[204] Holbach is as firm as Turgot in disallowing historical precedents to decide arguments over political right,[205] but a heartfelt craving to rid us of our itch for change is evident in the baron's most politically challenging works. To him it was a measure of how shallow and uprooted the Athenians were and the moderns are that conversations began with the question, "What's new?"[206]

Away, then, from the whirl of life in high society; back to the country-side, back to traditional values, with special attention paid to the revital-ization of the family—such are Holbach's recommendations. "The more a nation is corrupt, the more the reasonable citizen will take precautions to protect himself from the public infection. In the event he cannot remedy the ills of his *patrie,* he should at least search to procure domestic happiness."[207] *Le Père de famille,* set by Diderot in Paris, was moved by Holbach to the "fields of our fathers,"[208] possibly with Diderot's support since he shared Holbach's worry about the well-being of the family in the contemporary social setting.[209]

At first the philosophes avoided attacks on nobility, the better to gain support for their crusade against Catholicism; later, they worked up the courage to place merit above titles. Never, however, did they repudiate the gentlemanly ideal, and now it was the enlightened *honnête homme* on whom they pinned their hopes. On the assumption that the people look to their social superiors for models of praiseworthy behavior, it follows that the many, at present corrupted by their betters, could be regenerated by a reformed aristocracy.

Holbach's proposed rural refuge will be inhabited by persons well to do but unconcerned to increase their wealth; commerce will be shunned not as ignoble but as threatening to disrupt the "happy mediocrity"[210] that leaves country folk content with what they have. Neither great nor glam-orous but happy and fulfilled, Holbach's aristocrats will be as devoted to their families as their urban counterparts are to fleeing their homes, yet his titled provincials will always find time to aid needy neighbors. Rural gentlemen should live in accordance with the best traditions of *noblesse oblige,* engaging in charitable and philanthropic acts, accepting all the duties that inhere in their social station while remaining indifferent to their titles as such.

Women, Holbach realized, were critical to the success of his scheme; yet he was far from convinced that they were adequately prepared for the great task of moral regeneration. "In all countries the lot of women is to be tyrannized,"[211] and not only in the sense of suffering from the overt brutality of men. Even worse, it seems, is the miseducation of the fair sex, such that they willingly act as the most frivolous persons in a frivolous society. Through no fault of their own women are all that is wrong with *le monde.* The French pride themselves on knowing how to enrich everyday life by means of the *art de plaire,* and expect women, above all, to enliven the game of pleasing. The playfulness[212] of the aristocratic code held little charm in Holbach's eyes, who saw it as an evasion of responsibility, an institutionalized childishness that revolved around women, the most infantile members of a society that shirked the burdens of maturity. When defending worldlings against charges leveled by otherworldly religion, Holbach warmly commends the art of pleasing; but when he rejects *le monde* he is bound to condemn women, spoiled and vain, who please and are pleased by childish modes and fashions.

Given the arranged and loveless marriages of aristocratic society, women pleased most of all when they committed adultery. Often the members of the highest classes did not bother to hide their extramarital affairs, and the philosophes, in this instance, were only too happy to follow the example of their social superiors. As Madame du Châtelet lay dying, her husband, her former lover Voltaire, and her current lover Saint-Lambert comforted her and one another—a scene that speaks eloquently about the marital mores of the day.

Celebrations of sexuality are not the entirety of what may be found in the writings of the philosophes on the relationships between men and women. As Holbach's case reveals, another dominant theme is the condemnation of adultery, accompanied by eulogies of domestic virtue. Under current circumstances women are central to what is wrong with society; women are no less critical to the project of social rebirth. "Contribute by your example," he urges women, "to the reform of these wasted and idle beings who infest society. Restore them to the *patrie;* lead them back to virtue."[213] By returning to the family, Holbach believes, women can save men.

Hearth and home is where women should be found, not in society, not outside the confines of what should be a familial fortress fending off a dissolute world. The free, aristocratic lady of *le monde* must yield to her better self, the mother and wife of the patriarchal family. During the Enlightenment the most radical political thought sometimes had a way of fostering a fervent revival of conservative familial ideals. If true of Holbach, this is especially marked in Rousseau, who attacked the philosophes as vigorously from the conservative direction as from the radical.

Haven in a Heartless World

Where are the French who still have the *moeurs* that are necessary to build a haven in the heartless world? Duclos had given one answer in his highly successful *Considérations sur les Moeurs:* "It's in Paris that one must consider the French, because they are more French there than elsewhere."[214] Rousseau gave the opposite answer in his writings, most notably in *Emile* and *Julie:* "One must go to the remote provinces—where there is less movement and commerce, where foreigners travel less, where the inhabitants move around less and change fortune and status less—in order to study the genius and *moeurs* of a nation. See the capital in passing, but go far away from it to observe the country. The French are not in Paris."[215]

In the preface to his novel Rousseau is at pains to explain he has written both about and for country folk. It is they, after all, who are the most avid readers of novels, a literary genre not completely respectable in aristocratic France. But up till now the characters encountered in love stories have been drawn not from the provinces but from *le monde;* hence, each novel consumed by provincials makes them that much more dissatisfied with their customs, mores, and way of life. After reading Rousseau's novel, rustics will understand that the happiness they seek has been at their doorstep all along. They have no reason to envy Parisians; on the contrary, Parisians should envy them.[216]

Ever the spokesmen of citified prejudices, philosophes ridicule the village dweller on the grounds that if he had a thought it would surely die of loneliness. "This is an error," writes Rousseau, "that could easily be corrected if it were remembered that most of the literary men who shine in Paris and most of the useful discoveries and new inventions come from these despised provinces." In a little town people have fewer models, are less imitative, and "each draws more from himself";[217] it is in Paris that the residents are little more than "puppets."[218] Wolmar, Rousseau's ideal aristocrat, enjoys conversing with simple peasants; in their humble villages he finds "more men thinking for themselves than under the uniform mask of inhabitants of cities." Man in the urban setting is merely *l'homme de l'homme,* in contrast to *l'homme de la nature* who is not yet extinct in the countryside.[219]

Of all places under the sun, the last one from which the philosophes expected something worthwhile was the mountainside of Switzerland, whose isolated inhabitants had indeed been mentioned by d'Alembert in the *Encyclopédie* but in an article entitled "Cretin."[220] Naturally Rousseau decided to make a great deal of these rough and ready people, and went so far as to turn them into beings who did not need to construct a familial haven well preserved from the corruptions of society, since they were born to so admirable a condition. Having informed the republican philosophes that crude Corsica, relatively untouched by the high culture of France, was the best possibility for the fulfillment of their political aspirations, he added that the supposedly primitive *montagnards* were already in full possession of the familial ideal espoused by some of the champions of light.

"Both the tranquility of a retreat and the sweetness of society" may be relished in the High Valais. During the long winter, when cut off from the outside world, each mountain dweller is "warmly closed up with his big family." Self-reliant by necessity, the father is his own carpenter, glazier, locksmith; "each is everything for himself, no one is anything for another." As in Geneva some residents are watchmakers, with the significant difference, however, that "each mountaineer joins in himself all the various crafts into which watchmaking is divided and makes all his tools himself." Elsewhere artisans are taught by masters, but not in these snow-capped regions where the arts and crafts are passed down by tradition. Independence comes naturally where there are no masters or division of labor.[221]

What nature gives the mountain people, Wolmar and Julie create by self-conscious artistry at Clarens in rural Switzerland. Only a few years earlier Rousseau had published his thoughts on "political economy" in the *Encyclopédie;* now, as he set forth his thoughts on "domestic economy," he proved that many of his proposals for the public realm could and should be rewritten for the family. Apparently Diderot and Rousseau were still in agreement on one point, that women are the ideal preachers, because Julie is known to the other characters as *la prêcheuse.*[222] She is that and she is infinitely more: much as a political constitution must be internalized, loved, and willed, the domestic life of Clarens is willed by all its participants because of Julie. "You are made to rule," Claire writes her dearest friend; "your empire is the most absolute that I know. It extends even to the will."[223] Neither vain nor self-deprecating, Julie acknowledges that Wolmar "is the understanding and I the will" of the household.[224]

For his part Wolmar is the direct counterpart in the private world of the Great Legislator in the political realm.[225] The founder of a republic should be a man of "superior intelligence who sees all of men's passions yet experiences none of them,"[226] a perfect description of Wolmar's character. Blessed and cursed with a "cold heart," he is a born Stoic; too insensitive to base his humanitarianism on pity, Wolmar is concerned for others because, like the divinity, he wishes order to prevail.[227]

Yet the God-like Wolmar can accomplish nothing without Julie. "He enlightens me," she tells Saint-Preux, "and I animate him."[228] Modesty prevents her from adding that her expansive soul animates the whole community of Clarens.[229] Love of Julie forges the ties between the residents, from top to bottom of the social scale, much as love of country obliterates social distinctions in a well-governed republic. In the haven built by the Wolmars in rural Switzerland the *moeurs* of Julie integrate the social order as surely as the *moeurs* outdo the laws in forging the communal identity of a republic.

In the domestic retreat as in the healthy republic *égalité* is the foremost objective of all social arrangements, but it is important to remember that "equality" is not always the best translation of *égalité*. Saint-Preux admires the "*égalité* of soul"[230] of the mountaineers, their psychic equanimity and tranquility, itself the result of an even, flowing existence, free from the shocks and disruptions suffered by the French. Visiting Paris, where *égalité* of soul is unknown, Saint-Preux notes that as each coterie has its rules, a socially successful person must be a different man as many times a day as he moves from one group to another. Upon entering each house he leaves his soul behind, not realizing the day will come when he has no self to retrieve.[231] Ranks may be relatively stable in France but no one knows who he is, nor, for that matter, in what rung of the social ladder he will find himself tomorrow. "Given the unsettled and restless spirit of this age which upsets everything in each generation,"[232] not even the nobles are exempt from the blows of fortune. Born to the aristocracy, Emile must learn a trade so that, come what may, he can be self-supporting.[233] Diderot visited the workshops to observe the artisans plying their trades; Emile will know what an artisan knows because he will do what an artisan does. Under all circumstances independent Emile will enjoy psychic *égalité*.

"The great maxim of Madame de Wolmar is not to encourage changes of condition, but to contribute all she can to rendering each person happy with that already his." When Saint-Preux enters a plea in favor of talent and personal merit, Julie quickly corrects the error of his ways. Pernicious in its narrow individualism, harmful in the stimulus it gives to social climbing, a meritocratic world fails to respect humans in that it assigns persons to places when it is more fitting that places be assigned to persons. Julie also notes—as had d'Alembert—that a meritocratic society is conducive to fraud, it being so unclear who has merit and so necessary to feign its possession. In any case, "good and simple people do not need so many talents." Clarens has succeeded in the measure that its peasants do not want to leave the village to seek to better themselves in the city.[234]

Not many years after the publication of *La Nouvelle Héloïse* Voltaire set himself up as the *patriarche-philosophe* of Ferney. What Rousseau had done in imagination Voltaire undertook in fact, and his actions should be studied by anyone desiring to understand how thoroughly Rousseau had rejected the philosophical mainstream. As lord of the manor Voltaire turned his lands and its residents into a miniature market society: on his properties there were factories for turning out silk stockings and lace; a tannery, tile works, and a quarry; watchmakers, competitive with Geneva's, whose wares were destined by Voltaire to be shipped as far as Russia. If his plans for a port succeeded, as much produce would leave his community as distinguished visitors entered his sumptuous quarters.

Clarens is a community in every way antithetical to Ferney. Few outsiders enter Clarens, fewer still care to leave; Clarens is as much a closed community symbolized by the peasant as Ferney is open and typified by the artisan. Everything about the world forged in the image of Wolmar and Julie exudes a combination of intense activity and deliberate immobility. Economically, the strategy of Wolmar is to make his expanded family self-sufficient; trade is to be avoided as a matter of principle because no monetary profits are worth disrupting the oneness of Clarens. Barter is preferred to monetary exchanges, and middlemen are eliminated.[235] Luxury is not the aim of this noble family; the Wolmars prefer to multiply the necessary while disdaining the superfluous, thereby placing the brake of nature on their desires.[236] Having more of what is truly necessary than they are able to consume, they can afford to bring more unfortunates into their household.[237] Unmarried Emile, as part of his training in independence, learns that a meal is worthless if it passes through too many hands;[238] the married Wolmars, by contrast, place their fortune in labor-intensive viniculture, so that their autarchical household can support the greatest number of hands. None of the peasants under their protection will ever experience equality but all enjoy the benefits of *égalité,* that is, "the uniformity of a steady life."[239]

In a republic the citizens are brothers to one another; brotherly love thrives likewise in the household of the Wolmars, but the servants love one another only insofar as they love and are loved by their masters.[240] All the fraternity of Clarens is the creation of its patriarchal and paternalistic rulers. To Julie and Wolmar each servant is another of their children; to the domestics nothing is more reassuring than to acknowledge that the Wolmars are their true parents.[241] So little is the leadership of the masters a matter of power, so much is it one of authority well exercised, that their servants "will" their servitude.[242] Servants in other households curse their masters; those at Clarens thank God "for having placed the rich on the earth to make those under them happy, and to be a comfort to the poor."[243]

As Rousseau sees it, the best master will take measures to ensure that his charges govern themselves as much as he governs them. Whereas ordinary masters encourage their domestics to spy on one another, the Wolmars arrange matters such that each servant has a "palpable interest in being loved by all his comrades." Favors are never granted when asked for oneself, only when the master is beseeched to intercede in behalf of another. Asking for a fellow servant is compatible with self-love because it is a way of earning the esteem of the master. All this is done in secret and in the strictest confidence; thus the recipient of the good graces of the head of the household, not knowing whom to thank, must be grateful to all. Moreover, since love of the master supersedes love of one's fellow servants, the domestics feel obliged to take the initiative in expelling anyone who shirks his duties; they do so not from spite but because anything less is a betrayal of Julie and Wolmar.[244]

Inequality, the Wolmars agree, even the inequality that maximizes *égalité,* is always potentially burdensome. What better way to combat the sting of inequality than song, dance, and games? "By what means," Rousseau the republican asked, "are we to move men's hearts and bring them to love their fatherland? Dare I say? Through the games they play as children."[245] In the case of the Genevan republic Rousseau praised the ritualized public dances, where under the watchful eyes of the elders, the youngsters meet and pair off for marriage.[246] It just so happens, we learn in his novel, that what is good for a republic is equally serviceable in a nonpolitical familial haven. Rather than have the peasants go off to drink and swear on the weekends, the Wolmars provide them with amusements superior to anything the nearby village has to offer. Not the least of the entertainments are the informal balls at which the Wolmars play matchmakers and Julie sometimes joins in the dancing. "I find," she explains, "that such moderate familiarity . . . restores a little of our natural condition, in tempering the baseness of servitude and the rigor of authority." Saint-Preux confesses his admiration for the Wolmars, willing so often "to descend to the level of their domestics while avoiding that the latter should ever be tempted to take them at their word."[247]

The grape harvest is another excuse for the momentary revival of primitive equality. "We sing, we laugh the whole day long, and the work goes all the better. All live in the greatest familiarity; everyone is equal, and yet no one forgets himself."[248] At mealtime during the harvest, service is self-service or is done by anyone and everyone, sometimes by the lord and his lady. Work is play, a great ongoing "festival" reminiscent of saturnalia but without the theme of the world turned upside down, of servants acting as masters, masters as servants. Rousseau held such role-reversal against the comic genre when discussing drama,[249] and was no more sympathetic to it in his novel. The "reunion of estates," not the temporary overthrow of social order, is the objective of the Wolmars, who realize that *égalité* as equanimity has nothing to gain and much to lose from a ritualized kicking over of the traces. What joy to share collectively, however briefly, the delights of equality restored; what misery to dream, even momentarily, of ourselves becoming masters.[250]

Games, dances, drinking, laughter—Rousseau's haven hidden away from the corruptions of society is as exuberant as Holbach's is sober. Hostile to the childish adults of Paris, Holbach fails to understand that mature persons protected from society are childlike in their innocence, just as the adults of *le monde* are spoiled children. Emile and Sophie in France, the inhabitants of Clarens in Switzerland, have not been denatured by society; living away from the city, engaged in farming, they are the rarest of species: social and yet close to nature. The longer they remain childish, the better. Because the Wolmars deal with innocents, they do not need to force virtue upon their "children." Simply by attending to the pleasure and interest of their "family," the masters of Clarens rule effectively without resort either to punishment or to moral exhortation.[251] The age of gold mocked by Voltaire in *Le Mondain* is no figment of the poetic imagination, nor is it a period lost in the past. Julie and Wolmar have made it a reality, as will Emile and Sophie.[252]

The primary complaint about the Golden Age in *Le Mondain* is that it was crude, unpolished. Voltaire the man of taste, the connoisseur and would-be aristocrat, surrounds himself at Cirey with Gobelin tapestries, works of art, the finest silverware, and the most ornate carriage—with everything Parisian available to someone exiled from the center of taste.[253] The philosophes insisted upon philosophizing about taste, despite the claim of aristocrats such as Saint-Evremond that taste is bound so ineffably to social class that it cannot be abstracted into concepts.[254] Even d'Alembert, usually so insistent on the limits of reason, wrote about taste in the *Encyclopédie,* as did Montesquieu and Voltaire,[255] the first two discussing it in universal psychological categories that admitted men of letters to a domain hitherto the prerogative of a privileged few.

Rousseau recognized from the outset that snobbery was the essence of philosophical discussions of taste. Even though prowess in matters of taste might not earn the philosophes entry to the aristocracy, their ease with a topic so exclusionary sufficed to enable them to join the ever widening numbers of those who rose socially by removing themselves from the ranks of *le peuple.*[256] Initially Rousseau denounced taste as "the art of being knowing about petty things";[257] upon further reflection he added, "but since the agreeableness of life depends on a tissue of petty things, such concerns are far from being matters of indifference."[258] Among other things *Emile* is "a kind of essay on true taste,"[259] and *La Nouvelle Héloïse* offers an illustration of what had been regarded as unthinkable: taste that is as inclusionary as it is refined.

Reversing Voltaire, Rousseau held "there is perhaps not a civilized place on earth where the general taste is worse than in Paris."[260] Wolmar and Julie have built an anti-Paris in the backwoods that far surpasses the French capital in everything concerning taste. "All the true models of taste are in nature," Rousseau argued, and nature as he understands it is within everyone's reach. It follows that "wherever taste is expensive, it is false."[261] No expanded family could be more aristocratic than that of the titled

Wolmars; no enclosed community could be more dedicated to *égalité* than Clarens, which has borrowed dances from Geneva, autarchy from the High Valais, and supplemented these with a home-grown but exquisite taste, as common in its resources as it is extraordinary in its elevation of soul.

Voltaire's letters at the time of his installation at Les Délices, just inside the Swiss border, show a man whose taste obliges him to send to France for items ranging from a coach to seeds and wine.[262] The Wolmars do the opposite: the vines of Clarens are their sole source of wine but are handled so skillfully as to conjure up the flavors of the grapes of several countries.[263] At Clarens one drinks excellent wine but purely for the pleasures of palate and companionship, never to prove one has taste.

The fountain mentioned in Voltaire's poem celebrating luxury shoots jets of water into the air. Its equivalent at Clarens was placed there by Julie's father, a man of extreme aristocratic prejudices; Wolmar and Julie have rechanneled it to water her garden, a place of wonderment without show or grandeur. Within this garden there is an aviary, but it is without bars to hold the birds prisoner; the flower beds and trees are not symmetrically situated because such is not the way of nature; nor is there a special viewing area overlooking the whole—because any such vantage point suggests dissatisfaction with where we are. The French disfigure nature; Julie accents its beauty with artistry, carefully hiding all traces of the work of the artist.[264] As the second half of the century unfolded Rousseau's thoughts on gardens led to the vogue of the *jardin anglais;* he himself, however, was merely following Boileau's command to "be simple with artistry, sublime without pride, attractive without make-up."[265] Rousseau's ideal is impeccably and classically French, even as it discredits sculpted French gardens.

Spartan as a republican, Rousseau is a voluptuary as an advocate of social salvation through withdrawal into the family. Dealing with dress, food, furniture, and the like, the Wolmars make exclusive use of materials that are plentiful and inexpensive; yet by the time they have finished preparing the trout or arranging a room, all is delightful and comfortable, "agreeable and useful"—the standard of utility serving as a safeguard against the encroachments of vanity. By such means the household answers to the initial formula of abundance without luxury.[266]

However fulfilling this abundance, it does not exhaust the pleasures savored by Julie. Hers is a code of sensual, Epicurean enjoyment, of indulgence of the self that never degenerates into self-indulgence. That *art de jouïr* in which the French take pride is Julie's concern as well, but unlike Parisians she understands that any sensual pleasures beyond those immediately granted by nature eventually induce boredom and disgust if permitted to become a habit. Hence she limits the frequency of her pleasures, only drinking the coffee she loves on occasion. She abstains as a voluptuary, not as a nun.[267] Much the same may be said about the sleeping arrangements of Sophie and Emile. At the urging of the tutor, Sophie refrains from frequent sex with her husband. "You will reign by means of love for a long time," the tutor tells her, "if you make your favors rare and precious."[268]

Rousseau's masterstroke was to purge the high culture of France from his republic, relocating it, transfigured and transmogrified, in his apolitical familial refuge. Whereas the high taste of Paris was the death of nature, his taste would be the highest development of human nature preserved from social corruption. Perhaps the single most powerful example of Rousseau's strategy is Saint-Preux's recollection of a morning spent with Julie and Wolmar in perfect communication, a mutual meeting of hearts and souls, absolute in its intimacy. Not a single word is spoken because language, a social institution, could only diminish the bond between three such beautiful souls.[269] Implicitly, this remarkable passage is a commentary on the art of conversation, invented and perfected by French society. All is *politesse* and wit in the verbal exchanges of salons; nothing reaches the *fond du coeur*.[270] French society has succeeded in removing itself from primitive nature, but does not realize it has failed to nurture—and has in fact killed—the nature that is compatible with society.

"One must not confound what is natural in the savage state with what is natural in the civil state."[271] Especially for women and children there is reason to believe that nature may yet flourish in the midst of a degraded society. On his visit to Paris Saint-Preux discovers that its women, despite their central place in a world of depravity, have not completely lost their natural goodness.[272] Were women to leave *le monde*, reclaiming their place in the family, "*moeurs* would reform themselves, nature's sentiments would be reawakened in every heart."[273] Mothers who breast-feed their children have a better chance than men to reestablish our ties to nature; women are our last chance because once restored to nature, our original mother, they may bear many Emiles and Sophies.

If anyone bothers to take care of the unfortunate it will surely be women, for their natural pity has not suffered damage as decisive as that society has inflicted on men.[274] Acts of charity should take women out of the home but never into *le monde,* and the end of each day spent assisting the poor should find the most high-born lady surrounded by her spouse and children, far away from the glitter of salons, theaters, operas. No more than men, or rather less than males, should females seek to have their talents recognized; for not only will competition make women as bad as men but it will obliterate distinctions of gender—the last thing desirable for persons already so uncertain who they are.

Not satisfied with stealing the conservative familial program of the philosophes, Rousseau topped off his performance with a crescendo of accusations at their expense hardly distinguishable from the rhetoric of Palissot or the other antiphilosophes. At the very moment the philosophes were protecting themselves by taking stands conspicuously traditionalist, he portrayed them as "dignified advocates of crime." Their advocacy of sexual pleasure, in his interpretation, was the same as granting a license to adultery and to the destruction of whatever remained of *moeurs.* "These *dangerous reasoners,*" he writes, deliberately taunting Diderot, "have resolved to annihilate in one fell swoop all human society ... Look how they exonerate secret adultery!"[275]

The violent reasoner, be it recalled, cannot be answered short of a rebirth of ardent republicanism, because in existing societies it will never be in one's interest to be virtuous. Rousseau therefore turns to religion in *Emile,* arguing that "without faith no true virtue exists." Consistently and brutally he concludes that faithless philosophes, despite their moral rhetoric, are not virtuous.

> Let everything be related to me alone; let all mankind, if need be, die in suffering and poverty to spare me a moment of pain or hunger. This is the inner language of every unbeliever who reasons ... Whoever speaks otherwise although he has said in his heart, "There is no God," is nothing but a liar or a fool.[276]

Fittingly, it is Julie who makes an identical argument in Rousseau's novel. Here was Diderot's feminine preacher delivering a sermon against him; here was the most sensitive of women defending morality the only way it can be sustained, by uncorrupted sensibility coming to the aid of insufficient reason.[277] Rousseau's conclusion, philosophical and antiphilosophical at the same time, that reason is nothing without sensibility, was especially persuasive when uttered in a feminine voice.

Julie does not know whether religion is true or false. What matters is that we should act as if it were true—for two reasons. The first is that we cannot be happy, whole, and content in this life, at peace with ourselves, free from vile social passions, unless we believe in happiness in the next life. Second, we should not help the rich and their philosophical domestics rob the poor of their one remaining consolation, faith. Atheism is not the least of the luxuries for which the philosophes, "under the haughty pretext that they alone are enlightened," serve as diligent and well-compensated apologists.[278]

WHEN THE PHILOSOPHES glanced to the "left" they saw Rousseau, his republicanism a devastating critique of theirs, not to mention those of their ranks whose sympathy for monarchy expanded with their waist-lines. Turning to the "right" they again collided with him and concluded he had joined the camp of the enemy. Looking into the mirror, it was difficult to deny they had met the enemy and he was they.

Religious metaphors came readily to the philosophes, weaned on religious texts and always ready to use the words of the Church against the priests and for themselves. They countered the Christian belief that Jesus brought light into the world by viewing their movement as enlightenment, Christianity as darkness. Voltaire, addicted to religious imagery, liked to call his group the Apostles, which predictably led him to dub Rousseau "Judas."[279]

Diderot was especially fond of the image of the Trinity, and insisted it was less hatred of the infamous that united the enlightened "brothers" than dedication to their own trinity, the true, the good, and the beautiful.[280] Eventually he learned that he and his comrades were faced with another trinity, more disconcerting than the religious mystery of three persons in one God. Rousseau was three enemies in one person, each directed at the philosophes: the enemy on the left, the enemy on the right, and the enemy within.

CHAPTER FIVE

Generation, Degeneration, Regeneration

In one fashion or another all the thought of the Enlightenment revolves around theories and applications of science, so much that the very philosophy articulated by the philosophes often seems virtually identical to the epistemology and methodology of science. With regard to applications, the philosophes were especially concerned to stress the promise of science to better the lot of humanity, to promote the progress that more frequently than not has eluded our grasp; and progress, in their sense, went far beyond an improvement of material conditions: Diderot spoke for all the philosophes when he said that scientific reason could make us not just less ignorant but happier and more virtuous.[1] Science is not everything, but without it we lack the confidence and hope that come with visible, incontrovertible success; with science, we can resolve whatever of our discontents are amenable to remedies.

Unless we appreciate how vigorously Rousseau pursued scientific studies and enlisted scientific arguments in his campaign against his philosophical contemporaries, his full stature as autocritic of the Enlightenment will remain understated. Rousseau, man of science, is, however, an expression that does not roll readily off the lips, so trained are we to see him through lenses inherited from the romantic movement. Once it was literary critics who obliterated all traces of Rousseau's scientific interests by treating him as a romantic before his time, a sentimental worshipper of nature whose exclamatory responses to breath-taking natural settings are totally foreign to the detachment of the scientist. More recently, historians of science have taken up where literary critics left off: nothing is more common in accounts of eighteenth-century scientific thought than the omission of Rousseau or a brief, unsubstantiated characterization of his thought as preromantic, followed by his early dismissal from serious discussion.[2]

Any traces of Jean-Jacques' commitments to science that survive the historians of science meet their demise in the Kantian Rousseau of Ernst Cassirer. To qualify for the honor of having anticipated Kant, Rousseau must be lifted entirely out of his French context, his determination to ground moral criticism in a science of humankind overlooked or treated as a mistake, until at last one arrives at Kant, for whom the autonomy of moral philosophy means that anthropology and other scientific studies have no direct bearing on ethics.[3]

In this chapter I shall attempt to restore Rousseau to those scientific debates of his era in which he participated. The Rousseau who will emerge contradicts both the figure unjustly maligned or neglected by historians of science and the man praised by Kantians for all the wrong reasons. My undertaking shall be all the more manageable thanks to the contributions that some of the ablest Rousseau scholars have made to the interpretive literature in recent years. These reconsiderations come in various shapes and sizes. There is the self-admitted failure of a distinguished historian of physical science to find any evidence to confirm his thesis that Rousseau is to be blamed for Jacobin attacks on science.[4] More subtly, it has been noted that in the second of the walks recorded by Rousseau during his last years, he is as delighted to identify three rare plants and to specify their Latin names as to evoke a sentimental response to nature.[5] Supplement this observation with Rousseau's prompt disavowal of any intent in the *First Discourse* to belittle science, and one has a thinker who from beginning to end shared the high estimate of the philosophes for scientific endeavor.[6]

Most important of all, however, are Rousseau's efforts—only now beginning to receive the attention they merit—to place his social and political thought in intimate connection with the budding life sciences of his day, Buffon's natural history most of all.[7] If the first half of the eighteenth century was marked by the fulfillment of a Newtonian research program, understood as experimental science in England and Holland, as rational mechanics in France,[8] the second half was that of the life sciences, with France in the lead and Rousseau a leader among the French in extending the new science to the examination of human history and society.[9]

France was also the home in the eighteenth century of bold, unabashed scientific materialism; it was the birthplace of such noteworthy and notorious personages as La Mettrie and Helvétius, intellectually very different and even contradictory, but alike in that both were denounced by the authorities for the shocking conclusions they drew from their respective materialist premises.[10] Then there was Holbach, author of a torrent of repetitive, scandalous works, atheistic, materialistic, and fiercely anticlerical, all published anonymously. Finally there was Diderot, greatest of the French materialists, a brilliant writer, and once the friend of Rousseau.

Always attuned to his age, if only to sing his own tune, Rousseau vehemently denounced materialism but filled his works with illustrations of an unfinished project, which if published in its own right would have borne some such title as "The Materialism of the Sage."[11] Rousseau could thunder against materialist philosophy in his mature works and look to botany during his final, tormented years for emotional and perhaps religious solace; but the most vital of his stands for and against materialism lie elsewhere. His was a lifelong project, completely in keeping with the Enlightenment, of criticizing materialism as a "system" while employing it as a program of social action; his was a discerning critique of materialism, one that carefully noted both its proper and its improper uses.

Not the least ironic aspect of the Enlightenment is that it is Rousseau who, after denouncing materialism in the words of a clergyman, successfully grounds his most lofty ideals in matter; in striking contrast it is Holbach, the flamboyant materialist, whose ethics and politics drip with excessive idealism. On questions of matter and antimatter Rousseau repeated his pattern of duplicating traditionalist polemics against the philosophes while simultaneously outdoing them at their own game.

Analysis and Genesis

"Analysis," championed by Newton and later hailed by Voltaire in 1734,[12] the same year the *Lettres philosophiques* introduced his countrymen to English thought, is perhaps the favorite scientific method of the eighteenth century, and the one most frequently designated by the philosophes as a model for all thinking.[13] Voltaire, Condillac, d'Alembert, Turgot, zealots all of mathematico-physical science, partisans also—in Rousseau's eyes—of monarchy, and proclaimers of the cultural finality of Louis XIV's epoch, were strong advocates of the analytical method. Rousseau challenged the intellectual imperialism of analysis with the genetic approach he found much more fruitful when dealing with questions of human nature, culture, and politics. Respectful of the analytical method within its proper sphere, Rousseau nevertheless realized, even more than Diderot, that to prevent the transgressions of analysis and to give genesis its due was to open up new political and cultural possibilities.

The philosophes did not dogmatically affirm that a commitment to the analytical method rigorously entailed a monarchical position on politics or the conclusion that the art and literature of the Grand Siècle could never be surpassed. But they certainly were slow to note the way misplaced analysis sometimes shaped their thoughts on politics and the arts, and slower still to appreciate what genesis had to offer. Even on those occasions when their philosophical histories seemingly beckoned for a genetic account, they fell short; what stands out is the timidity of their efforts, the premature halt they call to such reasoning, and their inclination to term "genetic" a form of thinking that is ahistorical and analytical.

Consider the cases of Voltaire and d'Alembert. Nature as Voltaire understands it is fixed and atemporal, just as Newton taught. When Buffon ventured a conjectural sketch of the origins and history of the earth, Voltaire responded at first with his usual sarcastic sneer, a position from which he retreated only after discovering how well placed Buffon was in the social order. Similarly, all his life Voltaire shied away from the ongoing debate on the origins of language, debunked the historicity of the state of nature, and began to address the prehistorical period of humanity only in his late years, seemingly out of fear of becoming so unfashionable as to lose his audience. Nothing, perhaps, is more characteristic of the man than his refusal to take seriously reports that marine fossils had been found on mountainsides. How could any such tales be true, given that they gave credence either to the Flood or to the emergent theories of geological evolution that threatened his comfortably static world.[14]

Voltaire's cultural universe was as frozen as his view of the physical environment. Just as he spent the last thirteen years of his life polemicizing against atheism and the support it received from the life sciences,[15] so did the elderly Voltaire embroil the French Academy in a rear-guard attack on Shakespeare's dramas. Empiricism in a timeless universe leads to Voltaire's conviction that since we have seen all there is to see, and the culture of Louis XIV's reign is the most outstanding of the fixed number of lots, the best we can do is hold on to the past, seeking to adapt it to the present, even when this means, as it did to Voltaire, writing tragedies he knew were inferior to Racine's. Characteristically he sat out the debate on Italian versus French opera, music rating so low on the seventeenth-century hierarchy of artistic genres that he deemed his participation unnecessary. Why bother to comment on the birth of a new genre, the successor to classical drama, when it has been decided in advance that no such development is possible?[16]

It was the fate of Voltaire, the leading representative of French poetry, to preside over its demise in an age of prose. Not for Voltaire the suggestion of Fontenelle that the "spirit of geometry" be extended to criticism and eloquence,[17] a proposal that could only make matters worse. Impeccable taste, a capacity slowly acquired by a man or a nation, makes the connoisseur, not prowess in mathematics. Judgments in art, it seems, are not all that different from those in politics. In both cases a discriminating intelligence is needed, one polished by experience so that it can tell a good work of art from an inferior one or recognize that for the circumstances of a large country, such as France, luxury is as appropriate as it is out of place in a small republic.[18]

Sometimes Voltaire's focus is analytical, as in the *Treatise on Metaphysics;* at other times it is historical, as in the *Century of Louis XIV;* in matters concerning beauty he deliberately shuns philosophical labels, but presumably would admit to an implicit empiricism in all that relates to taste and judgment. Never is his approach genetic, nor does he ever delve beneath the surface to ponder what escapes all eyes, even those assisted by a microscope, that lack the vision provided by a hypothesis or a conjecture. Rousseau and Diderot agreed that Voltaire, for all his boundless energy, had aged prematurely.

Voltaire the advocate of mathematico-physical science knew little mathematics; d'Alembert, in marked contrast, was a great mathematician, his glory especially evident in the rational mechanics that was the pride of France. Who better, then, than d'Alembert to contribute the article "Analytique" to the *Encyclopédie*? Yet however remarkable his mathematical prowess, d'Alembert always insisted on the limits of mathematical methods and was a severe critic of those who mathematized beyond their means. It is, therefore, not surprising to find him trying his hand at genetic reasoning in the first half of the *Preliminary Discourse.* The failure of his efforts indicates how unready the age was to relinquish its analytical bias.

Rational mechanics—the mathematical study of idealized, frictionless movements of celestial bodies—was carried out by investigators who never set foot in a laboratory, but that did not prevent d'Alembert from having a deep appreciation of experimental science.[19] Nor did his mathematical predisposition induce him to forgive the abuses of quantitative methods that were becoming all too common. Medicine such as it was in his day needed to take heed of the Hippocratic injunction to observe and record, in low-grade, humble fashion,[20] rather than continue down the path of the "algebraic doctors,"[21] so forgetful that mathematics thrives on a simplicity that has nothing to do with the human body.[22] At times, of course, the doctors were justified in stretching beyond immediate experience with the aid of "conjectures," but only because we frequently must act before we are adequately informed when lives hang in the balance.[23]

Eventually some of the mathematical philosophes, Condorcet most of all, turned to probability theory for solutions to vexing social problems. If in the end natural science comes down to probable truth, the emerging social sciences need not suffer from an inferiority complex, argued Condorcet.[24] Indeed, the uses of probability in securing justice in the courtroom or in vindicating inoculation for smallpox were enough to convince social mathematicians of the grandeur of their mission. One quantifier of stature, d'Alembert,[25] did not support their efforts, because he spied the vanity of intellectuals and little more in such proceedings. Of what worth, asked d'Alembert, were these mathematical weights, so arbitrarily attached to judicial evidence, save to foster a false sense of near certitude? Even inoculation was not properly a matter for the calculus of probabilities to decide, the risks of dying from the preventative measure being sufficiently high to muddle the question of rational choice.[26] What are we to say if what is rational for society taken as a whole is less clearly so from the standpoint of the individual person?

Diderot argued that in separating private and public interest d'Alembert was "a good mathematician but a very bad citizen."[27] It might be more accurate, however, to say that d'Alembert believed each citizen has rights no mathematician should override. One may add that, from d'Alembert's point of view, mathematicians themselves lose when they brazenly impose their views on society. As someone who had always admired mathematicians for their immunity to opinion, d'Alembert naturally worried that probability theory would tempt them into the world, where they would soon become as prideful and sullied by ambition as the literary intellectuals.[28]

On the arts d'Alembert was both with and against Voltaire. Much as his mentor had, d'Alembert condemns the intrusion of the analytical spirit into belles-lettres. "Our century," wrote d'Alembert, "which is inclined toward combination and analysis, seems to desire to introduce frigid and didactic discussions into things of sentiment."[29] Up to this point Voltaire, the man of inbred, anticonceptual taste, can wholeheartedly agree with his pupil, but not with d'Alembert's subsequent statement that "the true philosophic spirit . . . is the most firm support [of good taste]."[30] Though skeptical of intellectual power-seekers, d'Alembert was forever open to the discovery and exploration of new mental continents. Hence after removing taste from the mathematician, he gladly added it to the list of topics on the philosopher's agenda.

Though an ideal candidate to break out of the artistic hegemony of Louis XIV's era, d'Alembert ultimately fell short of doing so, and his failure underscores the boldness of Rousseau and Diderot. It was d'Alembert's explicit claim that we must never fix in advance the limits of the mind; ultimate metaphysical questions may be ruled out but little else. Many another physical scientist outlawed conjecture and used analogy merely to assume that what we have not seen is the same as what is before our eyes; d'Alembert, however, applauds "that spirit of analogy . . . which pierces beyond what nature seems to want to show us, and foresees facts before they are seen."[31] From such a man we do not expect the cultural stodginess into which he settles.

In the debate on music d'Alembert exposed another false application of mathematics and displayed his openness to new cultural trends; even more, however, he revealed his inability to transcend the artistic legacy of the Grand Siècle. Along with the other philosophes he sided with the Italians in the quarrel over opera. When it was no longer possible to keep Rameau from attacking Rousseau's entries on music in the *Encyclopédie*, it fell to d'Alembert to deflate the great composer's misguided attempt to reduce harmony to mathematics. Yet d'Alembert unthinkingly accepted the conventional ranking of music in the "last place" in the arts;[32] quite consistent with that view, when the king's corner at the opera transformed a musical disagreement into a charge of philosophical disloyalty to country and throne, d'Alembert came to blame Rousseau for starting and involving the philosophes in a meaningless civil war. To Rousseau the loss of musical speech, as delineated in his philosophical history, was the demise of the better part of our humanity; to d'Alembert the height of absurdity was for the party of humanity, over something as trivial as music, to be denounced as Bouffonists, republicans, Frondeurs, atheists, and materialists "as if they were synonymous terms."[33]

The closest d'Alembert ever came to the genetic reasoning that characterizes the *Discourse on Inequality* is in the first half of the *Preliminary Discourse*. Unlike the second half, which, beginning with the Renaissance, repeats Voltaire's sketch of pre-Enlightenments, d'Alembert in the opening section sets about the Lockean task of tracing the "origin and generation of our ideas."[34] Strange happenings soon beset this hypothetical mind of the species, not the least odd d'Alembert's habit of falling back into Cartesian formulas while ostensibly historicizing Locke. For instance, he maintains that the senses refer only secondarily to our bodies and the external world, our first sensations being those which concern the "thinking principle which constitutes our nature."[35] D'Alembert's uneasiness with genetic reasoning is again evident when he places imagination after reason in the hypothetical developmental order, then points out in the second section that in the history that actually occurred imagination and poetry preceded reason and science.[36] Barely has early man begun to think, moreover, than he is frustrated in his purely utilitarian search for knowledge, excuse enough for d'Alembert to laud pure science and launch into a mini-treatise on mathematics and physics. It is some measure of d'Alembert's failure to carry through a genetic account that one sometimes comes across a passage in which his primitives appear to be engaging in analytical examinations of nature.[37]

Perhaps d'Alembert's foray into genesis is so brief and awkward because he learned that what he asked of it, it could not give. He had intended to chart a "genealogical or encyclopedic tree which will gather the various branches of knowledge together under a single point of view and will serve to indicate their origin and their relationships to one another."[38] Now and then he tries to paper over the gap between expectation and results, but in the end admits that he and Diderot must link together the various fields of study as best they can.[39] Hypothetical, conjectural, genetic history falls short in the task of integration d'Alembert has assigned it; try as we may, we cannot effectively expound the "chain"[40] linking the arts and sciences by recapturing the moment of their genesis. Presumably, d'Alembert might have concluded that he had asked the genetic method to answer the wrong question; instead, he abandoned it.

Condillac and Turgot proved exceptionally adept in advancing accounts of the genesis of science and the arts, but the upshot of their genetic labors, fully intended, was to strengthen the stranglehold of analysis in the circles of advanced thinkers. As we have seen, Turgot employed Locke to depict human history as a progressive development, the opposite of the repetitive and closed movements of nature. Over time the mind of the species unfolds, its various faculties come into play, as do those of the individual mind, culminating in reason, which has at its disposal an ever-growing storehouse of experience. The more we know about nature, the more the mind dismisses the myths of early mankind and the caprices of imagination that lead away from truth. Rightfully, the poet must yield to the scientist, the "agreeable" arts to the useful sciences, as language becomes ever more rational, precise, and analytical. All that is required to ensure the irreversibility of progress is to encapsulate the entirety of human knowledge in mathematical symbols.[41]

With Condillac, too, a genetic investigation serves only so long as necessary to vindicate analysis, after which analysis is everything, genesis nothing. As a good disciple of Locke, Condillac blamed linguistic befuddlement for most of our errors, and sketched a history of language to learn where we went wrong and how we might go right. During the course of his research Condillac drew a picture of earlier societies, upon which Rousseau borrowed heavily, wherein music, poetry, and language were one and the same, writing did not exist but public memory did, because accented and musical words projected to a large audience are unforgettable.

Condillac bid adieu to that benighted age with a minimum of regret and embraced the modern world wholeheartedly, especially its principal language, French, so crystalline in its clarity, so conducive to analysis,[42] the only worthwhile mode of thought. Condillac could ask only one thing more of modern language, that it become even more uncompromisingly analytical. Accordingly he devoted much of his later philosophical endeavors to the elaboration of a language that would be modeled on algebra and calculus. "To speak understandably," he argued in his *Logic,* "we must conceive and render our ideas in the analytic order, which decomposes and recomposes each thought."[43] Reasoning well and having "a well-made language" turn out to be identical,[44] just as there is no distinction among logical, philosophical, and mathematical analysis.[45]

"Analysis and imagination," Condillac noted, "are two operations so different, that they generally obstruct the progress of each other";[46] whence it follows that in giving all to analysis, he was embracing the decline of the arts. Why, he asks, bemoan the "loss of a few beauties" for which we are amply indemnified by the "progress of sound philosophy?"[47] Not for him Voltaire's nostalgia for the lost glories of poetry; not for Condillac that disturbing sense, quite common in the eighteenth century, of living off the dead literary glories of the Sun King's reign. Turgot had accepted a combination of scientific progress and cultural petrifaction; Condillac went him one better in uncovering and then applauding a strong connection between the forward march of science and the irreversible decline of culture.

Rousseau commended the role of analysis in mathematics and chemistry,[48] briefly indicated that it may have its uses in the examination of texts,[49] and took care to include analytical thinking, broadly conceived, in Emile's education.[50] Yet when it came to the great questions of politics and culture he found the analytical method not just misplaced but positively pernicious. "This analytical method," he wrote in exasperation, is the one that leads "the wisest person to comprehend the least." Why mores are corrupted in direct proportion to the enlightenment of minds, why savages transported to Europe do not partake of our passions and pleasures—none of these vital matters is understood by those who pride themselves on their prowess in philosophical analysis. "They know very well the bourgeois of London or Paris; but they will never know what a man is."[51]

Discussions of natural rights, insofar as they are based on the analytical method, have gone wrong from the beginning. Take the example of Hobbes. When he resolves society into its individual parts, what is the result?—the narrowly and viciously self-interested actor, totally social in his craving for honors, who is then erroneously termed natural. Rather than clarify the distinction between the social and the natural, analysis destroys it; instead of uncovering causes, it leads us to mistake effects for causes, to blame human nature for conflict when war is a social institution. Under the spell of analysis, theorists of natural right decompose the social whole into its socially created, individual constituents, each the enemy of his fellows; then they recompose society and establish the rules of right by outlining the agreement the worst of these unnatural beings foist upon their guileless neighbors.

Between Grotius and Hobbes, between two versions of natural right, one grounded in history, the other in analysis, there is a difference of method but, Rousseau points out, no difference in result.[52] Each takes the person before our eyes, the bourgeois of London or Paris, and assumes he is "man." Sometimes the philosophes followed Grotius, as Diderot did when he appealed to history in "Political Authority" and "Natural Right"; sometimes the model was Hobbes, or at least the Hobbesian mode of analytic thought, as when Holbach suggested that right should be decided by looking at the "qualities and properties found visibly and constantly in [social man]."[53] When the best minds perform so inadequately we must be prepared to draw Rousseau's depressing conclusion: "The science of political right is yet to be born, and it is to be presumed that it never will be born."[54]

Many of the polemical exchanges following the publication of the *First Discourse* centered on the question of causality. Were the arts and sciences the cause or the symptom of corruption, the underlying cause or a contributing cause? What precisely was the argument? Rousseau was willing to admit that high culture could not be isolated as the exclusive driving force behind moral decline, but he was determined not to back away from his fundamental position; to that end, he enlisted the assistance of a more rigorously formulated method. At first he looked to comparative analysis;[55] then, finding "comparisons between one people and another are difficult, since a great many factors have to be taken into account, and since they are always in some respect imprecise, [he decided that] one is far better off tracing the history of one and the same people, and comparing its progress in knowledge with the revolutions in its morals."[56] By his account, he was out to chart a "genealogy," according to which "the first source of evil is inequality."[57]

It was several years later, when Rousseau attempted a conjectural and genetic explanation of inequality in the *Second Discourse,* that he found himself in full possession of the method he needed to plumb the depths of the human condition. Recorded history was no longer his concern; what preceded it was, man before society deformed and denatured him, the natural man so much spoken of but totally unknown, social impostors having taken his rightful place. Only a genetic account can unearth the long extinct natural man and confirm how impossible it now is, save perhaps for Corsicans, to base right on our original pity and goodness. Rights must henceforth be reinforced by duties, duties that can match our inclinations only if the polity catches us up in a whirl of civic activities, quite unnatural and manufactured, but conducive to love of country and countrymen.

After analysis came synthesis, after decomposing society it was time to recompose it by adding together the elements that had been isolated during the prior analytical procedure. For the utilitarians and the physiocrats, and in a larger sense for all those addicted to the analytical method, society was nothing more than the sum total of the individuals composing it—a view Rousseau found fundamentally misleading. Truth be known—and he was adamant it would be—society is both more and less than its individual members arithmetically totaled, because in society we enter into and are shaped by relationships that make us other than we would be left to ourselves—sometimes better, frequently worse, sometimes more and often less than if left to vegetate in our natural state.

Utilitarians, it appears, have described society as an "aggregation," which it is under despotism; not as the "association" it should be.[58] Formed in accordance with the agreement prescribed in the *Social Contract,* society is "a moral and collective body, composed of as many members as there are voices in the assembly, which receives from this [contractual] act its unity, its common *self.*"[59] From natural to social man there is a qualitative transformation that escapes the quantifiers: "This passage from the state of nature to the civil state produces a remarkable change in man, by substituting justice for instinct in his behavior and giving his actions the morality they previously lacked . . . If the abuses of this new condition did not often degrade him beneath the condition he left, he ought ceaselessly to bless the happy moment that tore him away from it."[60] How the social whole, greater than the sum of its parts, produces individuals superior to natural persons may be seen in the actions of Spartans or Romans; how society generates individuals inferior to what they were on leaving the womb may be seen in observing Europeans, much more selfish, vicious, and inhuman in groups than when acting alone.[61]

On occasion Rousseau found that all he need do to highlight the political implications of the genetic method was to revisit Condillac's first book, specifically the genetic account of linguistic development that preceded the later plea, in the same volume, for an analytical language. "In the prosody of the ancients I find the reason of a fact hitherto unexplained," Condillac proclaimed. "The question is, in what manner the Roman orators, who harangued in the public forum, could be heard by the whole people?"[62] Condillac's answer was that a musical, poetic language carries well, unlike French. "As the French language has hardly any such thing as prosody, it follows that . . . our public spectacles are confined to buildings where only an inconsiderable part of the people assemble."[63] Despite his monarchical bent, Condillac unwittingly handed republicans a wonderful critical device.

Rousseau was not about to waste so useful a weapon, even if to wield it he had first to revise the denigration of oratory, borrowed from Montaigne, that pervades his early writings. An inviting way to reverse his stand while appearing to stand fast was to slide from Sparta, the republic of silence, to Sparta, home of laconic speech: "the Athenian babblers feared the words of Spartans as much as their blows."[64] Both in the *Essay on the Origin of Languages* and in the *Social Contract* he purloined Condillac's genetically derived insights, the better to condemn the modern period in which the very manner in which words are uttered, regardless of content, militates against republicanism. French is suitable for the salon, suitable also for a polity in which the king need only justify his acts by invoking the formula, "because such is my good pleasure"; but we gain some sense of the limits of the French language when we observe that an academician reading a paper cannot be heard at the back of the hall. "I maintain that any language in which it is not possible to make oneself understood by the people assembled is a servile language."[65]

Condillac's genetic findings might have been forgotten, had it not been for Rousseau. For not only did the good abbé end such researches prematurely; he also—to Rousseau's mind—blurred the distinction between analysis and genesis, such that the genetic method disappeared, its very name usurped by its analytical competitor. The original, the natural, the primitive, as attained through the analytical procedure, has nothing to do with early society or the state of nature; it is not the crude and prerational mind that Condillac seeks but the purely rational mind, capable of decomposing and recomposing its ideas instantaneously, the mind which is ideal because it is free from error. Condillac's concern is the genesis of clear and distinct ideas, which means his "natural" man is an ahistorical calculating machine.[66] What, Rousseau would surely ask, can be less genetic than Condillac's account of the genesis of ideas; what less natural than his natural man?

Out of touch with nature, Condillac and his kind were likewise insensitive to the grandeur and glory of the passions. Unknown in the pure state of nature, elevated passions characterize the nascent humanity of a later age, not yet corrupted by society; the youthful era of musical and poetic language described by Rousseau was the one Condillac had portrayed, though the good abbé failed to understand that it was love which loosened previously inactive tongues and filled the air with music. Philosophically, Rousseau recaptured the memory of that lost age with one of his exercises in genetic thinking, the *Essay on the Origin of Languages;* artistically, he resorted to his opera and his operatic novel,[67] *La Nouvelle Héloïse,* to make his degenerate audience feel the power of purified passions. Analysis cannot fathom emotions such as these, nor can the desiccated artistic orthodoxy of the Grand Siècle. Hence Rousseau used music, at the bottom of the hierarchy of the arts, and the novel, still struggling for recognition in France, to give voice to passion;[68] new forms of art were needed to create contemporary surrogates for a world lost and gone forever. We do not know all that human nature is capable of,[69] but we do know it does not regress;[70] that is why it falls to art to offer compensations, however inadequate, to artificial moderns who can never go home to nature again.

Diderot's position on the links between science, the arts, and politics is of interest both in its own right and for the new light it shines on Rousseau. Obliged during his early bohemian years to learn the mathematics he was teaching under false pretenses, Diderot continued long after to follow certain debates on quantification, for instance, the discussion of probability and inoculation. Fundamentally, however, he turned against mathematics when he took up the life sciences, doubtless following the lead of Buffon, who in the "Initial Discourse" (1749) of his *Natural History* complained that insofar as mathematics was tautologies and pure logic, it had little to offer biological science. Diderot began his *Interpretation of Nature* (1753) with the stunning proclamation that the day of mathematical science was over. Because mathematics abstracted away all the properties that make something alive, Diderot was convinced it had no bearing on the emerging sciences of organic nature.[71]

He even dared question, at this early date, the ultimate worth of rational mechanics, and commented in passing that anyone who could be a mathematician without having his artistic taste ruined was a rare person.[72] Perhaps d'Alembert was already his target, as he definitely was many years later in *D'Alembert's Dream* (1769). What better way to deride the man who abandoned the *Encyclopédie* during its time of political trouble; how better express, at the same time, the blindness of mathematicians to the life sciences than to have d'Alembert gain compelling insights on generation and reproduction while dreaming and masturbating? Clearly Diderot could occasionally be as malicious as Voltaire.

Innovative in science, Diderot was equally so in the arts. For a brief moment in 1751 he accepted Condillac's argument that the progress of science entails the demise of imagination.[73] Soon he did an about-face: "Imagination!—there's the quality without which one cannot be a poet or a philosopher . . . or simply a man."[74] Receptive to Richardson's novels and himself a novelist, an experimenter in new theatrical genres, the father of art criticism—Diderot brought as much of his verve and genius to the arts as to science. It was he, above all, who advocated that the creative genius should overthrow Voltaire's caretaking reign of taste. "A nation is old when it has taste,"[75] wrote Diderot, probably thinking of the aging Voltaire. In an unpublished work he remarked that Voltaire still turned out tragedies the way some old men continued to run after young women.[76]

We need to take analysis out of art and infuse imagination into science. Philosophical analysis, in Diderot's opinion, introduces "an exactitude, a precision, a method—forgive the expression—a kind of pedantry that kills everything [artistic]."[77] As for imagination, its normal residence is the garret of the artist; yet there are times when it is just what the scientist needs in his study or laboratory. In the original edition of the *Interpretation of Nature* Diderot presented his mind-stretching "conjectures" under the word "reveries." Directly contradicting Condillac, who in his *Treatise on Systems* (1749) had denounced metaphysicians as dreamers,[78] Diderot defended "conjectures founded on oppositions or resemblances so distant . . . that the dreams of a sick man do not appear more bizarre or disconnected."[79] Possibly his greatest, certainly his most audacious, work on science is later offered as the "dream" of d'Alembert. The spider and its web as an image of the brain and nervous system, a swarm of bees representing what later science would call a creature composed of cells— Diderot constantly and deliberately resorts to the metaphorical expressions ruled out of philosophy by Condillac.[80] Only a mind as opened as most are closed by attention to method can hope to begin to unravel a world so alive and complex as ours. The scientist must "interrogate nature, which often presents him with a quite different phenomenon from the one he had been counting on. And then he realizes that analogy has been playing tricks on him."[81] Diderot's are imaginative analogies—a far cry, indeed, from Newton's.

In social and political thought, it is not surprising that Diderot came to view the utilitarianism of Helvétius and the economics of physiocracy as failures, and in both cases laid part of the blame at the doorstep of the analytical method.[82] It was a fatal mistake, he was convinced, to believe that social complexity could be understood by isolating individuals and adding them together by a kind of political and economic arithmetic.

On the question of natural rights, there are indications that both the mathematical and the biological philosophes conjured up moral doctrines that complemented their scientific outlooks. When d'Alembert, Turgot, or Condorcet speak, they uphold the Lockean view of nature as consisting of individuals, which leads them to view natural rights as the claims of individual persons who in a moral sense are anterior to society, and whose rights take precedence over duties. For the life scientists Diderot and Holbach, by contrast, rights of individuals are immediately translatable into social duties, not so much because they follow Pufendorf and Shaftesbury servilely, but because the words of these philosophers of an earlier age rang true to new philosophes who had learned to deny that anything individual exists in organic nature.[83] Not for Diderot and Holbach the view of Locke that the notions of genus and species are mere "artifice[s] of the understanding."[84] Turgot's disdain for the corporate spirit extended, beyond the guilds, to the very academies where many philosophes sat;[85] Diderot, however, owing to his addiction to organicist modes of thought, called upon the unlikely analogy of a monastery to indicate how in nature a body continues to live, even as its components, one by one, die and are replaced over time.[86] For Diderot and Holbach the whole was so much more than the sum of its parts that the parts were in danger of losing their individual identity.

For life scientists, organicism in social thought came naturally, just as mathematico-physical scientists were wont to see society as a mechanism. "The universe is just a huge machine," Condillac suggested; applying that outlook to society, he held that "a people is an artificial body" and the magistrate is "the mechanic who must restore the springs and wind up the whole machine."[87] In the cases of Diderot and Holbach, it is remarkable to see how little volition enters into the meaning of their constantly used expression, the "general will." Reason and organism are their concern, and by "reason" they mean comprehension of the interests of the species—that biological entity to which they refer when speaking of the "general will of the human race [*genre humain* or *espèce humaine*]."[88]

Rousseau was no less critical of misplaced organicism than of the excesses of analysis, as his attack on Diderot's conception of the general will proves. Sounding much like Condillac, for whom the best way to deflate an overblown and reified abstraction was to decompose it, Rousseau noted that "the term *genre humain* suggests only a purely collective idea which assumes no real union among the individuals who constitute it." Again like Condillac, Rousseau offered an empiricist's account of the origin of the idea of humanity: "It is only from the social order established among us that we derive ideas about the one we imagine. We conceive of the general society [of the human race] on the basis of our particular societies; . . . and we do not really begin to become [cosmopolitan] until after we have been citizens."[89] For Diderot and Holbach the general will is already there, given by nature; for Rousseau it must be constructed, with painstaking effort and at a high human cost, within the walls of a republic.

This republican general will is not natural; it is conventional and always somewhat painful, because our mixed condition, part social, part natural, must give way to such fully civic and "denatured" persons as the Spartan mother who was more uplifted by word of victory than devastated by reports her sons were killed in battle. She knows who she is and what she must do, but is unaware how much she has forfeited to become whole.

One cannot imagine a view more distant from Diderot's and Holbach's than Rousseau's, nor can there be a greater distortion of the thought of Rousseau than the interpretation, once seriously maintained, that he is a precursor of the organicizing romantic nationalists of the nineteenth century.[90]

Natural (and Unnatural) History

Without question Rousseau's single most pathbreaking exercise in genetic thinking is his *Second Discourse*. Deeper than the old political history, deeper than the succeeding cultural history of the philosophes, deeper even than Rousseau's merger of political and cultural history in the *First Discourse* is his effort in the second to write the "history of the [human] species."[91] Though the scholars of our day have a penchant for calling Rousseau an anthropologist,[92] I shall refer to him as a natural historian, because he intended his work to be read as a contribution to Buffon's ongoing and exceptionally popular *Natural History*. The purpose of Rousseau's remarkably daring essay, as he immediately informs us, is to heed the words of the Delphic oracle: "Know Thyself."[93] He could not imagine a more worthy admonition, nor one less obeyed.

Perhaps no thinker in his age matched Rousseau when it came to insisting on understanding humans as animals that had evolved, ever so slowly, halfstep by almost imperceptible halfstep, over an enormous span of time, changing fundamentally in the process, physically, mentally, emotionally. Just before Rousseau wrote the *Discourse on Inequality,* his then close friend and fellow life scientist Diderot published his *Interpretation of Nature,* a brief book that illuminates Rousseau's only in that it revealingly figures nowhere in the notes of the *Second Discourse,* whereas references to Buffon's volumes are plentiful. It is not difficult to see why Buffon was so important to Rousseau, Diderot so insignificant. The pages of the *Natural History,* unlike so many previous ones written under that rubric, were much more than an inventory of nature or a collection of the information that would help the scientist perform experiments.[94] Instead, Buffon's writings gave indications of what Rousseau sought, a genuine history of nature. Diderot's view of the world, in marked contrast, was already headed toward his later formulation: "The world is ceaselessly beginning and ending; at every moment it is at its beginning and its end."[95] When each instant starts the world anew, all is change but nothing is history.

Buffon the historian of nature is clearly Rousseau's man, but the prideful and self-absorbed author of the *Natural History* was unwilling to practice reciprocity. Briefly, he bothered to take notice of Rousseau in his seventh volume (1758) but only to dismiss the *Second Discourse* out of hand. "We do not suppose with a philosophe, one of the most fierce censors of our humanity, that there is a greater distance from man in the pure state of nature to the savage, than from the savage to us."[96] Buffon then added in his self-assured manner, "the state of nature is a known condition: it is that of the savage."[97] Not for a moment is Buffon willing to entertain the possibility that the history of society needs to be supplemented both by an account of a presocial age and by conjectures on the gradual coming to be of society. He goes so far, in his determination to discredit Rousseau, as to utter the word no Lockean should ever allow to fall from his lips: society belongs to "the very *essence* of the species" (emphasis added).[98]

Despite the rebuff, Rousseau never ceased to admire Buffon; in 1770 the philosophical outcast visited the celebrated natural historian's estate in Burgundy, kneeling down in homage at the threshold of Buffon's study. Of course Rousseau had his own reasons, over and above generosity, to continue praising the intellectual achievement of Buffon, not the least of which, in all likelihood, pertained to those occasional comments in the *Natural History* after 1758 that gave Jean-Jacques new proofs that the *Second Discourse* was a rightful and courageous fulfillment of the thought of perhaps the most widely read scientist of his day. Now and then Buffon inadvertently let slip comments confirming what Jean-Jacques had known all along, that Rousseau was more Buffonian than the fastidious Buffon.

In his fourteenth volume (1766) Buffon offered judgments, apparently without recognizing their significance, that directly contradicted his grounds for criticizing Rousseau eight years earlier. Sounding for all the world like Rousseau in 1755, Buffon now wrote, "there is a greater distance from man in the pure state of nature to the Hottentot, than from the Hottentot to us."[99] An avid reader of the *Natural History*, Rousseau presumably saw in this relatively late Buffon a return to the man who was already occasionally visible in the first three volumes published in 1749. Familiar with the "Natural History of Man," which appeared in volumes two and three, Rousseau undoubtedly encountered the passage wherein Buffon was virtually Rousseau: "We distinguish so poorly what nature alone gives us," wrote Buffon, "from what education, imitation, and example communicate, that it would not be astonishing were we to fail to recognize the portrait of a savage presented us in true colors."[100] A Buffon with the courage of his convictions becomes Rousseau, or so Jean-Jacques believed.

Rousseau found in the Buffon of 1749 everything he could possibly ask for to initiate his history of the species. In the three volumes Buffon released that year he included a sharp attack on analysis, both its decompositions and its recompositions. The shortcomings of the analytical procedure, Buffon charged, should be painfully obvious to anyone interested in life-forms.[101] Criticizing analysis, of course, is not the same as vindicating the long-term genetic outlook Rousseau favored; still, it opens the door, and Buffon at times walked through to view a natural world incrementally undergoing major transformations over passages of time previously regarded as unthinkably long.

Volume one of Buffon's *Natural History* featured a sketch of a "history and theory of the earth," followed by a conjectural essay on "the formation of the planets." The heavens themselves, no matter what Newton thought, came to be; as for the earth, its history could be recounted with the assistance of physical evidence indicating how fundamentally it had been altered by natural laws constantly at work for eons. When applied to humans such a view of the world indicates that beneath the political history occurring on the surface there is a more fundamental development at work. Immersed in the travel literature of his day, Buffon tried to explain the "Varieties of the Human Species" as slowly derived mutations stemming from a single original stock—climate, nourishment, and mode of life serving as the agents of change. With no paleontology to call upon, he resorted to the literature on travel across space to draw lessons on the human effects of the passage of time.

After so promising a start Buffon prematurely finished his labors with a thoroughgoing rationalization of the prejudices of his age, the ones most despised by Rousseau. European man is for Buffon the masterpiece of existence, the type against which all others are measured; non-Europeans are degenerate forms of the same stock from which Europeans hail, and black skin is a decline from an originally white appearance.[102] With his upright carriage and eyes lifted to the heavens, man is by divine right born to command animals.[103]

Obviously nothing could be more delicious, from Rousseau's point of view, than to use Buffon's method and evidence to draw conclusions opposite the master's, all the more so considering how much Buffon was a pillar of the establishment. Director of the Jardin du Roi, his books published on the king's press, member of both the Academy of Sciences and the French Academy, seigneur of Montbard, assisted by amateurs many of whom were gentlemen, himself eventually named a Count, Buffon was precisely the kind of man Rousseau loved to challenge. Naturally one must not forget one last title, that of philosophe, which was attributed to Buffon by the public, much to Rousseau's polemical satisfaction.

Out to visualize an original species far removed from anything his contemporaries would recognize as human, Rousseau immediately draws a parallel between his undertaking and Buffon's conjectural *Theory of the Earth*. Readers of the *Second Discourse* are assured that the "hypothetical" reasonings Rousseau is about to set forth are comparable to "those our physicists make everyday concerning the formation of the world."[104] Another way for Rousseau to enhance his scientific credentials is to announce his intention to conduct "experiments"; he is shrewd enough, however, to note the difficulty the investigator faces when he cannot place himself outside the experiment. "What experiments would be necessary to achieve knowledge of natural man, and what are the means of making these experiments in the midst of society?"[105] It is extremely unfortunate but not in the least surprising that Buffon regarded the denatured society of his day as the fulfillment of nature; for, as Rousseau explained, "all that men do appears natural to us because we are outside nature."[106]

Humans have a natural but also an unnatural or post-natural history, which is why it is so difficult for us to conceive of natural man without projecting acquired traits into his being. At best, as Buffon did when repudiating Rousseau, we mistake the savage for the natural man, and then rush to the conclusion that aggression is a given of human nature.[107] Though our reading of Locke bids us ask how that aggression got there in the first place, our determination to congratulate ourselves on our civilized superiority prevents our making the correct inquiries.

Before we became savages we were something else, something we can only begin to understand on the condition that we look anew at our present condition. What are we, if not exiles from nature imagining our-selves its fulfillment? Physical evidence indicates that the degeneration of the varieties of the human species should not be measured, despite Buffon, in terms of movement away from ourselves to primitives and animals; rather, it is Europeans who may constitute the degenerate stock, reduced by the civilization they cherish to their current lowly status.

Take the example of domesticated animals. Buffon's view, the conven-tional one, is that humans rule animals by a "right of nature" and as a manifestation of the "empire of mind over matter." Rousseau countered with the assertion that since animals "share something of our nature through the sensitivity with which they are endowed, . . . they too ought to participate in natural right."[108] Buffon held animals are here so that "man can recognize at every instant the excellence of his being"; Rousseau believed, on the contrary, that the vicious reign of *amour-propre* dawned the day a natural man, "considering himself in the first rank as a species, prepared himself from afar to claim first rank as an individual."[109] The critical point, however, is that even when treated well, domesticated ani-mals are only half what they were in the wild. "It is the same for man," Rousseau argued forcefully. "In becoming sociable and a slave he becomes weak"; weaker, in fact, than the domesticated animal, because we expect animals to do many of the things for us that we should do for ourselves. Fat and slack, we are as far removed from nature as our original predecessor was lithe, sinewy, and nature's child. Domestication and "degeneration" are the same, and the most domesticated and "degenerate" of all creatures are humans.[110]

Neglected and unused limbs enervate our bodies, but that is only the beginning of the harm social existence does to our physical constitution. Excesses of every kind, the pursuit of needs having no foundation in nature, "the extreme *inégalité* in our way of life, excess of idleness in some, excess of labor in others," result in a plethora of physical maladies unknown to *l'homme sauvage*. From which it follows both that "most of our ills are our own work" and that "the history of human illnesses could easily be written by following that of civil societies."[111] Interestingly Buffon agrees, albeit without recognizing that he has thereby compromised his glowing portrait of *l'homme civil;* all that is necessary, so he thinks, to restore the prestige of civilized man is to praise the sage, "master of himself, . . . self-sufficient, with only a slight need of others."[112] Rousseau, too, admires the Stoic but finds that the only person worthy of that designation is natural man: he alone lives in indifference to opinion and in accordance with a regimen of strictly natural needs. No philosopher can say as much.[113]

On the subject of peasants the differences between Rousseau and Buffon could hardly be greater or more typical of their overall disagreement. For Buffon the ugliness of peasants proves his generalization that "crude, unhealthy, or poorly prepared food can cause the human species to degenerate."[114] First-hand experience with peasants, other than to command them as lord of the manor, was, however, not one of Buffon's strengths. Rousseau feels justified in commenting extensively on peasants because, as he informs the reader, he has spent a great deal of time living with them as one of their numbers.[115] Their diet is superior to that of city folk, he assures us, because their women prefer vegetables to meat; and from their healthy bodies flows the milk refined women withhold from their children.[116] The offspring of peasants have stronger stomachs, and bodies better exercised and healthier, than their urban counterparts.[117] Only in comparison with savages do they fare badly,[118] because true primitives have not yet had their spirits and bodies crushed by inequality, the foremost wonder of civilized existence.

Even the most brutalized peasant breathes clean air, which is more than the wealthiest city dweller can say. There is nothing quite like a visit to a crowded city to convince a natural historian how unnatural our socially constructed lives are.

> The infirmities of the body, as well as the vices of the soul, are the unfailing effect of this overcrowding. Man is, of all the animals, the one who can least live in herds ... Man's breath is deadly to his kind. This is no less true in the literal sense than the figurative.

"Cities are the abyss of the human species"; the countryside its renewal.[119]

Buffon admired "a civilized society, where the mind does more than the body, and work with the hands is restricted to men of the lowest order."[120] Beyond the snobbery of Buffon, Rousseau objected to this separation of mental from physical activity, which can only make us unhealthy, the intellectuals most of all. Repeatedly he warned that men of letters belong to "the most sedentary, the most unhealthy, the most reflective and therefore the unhappiest" occupational group.[121] "Work in the study causes men to grow frail, it weakens their temperament, and the soul's vigor is difficult to preserve once the body's vigor is lost."[122] Hence Rousseau's statement in the *Second Discourse,* so often misunderstood: "I almost dare affirm that the state of reflection is a state contrary to nature and that the man who meditates is a depraved animal."[123] Possibly Rousseau's comment raised less of a furor in his day than subsequently, since his contemporaries sometimes made the same point, Dr. Tronchin for one, Diderot for another and with a typical sexual flourish: "One must not break away completely from the animal condition ... I would be in better health had I bent over a woman part of the time I have spent bending over my books."[124]

So slow and imperceptible is the pace of collective degeneration, so rapid and obvious the development of individual humans from infancy to maturity, that we readily believe in progress and fail to recognize the tell-tale signs of the decrepitude of our species.[125] It is consequently imperative that we travel, if only in thought, with the voyagers who have brought back to Europe descriptions of peoples representing an earlier stage of mankind; it is essential that after visiting savage peoples we raise anchor and set sail again, this time in search of creatures who exemplify an even earlier era in the history of our species, for as Buffon said on occasion and Rousseau consistently held, the passage from natural man to the Hottentot may have taken longer than that from savage to civilized humanity.

We must study the first man, the one preceding the savage, already much too cruel and social to be our originator.

Previously we saw how Rousseau, to avoid the arbitrariness of taking sociability as something innate, emptied human nature of all its traits and then showed how the faculties developed with experience. Where Condillac had spoken of a statue brought to life by sensation, Rousseau spoke of natural man evolving into social humanity. The travel literature afforded Rousseau a chance to cover Condillac's statue with living flesh, the hairy flesh and visage of the most manlike of apes, the orangutan. In a lengthy note appended to the text of the *Second Discourse* Rousseau speculated on the possibility that Buffon's "Varieties of the Human Species" should include a chapter on the orangutan "whose race, dispersed in the woods . . . , had not had an opportunity to develop its potential faculties, . . . and was still found in the primitive state of nature."[126]

Neither the state of comparative anatomy[127] in his day nor the reliability of the travel literature, Rousseau fully realized, was adequate to substantiate his hunch, and he does not claim for it anything more than the status of a hypothesis. One can have little confidence in the reports of sailors, merchants, soldiers, and missionaries; as for philosophers, they travel to Lapland only to prove Newton's law of gravitation,[128] not to observe the mores of peoples utterly unlike Europeans. Hence the view "so often repeated by the philosophical rabble: that men are everywhere the same."[129] Such information as we have on the orangutan, he notes, is far too brief and filtered through prejudices. Yet insofar as we can tell, no animal resembles man more physically; and though much too little is known about the orangutan's way of life, Rousseau speculated with what turns out to be uncanny accuracy that this ape lived peacefully and alone.[130]

About a decade after Rousseau's *Second Discourse* Buffon toyed with the idea that orangutans and humans were related, and went so far as to chastise those who falsely settled the issue by comparing this ape with *l'homme des villes*. "It's beside the savage man . . . that one must place [the ape] to judge one and the other."[131] Nevertheless Buffon wastes little time before retreating to his standard position, that the gap between humans and animals is unbridgeable, his evidence consisting in the fact that even savages speak whereas orangutans are silent.[132] Unnoticed by Buffon, who had conveniently forgotten Rousseau, was the argument in the *Second Discourse* that language is conventional, not natural, a historical acquisition rather than an emanation from a human essence. Buffon's reasons were "weak reasons for those who know that although the organ of speech is natural to man, speech itself is nonetheless not natural to him."[133] Until the orangutan is given the opportunity to speak, we are not entitled to pronounce him a dumb being. What of the speechless child found in the woods in 1694, raised there by animals or by himself? Should he have been locked up in a cage at the zoo? asks Rousseau.[134]

Rousseau ends the *Second Discourse* where he began, with the problem of our lack of self-knowledge. Buffon's explanation, quoted by Rousseau, is the one Voltaire used against Pascal, the empiricist argument that our senses naturally take us away from ourselves and into the world, where they gather the information needed for survival;[135] by our very nature, then, we neither have nor need self-knowledge. Rousseau's alternative formulation, directed to individuals, is that each person is a stranger to himself because, having become social beings, we all live outside ourselves in the eyes of others. There was a time when our senses centered on the natural environment, but now their concern is the social world which denies us a self to know.

Backed by natural history we can go one step further. Just as the individual lacks a self to understand, so does the species lack a human nature. No person remembers when he forfeited his self, nor does the species recall when it placed itself outside nature. We are constituted and defined by our forgotten historical journey, from the original human to the savage, from the savage to the golden age, from the golden age to our present condition. Most of our "progress" has gone hand in hand with the demise of nature, with the upshot that the human animal is now "the tyrant of himself and of nature."[136]

Obviously Rousseau would concede that Turgot was right to depict recorded history as the frenetic movement of a humanity set apart from the rest of lethargic and repetitive nature. But he would add that Turgot failed to appreciate how much mankind was once itself caught up in that lethargy. One mistake breeds another, and so it is that Turgot, who saw change everywhere, foolishly believed that human nature itself stands still. Had Turgot made an effort to understand our unrecorded natural history, he might have realized that our recorded history is one of radical denaturation.

No longer to have a nature is very different from never having had one. To Helvétius, for whom the environment has always been everything and human nature nothing, it is within our power to build a civilization that exacts no pain, loss, or renunciation. Rousseau could not disagree more, unless it be with those organicizers, Buffon, Diderot, Holbach, for whom our nature is always already there, such that to eliminate ascetic morality from society is to remove unhappiness. Rousseau the natural historian keeps company with such later figures as Nietzsche and Freud who acknowledge the inevitablity of our loss of nature but insist we face up to the depths of the miseries that ensue.

System and Antisystem

All the philosophes denounced speculative metaphysics, yet one by one they "anticipated" nature on occasion, in direct violation of Bacon's rules of method. All were empiricists who chose at times to view nature not with their eyes but with what Buffon and Marmontel called "the eyes of the mind."[137] Despite Newton's malediction, the philosophes found a place in science for hypotheses; despite the malediction they themselves pronounced against the "spirit of systems,"[138] the philosophes deliberately used systems as ways to interpret nature. Their goal, to possess a system without being possessed by one, takes on an especially nuanced meaning in the case of Rousseau.

Diderot set forth a system of sorts in *D'Alembert's Dream,* then characteristically modified its import several years later; "the general sensibility of material molecules is just a supposition that draws all its force from the difficulties it removes, which in good philosophy does not suffice."[139] The early *Interpretation of Nature* took its title but only part of its method from Bacon, who would have objected to Diderot's distinction between the observer and the interpreter of natural phenomena.[140] When the senses and instruments meet their limits the observer has finished, Diderot explained, but the interpreter has only begun.[141] Then is imagination temporarily set free to dream its conjectures, each a kind of "system" by which phenomena are linked together in a thought experiment.[142] Eventually these conjectures are checked and brought under control, sometimes by inversion, at other times by allowing them full play, which both brings their shortcomings out into the open and prevents the scientist from prematurely abandoning his research project.[143]

Before the polemical aftermath of the *First Discourse* subsided Rousseau was already referring to his "system,"[144] probably as a way to underscore the earnestness of an argument his critics responded to vigorously but without taking it quite seriously. Throughout his career he continued to maintain that his writings were systematically interrelated,[145] but he vehemently proclaimed himself a man who had "no system to sustain, . . . no furor of party, and who does not aspire to the honor of being chief of a sect."[146] The culminating point of Rousseau's labors in epistemology, beyond which nothing more may be said, was the starting point of Descartes: I think (or feel), therefore I am.[147] No one who knew his Montaigne as thoroughly as Rousseau could be anything other than a skeptic; hence systems were abhorrent to Rousseau, all the more so because he saw a rebirth of the fanatical spirit they engendered in the philosophes, a party indeed, but not of humanity as they declared.[148]

In his reluctance to grant anything to the *esprit de système* Rousseau advanced a position close to Condillac's, whose many restrictions on the proper use of systems ruled out just about everything except Newtonian physics.[149] Specifically, Rousseau the life scientist and master of the genetic method said no to the great debate on the generation of animals. Where is our epistemological warrant for discussions of organic molecules, pansensitive matter, or the supposedly many botched attempts of nature at creating species? he asks.[150] Without the slightest reluctance, Rousseau granted Buffon's point that there may be qualities and powers internal to matter unknown to us but perhaps knowable to a being with senses other than the five that are ours.[151] Nevertheless we must play the hand we have been dealt, and it is far too weak to answer the questions posed by Buffon. Diderot designated the generation of animals "the most incomprehensible mystery of nature,"[152] and then proceeded to spend the rest of his days solving the mystery of life. Rousseau pronounced "the generation of living and organized bodies . . . [the] abyss of the human mind"[153] and devoted his attention to other matters.

When to conjecture, when not—that was the question the philosophes had to answer, since even those most given to epistemological skepticism, d'Alembert and Rousseau, admitted that our vision must sometimes come from the eyes of the mind. D'Alembert scorned the prideful and dangerous doctors who advanced their careers by infecting medicine with dogmatic "systems";[154] still, he admitted, conjecture cannot be ruled out of medical practice when to wait on the evidence is to bury the patient. Similarly, Rousseau complained about the inadequate state of natural history[155] but nevertheless decided to risk a conjectural history of the human species, because when political leaders and philosophers generalize on the basis of what is before their eyes, they rationalize a social and political order that must be condemned.[156] Observation is the best prescription for doctors, thought d'Alembert, best for the imperfect science of medicine and for the patient. Rousseau's position was much the same: "Instead of yielding to the systematic spirit, I grant as little as possible to reasoning and I trust only observation."[157] It was Rousseau's constant cry that observation was both the way to crush systems[158] and to learn how to heal divided souls. "I am an observer, not a moralist."[159]

Disappointed by the absence of an adequate treatise on the art of observation,[160] Rousseau supplied one himself by fits and starts in his writings, beginning with the depiction of an ideal albeit almost inhuman observer. Perfectly suited for social observation by virtue of his dispassionate nature, Rousseau's fictional Wolmar has dedicated his entire life to reading hearts and characters.[161] "I do not like to play a role," Wolmar explains, "but only to see others play theirs. Society to me is agreeable not to be a part of, but to contemplate." Permitted to choose his fate, he would not hesitate to be a "living eye";[162] those who surround him learn that in his present incarnation he already possesses a "penetrating eye"[163] which pierces the depths of their being.

The method of observation would have no chance if it depended on persons as superhuman as Wolmar, born rather than trained to observe. Rousseau was comforted to realize that although he himself was as human, weak, and passionate as Saint-Preux,[164] his deficiencies did not prevent him from being a good observer. In one regard weak Rousseau was similar to strong Wolmar. Both men lived at one time or another in every estate of society, top to bottom, bottom to top, as peasants and servants, as a noble in Wolmar's case and as someone intimate with nobles in Rousseau's. Observation is situational; where we stand, kneel, or bow conditions what we see. Most persons can view the world only through the eyes of their estate; Rousseau and Wolmar, moving up and down the social scale, are able to see society and humanity in the large.[165]

"What would be required in order to observe men well?"[166] Rousseau's answer was that one must know the passions while keeping them at a distance. Unable to be dispassionate by nature, Rousseau believed he had become so as a result of withdrawing from society; his self-imposed isolation had cured him of prejudices and social passions and had allowed him, when viewing society, to distinguish between appearances and realities.[167] According to Saint-Preux, a foreign visitor has special advantages as observer, because his circumstances make him an insider and outsider at the same time.[168] It need hardly be added that Rousseau himself was a resident alien who learned the mores of Paris first-hand without aspiring to the honor of becoming a Parisian.

Age and gender also have a say in who is prepared to observe well. A discerning eye comes naturally to women and can be of service both to them and to their families. Rousseau dwells at some length on his image of the ideal hostess at a dinner party: "Hardly a meaningful gesture is made for which she does not have a ready interpretation, and one almost always in conformity with the truth."[169] Less adept than women at social observation, men can learn to see if trained at the correct moment in the life cycle. Every man is a Wolmar just before puberty—self-sufficient, psychologically strong, with few wants and more than enough power to fulfill them.[170] As puberty dawns there is a brief period preceding the onset of strong passions, when the youngster is ready to be pulled outside of himself but not yet weakened by the need for a sexual partner. This is the time for Emile to be taught how to interpret human action.[171]

The author of the *Encyclopédie* article "Observation" believed the veil could be lifted from nature without affecting "the slightest alteration in the nature of the observed object."[172] Rousseau knew that when human eyes fix upon other persons the "object" does change; a social performance takes place that inevitably leads us to speak of actors on a stage. Emile's tutor takes his charge backstage, so to speak, where the lad sees the actors donning their masks.[173] Any potential observer should be forewarned, Rousseau thought, not only that the person observed is altered by being observed but also that the observer may find himself changed. This is especially true because, as Saint-Preux and Wolmar agree, one must be an actor in order to be a spectator.[174] For Saint-Preux the lesson is more than one in method; finding himself in a Parisian brothel, he elects to adopt the attitude of an observer but wakes up the next morning dissatisfied that he has so faithfully followed the rules of participatory observation.[175]

When Rousseau set about controlling his most audacious conjectures with observation and interpretation of human behavior, he found that the ground had been well prepared for his efforts. Buffon's *Natural History of Man* contains a section on the way the varying passions paint themselves on faces.[176] In his very early *Letter on the Deaf and Dumb* Diderot reported how he stuck his fingers in his ears at the theater to judge how well the actors spoke with their bodies; throughout his life Diderot periodically returned to the theme of reading character through studying gestures, physical appearance, casual conversation, and professional training.[177]

Learning to read faces, gestures, and voices takes time,[178] Rousseau noted. Applying what one has learned takes even longer since no two persons are alike,[179] and character must be studied early, before the child has learned to feign.[180] Our most seemingly insignificant gestures give us away, but only to the interpreter who knows where to look: to the facial muscles, not the eyes, of the baby;[181] to the eyes of an adolescent;[182] to both eyes and mouth when addressing a woman, while understanding that what she says may not be judged by her words alone.[183] The best of tutors will "spy" on his pupil "without letup and without appearing to do so"; normal tutors are spied on by the child, eager to discover the weaknesses of the person charged with curtailing his freedom.[184]

Throughout Rousseau's account of observation his constant claim is that the better we interpret the meaning of human action, the more dissatisfied we are with the maxims and rules of philosophers, which are bound to be wrong because they overgeneralize.[185] In the *Second Discourse* Rousseau reads the "book of nature" to study *"man"*; in his later writings he finds that the "true book of nature is the heart of *men"* (emphasis added).[186] Consequently Rousseau does his utmost to base his own thought and recommendations on specific observations. "My reasonings are founded less on principles than on facts; and I believe I cannot better put you in a position to judge of them than to report to you some example of the observations which suggested them to me."[187] Such is his method in *Emile,* his most comprehensive work.

Intellectual modesty, however essential, is no excuse for running away from the questions we must strive to answer. For the individual and for society the process of healing can only commence if we think both in the small and the large: "society must be studied by means of men, and men by means of society."[188] Just as Wolmar strives to administer a therapy that will "cure" Saint-Preux of his nostalgia,[189] Rousseau offers a therapy for the entire social order in his *Social Contract* and related political works. It should be noted, moreover, that in *Emile* no less than in the *Second Discourse* Rousseau seeks to find qualified travelers to navigate the world—trained observers who will collect information on species of animals and early humans, thus making it possible for someone to write the "history of the human species." In this matter there is only one difference between the earlier and later Rousseau; initially he nominated philosophes to see the varieties of the human species with an unjaundiced eye,[190] but by the time he wrote *Emile* he was convinced that no one was more prejudiced than the philosophes,[191] those self-admittedly partisan thinkers who nevertheless prided themselves on uprooting prejudices. "When the aim is a system of philosophy, the traveler never sees anything but what he wants to see."[192]

Philosophy must be for the individual person, not the person for philosophy. In his book on education Rousseau takes his grand adventures in philosophical history—the *Discourses*—and transforms them into a program of action to save at least one human from social debilitation. Emile shall have what society has denied everyone else, a *natural* history. For the rest of us ontogenesis sadly recapitulates phylogenesis, as each individual inherits the loss of nature that has come to define the human species. Emile, however, will be a man apart, raised to be a natural man in society. All the lessons of philosophical history must be remembered if Emile is to be spared the fate of other humans, which means that Rousseau continued to be a systematic thinker even when he was most insistent upon deflating systems.

Under current circumstances, Rousseau repeatedly warns, nothing can possibly be so unnatural as the education of a natural man.[193] From the moment of birth, therefore, Emile's environment must be completely controlled by the tutor.[194] How strange that Helvétius the determinist and Rousseau the believer in free will should, in this regard, find themselves in agreement. But while Helvétius would choose the character with which to fill the child's empty interior, Rousseau would protect Emile's original nature until the day the young man is able to choose freely the social surroundings he will make his own. The offspring of Helvétius is the child of heteronomy; Rousseau's of autonomy. With the greatest of efforts on the part of the tutor, Emile in the period immediately preceding puberty will be a youngster whose traits exactly parallel those of the original human in the state of nature. After puberty he will be trained to be someone as yet unseen, a natural man living in the midst of society, enjoying its benefits, contributing to its well-being while avoiding its disabilities.

By the time he approaches puberty the normal child, vain, spoiled, selfish, bears not the slightest resemblance to his original progenitor, the creature who once lived in the woods. Emile, by contrast, is a less hairy likeness of his ancestor. "If [Emile] is tired, he stretches out on the earth and sleeps. He sees himself everywhere surrounded by all that is necessary to him." Virtually the same description may be found in the *Second Discourse:* "I see . . . [natural man] quenching his thirst at the first stream, finding his bed at the foot of the same tree that furnished his meal; and therewith his needs are satisfied."[195] Both Emile and the man of nature are indifferent to opinion, strong enough to provide for their few needs, hence self-sufficient. Natural man, however, simply is, whereas Emile is made.

Like the man of nature Emile lives in the present, without a thought about yesterday or tomorrow, his imagination dormant.[196] Physically he is strong, agile, and healthy because he washes in cold water and exercises his limbs vigorously in unrestrained play.[197] Emile's senses, developed by the tutor who trains one organ of sensation to come to the aid of another, are keen like an animal's.[198] Morality was unknown and unnecessary in the presocial state, where natural innocence more than sufficed; and so it is that Emile, a purely physical being in his early years, has no concept of virtue or duty.[199] Whenever discipline is necessary the tutor so arranges matters that the rebuff appears to come "from the thing itself," as a seemingly natural and inevitable consequence of the child's act, never as a punishment or an act of human will.[200] Unlike other humans, Emile is not a domesticated animal. His will has not been broken.

"There is a great difference between the natural man living in the state of nature and the natural man living in the state of society."[201] Destined for society, Emile must be taught those very arts and sciences that philosophical history designated as central to our downfall. Emile's tutor knows that the learning within the reach of everyone is of incomparably greater significance than the learning limited to the few; he also realizes that in society knowledge is nevertheless prized only as a means of fostering the inequality of distinctions.[202] Therefore Emile's education will consist in learning for personal physical use or to satisfy natural curiosity, never to show himself off to others.[203] All his education may be summed up in the example of his determination to learn astronomy so that he can find his way through the woods.[204] A perfectible animal, Emile comes to know infinitely more about nature than did man in the state of nature, but he continues to be like natural man in that both have self-contained selves.

Inevitably Emile, as he comes into contact with other persons, will be

tempted to seek their applause. Therefore the tutor takes the scientifically
adept boy to a country fair and permits him to win the crowd's approval
by revealing the trick of a conjuror. The next day the "proud little natu-
ralist" returns to the scene of his triumph and is publicly humiliated by
the performer, who on the advice of the tutor has resorted to the use of
a magnet, about which Emile is ignorant. Every time scientific knowledge
and vanity begin to fuse the tutor repeats, under different guises, the
adventure with the magician.[205] It may be that Emile must compete with
and outdo someone; if so, let it be himself, let him strive to outdo his
previous performances in a skill or art.[206]

For better and for worse the post-pubescent Emile is no longer a self-
contained being. Sexual yearnings awaken his imagination; incomplete,
longing for he knows not what, Emile recognizes his vulnerability and is
ready to identify with and feel pity for those who suffer. Commiseration
is naturally given but largely irrelevant to isolated natural man. The dis-
persion of population, more than natural pity or goodness, is responsible
for the peace of the golden age, wherein the arousal of glorious passions
is also the awakening of jealousy.[207] Emile must be trained at the critical
moment of the life cycle to feel pity, because before long society will do
its utmost to override his most worthy sentiments. "Adolescence is not
the age of vengeance or hate; it is that of commiseration."[208] The tutor,
by exposing Emile to the sight of human suffering, develops the lad's
natural capacity for pity, after which he makes certain the young man
learns to abstract from the particular case to humanity. "To prevent pity
from degenerating into weakness, it must be generalized and extended to
the whole of mankind."[209] It was pity, not uncontrollable passion, that led
to Julie's fall.[210]

Emile can only settle down with a wife and remain a natural man if she
is a natural woman, as opposed to a socially created person. Woman
threatens man's autonomy no less than he threatens hers; she is dominated
by men's laws but dominates men with her feminine ruses.[211] The segregation of the sexes is Rousseau's solution, separation by mores and way
of life. Anything and everything must be done to accentuate distinctions
of gender because society is busily confounding the sexes; Parisian men,
spending all their time in the circles of women, are becoming female, just
as women aspire to become male.[212] Helvétius and Diderot wanted more
sex, Rousseau more gender, without which our uncertainties as to who
we are grow from disturbing to overwhelming proportions. Even a caste

system is preferable to a world in which no one has a place, Rousseau maintained.[213] Knowing who one is begins with assurance as to what is male and female, no matter that distinctions of gender are social constructs as well as natural givens.

Marriage based not on the largely social institution of romantic love but on companionship completes Emile's natural history. Love does not last long and undermines our autonomy throughout its brief duration. A successful marital union lasts a lifetime and is a message to everyone that humans can sometimes mutually fulfill one another.[214] Each couple has an opportunity to show that nature and society can be one, provided man and woman join together, as Emile and Sophie do, in shutting out the larger social order.

How could Rousseau, for all his skepticism, not have a "system"? So systemic is the problem of the human race that only a comprehensive solution can be of significance. The debate over the generation of animals transgresses the intellectual limitations of mere humans and is pointless to all but those interested in sustaining atheism. By contrast, the debate over human degeneration and possibilities of regeneration does have a point. Imagine a person such as Emile, "the same in a group as when alone";[215] one such person proves that the educational program derived from the joint venture of observation and philosophical history can overcome the degenerative history of the human species.

Matter and Antimatter

No one denounced materialism as a "system" more bitterly than Rousseau; no one made better use than he of materialism as a program of action. Although he abandoned the book tentatively entitled *La Morale sensitive* or *Le Matérialisme du sage*,[216] Rousseau inserted illustrations of his intent in works such as *Julie* and *Emile*. Though *of* the sage, Rousseau's materialism was *for* the many, for them one by one as protection against contamination by contemporary society, for one and all as a way to strengthen a regenerative political order, should it ever materialize.

Whereas most materialism threatens to destroy the very notion of personal autonomy, Rousseau's aims to restore us to ourselves. Why do we so often act "unlike ourselves"; is it not, he suggests, due to the "impression which external objects have previously made upon us, and because we, continually modified by our senses and bodily organs, unknowingly exhibit the effects of these modifications in our ideas, feelings, and even in our actions?" High in the mountains Saint-Preux discovers that "a pleasing climate causes the passions, which elsewhere constitute man's torment, to contribute to his happiness. I doubt whether any violent agitation . . . could withstand a prolonged stay in the mountains, and I am surprised that baths of salutary and beneficial mountain air are not one of the great remedies of medicine and morality." Rousseau generalizes Saint-Preux's passing comments in the *Confessions:* "Different climates, seasons, sounds, colors, darkness, light, the elements, food, noise, silence, movements, repose—all effect the bodily machine, and hence the mind." With the help of a sensitive materialism, it is possible to "place the mind in the condition most favorable to virtue" and thus to "compel the animal economy to support the moral order."[217]

One after another the French materialists boldly announced that "the word liberty is void of sense,"[218] and then found themselves engaged in floundering efforts to save the notion of moral responsibility. A believer in freedom from the start, Rousseau came to appreciate materialism for its insights into the sources of our unfreedom, insights which could be converted into a program to reclaim the lost freedom that—in conjunction with perfectibility—distinguishes humans from animals.[219]

Condillac's device of the statue gradually brought to life by outside stimuli served the philosophes well when they were out to disprove innate religious ideas, Rousseau well when he was out to disprove the philosophes' idea of innate sociability. To embrace Condillac's research program, however, was not to commend his *Treatise on Sensations* as a complete philosophy, especially not after Helvétius took Condillac's endpoint, an externally constructed human, and made it the starting point of his notorious *De l'Esprit* wherein the environment is the entire person. If nothing else Helvétius did clarify the question Rousseau had to answer: how can a disciple of Locke conjure up a "will" strong enough to make autonomy possible?

All the manifestations of will, to Condillac, stem from a desire to re-experience pleasurable and avoid painful sensations; through experience, he held, desire yields love and hate, hope and fear, and all the passions. So much is will regarded as an effect in this scenario that it is anyone's guess as to how it can ever be a cause. Rousseau the Lockean therefore beat a hasty retreat to Malebranche, whether directly or through the good graces of the Oratorian Father Lamy, voraciously read and appreciated by the youthful Jean-Jacques.[220] There was much in Malebranche to Rousseau's liking: a Christianity that downplayed sin, posited an inner light not unlike natural goodness, and accepted the legitimacy of the human quest for pleasure;[221] in Malebranche there were the specific claims Rousseau repeated, that inventors of systems were solely concerned to promote their reputations; and that women are ideally suited to preside over matters of taste but not to grapple with abstract truths.[222] Most of all, Rousseau could find in Malebranche a recognition the philosophes of his day lacked, namely, that consent to truth is an act not of the understanding but of the will.[223] Saint-Preux knows Julie de Wolmar is no longer Julie d'Etange, the woman once his. He is a well-educated, enlightened man, a philosopher; he knows, but his knowledge is of no use to him because his will is weak. With Malebranche in mind Rousseau could search for a way to turn Locke into a philosopher whose sensationalism supports the development of a firm will.

Oratorian education aimed to regulate the will by developing precise judgment.[224] Although this objective could be pursued through formal studies in the sciences, Malebranche made clear that it should begin in earliest childhood with proper attention paid to the use of the senses. It was his contention, faithfully repeated by Rousseau, that error stems not from the senses but from judgment.[225] Few themes recur so frequently in *Emile* as that of training the senses to judge correctly;[226] however Lockean on the surface, Rousseau's concern was to train the boy's will. It is telling that the first objection Rousseau made to *De l'Esprit* was on the grounds that Helvétius had reduced active judgment to passive sensation.[227] Morality no less than epistemology is at issue, for if our judgment is passive we cannot will and are nothing. By the time he wrote *Emile* Rousseau was ready to state his position in a more positive voice: when the educator activates the pupil's judgment, the young man's will becomes self-caused rather than determined by outside forces.[228]

A weak will is willful, capricious, arbitrary; it accedes to every compulsion of *amour-propre* and debases our reason into the tool of selfishness. Because Emile has a strong will he knows when to will, when not; accepting the findings of his well-trained judgment, which is all our senses working effectively together,[229] Emile never wills what is outside his power. His strong body, able to withstand whatever the natural environment sends his way, saves his soul from many physically induced torments; his purely physical, antisocial education saves his will from contamination by *amour-propre*. When at last he enters into social and moral relations he possesses a regulated will, prepared years in advance by his education in sensual judgment.[230]

In typical empiricist fashion Rousseau understands reason as the comparison of sensations, or sees it as the composite of all the mental faculties.[231] But what is it the child compares? Not primarily objects, as the philosophers think, but rather himself with other persons, with the result that the combined workings of his mind produce a divided person, neither natural nor social, neither for himself nor for others. Emile, however, is whole; whole because he is removed from society, his judgment and reason brought to fruition before he enters into social relationships, his imagination suppressed as long as possible, so that no sensation reaches him before his judgment is there, ready to evaluate it. Rousseau's young man has the will to be his own person or, under the right conditions, the will to sign a social contract and abide by its terms.

Knowledge is virtue, the philosophes maintained, but Rousseau had trouble understanding how they arrived at their conclusion.[232] First, they repeated Condillac in denying reason a capacity for autonomous action; then, even so innovative a thinker as Diderot dusted off the time-honored notions of natural law and "right reason" in order to hang on to his idol of virtue.[233] Rousseau responded, in effect, with the contention that reason can never be "right" unless the will is "upright," as is true of the general will.[234] Civic rituals, in collectivizing *amour-propre,* free each citizen to will the public good. The same end is achieved by the opposite strategy of forbidding citizens to communicate with one another before voting.[235] Both techniques, isolation from subgroups and identification with the collectivity, free the will from the compulsions of *amour-propre.*

In the absence of a republic, what means does Emile have to force himself to remain free when he enters society? Even a reason such as his, healthy because divorced from *amour-propre,* will not be strong enough to sustain him in his precarious new condition. Rousseau visualized one plausible solution. Let the passions that enter into partnership with reason be such as come from within, as opposed to the passions of *amour-propre,* those hostile intruders from without. Then Emile may find the strength to will the good. According to Rousseau the active principle missing from Condillac's statue is present in humans in the form of sensibility. When the environment pushes in, we push back. Inherent sensibility shapes the senses as much as the senses shape sensibility.[236]

To make his case Rousseau called upon two topics dear to him, music and the uses of observation. Listening to music, Rousseau contended, is one of the best ways to refute materialism. Speak endlessly about nerves, vibrations, air; bring to bear the most brilliant discussions of physiology, and you still will not have begun to explain the power of music. "It is not so much the ear that conveys pleasure to the heart as the heart that conveys it to the ear." Whoever wants to write a treatise on the sensations must "distinguish between exclusively sensory impressions and the intellectual and moral impressions which we receive by way of the senses but of which the senses are merely the occasional causes." Always objectionable, the "systematizing spirit" is especially pernicious when it takes the form of an effort "to materialize all the operations of the soul"; neither morality nor music can survive such fanaticism.[237]

Observation is a second way Rousseau made his argument for re-filling human nature, after initially emptying it in the manner of Condillac. On one occasion Rousseau saw a nurse attempt to silence a baby by striking it; for a moment the child was quiet but only because overcome by the rage to which he soon gave unforgettable voice. "All the signs of the resentment, fury, and despair of his age were in his accents ... If I had doubted that the sentiment of the just and the unjust were innate in the heart of man, this example alone would have convinced me."[238] In his early writings Rousseau outdid the philosophes in searching for the external sources of everything in the mind; in his later works he blamed them for construing conscience as an acquisition. Determined to dramatize his break with the philosophes, he dared utter that most dreaded of nouns, "instinct"; and, as if to maximize the outrage, simultaneously invoked the most forbidden of adjectives: conscience is a "divine instinct."[239]

All the conscience and internal sensibility in the world are unlikely to be enough, however, unless we situate ourselves or are situated by someone else in a worldly condition that reaffirms good will. No sooner, therefore, has Rousseau crushed materialism as a philosophy than he turns it into a program of action. The most effective of all medicines—and the kind with the fewest side effects—is preventative; "for it is unquestionably more difficult ... to resist desires already fully formed, ... than it is to prevent, change, or modify these same desires at the fountainhead."[240] Before entering society Emile has no vices to overcome and no need of virtue; his untainted natural goodness was perfectly adequate in his presocial condition. Once virtue becomes necessary to cut out corruption, it causes fewest scars when imposed upon everyone. The great advantage of living in a republican polity is that moral and physical causes—symbols, rituals, and circumstances—combine forces to force us to be free, to will our good as part of the public good.

Madame d'Houdetot, an aristocratic lady, is neither the natural woman of *Emile* nor a citizen. For her moral renewal and regeneration there is no better treatment, thought Rousseau, than periodic withdrawal to the countryside where, away from *le monde,* she can retreat to the inner citadel and rediscover the innate sentiments that are the foundation of our moral being. Upon her return to Paris she will be better positioned to fend off urban temptations and to exercise her will.[241]

Saint-Preux's malady would be incurable, were it not that Wolmar, the greatest of all therapists, decides to try his skills on so difficult a case. A good man, Saint-Preux has been destroyed by the social prejudice which forbids the marriage of a commoner to a noble. Condemned to yearn forever for the woman once his but whom he shall never again embrace, he is dissuaded with difficulty from suicide. Usually love is the illusion that one man or woman is distinctly superior to all other persons of his or her sex; Julie, as Saint-Preux realizes, is the illusion become truth. After her there cannot be another woman. Under the watchful and all-seeing eye of Wolmar, the young man—against all odds—is "cured"[242] of his seemingly terminal malady.

Wolmar's treatment of Saint-Preux is not only a remarkable example of the "materialism of the sage"; it also affords us an excellent opportunity to underscore the profound differences among the materialisms of three different authors, Rousseau, Helvétius, and Diderot, each of whom works the significance of the past into his account in a distinctive manner. History is unimportant in Diderot's thoughts on nature and human nature. Perpetually nature begins and ends, allowing no history to take place; human nature, too, is largely ahistorical: for although "the Tahitian is close to the origin of the world and the European close to its old age,"[243] Diderot's natives are not very different from the inhabitants of the old world, just less sexually inhibited. For Helvétius, a strict environmental determinist, the past does matter. It is important in the sense that we are our past and nothing more; our previous experiences have filled our once empty and forever passive being.

Saint-Preux's history is all important, not because it defines him but because he remembers it, and lacks the will to stop living in the past. The materialism of the sage Wolmar frees Saint-Preux's will from the compulsion to continue chasing after what is lost and gone. Never to see Julie again would confirm Saint-Preux forever in his enslavement to her memory; he must therefore be placed in her presence but under conditions that force the passionate man to see a mother and wife in the woman once his lover.[244] Every physical landmark of their passion must be revisited, desanctified, "profaned,"[245] until what was extraordinary is such no more.

For individuals as for states, virtue is sometimes restored by a sudden revolutionary eruption that destroys the past. Politically, Rome after the Tarquins, Sparta at the time of Lycurgus, and Holland and Switzerland after their wars of liberation offer examples. On a personal level, Julie credits some such upheaval on the day of her marriage[246] with her determination to be a model wife for Wolmar, the man she does not love. The crisis that breaks the hold of the past on Saint-Preux's psyche is precipitated by a visit to a place where he sees the many physical emblems of his love that he carved in the rocks years ago. At first he longs for death but soon correctly reckons himself cured of his malady by the very violence of his catharsis.[247] Henceforth he shall live in the present and actively will the new situation in which he finds himself. So confident is Wolmar in the young man that he charges Saint-Preux with the responsibility of educating Julie's children.[248]

Both Diderot's Tahitians and Helvétius' Spartans are robust, healthy, and happy because they enjoy the gratifications of carnal desire. It is high time, Diderot believed, that we stop "attaching moral values to certain physical acts which carry no such implications."[249] Morality will lose nothing, and we shall gain in well-being, from the frank admission that "there is a bit of testicle at the bottom of our most sublime sentiments and purified tenderness."[250]

Rousseau's position on sexuality sets out from Buffon's passing comment that only the physical in love is good,[251] and builds to the conclusion that society has so radically altered natural sexual drives that physical and quantitative solutions do not even begin to address the sources of our unhappiness. For natural man any woman is good on a given night; for Saint-Preux all the women in the world would not compensate for the loss of Julie. In milder form the same malady besets everyone; from the moment we enter society we seek the inequality of rank-ordering, not least in our sexual preferences.

The contrast between Rousseau and the French materialists on sexual matters illustrates their overall differences. "Properly speaking," wrote Diderot, "there is only one kind of cause, physical causes."[252] Therein, to Rousseau's way of thinking, lay the crux of the failure of the materialists. One need not be moralistic to recognize that "moral causes" are as important as their physical counterparts. Memory, imagination, reason; gestures, signs, symbols, language; art, literature, music, religion—all these are social artifacts. Not one belongs to the original state of nature. The environment that overwhelms the individual is partly physical and given, but the other part is constructed by humans themselves who then lose control over and are themselves controlled by what they have created. Strict materialism is right to believe that we are unfree, wrong to cite nature when it is we ourselves who are the authors of our unfreedom. Culture may be our glory but it is even more our enslavement.

Condillac's *Treatise on the Sensations* was a triumph for his analytical method, but his book inadvertently prepared the way for the narrow materialism of Helvétius. Rousseau's genetic method uncovered both our attachments to nature and our flight from her; the so-called second nature we have superimposed on the first has suffocated our original nature. Society is the source of many of our physical and all our psychological maladies. More sex will not revitalize Saint-Preux, whose problem extends beyond the needs of nature; only his "restoration" to himself can cure him. Most of us have no Wolmar to turn to, and are thus fated never to return to ourselves. Less a material than something bordering on a social determinism is what makes us act "unlike ourselves."

Significantly, Rousseau speaks less about freedom than about the need to "capture the will." The tutor must capture Emile's will, the magistrate capture the will of the citizens, the Wolmars capture the wills of their servants and peasants.[253] This theme of capturing the will may initially sound peculiar coming from someone who posits free will against the determinists of his day. Yet it is just another formulation of his notorious proclamation that we must be forced to be free. Autonomy is not what we desire, but with the right conditioning we can learn to live without a master. "Liberty consists less in acting according to one's will than in not being subjected to the will of another."[254]

In no way am I diminished when asked to abide by a law with which I disagree but which is procedurally the expression of the general will. To obey such a law is much like the boy Emile's submission to the law of natural necessity,[255] under which pretext the tutor hides many items that are in truth social rather than natural. Strange as it may sound, submission to necessity strengthens the will because it protects us from feeling dependent on the wills of others. Dependence on things exacts no psychological price, nor does dependence on a faceless general will, which is the human equivalent of a "thing."

If only materialistic determinism were true our lot might be much happier; in its absence we must invent the functional equivalent thereof, which is submission to the general will. Near the end of *Emile,* at the precise moment when we expect Rousseau to throw away the pretext of necessity, the tutor surprises us with the opposite maneuver: "Extend the law of necessity to moral things," he urges young man Emile.[256] Although natural man, Emile, and the citizens of Rousseau's republic do not know what a Stoic is, theirs is a resignation to necessity any Stoic might admire. Citizens and natural men living in society can learn to will the necessity that for the original natural man simply is. It must be remembered that the *Social Contract* attempts to legitimize our "chains," not to remove them.[257]

The Ideal Materialist

Rousseau's materialism places him at the heart of the French Enlightenment, not with its most famous materialists, La Mettrie, Holbach, and Diderot, however, but with thinkers such as d'Alembert and Voltaire who love to point out that what we eat in the morning has a direct bearing on how we think in the evening. When healthy, Voltaire could brush Pascal aside; when sick, the smiling skeptic repeatedly felt tormented by the sublime misanthrope.[258] Rousseau agreed with Voltaire that "we do not understand either mind or body," much less the exact nature of the link between the two.[259] The one indisputable fact is that the link is intimate; the one reasonable inference, that all philosophy must begin with the human body, its care and treatment.

Diderot was the greatest materialist of the age, Holbach the most strident, Helvétius and La Mettrie the most notorious, but not one of them was a successful materialist during his lifetime, and taken together they did not succeed in making materialism an influential part of the French Enlightenment. It may well be that whatever popularity materialist modes of thought attained in the eighteenth century owes more to Rousseau than to any of the recognized materialists.

Unlike Diderot, whose greatest works were not published until long after his death, Rousseau fed his materialism to the public in two best sellers, *Julie* and *Emile*. In the pages of books the French could not wait to read, Rousseau inserted extensive commentary on the best ways to secure physical and hence mental health. Hygiene, fresh air, exercise, and diet figure prominently in his prescriptions.[260] Chemistry, ever the science most called upon to attend to practical needs, was used by Rousseau to detect tainted wines and to examine the composition of foods.[261] Like La Mettrie, Rousseau warned the public against eating too much meat, a substance unhealthy not just to the body but to character. How gentle in truth can the English be, Rousseau inquires, a people that consumes so much roast beef?[262] All overeating, he adds, is a social disease, since peasants surrounded by foodstuffs never eat beyond their needs.[263] The easiest way to learn what to eat is to examine the diet of peasants, closer to nature than the rest of us.[264] The peasant way of life, in general, is worth studying to discover how to make body and mind function harmoniously. Emile "works like a peasant and thinks like a philosopher."[265]

It was unfortunate for the materialist cause that Diderot did not publish his best works, and possibly even more harmful that the works of Holbach, La Mettrie, and Helvétius did appear in print. The anonymous works of the baron forced the public to choose between Catholicism and ardent atheism, hardly the most likely road to success. To make matters worse Holbach set forth a "system of nature," leading Galiani, an enlightened skeptic, to remark that "at bottom, we do not know nature well enough to form its system."[266] Rousseau's advocacy of materialist proposals appeared in works that allowed the public to have its deism and eat it, too; and he made no pretense to setting forth a system of materialism in defiance of the epistemological ban on such grandiose endeavors. When it came to a practical program, Holbach's books were as lean in content as they were fat in bulk, and they fare poorly in comparison with the many specific recommendations sprinkled throughout Rousseau's writings.

There are strong indications that the materialists hesitated to advocate their strongest intellectual position, not so much from faintness of heart as from fear of compromising the Enlightenment. Under close scrutiny by the Church and its journalistic allies, both Diderot and Holbach frequently bracketed off their materialism and substituted high-blown idealistic tracts for intellectually more gratifying explorations of linkages between materialism and morals. Holbach's *La Morale universelle,* a treatise on "the duties of man founded on his nature," provides a striking example. The author is concerned in the preface to assure his readers that they need not worry whether materialism or dualism is true; "to know what man must do in society it is not necessary to go back so far."[267]

Segregation of essays on morals and politics from those on materialism was one way Diderot and Holbach sought respectability and influence at the expense of their materialistic program. A second tactic was to moralize excessively, especially though not exclusively when the mask of anonymity was dropped. "There is in the heart of man a taste for order more ancient than any reflective sentiment"—words from *Le Fils naturel* that Diderot borrowed, almost word for word, from Malebranche's *Traité de morale.*[268] Much the same formula was employed by Holbach, even though he enjoyed the protection of anonymity.[269] Add the many references in Diderot and Holbach to "right reason," their vindication of natural law, their eulogies of the duties that inhere in each station, their hymns to the family, and the result is the most idealistic materialism imaginable.

What has happened? In a word or, rather, in two names, Helvétius and La Mettrie. The black sheep of the French Enlightenment, Helvétius and La Mettrie embarrassed their materialistic brethren, forced them to go underground or to stay out of print, and gave Diderot and Holbach compelling reasons to up the idealistic ante. It was one thing for Diderot to play with the notion of free sexuality in a work he kept to himself and quite another for Helvétius to publish a book advocating a platonic community of wives for republican heroes whose lovemaking was anything but platonic.[270] How appalling, thought Diderot, that one book should both reduce materialism to a small-minded environmental determinism and vindicate the standard caricature of materialist ethics.

Diderot excoriated La Mettrie as "dissolute, impudent, a buffoon," a scandal to philosophy even in his materialistic death, brought on by over-indulging his taste for fine food.[271] Judging by such a vituperative litany, one would never know that Diderot's biological materialism owed much to the author of *L'Homme machine.* Against the passive human nature postulated by Helvétius, Rousseau asserted the claims of the "will" and internal sentiment, which push back when the external world impinges on the organism. To Diderot and earlier to La Mettrie it is bodily instincts, temperament, and hereditary dispositions that fend off the surrounding world; working with a physiological psychology, they were feeling their way to the conception—in the terminology of a later age—of the body as a self-adapting biochemical machine.[272]

Occasional echoes of La Mettrie's ethics may be detected in Diderot, as when the Nephew blames his perversity on the lack of a certain "fiber"[273] in his organic constitution—an adaptation of La Mettrie's earlier comment that "a tiny fiber could have made idiots of Erasmus and Fontenelle."[274] La Mettrie also stands behind Diderot's growing doubt that criminals can be rehabilitated.[275] As the Nephew and La Mettrie know, we are what we are and can never be otherwise, because our constitution defines our being.[276]

Indebted to La Mettrie, Diderot ungratefully denounces his predecessor to the world as the "apologist of vice and detractor of virtue."[277] More than anything else Diderot and Holbach condemned La Mettrie for showing the uselessness of guilt, which weighs heavily only on those who least need it.[278] Without the sanctions provided by guilt, Diderot and Holbach were in an ethical quandary; constantly repeating the standard materialistic argument that excess destroys the bodily machine, they could never overcome Buffon's observation that longevity correlates poorly with lifestyle.[279] Hence Diderot and Holbach buried their materialism under prophecies of guilt and a mound of moralizing: virtue and more virtue, followed by yet another installment of virtue. The most materialistic philosophes spoke the most idealistic language.

Diderot and Holbach were idealistic materialists, Rousseau the ideal materialist. Free from the burdens of the official materialists, he could interpolate strategies for promoting the health of the body in texts dealing with love, natural goodness, breast-feeding, and the reinvigoration of the family. Readers of *Emile* learned how to attend to the body without becoming dependent on doctors;[280] they also learned how to avoid the dependency that comes with ordering servants to attend to one's material needs: Emile will shop for his own groceries.[281] A strong "will" in a strong body is the greatest of blessings; it is the fulfillment of Rousseau's version of enlightened materialism.

CHAPTER SIX

Judging Jean-Jacques

THUS far we have tried to determine how Rousseau criticized the philosophes. Now it is time to ask how the philosophes criticized Rousseau. Up to this point it has been my objective to show that two benefits accrue when Rousseau is wrested from the romantics and restored to the Enlightenment: the first is the recovery of his intended meaning, the second the recovery of the autocritique of Enlightenment. In one sense the present chapter will work at cross-purposes with all my preceding efforts, for it is doubtful that anything can be learned about Rousseau's thought from reading the attacks unleashed by the philosophes. Rather than criticize his works they excoriated the man and invited the public to sit with them as they passed judgment, not on the writings of Rousseau, but on the person of Jean-Jacques. On trial, Rousseau did not have to be insane to compose a work entitled *Rousseau juge de Jean-Jacques* during his final years; better to place himself before the public as the accused than to be denied a chance to conduct his defense.

The immediate outcome of the conflict between Rousseau and the philosophes was the initiation of the literature of sincerity and authenticity[1] that has absolutely nothing to do with Voltaire, the man most representative of the age, and everything to do with the literature of the nineteenth century and beyond. Accused of insincerity, Rousseau responded with his confessional writings, which set the pattern for authors of the future and forever altered the relationship between writer and public. Arguably the debate between Rousseau and the philosophes marks both the intellectual culmination of the Enlightenment and the initial moment of transition to the succeeding age of romanticism. One need not be enamored of dialectics to recognize a historical basis for the claim that there is a "dialectic of Enlightenment."[2]

Dialogue or Two Monologues?

Less a dialogue than two monologues emerged during the protracted disagreement between Rousseau and the philosophes, which began politely enough but degenerated into a full-scale war. Rousseau questioned the beliefs and aspirations of his fellow encyclopedists in his earliest works; he initiated what might have been a fascinating and momentous exchange of ideas. When they refused him an intellectual answer his tone changed and so did theirs. From then on each side spoke *of* but not *to* the other; it was the public they addressed, cajoling readers to take sides, either with Rousseau or with his former comrades. A partisan debate ensued, the first of its kind, not between the hired pens of political factions but within the ranks of self-proclaimed independent writers, who regarded the newly arrived reading public both as the witness to their conflict and as the prize awaiting the victor.

On the surface it would seem that every prerequisite of a dialogue was present when Rousseau began to question the conception of enlightenment upheld by the philosophes. As an insider of the philosophical movement, Rousseau spoke the language of his fellow encyclopedists; he shared their antipathy to Catholicism, introduced Diderot to Condillac and to Grimm, joined with his fellow philosophes in viewing Locke as the starting point of any meaningful work in philosophy, and built his initial reputation on two essays written in the familiar genre of philosophical history, the *First and Second Discourses*. Surely with credentials such as his he deserved an answer.

Initially the philosophes pursued a policy of containment in their response to Rousseau's two discourses, which had proved disturbingly successful in arousing the interest of the reading public. As long as Rousseau remained a member of their party, they had little to gain and much to lose by attacking his *Discourse on the Sciences and Arts*. The rule of rules was to maintain unity within their ranks—to keep the "brothers" together despite the notorious propensity of writers to destroy one another and to discredit their calling through petty in-fighting. In any case the storm of controversy sparked by Rousseau's denial that learning enhances morality presumably allowed the philosophes to remain aloof; other writers would refute Rousseau without the encyclopedists' entering the fray.

With the first volume of the *Encyclopédie* about to appear, d'Alembert was faced in the *Preliminary Discourse* with the ticklish problem of how best to handle Rousseau, a contributor who had placed himself on record as opposing everything represented by the great undertaking in collective publication. Adept as always, d'Alembert praised the "eloquent and philosophical writer who has accused the sciences and arts of corrupting human mores." After congratulating the author of the prize-winning essay, d'Alembert noted with satisfaction that "the worthy man of whom we speak seems himself to have given suffrage to our work by the zeal and the success of his collaboration on it." The famous mathematician then minimized the import of Rousseau's main argument by pointing to the difficulties of assigning causal weights when explaining complex historical phenomena.[3] On any reasonable account corruption has many causes, most of which are only tangentially related to learning.

D'Alembert's was the official rejoinder to Rousseau. Off the record Diderot was happy to encourage Jean-Jacques, his best friend, to give free vent to what appeared to be a rhetorical strategy to win a contest, or at worst was no more than a passing fancy for an extravagant position. Ever open to intellectual paradox, convinced of Rousseau's loyalty to philosophical ideals, Diderot saw nothing to fear in a harmless *jeu d'esprit*.[4] Grimm, however, regarded Rousseau as a threat from the start, especially since Rousseau repeatedly affirmed in the *Preface to Narcisse* (1752–53) that he meant every word of the *First Discourse*. For all practical purposes Grimm was free to speak his mind in his *Correspondance littéraire*, addressed at any given moment to a non-French audience of no more than fifteen princes and potentates, mostly German. How unfortunate, Grimm lamented, that no worthy adversary had bothered to refute "so dangerous an enemy." At this early stage, before the other philosophes were willing to acknowledge a conflict, Grimm was already exercising what would prove to be his favorite verb whenever dealing with Rousseau, *outrer*, which served to place Jean-Jacques beyond the pale of respectable opinion. The only compliment he paid Rousseau was to admit that the *First Discourse* was eloquently written; each time another of Rousseau's works appeared Grimm immediately singled out its eloquence for praise, always with the transparent objective of encouraging the reader to conclude that the writings of Jean-Jacques were all style and no substance.[5]

What the *Correspondance littéraire* did not tell its readers was as revealing as the ground it covered. Grimm, who coveted the title of baron, neglected to inform his princely audience that Rousseau had, in the *Preface to Narcisse*, suggested that the vices denounced in the *First Discourse* "belong not so much to man as to man badly governed."[6] As the ever more successful courtier, at first of lesser royalty, later of Catherine the Great, Grimm omitted the political and republican dimension of Rousseau's argument.

Presumably those philosophes who, as time passed, became increasingly sympathetic to republican thought might have come to appreciate the *Discourse on the Sciences and the Arts.* Many years later, some philosophes did in fact find themselves advocating positions paralleling Rousseau's earliest findings; but by then the break between philosophes and ex-philosophe had so hardened that it was impermissible to recognize an intellectual debt to the man who had abandoned the movement and whose republic, like Savonarola's, would burn all the vanities, especially every hint of high French culture.

D'Alembert's case is particularly striking. Like Tacitus, his hero, he was unable to believe a republic possible, but equally unable to refrain from regretting its absence. He ended the *Preliminary Discourse* with the political and perhaps self-deprecatory remark that "there should be more orators, historians, and philosophers in a republic and more poets, theologians, and geometers in a monarchy."[7] Continuing along these lines of thought he argued in the *Elements of Philosophy* that abstract and speculative studies, presumably including mathematics, were inappropriate for citizens but fitting in a monarchy where the government obliges subjects "to remain useless and to seek to sweeten their idleness with occupations that have no consequences."[8]

Never was d'Alembert willing to join his friend Voltaire in apologizing for luxury, "the scourge of republics and the instrument of despotism." Yet he does sanction the luxurious "arts of agreement," because in certain states they can "occupy a great number of idle subjects, and prevent them from rendering their idleness harmful."[9] Precisely this same contention, in virtually identical words, had been used by Rousseau in the *Preface to Narcisse* to explain why he continued to write after denouncing the arts;[10] within recent memory, moreover, d'Alembert had read in Rousseau's letter on the theater that the arts were appropriate for monarchies. In spite of himself d'Alembert was now in agreement with and perhaps intellectually indebted to Rousseau, whom he nevertheless refused to name. Usually so generous, d'Alembert could not give credit to the man whose life was devoted to discrediting the philosophical party.

Similarly, when Holbach in the 1770s cited the literary glories of the ages of Alexander, Augustus, and Louis XIV as proofs that tyrants use the arts to throw garlands of flowers over our chains, he was merely replaying, some twenty-three years after the fact, Rousseau's refutation of the philosophical history of Voltaire. Nevertheless the baron does not name either of the two authors who are so obviously on his mind: Voltaire is unmentioned because it would not do to disagree fundamentally and in public with the most famous philosophe; Rousseau unmentioned because he was unmentionable. Lest anyone recall the source of his argument, the baron hastens in a contemporaneous work to denounce Rousseau by name for supposedly demeaning science in the *First Discourse*.[11]

Philosophical responses to the *Second Discourse* demonstrate what the philosophes themselves frequently stated: that the author who questions the fundamental assumptions of his time must expect to be misunderstood.[12] So it was with Rousseau's denial that sociability should be regarded as an irreducible given. Reared on Cicero by Jesuits, the philosophes took for granted the classical view that society, cities, and civilization set the boundary between humans and animals. Why should they give a second thought to a doctrine congenial to all they stood for, especially their hatred of the monastery and their determination to find fulfillment in social life? To them the state of nature was always the most expendable part of the literature on natural rights; d'Holbach spoke against Rousseau and for all his comrades when he proclaimed, "What is called the state of nature would be a state contrary to nature."[13] Not the pact of association, the social contract, but the pact of submission—the governmental contract—was the initial concern of the philosophes, later supplanted by the Lockean notion of government as a popular trust. Their state of nature was a juridical concept if it was anything at all.

Grimm applauded Rousseau's argument that when Hobbes and Pufendorf spoke of the presocial state, they invariably read social traits into the natural condition.[14] It was Grimm again who, following publication of the *First Discourse,* suggested that its author could profit from reading Buffon's *Discourse on the Nature of Animals,*[15] which is precisely what Rousseau set about doing before writing the *Second Discourse.* Ideally prepared to appreciate Rousseau's argument, Grimm elected to ignore Rousseau's recourse to Buffon, and prematurely and peremptorily announced that "it is by instinct that man speaks, thinks, and seeks society." Slightly embarrassed, he admitted "this instinct explains nothing,"[16] but took refuge in his constant theme that whatever is, is natural[17]—which placed him closer than he realized to "whatever is, is right."[18]

What makes a truth self-evident is that even when questioned no one bothers to answer. If someone so well situated as Grimm was unwilling to comprehend the *Second Discourse,* other philosophes were also bound to miss its argument. Rousseau had shattered the untouchable philosophical idol of natural sociability, but the enlightened thinkers continued to worship at its throne as if nothing had happened. What could be more dogmatic or more typical of the age than Voltaire's famous riposte to the *Second Discourse?* "No one has ever been as witty as you are in trying to turn us into brutes: to read your book makes one long to go on all fours."[19] Ridicule such as this is devastating, not because it is intelligent, but because it invites everyone to join with a famous man in his refusal to exercise his intelligence when faced with a challenge.

One can say of the *Second Discourse* and all Rousseau's subsequent writings what we have previously said of the *First Discourse:* that many of the positions set forth by the Citizen would eventually be shared by some of his estranged Parisian comrades, but at a date too late for the philosophes to reconsider his writings. Unrecognized convergence is especially evident on the question whether it is possible to silence the "violent reasoner." Briefly in the *Letter to D'Alembert,* more in depth in *Julie* and *Emile,*[20] Rousseau denied that morality can be sustained on the basis of a doctrine of pure self-interest in society as presently constituted. When Diderot and d'Alembert, each laboring independently of the other, arrived at the conclusion that under current circumstances an ethical treatise reconciling interest with virtue could not be written,[21] they recapitulated Rousseau's intellectual journey. To point out that they failed to acknowledge their affinity with the man they now saw as their most dangerous enemy would be to understate the case. Unwittingly Diderot engaged in a procedure of philosophical reversal, as he attributed his former position to Rousseau and availed himself of Rousseau's counterposition to defeat Jean-Jacques. In a paroxysm of righteousness Diderot pitied his enemy brother for consulting interest, when it is "our heart" we should consult to discover "the eternal and ineffaceable notion of the just and unjust."[22] To overhear Diderot in 1762 one would think that he was Rousseau and that Rousseau was the Diderot of "Natural Right." However absurd such posturing, it had the desired effect of permitting the philosophes to relocate rather than face up to the significance of the conflict between the two greatest figures of the French Enlightenment.

It is also clear that the republicanism Diderot came to share with Rousseau, far from fostering dialogue, made their differences irreconcilable. Every time Diderot moved in Rousseau's direction by interpreting enlightenment as civic education, Rousseau pulled away by denying that the good republic should encourage the social mobility of careers open to talent; for every bright young man from the provinces Diderot welcomed to Paris, Rousseau urged a would-be writer to return to the plow. It was so easy for Rousseau, who was Swiss, to publish his republican essay "Political Economy" in the *Encyclopédie;* it was so difficult for Diderot, burdened with keeping the censors of the *Encyclopédie* at bay, to be a republican. Doubtless Deleyre was right when he told Rousseau that the tame ending of Diderot's "Political Authority" (1751) was at odds with its bold opening;[23] but shortly after that article appeared it was savagely attacked by Jesuits and proponents of absolute monarchy, and it continued to be a target of traditionalist critics for the next twenty years.[24] Rousseau, a foreigner, could submit a bold *Discourse on Inequality* to the Academy of Dijon; Diderot found it impossible for a subject of the monarchy to treat the question of inequality properly.[25] Rousseau could deny property was a natural right and place its disposal at the discretion of the republic; Diderot's doubts about mine, thine, and the priority of property over human rights could never see the light of day in his lifetime.[26]

Most of all the figure of Catherine caused common republican sentiments to sharpen the animosity between the two one-time friends, now bitter rivals. In his last major work, the *Essai sur les règnes de Claude et de Néron,* Diderot interrupted the narrative to interpolate a series of gratuitous and violent personal attacks on the deceased Jean-Jacques.[27] Ostensibly writing to defend the actions of Seneca at the court of Nero, Diderot's real concern was his own relationship with Catherine. Rousseau could not be forgiven for holding himself aloof from all despots as effectively as Diderot did from Frederick but failed to do with Catherine. Whenever Diderot's troubled republican conscience got the better of him, Rousseau was in for some abuse.

Making matters all the worse was the strongly democratic character of the republic Rousseau espoused. To a man the philosophes regarded the intolerance of the wars of religion as the pure expression of the essence of popular political movements. Their eventual commitment to popular sovereignty was most definitely not to be construed as an endorsement of democratic government; therefore, they repudiated Rousseau's pro-democratic *Letters Written from the Mountain* as a seditious tract[28] and reaffirmed their alignment with the ruling Genevan oligarchy, which was pro-French culturally and ever willing to invite the government of France to intercede in its behalf against the Genevan democrats.[29] Reform, the philosophes believed, had to come from above; thus the arch-republican Helvétius, reduced to despair by Maupeou, dedicated his posthumous *De l'Homme* to Catherine and Frederick. D'Holbach addressed the final pages of his *Éthocratie,* a book that advocated representative and constitutional government, directly to Louis XVI at the time of his accession to the throne. Rousseau's democratic politics was a scandal that threatened to discredit the philosophical party.[30]

The philosophes were forever responding to Rousseau in terms of their movement, rarely in terms of his thought. Crush the infamous, a wrathful Voltaire shouted against the Church; the same slogan is just as fitting for his attitude to Rousseau. It was one of Rousseau's gifts that he always succeeded in bringing out the worst in the philosophes, and Voltaire's worst was worse than most. Repeatedly and endlessly Voltaire polemicized against Rousseau in a series of pamphlets that ranged from the wittily dismissive to the most despicable and vile personal attacks imaginable. Historians have sorted through these documents, dated and catalogued them; but no one has ever offered proof that Voltaire wrote a single line of intelligent criticism of Rousseau's writings.[31] Grimm worried with good reason that the heavy-handed libels of Voltaire might arouse public sympathy for Jean-Jacques.[32]

Occasionally one or another philosophe initiated what might have been an intellectually rewarding critique of Rousseau, but such insights were never sustained and usually were upheld by artificially isolating a single strand from the web of Rousseau's thought. In finding too much of the innate in *Emile* Helvétius opened a promising line of inquiry.[33] For when Rousseau refilled human nature after emptying it in the *Second Discourse,* he may well have dogmatically overfilled it in his determination to break away from his philosophical past. His deliberate backsliding into Cartesian dualism in the *Profession of Faith* comes immediately to mind;[34] possibly he was also guilty of polemical overcompensation when he termed conscience an instinct. Instead of attacking Rousseau where he was vulnerable, Helvétius embarrassed himself trying to prove that the genius of Jean-Jacques was not innate—that anyone with his personal history would have written *Emile.* An exasperated Diderot complained that Helvétius spent so much time "proving his kennelman could have written *De l'Esprit.*"[35]

Both d'Alembert and Grimm raised objections to Rousseau's treatment of women[36] that were well taken but not taken very far. To decide in advance that women are incapable of abstract thought, as Rousseau did, was to overfill women's nature during the process of refilling human nature. There is no question that as they read Rousseau, some of the philosophes, d'Alembert most explicitly, were driven to pay more attention to the issue of women's rights, an item on their agenda from the start[37] but usually placed near the bottom, perhaps because it is difficult to advocate more freedom for women when under attack by the Church for undermining the family. That said, it should be noted that they concentrated on Rousseau's gratuitous insults in the *Letter to D'Alembert* and *Emile* without examining his underlying rationale for advocating that women retreat from *le monde* to the family. Neither d'Alembert nor Grimm faced up to Rousseau's argument that what was called freedom for women would amount to the final capitulation of human nature to society. Nor did Holbach, who shared Rousseau's view, acknowledge his affinity with the unspeakable Jean-Jacques; one searches in vain in the pages of Holbach for an admission, however veiled, that his proposals for constructing a haven in a heartless world were in any way indebted to Rousseau's writings a decade or more earlier.

When Rousseau categorically denied the moral worth of "progress," he issued a challenge to the world view of the philosophes at the precise point where they were least certain of themselves. Although Diderot affirmed in the *Encyclopédie* that more knowledge guaranteed greater virtue, his private letters expressed strong reservations about his official stand: "It is quite certain we are less barbaric than our forebears. We are more enlightened. Are we better? That's another matter."[38] Faced with the possibility Rousseau was right, Diderot might have sympathetically reappraised the *First and Second Discourses.* Nothing of the sort; because Diderot's doubts threatened to place him in the camp of Jean-Jacques, he brushed aside his misgivings and vigorously reaffirmed the blessings of progress: "Whatever Jean-Jacques Rousseau and the fanatical enemies of the progress of *l'esprit humain* say, it is difficult to read the history of the barbarian centuries of any people without congratulating oneself on being born in an enlightened century and a civilized nation."[39] Hard put to sustain his position, Diderot, after several efforts, hit upon average life-expectancy as his evidence for the superiority of the social state.[40]

It is perhaps some measure of Diderot's uneasiness that he characterizes Rousseau's position in a way that is doubly misleading. "If Rousseau, instead of preaching a return to the forest, had occupied himself with imagining a type of society half civilized and half savage, one would have, I believe, a great deal of difficulty responding to him."[41] Now Diderot, who discussed the *Second Discourse* with Rousseau at considerable length, knew perfectly well that Rousseau had not advocated a return to the forest; he also knew his erstwhile companion had, in truth, designated a lost stage of human history, halfway between civilization and the pure state of nature, a world we have lost but which was recaptured and perfected by the Wolmars. Diderot was also well aware that Helvétius and Holbach wanted to limit economic "progress" and the corruption of *moeurs* that accompanies abundance. How disconcerting it must have been for Diderot to find his comrades and sometimes himself enticed by a vision strikingly similar to Rousseau's; all the more important, therefore, to misread and denigrate the writings of the renegade Rousseau.

In this task of denigration Diderot could count on all the philosophes as allies, even those whose affinities with Rousseau were most pronounced. One after another the most "enlightened" thinkers judged Rousseau an eloquent but confused, contradictory, incoherent thinker, "whose philosophy, if he has one, is in pieces and morsels."[42] At the risk of being incoherent themselves, they then turned around and accused Jean-Jacques of addiction to the "spirit of systems"; how appalling, they wrote, that Rousseau should prove so remarkably persistent in expanding a brief, paradoxical discourse into a system of thought.[43] Heads, Rousseau lost; tails, he did not win.

Decades after the *First Discourse* the philosophes were still returning to the scene of Rousseau's first antiphilosophical crime, always with a rehash of d'Alembert's original refutation.[44] By accusing Rousseau of making a bad causal argument, when he blamed the arts for the corruption that was not their responsibility, the philosophes sought to deny his scientific credentials. The same end of portraying Rousseau as scientifically deficient could be achieved, Diderot realized, by designating him a moralist.[45] The moralist label, moreover, had a second advantage in that it permitted the philosophes to trace the sources of Rousseau's ideas to Montaigne or Seneca,[46] as if that were enough to discredit Jean-Jacques. One wonders if they ever remembered d'Alembert's words in the *Preliminary Discourse:* "At the beginning great men are accused of being mistaken, and at the end they are treated as plagiarists."[47]

None of the philosophes ever conceded that Rousseau was a great thinker; nor did any of them ever admit that he had issued a fundamental challenge to their intellectual position. Dialogue was out of the question, but a shouting match might well be in order with the man who had betrayed their movement. Both early and late Grimm noted that no worthy adversary had engaged Rousseau in debate; initially he bemoaned this intellectual void, later he welcomed it. Why should anyone, asks Grimm, answer a person writing in bad faith?[48] Let the mudslinging begin.

High Muckraking

Historians of the low Enlightenment have argued that the legitimacy of the monarchy was undermined by *libellistes* who fed the insatiable hunger of the reading public for stories of scandal at court.[49] Less noticed is the extent to which Rousseau and the philosophes, the leading personages of high Enlightenment, proved as adept as any hack writer in penning mutual exposures, accusations, and recriminations. At the same time that muck-raking journalists were publishing the *Vies privées* of the royal family and highest aristocracy, the philosophes and one ex-philosophe were engaged in an ever more acrimonious and personal quarrel, consisting of charges and countercharges that invariably found their way into print, sometimes in the words of the actors themselves, the rest as reported by journalists who sensed that the philosophes, perhaps no less than courtiers, were figures who fascinated the public. The representatives of high Enlighten-ment, muckrakers themselves, frequently assisted the efforts of ordinary scandal-mongers; so exclusive a newsletter as Grimm's *Correspondance littéraire* could be used to leak unfavorable rumors about Jean-Jacques to popular journalists.[50] By fair means or foul, public opinion had to be shaped and molded, either for Rousseau or for the philosophes.

When Rousseau and his former comrades attacked one another, the "philosophical party" inadvertently demonstrated that it had internalized the tactics of highly publicized personal abuse which the conservative journalists and pamphleteers Fréron, Palissot, and Moreau had long been employing against them, not excepting Jean-Jacques. Because their enemies commanded a large audience through the popular press, the philosophes found themselves constantly in the public eye, compelled to perform before the gaze of a reading public that monitored their comings and goings more eagerly than it read their works. Hence the exhortations of one philosophe to another to keep up appearances in private life because someone was watching and the reputation of the movement was at stake. From the moment Rousseau bolted the philosophical ranks, the threat was that he might become an informer whose revelations would thoroughly discredit the philosophical party. The philosophes had to ruin the reputation of Rousseau and he, tied to them by rebellion as closely as he had previously been by collaboration, had to ruin theirs. What churchmen and traditionalist journalists had done to the philosophes and Rousseau would now be done by the philosophes to Rousseau and by Rousseau to the philosophes.

To the members of the party of light, Rousseau's defection tilted the balance in their struggle against the Church because they had henceforth to fight on two fronts, one of which was behind their own lines. With each passing year it became more urgent that they gird themselves for a civil war at the very moment they were preparing to take Troy. A standard vocabulary of vituperation, chiefly but by no means solely the work of Voltaire, took root in their correspondence about their erstwhile companion: they pronounced an anathema against Rousseau the "traitor," the "renegade," the "deserter," the "apostate," the "Judas" of the church of the philosophical faithful.[51] History had to be rewritten, all traces of one-time solidarity obliterated: no one was to remember, Voltaire insisted,[52] that in the article "Encyclopedia" Diderot had uttered the words "Oh, Rousseau, my dear and worthy friend." After the break, with the possible exception of d'Alembert, the philosophes never had a kind word for Jean-Jacques unless he was suffering persecution at the hands of the Catholic Church, under which circumstances to speak in favor of Rousseau was in reality to speak for themselves and against the forces of darkness.

If at one level the conflict between Rousseau and the philosophes was personal, at another their quarrel was over nothing less than the definition and safekeeping of the Enlightenment. Each side posed as the champion of humanity and the foe of the intolerant and reactionary Church. Rousseau was as staunch a defender of reason against miracles and clerical authority as any encyclopedist; to reason he turned again in the *Second*

Discourse, with the suggestion that the good offices of rationality are our only means to arrive at the equivalent of natural right in our post-natural state.[53] In the first version of the *Social Contract* Rousseau counted on reason to show the violent reasoner that in a polity governed by the rational "principles of political right," it will be in his interests to obey the law.[54] Conscience, to Jean-Jacques, far from an invitation to abandon reason, was a way of coming to the aid of individuals struggling to lead moral lives despite living in a social order that honors evil persons and treats good persons as fools. Not in the least did Rousseau's turn inward signify an abandonment of the Enlightenment project of human betterment through science; in *Emile,* which contains his most famous invocation of conscience, he remains as attentive as ever not just to natural history but even to the encyclopedic "chain" by means of which d'Alembert and Diderot sought to relate one science to another;[55] his reason for not following its links in the boy's education is that Emile is not yet ready for a concept so abstract and far removed from the experiences of childhood. In sum, Rousseau's thought from beginning to end is that of a fervent advocate of Enlightenment.

The struggle between Rousseau and the philosophes was bound to become vicious. Each party was convinced both that it embodied the Enlightenment and that the opposition was a second source of fanaticism almost as dangerous as the Church. It would be true but only a half-truth to declare that from the late 1750s onward Rousseau and the encyclopedists inflated personal animosities and feelings of betrayal into a grand contest of principle; the other half of the truth is that each party regarded its muckraking as the faithful discharge of a duty to humanity. The personal and the impersonal blend to the point where one cannot be distinguished from the other when dealing with intellectuals who universalize everything, whose everyday actions have become a part of the public record, and who have learned that there is more to persuasion than the printed word. All parties agreed that how one lives is as important as what one publishes. Unless the enlighteners lived the ideals of the Enlightenment, they discredited their beliefs.

On Rousseau's testimony it was because he made so conspicuous a show of living in accordance with the slogan "Liberty, Truth, Poverty" that the philosophes first became suspicious of him.

> It was the change in my character, . . . rather than my literary celebrity, that drew their jealousy upon me; they would perhaps have forgiven me for

distinguishing myself in the art of writing; but they could not forgive me for setting an example in my change of life, which seemed likely to cause them inconvenience.[56]

After the spectacular success at court in 1752 of his *Devin du village*, he refused an audience with the king that would almost certainly have led to a pension. He likewise rejected the position of cashier for a receiver-general of finance, a post that would have made his fortune at the same time that it provided leisure for writing. Born to the world of tradesmen, to the trades he would now return, henceforth eking out a meager living as a copyist of music, writing only when necessary "to tell the public harsh but useful truths"[57] or to save his native city from Voltaire's theater. Offered a lucrative and undemanding position with the *Journal des Savants* in his later years, Rousseau declined the generous offer on the grounds that writing should never be a profession.[58]

How his mode of life was "inconvenient" to the philosophes Rousseau did not need to explain. His Parisian comrades had only to look at him to realize that he was living what they professed, and they were not; or such at least was the message Rousseau conveyed more eloquently with an unkempt appearance than with words during the years immediately preceding his departure from Paris. Later, from the Hermitage, Rousseau wrote letters that implicitly invited Diderot to draw a parallel between the Citizen, who chose the independence of poverty, and the Philosophe, whose yearnings for *embourgeoisement* would sooner or later be fulfilled by placing himself in debt to someone rich and powerful.[59] In the early 1760s, at the very time d'Alembert was winning the fight to stack the French Academy with philosophes, Rousseau rejected the overtures of Madame de Luxembourg that might have led to an academic position. Though d'Alembert himself might remain lean, the minor philosophes who entered the academy under his leadership fattened themselves at the trough of privilege and grew conservative, even as Rousseau held fast to the image of the incorruptible outsider.

Before his public break with Diderot in 1758, Rousseau troubled the philosophes infinitely more with one action in 1756 than with all his publications prior to that date. The day he left Paris Rousseau symbolically asserted that his writings were not intellectual games, harmless paradoxes, or the rhetorical flourishes, as Palissot would have it, of someone determined to be an "original."[60] Rousseau's meaning was not entirely clear until he clarified it with his feet. And if he was right to leave, the philosophes were wrong to stay; if he was virtuous because he withdrew, they were corrupt because they remained in *le monde*. One philosophe after another, acknowledging the writer's need to keep society at a distance, recommended that the author divide his time between retreat and social activities;[61] Rousseau, in effect, asked why men of letters who had observed Parisian life, learning all the lessons about taste it had to offer, should remain in such dangerous surroundings.

Barely had Rousseau departed than the philosophes began to place an interpretation on his actions supportive of their principles, their favorite ploy being to predict that a life outside society would drive Jean-Jacques to madness. Grimm remarked that Rousseau "would end by being completely mad, and that the madness would be the result of his stay at the Hermitage. It is impossible for such a fiery and badly organized character to tolerate solitude."[62] After the rupture, Diderot was surely thinking of Rousseau when in *The Nun* he supplemented his usual attack on asceticism with a sharp rejection of seclusion: "Man is born for life in society; separate him, isolate him, and his ideas will go to pieces, his character will go sour, a hundred ridiculous affections will spring up in his heart, extravagant notions will take root in his mind."[63] The notion of the mentally unbalanced if not insane Rousseau was destined to be one of the staples in philosophical denigrations of the troublesome Jean-Jacques; *"le fou"* was to find its place in the list of the standard epithets.

Only a beast (or a God) can live outside society, Aristotle had written, and his words were paraphrased by every philosophe, some of whom went so far as to deify society.[64] Morality in the thought of the encyclopedists amounts to living in accordance with our social nature, honoring our duties to our fellow men and serving a useful social function. Rather predictably, Diderot and Grimm began by reminding Rousseau of his obligations to Madame d'Épinay and ended by declaring him an unnatural being; Rousseau the "monster" became a second standard epithet.

Rousseau's unwillingness to accompany Madame d'Épinay on her journey to Geneva, where the famous Doctor Tronchin awaited her, exasperated Diderot and Grimm, who foolishly took to preaching to Jean-Jacques about his duties to his benefactress. The more they cajoled him, the more adamant his refusal, which he justified with the assertion that Madame d'Épinay was indebted to him, not he to her. "Compare her benefactions with my two years of slavery and the sacrifice for her sake of my plans to reside in my country, and tell me whether I or she is more obligated to the other."[65] Provoked beyond endurance by Rousseau's strange notions of independence, Diderot inserted in *Le Fils naturel* the words Rousseau believed were directed at him: "Only the evil man lives alone." Diderot's play was a public document, as was his final work, on Seneca and Nero, in which he lambasted by name Jean-Jacques Rousseau, the most ungrateful of men, a moral monster living outside society.[66]

It would be manifestly unfair to Rousseau to treat as evidence of insanity his repeated and agonized complaints that his enemies had transformed him into the "were-wolf"[67] of Europe. Madame d'Épinay, Grimm, and Diderot did in fact want posterity to remember Rousseau as "insane," "damned," "wicked and tormented."[68] Living alone, he was not Aristotle's God; therefore Diderot deemed him a "monster."[69] The epithet seemed warranted because even a beast belongs to nature, whereas Rousseau had rejected nature, and nature, in turn, had ostracized Rousseau. As a psychologist and scientist Diderot found that there was much to be learned about the "normal" by studying the "abnormal." He also believed that "monsters," far from unnatural, helped reveal nature. Sadly, these insights deserted him whenever he addressed the "monstrous" and "unnatural" Jean-Jacques.[70]

Though too personally involved to offer detached judgments, the philosophes by virtue of commenting so frequently on Jean-Jacques were bound, sooner or later, to hit the mark. Surely Grimm was right to say that Rousseau never praised except to blame.[71] Hardly a single arrangement in the household of the Wolmars can be cited that is not explicitly part of a scheme for an anti-Paris, and Rousseau's writings are ever more vehemently antiphilosophical. It was Rousseau's belief that a "gentleness of soul" could be felt in the works he wrote after leaving Paris; perhaps so, but he cannot be thinking of the obsessive and belligerent comments on the philosophes that permeate the pages of *Julie* or *Emile*.

Consider the following sampling of Rousseau's polemics. Given that the philosophes pride themselves on fighting against prejudices, Rousseau's philosophers are portrayed as the most prejudiced of men: "A savage," remarks Jean-Jacques, "has a healthier judgment of us than a philosopher does."[72] Why is it that a woman must be educated? Because, Rousseau answers, "in this philosophical age she needs a virtue that can be put to the test."[73] Why do philosophers love humanity? "A philosopher loves the Tartars so as to be spared having to love his neighbors."[74] Philosophers want fame and will do anything to obtain it; "where is the philosopher who would not gladly deceive mankind for his own glory?"[75] Before applauding the standard of utility the philosopher had better look in the mirror: "if all the kings and all the philosophers were taken away, their absence would hardly be noticeable."[76] Lashing out against his philosophical past, Rousseau went so far as to speak in favor of fanaticism.

> Fanaticism, although sanguinary and cruel, is nevertheless a grand and strong passion which elevates the heart of man, ... and gives him a prodigious energy that need only be better directed to produce the most sublime virtues. On the other hand, irreligion—and the philosophic spirit—makes souls effeminate and degraded, concentrates all the passions in the baseness of private interest, ... and thus quietly saps the true foundations of every society.

Rousseau would have us understand that "religion does many things that philosophy could not do."[77]

If Rousseau was singularly effective in portraying the philosophical opponents of prejudice as highly prejudiced in favor of the inegalitarian social order that sponsors the arts and sciences, he was also adept at exposing the intolerance of the champions of toleration. When he charged that the philosophes resembled the Jesuits they despised, Rousseau scored a palpable hit.[78] Voltaire in particular rarely spoke of the philosophical party without calling it a church staffed by apostles; and what he said off the record was placed before the public in *De l'Homme*, which contains long sections in which Helvétius speaks admiringly of the organization of the Society of Jesus, going so far as to recommend that philosophes and magistrates carefully consider the model provided by so effective a government.[79]

Rousseau himself proved wonderfully adept at performing publicly visible acts of toleration in behalf of his enemies. D'Alembert in 1755–56 would have King Stanislas expel Palissot from the Academy of Nancy for parodying Rousseau in a play entitled *Les Originaux*, but Jean-Jacques took advantage of the situation to teach the philosophes a lesson in toleration. Taking up his pen, he asked that Palissot be forgiven. Five years later Palissot afforded Rousseau a second opportunity to come to the assistance of an enemy, now a philosophical enemy, Morellet, whose counterattack on *Les Philosophes* had led to a stay in the Bastille. When d'Alembert pleaded with Jean-Jacques to seek the assistance of the Luxembourgs,

Rousseau acted swiftly and effectively, and Morellet was released. But the masterpiece of Rousseau's show of toleration came in 1770, when he announced his intention in the *Gazette de Berne* of joining with other writers in contributing to a statue honoring his arch-enemy Voltaire. One cannot imagine anything nobler or more brilliantly mischievous than for Rousseau publicly to support the man who had written so many repulsive libels against him.[80]

For their part the philosophes saw Rousseau as the head of a fanatical sect.[81] If they overcame their fears that he would join the *dévot* party, they did so on the grounds that his religiosity was a cover for his attacks on them.[82] Never for a moment did they accept his incessant claims that he belonged to no party—a view placing them in rare agreement with one of their most outspoken enemies, Lefranc de Pompignan, who observed that Rousseau added a third party to the previously existing two, the Christian and the philosophical.[83] On only one point did they disagree with their adversary's assessment of Rousseau: Lefranc de Pompignan was wrong to assert that Rousseau was destined to be the only member of his sect. Many members of the reading public, far too many, were rallying to Julie's new banner of passionate virtue.

Rousseau's colors might appear new but his message, the philosophes found, duplicated many of the positions held by churchmen and reactionaries. Even before reading Rousseau's essay against a Genevan theater, Voltaire was sarcastically inquiring whether Rousseau had become a church father;[84] imagine how he felt after the Jesuit Berthier and the anti-philosophical journalist Chaumeix applauded the *Letter to d'Alembert*. Rousseau's attacks on the abstract cosmopolitanism of the philosophes were again reminiscent of the traditionalists, Palissot for one;[85] worse, the comments calling into question the civic credentials of the philosophes were delivered by Rousseau during a losing war when the French government and Church were looking for scapegoats. Along the way the members of the philosophical cohort quite naturally forgot Rousseau's civic, non-Christian reasons for outlawing the theater, and his democratic reasons for disallowing a humanitarianism that neglected the *peuple* who make up the overwhelming bulk of mankind.[86] No philosophe could fail to be outraged against the former philosophe who repeatedly said there could be no morality without religion,[87] whose republic would not tolerate outspoken atheists,[88] who accused the philosophes of destroying the family and of constituting a tightly organized group, quite capable of conspiracy (especially against him[89])—all positions long maintained by the opponents of light.

Feasibly the philosophes could have gained enough self-control to ignore Rousseau, if his books had sold poorly. The ultimate insult and threat, however, was that he had placed his most strident antiphilosophical propaganda in his most popular works, *Emile* and *Julie*. Seventy-two editions of his novel had appeared by the turn of the century, a stupendous figure. Women, especially Parisian women, read and adored the author who publicly maligned them; the lovelorn of varying social stations wrote to Rousseau soliciting his advice. Diderot tried to stem the tide by launching a pro-Richardson, anti-Rousseau campaign,[90] but his efforts were like those of a child at a beach trying to drain the ocean into his freshly dug hole in the sand. Normally a good critic, Diderot was too blinded by hatred to appreciate what Rousseau had accomplished, which was to transplant Racine's genius for static but passionately charged situations from the theater to the novel, the genre Voltaire disdained as plebeian. Rousseau, who knew his French audience well, gave it the form it desired[91] filled with a content of his choosing. Opinion, the philosophes agreed, governs the world; how devastating that Jean-Jacques by himself should influence opinion more effectively than all the philosophes combined.

After suffering the antiphilosophical abuse contained in *Emile*, Grimm dredged up all the embarrassing incidents, past and present, that he could lay at the door of Jean-Jacques. *The New Dædalus*, Rousseau's 1742 scheme for an airship, was now revealed to Grimm's audience so they could have a good laugh at Jean-Jacques.[92] It was even more pleasing to remind readers that the same Rousseau who disallowed miracles in *Emile* had once been cited in a Catholic journal as a witness who had testified to the authenticity of a miraculous event.[93] Best of all was the revelation that Rousseau, living off the blue-blooded Luxembourgs, had stopped calling his dog "Duke" to avoid offending his patrons.[94] Diderot, writing for a much larger audience than Grimm's, informed his readers that the supposedly independent Rousseau had a history of accepting positions with tax-farmers and aristocrats. Thus were "charlatan" and "sophist" added to the list of standard anti-Rousseau epithets. Marmontel put the final touches to these efforts to disgrace Jean-Jacques when he credited Diderot with persuading Rousseau to write against the moral effects of the arts in the *First Discourse*, this despite Diderot's own account that he, knowing his Jean-Jacques, simply predicted the position Rousseau would take. Marmontel wanted the world to believe that Rousseau's entire life had been a lie.

Once intimate friends, now enemies, the philosophes feared that Rousseau, in Diderot's words, would "leave on his tomb the secrets confided in him."[95] It was not only for the public opinion of their day that the parties fought; Rousseau and the philosophes were engaged in an even larger struggle for the favor of future generations—the posterity Diderot came close to worshiping and to which Rousseau looked, perhaps more than to the afterlife, when he anticipated compensation for the woes of his earthly existence. Fearing the *Confessions,* Diderot toyed with what amounted to a *Counter-Confessions* when he helped Madame d'Épinay turn the René (Rousseau) character of her *Histoire de Madame de Montbrillant* into a consistent scoundrel.[96] Diderot, Grimm, and Madame d'Épinay thought better of publishing their collective libel, but so violent were Diderot's attacks on the deceased Rousseau in the final book he published that the gazettes sided with Rousseau and against Diderot.[97]

The final publications of Jean-Jacques and the philosophes ensured that the muckraking activities of their later years would continue indefinitely after their deaths—that from the grave they would reach back and compel the living to choose between the true and the false party of light.

The Paradox of Acting

Never, perhaps, have "men of letters" spoken so incessantly about acting as did the philosophes, whether as playwrights, dramatic critics, defenders of the rights of actors, proponents of a morality of role-playing, or as actors themselves, willingly or unwillingly, on the stage of the world. In Rousseau they had to contend with someone who wrote against their views on all these topics, even their campaign for the civic rights of actors; yet on the stage of the world Jean-Jacques was the supreme actor, incessantly upstaging his ex-colleagues and proving himself the consummate showman of the Enlightenment. Naturally the philosophes could not forgive Rousseau for "acting" so well in behalf of his Enlightenment and against theirs. The question is, could Rousseau forgive himself? Not the least of the paradoxes in which Jean-Jacques found himself embroiled was that he who denounced acting as the "art of counterfeiting oneself"[98] was constantly staging masterful performances.

Write a play, Voltaire told the young Marmontel, and you will "arrive in one day at glory and fortune."[99] Write a play with a message, the philosophes added, and you will advance the good cause; thus Voltaire's tragedies and Diderot's domestic dramas are saturated with humanitarian homilies, which seems only fitting given the intent to replace the pulpit with the stage. Of course, the theater is nothing without performers, and will never be all it might be if the Church is permitted to continue abusing actors; Voltaire praises the English for burying Mrs. Oldfield in Westminster Abbey and condemns the French for throwing the carcass of Mademoiselle Lecouvrer on the garbage heap.[100]

Diderot and Holbach transplanted the language of the theater to society when they outlined a morality of social roles and construed conscience as the internalized eyes of an imaginary spectator; then, as their critique of society grew more radical, they began to worry that they might be read as advocates of conformity and apologists for an unworthy status quo. One after another the philosophes repeated the familiar Stoic refrain that all the world's a stage and each person an actor; the vital point, for a philosopher, was to be in the audience watching the performances of others, while himself never setting foot on the platform. How dumbfounded the philosophes must have felt to realize they were on stage in spite of themselves, trapped there by the public they craved, unable to exit because the journalists were recording their every move. It was a sign of the times that when Rousseau left Paris, he was playing an exit scene rather than leaving the long-running philosophical play.

Not many of the philosophes followed Diderot's example in spending a lifetime commenting on declamation, scenery, costumes, and other matters pertaining to the art of acting; but even those least concerned about the theater were familiar with Condillac's claim in the *Essai* that the earliest language was one of gestures. "Speaking by action," the "dance of gestures," and the "discovery of pantomimes"[101] figure prominently in Condillac's path-breaking work of 1746 and, under his aegis, in the thought of the philosophes in general. Rousseau repeatedly stresses how deeply the Greeks and Romans appreciated the political uses of nonspoken speech: "What the ancients said in the liveliest way, they did not express in words but by means of signs. They did not say it, they showed it."[102] Because the Romans were attentive to signs in their public affairs, their political order had at its disposal the power of authority, whereas modern regimes have to govern through coercion, self-interest, and money. Rousseau could agree with Diderot's comment, "the gesture is sometimes as sublime as the word."[103]

To be an educated person in the eighteenth century was to be reared on the classics and to appreciate allusions to Greek and Roman personages, both when reading a formal treatise and again when chatting in an off-hand way. Voltaire was in no way unusual in his habit of passing out classical nicknames to the philosophes, Protagoras to d'Alembert, Apollo to Helvétius, Plato (compliment or insult?) to Diderot. The public at large, presumably, knew little about such names of endearment, but in the case of Jean-Jacques the popular journalists, conservative or simply sensation-seeking, did not need access to Voltaire's correspondence to discern that Rousseau was the modern incarnation of Diogenes.

For nature and against the city, nay-sayer to all the accepted beliefs, against luxury but luxuriating in his poverty, dispossessing himself of sword, watch, white stockings, gilt trimmings, and powder,[104] presenting himself unshaved and disheveled at Fontainebleau when his music was performed for royalty,[105] Rousseau may not have sought the role of Diogenes but he accepted it and played it for all it was worth. In his first years as a writer Jean-Jacques remarked that Diogenes failed to find an honest man because it was too late; in his later years, at odds with everyone, he liked to say the time had come "to put out my lantern."[106] Diogenes had been the showman of antiquity, the man who walked into the theater as the spectators were leaving, the philosopher as public figure whose social performances were his teaching. Typecast as the modern Cynic, Rousseau was granted a license, so to speak, to be a philosophical actor playing whatever parts and striking whatever poses best fit the varying messages he wished to convey.

Voltaire, author of *Le Mondain,* held in contempt both the old Diogenes and the new; Diderot proved markedly ambivalent, admiring the Cynic of bygone days sometimes, disdaining him others,[107] constantly disturbed by his best friend turned Cynic. D'Alembert alone gave Rousseau his due in the *Essay on Men of Letters:* "Each century and ours especially has need of a Diogenes; but the difficulty is to find someone with the courage to be him, and men with the courage to suffer him."[108] When Rousseau eventually identified the philosophes as the most corrupt of the denizens of the city, as figures who in their determination to guide opinion were themselves its foremost slaves, d'Alembert found himself ever more isolated in his willingness to tolerate Rousseau.

"Diogenes" was a name attributed to Rousseau; the name he chose for himself, first employing it in a letter to Voltaire,[109] was "Citizen." With the exception of *Julie*, Rousseau signed his publications "Jean-Jacques Rousseau, citizen of Geneva," a title noteworthy for both its brevity and its contempt for titles. Whenever writing against one of pillars of the regime, Jean-Jacques reveled in contrasting his simplicity with the pretense of his opponent. In his protest to Christophe de Beaumont, sponsor of a mandate against *Emile* and its author, Rousseau began by placing all the titles of his adversary on the first page: "Archbishop of Paris, Duke of St. Cloud, Peer of France, Commander of the Order of the Holy Spirit, Head of the Sorbonne, etc." It was the same tactic he had used against the philosophes at the time of the debate over the theater; the "citizen of Geneva" had addressed his letter to M. d'Alembert, "of the French Academy, of the Royal Academy of Sciences, of that of Prussia, of the Royal Society of London, the Swedish Royal Academy of Belles-Lettres, the Institute of Bologna." Simply by respectfully reciting d'Alembert's titles, Rousseau deprived him of his motto "Liberty, Truth, Poverty." In the case of Voltaire it is worth noting that Diderot expressed his hostility to the great lord of the manor by constantly addressing the patriarch as *de* Voltaire, whereas Rousseau in the *First Discourse* accomplished the same end by asking how many great works the "famed Arouet"[110] had sacrificed to the corrupt taste of his age. When dealing with Voltaire, either to withhold a title or to cite it conspicuously was to damn the man.

How would Rousseau play the role of citizen? Would he aspire to reincarnate Cato the elder, who dedicated his life to agriculture and to keeping the philosophers out of Rome? No doubt during the years of his "reform," when Rousseau combined his written censorship of morals with an ostentatiously austere life in Paris, he did remind some observers of the republican hero of antiquity. Diderot searched for Cato in La Tour's 1753 portrait of Rousseau and expressed regrets on not finding him: "La Tour has made his portrait of M. Rousseau a beautiful object, instead of the masterpiece he could have made it. I looked for the Censor of our literature, the Cato of our age, . . . instead I saw the composer of *Le Devin du village*, well dressed, well powdered."[111] Rousseau himself, it seems, was ill at ease with playing a part beyond the means of his less than Roman person. He settled for the compromise of claiming Cato for his cause with the printed word while acting on the stage of the world in accordance with the less demanding Genevan nature of his citizenship.

Within the pages of the *First Discourse* and during the ensuing polemical exchanges Rousseau upheld the dignity of Cato the elder against moderns who preferred a more supple ethic.[112] In the *Second Discourse* Rousseau hailed as the "greatest of men"[113] Cato the younger, who committed suicide rather than bend to Caesar. At the same time he included in *Political Economy* a comparison of Socrates and Cato, one the martyr of philosophers, the other of republicans, praising both but favoring Cato, who served the people, over the philosophical hero, who educated the gifted few.[114]

Rousseau knew he was no Cato, a leader of the people, but as Citizen of Geneva he could serve the many by being the one writer who—instead of putting as much distance as possible between himself and his humble origins—flaunted his common roots, claimed to be a practicing artisan, and gave it to be known that he was considering a return to his native city, its citizens, and their occupations. The weak Jean-Jacques, though more the exemplar of Genevan natural goodness than the living image of Roman austerity, did resemble Cato in one respect: "Someday our descendants will learn," remarked Rousseau, "that in this century of wise men and of philosophers, the most virtuous of [ancient] men was held up to ridicule and called a madman for having wished not to sully his great soul with his contemporaries' crimes."[115] These words, written about Cato at the beginning of Rousseau's antiphilosophical career, read in retrospect as a presentiment of his own fate.

The role of Citizen was Rousseau's by his own choice; the part of Diogenes, though thrust upon him, was one he played with panache. When forced against his will by philosophes and journalists to wear the mask of the Misanthrope, he wavered between making fruitless efforts to reject the role and rewriting the part to suit his needs. It was one thing, Rousseau realized, to reconcile the role of Diogenes with that of Citizen but quite another to convince oneself or others that the Misanthrope and the Citizen were the same man. Diogenes lived within the city and challenged its citizens to live virtuous lives; the Misanthrope, however, had abandoned his fellow men. Time and again Rousseau returned to the words of Diderot that stung him to the core: "Only the evil man lives alone." He was wounded all the more by Diderot's letter that contained no disavowal of the charge that his words were aimed at Rousseau; and Jean-Jacques, now living at the Hermitage, could never forget the closing words of the Philosophe: "Adieu, citizen! And yet, a hermit is a very singular citizen."[116]

It was in the *Letter to d'Alembert* that Rousseau attempted a rewrite of the *Misanthrope*. "After he had played so many other ridiculous characters, there remained to Molière the one which the world pardons the least, the one who is ridiculous because he is virtuous." Rousseau readily concedes that someone who reviles humanity is a "monster"; he insists, however, that we distinguish the man who hates mankind from the man who, "precisely because he loves his fellow creatures, hates in them the evils they do to one another."[117] Determined to please *le monde*, Molière fashioned a misanthrope so petty, spiteful, and untrue to himself that a degraded society could avenge itself against its accuser with volleys of malicious laughter. Rousseau's revised edition of the *Misanthrope*, by contrast, would dramatize the tragic fate certain to befall anyone who challenged his corrupt contemporaries.

Rousseau was well aware that his revisionist misanthrope had not carried the day—that despite his best efforts he continued to be portrayed to the public as the Alceste of the original script. In his darker moments, most notably *Rousseau Judges Jean-Jacques,* he obsessively complains that his enemies have succeeded in convincing the public he is a misanthrope and consequently neither citizen nor man but an unspeakable "monster."[118] Each of his autobiographical works contains a new rationale for his seclusion: at first his excuse is illness, then his love of freedom, next his need to flee men in order to love mankind, finally his need to flee humans in order to avoid hating them.[119] Through it all no one, not the philosophes, the journalists, or Rousseau himself, ever offered the most simple and compelling explanation of his withdrawal from Paris: while other philosophes might seek independence from patrons, Rousseau required independence from the philosophes, Diderot most of all, if he was to complete his early critical works with the positive program for an alternative enlightenment outlined in *Julie, Emile,* and the *Social Contract.*

Cast as Socrates both by the public and himself, Rousseau played the role for a number of years, until he discovered his message was better expressed by praising Cato or Jesus to the detriment of the patron saint of philosophers. The Socrates of the *First Discourse,* who knows more than other philosophers because he knows he does not know, is Rousseau's man; what makes this Socrates even more enticing is that, in a willful misreading of the *Apology,* Rousseau's gadfly scorns the pretensions of artists rather than artisans.[120] When Dancourt's *Les Fées* was being performed at the Théâtre Français, Rousseau attended as Socrates had *The Clouds,* and applauded the scene played at his expense. As early as 1753, at the time of the fracas over the *Letter on French Music,* Palissot, who would soon claim for himself the mantle of the modern Aristophanes, remarked that Rousseau was inviting a parallel between himself and Socrates. With the performance of *Les Originaux* and *Les Philosophes,* Palissot succeeded in identifying himself with Aristophanes, with the inevitable consequence that Rousseau, lampooned in both plays, was henceforth Socrates in the eyes of the public.[121] Perhaps the most striking commonality between Socrates and Rousseau was the one least appreciated, that just as Aristophanes mistakenly lumped Socrates with the Sophists he repudiated, so Palissot falsely portrayed Rousseau as a leading philosophe.

The year 1762 was both the period in which Rousseau strove most mightily to shed the Socrates label and the time when he was universally acknowledged as the living likeness of the Greek sage. Persecuted for the religious views of *Emile,* Rousseau appeared to everyone, even to the authorities, as the reincarnation of Socrates charged with impiety. Fearing allusions would be drawn to Rousseau, the government forbade performances of Sauvigny's *Mort de Socrate.*[122] During the period when Rousseau hesitated between fleeing and staying to confront the authorities, d'Alembert, Helvétius, and Rulhière worried that he would drink the hemlock.[123]

Martyrdom, the philosophes agreed, was properly the monopoly of their fanatical enemies. Holbach spoke for most of his comrades when he said Socrates should have availed himself of the opportunity to escape.[124] Diderot alone was enticed by philosophical martyrdom,[125] the martyrdom he refused in 1749 when incarcerated for the *Letter on the Blind.* In 1762 Diderot temporarily readmitted Rousseau to the philosophical faithful, so that he could beat his breast about the plight of modern philosophers, so similar to that of their great Greek predecessor, Socrates.[126]

Lost along the way was the parallel Rousseau had drawn in his outlawed educational treatise between Socrates and Jesus. Previously, when it dawned upon Rousseau that Socrates was the hero of philosophers, he had elevated Cato above the Athenian wise man; now it was the "son of Mary" whom he deemed more worthy of esteem than "the son of Sophroniscus," a choice certain to infuriate the philosophes.

> Socrates, dying without pain and without ignominy, easily sticks to his character to the end; and if this easy death had not honored his life, one would doubt whether Socrates . . . were anything but a sophist . . . The death of Socrates, philosophizing tranquilly with his friends, is the sweetest one could desire; that of Jesus, expiring in torment, insulted, jeered at, cursed by a whole people, is the most horrible one could fear.[127]

It did not take long for the exiled Rousseau, driven out of one sanctuary after another, to note that he, like Jesus, was "insulted, jeered at, cursed by a whole people." A year after the condemnation of *Emile* he bought a copy of Thomas à Kempis's *Imitation of Christ*.[128] In the later 1760s Jean-Jacques' comments on Jesus in his occasional writings[129] are difficult to distinguish from those about himself in his autobiographical works: a simple artisan, innocent, of gentle character, hoping to regenerate the people by the power of his example, Jesus/Jean-Jacques was vilified and disfigured by those who regarded his virtue as a reproach. By 1770 Rousseau could tell an acquaintance "I find nothing so grand, so beautiful, as to suffer for the truth. I envy the glory of martyrs."[130] Although most of Rousseau's uses of the persona of Christ were off-stage, the journals did report the view that he was the "apostle and martyr of humanity."[131]

Even though the philosophes wrote much of the dramatic script in which Rousseau was assigned the roles of Diogenes and Socrates, this did not prevent them from accusing him of being a mere actor, a *poseur* and a sensationalist, a man "without character."[132] For all his sophisticated understanding of the art of acting, Diderot could only see a contemptible quest for singularity in the Armenian costume Rousseau donned in 1763.[133] In common with all the philosophes, Diderot incessantly called his erstwhile friend a sophist, occasionally tempering his attacks with the stipulation that Jean-Jacques was the "first dupe of his sophisms."[134]

Grimm was especially intent upon unmasking Rousseau the actor, to which end the editor of the *Correspondance littéraire* paid particular attention to the role of "Citizen of Geneva." Forever considering a permanent installation in his native city, then balking whenever the occasion for action arose, drumming up one excuse or another for staying in France, Rousseau was vulnerable to the charge that his citizenship was more show than substance. Grimm, sensing an opportunity to embarrass Rousseau, invited his readers to "compare the *Letters from the Mountain* with the *Dedicatory Epistle* [to the *Second Discourse*], addressed to the republic precisely ten years ago."[135] In 1754 Rousseau's Geneva had been the best of all possible modern republics; by 1764 he had decided that it was ruled by "twenty-five tyrants" who wielded an absolute power quite unnecessary to prevail over a people who were "merchants, artisans, burghers preoccupied with their private interests, their buying and selling, their work and wages; persons to whom liberty itself is only a means to unhindered acquisition and to surety of possession."[136] To Grimm this about-face was only to be expected, given that the Geneva originally idealized by Rousseau was a pure concoction, totally at odds with the truth, which was that Genevans were money-grubbing expatriates, "the vagabonds of Europe."[137] Rousseau was a fraud, and his Geneva was part of his hypocrisy. Grimm cleverly noted how careful Rousseau had been in the *Letters from the Mountain* to avoid offending the French authorities: "One sees that M. Rousseau has not renounced the hope to returning to France."[138] Once Grimm went so far as to suggest that Rousseau "elevated his country to the skies while secretly hating it, and loved Paris passionately while heaping imprecations and injuries on it."[139]

Yet Rousseau did have good reasons for avoiding Geneva and remaining in France, even if he never acknowledged them in the most explicit terms. Had he settled in Geneva, Rousseau would not have been free to publish his works; residence in monarchical and unfree France, combined with a Dutch publisher, permitted him to flaunt his citizenship while circumventing its disadvantages. Moreover, all of Rousseau's works are contributions to the French Enlightenment, ever the dominant context of his thought, compared with which Geneva is a side show or a convenient battleground on which Jean-Jacques could joust with d'Alembert or Voltaire. The Hermitage to which he retreated in 1756 was only ten miles from Paris, and the *Reveries* of his final years were written "in the middle of Paris."[140] Surely the philosophes cannot be gainsaid for their caustic comments on Rousseau's inability to stop thinking about them or the Paris he so ardently discredited in his novel and in *Emile*. But why is that a fault, if his life's work was to respond to their Enlightenment with his?

Even if we find grounds to exonerate Rousseau, it does not follow that he would be ready to accept them. Excellent at unmasking the philosophes, Rousseau was afraid that he, too, might be wearing a mask. Self-doubt, which assumes many forms, visited him as the fear that he was "acting" before the public, in violation of his own imperative that "being" should replace "seeming." How could the same Jean-Jacques who condemned the actor for "putting on another character than his own, for appearing different than he is,"[141] turn around and play the part of Diogenes or Socrates? Emile is never to identify with someone else, not even Cato or Socrates, because "he who begins to become alien to himself does not take long to forget himself completely."[142] It was always Rousseau's claim that his every emotion immediately expressed itself on his face, a face that was not a mask but a revelation of the man and his innermost soul. Rousseau's genius for playing roles on the stage of the world raised the question whether he was thereby exemplifying his beliefs, as he hoped; or was he "acting," as he feared? To answer this question Rousseau did the same as everyone else; he sat in judgment of Jean-Jacques.

Rousseau Judges Jean-Jacques

Coming under constant attack, usually in the form of an attempt to discredit his thought by unmasking his person, Rousseau had to write an autobiographical defense. Philosophes, churchmen, and journalists might hate one another, but their cacophony was transformed into harmony whenever they sang the litany of Rousseau's contradictions: Jean-Jacques wrote a play that failed and then denounced the drama; he berated romantic love and wrote a love story; announced there could be no French music while performing *Le Devin du village;* denied revelation, miracles, and sin while proclaiming his fervent Christian faith; accepted the patronage of tax-farmers and the highest nobility even as he gloried in his poverty. By telling his own story Rousseau could show the public the whole that integrated and reconciled all his apparent inconsistencies; he could close the purported gap between his theory and his practice.

It was imperative that he do so, not only for himself but also for his doctrine, which had become inseparable from the man in the public mind. Never before and perhaps never since has an author been known to his readers by his Christian name; Rousseau was as much Jean-Jacques to persons he had never met as to his closest acquaintances. Other authors might hide behind assumed names, attribute their controversial publications to dead writers, and avail themselves of all the standard machinations of the clandestine book trade; Rousseau insisted upon signing his works because both he and his readers had come to expect nothing less. Candide, whose "face bespoke his soul," paid dearly for what Voltaire regarded as the foolishness of his candor. Rousseau's openness, far from naive, is tinged from the beginning with premonitions of a tragic fate; come what may, nothing and no one will prevent him from approaching each reader on a personal basis. His novel, especially, created a moral and emotional bond between author and reader quite unlike anything previously seen.[143]

Once he started down the road of autobiography Rousseau found he could not stop. After the *Confessions* came the *Dialogues,* or *Rousseau Judges Jean-Jacques,* followed at the end of his life by the *Reveries of a*

Solitary Walker, "an appendix to my *Confessions*"[144] that might better be termed a fresh start. Church and government persecuted him, and Voltaire tried to organize a philosophical conspiracy against him,[145] only to be thwarted by what d'Alembert had once referred to as the "anarchy"[146] of the republic of letters; above all, however, it was Rousseau who continued to accuse Jean-Jacques. Having chosen to make his self a statement of his principles, he was condemned to an endless struggle to bind his life and thought into a coherent whole. Not for him the easy way out of asserting that the truth of his writings was independent of the author—a proposition incompatible with his self-proclaimed status as the living truth. *Vitam impendere vero,* to dedicate life to truth, his life to his truth, was his motto.

Even in his earliest writings Rousseau had noted that the thinkers of his age constantly betrayed their books by their actions: "In every book of ethics and philosophy I had read, I believed I saw the author's soul and principles. I regarded all these grave writers as modest, wise, virtuous, irreproachable men ... Finally I saw them; this childish prejudice vanished, and it is the only error of which they have cured me."[147] Later, in his autobiographical writings, he struggled to explain why he was not guilty of the same offense.

At any moment his enemies might charge him with ingratitude to his benefactress, Madame d'Épinay; or with toadying to the Luxembourgs who were great even in the ranks of the *grands;* or—a particularly dark revelation—with failure to raise his own children. Appearances, he stated in the *Confessions* when discussing his relationship with the Countess d'Houdetot, are frequently on the side of the guilty and against the innocent.[148] Diderot's list of the Citizen's "rascalities" included the following item: "Rousseau fell in love with Madame d'Houdetot; and to prosper from his affair, what did he do? He sowed scruples in the mind of this lady regarding her passion for Saint-Lambert, his friend."[149] To all appearances Rousseau's objections to adultery had degenerated into an excuse for inviting Sophie to break with her lover, after which the "amorous citizen" would attend to her consolation. Since his actions created appearances he could not control, Rousseau searched for forms of self-definition that were independent of his deeds; doing gave way to being, body to soul, outside to inside, consequences to intentions in his thought.

Revealingly, it is in an essay written for Sophie that Rousseau pronounced the words, "all the morality of human life is in the intentions of man."[150] In a related move, Rousseau the astute practitioner of hermeneutics announced in the *Confessions* that because his "inner life" led an autonomous existence, his intentions could not be deciphered by studying his actions. As the "secret history" of his inner self, the *Confessions* were "less the history of the events [of my life] than that of the state of my soul at the time they took place." Whenever other persons interpreted his actions their "judgments were almost always wrong in the reasons they gave for my conduct, and usually the smarter the person, the more incorrect the explanation." Hence we find Rousseau proclaiming the notion of privileged access; "no one can write the life of a man but he himself." The novelty of the *Confessions* was that for the first time someone would "tell all" about his self, the "all" only he could know, but which Rousseau, unlike Montaigne, would not disguise or falsify through selective silences.[151]

"I have unveiled my inmost self,"[152] Rousseau told the world at the outset of his autobiography. His method for undertaking this project, as may be reconstructed from the original introduction to the *Confessions,* has much in common with philosophical history: "To know a character well it would be necessary to distinguish the acquired from the natural, to see how it was formed, what occasions developed it, what chain of secret affections made it such, and how it was modified sometimes to produce the most contradictory and unexpected effects. That which is seen is only the least part of what is."[153] Once again Rousseau undertook to peel away the social deposits in an effort to reach the bedrock of the naturally given, and as in the *Second Discourse* he sought to follow a "chain" linking the moments of time, from present to past until he arrived at his original self; and from past to present, as he related the story of his life. In the *Second Discourse* he wanted to show that what is visible is the worst of human nature; in the *Confessions* his objective was to show that Rousseau as seen acting in public was the most misleading part of Jean-Jacques.

There is, however, a fundamental difference between Rousseau's philosophical history of the species of 1754 and the one he applied to himself in 1764: in the *Second Discourse* society and history displace and destroy nature, whereas the individual nature of Jean-Jacques remains ever the same in the *Confessions.* For several years before he began writing his life's story, Rousseau had been conceptually refilling the human nature he had virtually emptied of content in his *Discourse on Inequality;* conscience, he had decided in retrospect, is innate, and in a deliberately provocative move, he rehabilitated the "moral sense"[154] that the philosophes had long since shipped back to Scotland. But when writing his autobiography Rousseau went much further; he presented his self as if it had always been there, preformed, waiting to display the essence that bound together all the moments of his existence into a unified whole. In a word, he denied change and history in the *Confessions* as much as he had insisted on the same in the *Second Discourse*.

This notion of an inexplicably fixed self served Rousseau well whenever he confessed a wrongdoing or explained why what appeared wrong was not as it seemed. The *morale sensitive* or materialism of the sage that Rousseau outlined in Book IX is integral to the apologetic strategy of the *Confessions*. Rousseau knew that we need to be "restored" to ourselves by a more favorable environment, because he had frequently acted other than himself; "there are times when I so little resemble myself that one would take me for another man of quite an opposite character."[155] Yet he staunchly maintained that even at his worst he never lost the original innocence that promptly returned as soon as his circumstances permitted the resurrection of his true being. As a philosophical historian, Rousseau was as concerned to trace the entry of vice into the human heart as the philosophes had been to discover the origins of error; as a man revealing the history of his soul, Jean-Jacques isolated those incidents which threatened to penetrate his being and end his goodness. Speaking of the species, he held that the onset of its vices radically altered human nature; speaking of himself, he held that his immoral actions were temporary lapses, errors, externally induced aberrations that had no lasting effect on his impermeable and petrified self.

Shame made the young Rousseau other than himself when he stole a ribbon and in his embarrassment falsely accused Marion of his misdeed. Not long afterwards it was not Rousseau but a pretender who, having borrowed his body, assumed the name Vaussore de Villeneuve and feigned the credentials of a composer before he knew music. Eventually Rousseau would proclaim in the bizarre and fascinating *Dialogues* that the ten years he spent writing his greatest works were an aberration having little or nothing to do with his true self, which had never belonged to the world of literature. By nature he was fit to copy music, not to write; the conversion-like experience on the road to Vincennes that inaugurated his period as author lasted a decade, following which he had returned to the nothingness that was his natural element. No one, therefore, should accuse him of inconsistency if he repeatedly wrote to denounce writing—not if his books were merely the most notorious result of those fits of "delirium" during which he acted other than he was.[156]

Though his actions might accuse him, his intentions and sentiments excused him. "Wicked intent"[157] was never further from Jean-Jacques than when he betrayed Marion. Intentions again came to his rescue when he confessed that he had sent his five children to the Foundling Home: "My fault is great, but it was due to error; I have neglected my duties, but the desire of doing an injury never entered my heart."[158] Whatever fault the morality of intentions left on his soul, the sentiments were certain to wash away. Sentiment acted as narrator, judge, jury, and proof of Rousseau's innocence: it was narrator in that Rousseau counted on the "chain of feelings" to remind him of the "succession of events";[159] it was judge in that the conscience that presides over moral judgment is a sentiment; it was proof of innocence in that the "sweet and lively emotion I feel at the sight of all that is virtuous"[160] vindicates him; and it was jury in that the audience which shares his moral passion when reading his books is instructed in the *Dialogues* to find him innocent. Should all else fail there is crying, which Rousseau frequently deems a social performance when viewing the tears of others, and as pure manipulation when the tears roll down the powdered face of Grimm,[161] but he never doubts that his own tears provide convincing evidence of his unspoiled natural goodness.

Never, perhaps, did the rift with Diderot cost Rousseau more than during the period of his autobiographical writings; for Diderot, too, had begun a project of sincerity,[162] only to abandon it because he discovered that motives are so complex, our most heroic undertakings so much the result of both worthy and unworthy intent, that to seek purity of heart is self-destructive. "This assiduous examination of the self serves less to improve the self than to teach that neither oneself nor others are especially good."[163] At the end of Diderot's autobiographical play of the 1770s one of the characters asks of the Diderot figure, "Is he good? Is he bad?" and receives the answer, "First one, then the other. Like you, like me, like everybody."[164] Unless we learn to live with our inevitably compromised selves, we shall be cursed to perpetual unhappiness. It is not surprising that the ethics of intentions found in Diderot's early essay on Shaftesbury has been supplanted in his later works by a more utilitarian concentration on consequences.

Before the break, at the time of Rousseau's refusal to accompany Madame d'Épinay on her journey to Geneva, Diderot had invited Rousseau to reconsider his ever more subjective conception of morality: "I am well aware that, whatever you do, you will always have the testimony of your conscience on your side; but is this testimony sufficient by itself, and is it allowed to neglect, up to a certain point, that of other men?"[165] Rousseau faithfully recorded in the *Confessions* both Diderot's letter and his rage upon reading it. Later, however, in the *Dialogues,* he summoned all his remaining strength and, escaping momentarily from his subjective ethic, wrote a sentence resembling Diderot's two decades earlier: "Our sweetest existence is relative and collective, and our true self is not completely inside us."[166]

Without exception Rousseau's remarks about La Rochefoucauld are disparaging, which is unfortunate because he might have learned much from the *Maxims.* "Nothing makes it so difficult to be natural as the desire to appear so," wrote the cynical duke whose insights Rousseau could not respect because they struck too close to home. It is the peculiarity of the human eyes, La Rochefoucauld continued, that they permit us to see everyone except ourselves: so much, then, for Rousseau's self-serving notion of privileged access. Most disturbing of all, brilliantly so, was this maxim: "Our enemies are nearer the truth in their opinion of us than we are ourselves."[167] Near the end of the *Dialogues,* convinced he was the victim of a "philosophical inquisition,"[168] Rousseau raised the plaintive question: "If men wish to see me other than I am, why should I care? Is the essence of my being in their looks?"[169] Despite his determined efforts, he could not free himself from the suspicion that the answer was at least half in the affirmative.

In common with the rest of Locke's progeny, Rousseau began with the premise that we are born to act.[170] To the philosophes our need to do something, anything, is a blessing, for it compels us to contribute to society and to ourselves; to Rousseau it is a curse. Whenever he acted, Rousseau sensed that others were pulling his being away from him, that his actions betrayed him and led to the charge that his deeds belied his principles. Others saw him with the Luxembourgs but could not see the sentiment of friendship that raised them above their privileged estate[171] and bound him to them despite their titles. Lodging provided by Madame d'Épinay or the Luxembourgs was not patronage but a simple display of friendship, no matter that philosophes, taking everything at face value, could not understand how friendship can make equality triumph where least expected. Because Rousseau acted like other writers in accepting gifts from the wealthy, his enemies unfairly took him for a man no better than those he denounced. If only he could somehow stop acting, his self would belong entirely to himself.

"I know that the only good which is henceforth within my power is to abstain from acting, lest unwittingly and unintentionally I should act badly,"[172] writes the solitary walker. The advice the imaginary Frenchman offers Jean-Jacques in the *Dialogues* is "entirely to avoid acting, to remain immobile if he can."[173] Inaction is Rousseau's obsessive motif: sometimes he declares he has been prevented from acting, on other occasions that he has chosen inaction or that he is passive by nature. When in 1765 Rousseau requested the authorities of Berne to place him "in prison for the rest of my days," Voltaire dismissed the incident as a publicity stunt.[174] In fact, however, Rousseau's desire to be imprisoned is one of two associated and constantly recurring themes in his letters and autobiographical writings, the second being that of the happiness and freedom he would enjoy within the walls of the Bastille as he fed off his own substance, dreaming, imagining, conjuring up beings to his liking.[175] Living in confinement, having no social relations, Jean-Jacques would at last be his own person, and never again the man accused of saying one thing and doing another.

"Human nature does not regress,"[176] Rousseau believed, and yet he strove mightily to exempt himself from the rule. For six years, by his account, he had been a paragon of virtue in iniquitous Paris, six years "during which I ceased to be myself and became another." Barely, however, had he left the city and returned to natural surroundings than he felt himself "restored to nature above which I had attempted to elevate myself."[177] At one with nature and with his own nature, Rousseau was not virtuous but he was good, naturally good. In the *Dialogues* he goes much further, declaring himself the one person who is still a natural man.[178] All the traits of man in the state of nature just so happen to be his as well; both Rousseau and natural man live in the present, are lazy, indolent, and inactive, find thinking difficult, and exist through their senses. Human nature does regress in the person of Jean-Jacques, who is neither the author nor the citizen but the man of nature living on the fringes of society.

As natural man Rousseau could fail to live according to his principles and still be fully in accord with them. "Never," he says of himself, "did a man conduct himself less by principles and follow more blindly his penchants."[179] Yet never was a man less guilty of violating his principles: natural man has no principles, he simply is. After playing so many other roles Rousseau assumed the part of the man of nature as his final performance. Appearing on the stage for the last time, he could convince no one, least of all himself, that the unthinking self presented to the public in the *Dialogues* was the real man.

Had he remembered his words in a letter of 1764, he would have known why his strategy of 1774–1776 could not succeed: "One can no more recover one's simplicity than one's infancy. Once the mind is in effervescence it remains so always, and whoever has once done some thinking will do so all his life. That is the greatest misfortune about the reflective state: the more one feels the evils thereof, the more one augments them, and all our efforts to come out of it only entangle us more profoundly."[180] The view expressed in this letter was merely an amplification of his words in *Emile:* "Man does not easily begin to think. But as soon as he begins, he never stops. Whoever has thought will always think, and once the understanding is practiced at reflection, it can no longer stay at rest."[181] Sooner or later Rousseau was bound to recognize how much thinking went into his attempt to convince himself and others that he was natural because he did not think.

Implicitly Rousseau recognized that since he could not simply *be* natural man, he would have to *make* himself a person who, like the man of nature, had a mind emptied of the faculties that are developed by social intercourse. During his daydreams he "yielded his senses entirely to the impression of exterior objects" and "nourished the pleasure of existing without exercising his faculties."[182] Thinking destroys revery; therefore all daydreaming is predicated on a light, evenly flowing sensation that permits the suspension of thought.[183] Although imagination is perfectly compatible with dreaming, the reveries Rousseau came to cherish most are episodes of pure sensation, during which all the faculties of the mind—imagining, comparing, thinking—have been annihilated. Because imagination calls up the future or reminds us of the past, it readily frustrates the bid for a "present that runs on indefinitely while this duration goes unnoticed."[184]

The eternal now that Rousseau experienced when floating on a boat or sitting by the shore was a state "where time is nothing" and he was "self-sufficient like God" or deliciously annihilated by the immensity of nature.[185] Unfortunately every dream is followed by an awakening, and then Rousseau found himself once again in a temporal and social world that reminded him he was forced to act and to do, no matter that his deepest desire was simply to be. Ostracized, his pathetic plight was to converse in the "society of vegetables" because he was the one botanist forbidden to talk to humans.[186] From the depths of his misery he then proclaimed how happy he was living off his own substance, because to admit his unhappiness was to vindicate the philosophical view that withdrawal from society can only lead to misery and madness. Most of all it was time that was his undoing, the flow of time from the fleeting present into the approaching future, that made him choose time and again what to do and who to be, instead of permitting him to coincide with himself as does the natural man. Once touched by society, we can never go home to nature again.

And so, in his last two years he reopened the question of the meaning of his life, this time approaching it experimentally,[187] descriptively, inductively instead of declaring in advance what his nature was and how it dictated the meaning of events. "One must be oneself," he had frequently stated. Now, it seems, it was not so certain he had a self to be. The *Reveries* opens with the question "What am I?"[188]

THE GREAT INTELLECTUAL debate that might have taken place when the philosophes responded to Rousseau failed to occur. Instead, the philosophes waged war on the person of Jean-Jacques and he fought back with the path-breaking autobiographical works meant to reveal the man, the truth, the man as truth, the man living the truth and claiming to set an example of how to remain unbroken by society.[189]

There can be no doubt that what we have just witnessed, the muckraking of the philosophes, the role-playing of Jean-Jacques, the appeals of both sides to the audience, and Rousseau's never-ending struggle to bind his life and thought into a coherent whole, constitute a significant part of the French Enlightenment. It is equally evident, however, that in recreating this dimension of the exchanges between Rousseau and the philosophes we have encountered the point at which the eighteenth century passed over into the nineteenth. During his final two years, Rousseau is no longer concerned with the question What is Enlightenment? The only question worth his attention, the one he strove desperately and unavailingly to answer before being overtaken by death, was Who am I?

Conclusion: Posterity Gained and Lost

BOTH Rousseau and Diderot, our two major protagonists, were concerned to persuade not only the audience of their day but that of all days to come. On Rousseau's orders his autobiographical works were not published until after his death because, as he fully realized, to tell his story was to tell that of all those who had once been his best friends and were now his worst enemies. He anticipated the vindication in the ages to come that he felt had eluded him during his lifetime, largely because the public was (mis)guided, in his view, by his philosophical adversaries who prided themselves on their prowess as opinion makers. Before he succumbed to delusions of a universal conspiracy against his name, he looked forward to the publication of his *Confessions* with as much hope as there was fear among the philosophes that his memoirs would besmirch their reputations with the hateful revelations that are the specialty of a former lover who can never forgive or forget.

Diderot, who had gambled all his hopes on posterity, was particularly apprehensive during the period leading up to the release of the *Confessions*, and as a result treated Rousseau so badly in his last published work that the journals saw fit to ask what *monsieur le philosophe* had to hide.[1] But though his actions might have been more politic, Diderot did have good reason to fear that all he had worked for was about to be snatched away by the irrepressible Jean-Jacques, still a threat even after his death. To Diderot posterity had always been everything, his reason for living, his purpose in sacrificing a life of leisure to the drudgery of the *Encyclopédie*, his consolation as he approached death. Convinced he merited the glorious name in ages to come that he did not fully attain among his contemporaries, he dreaded the thought that Rousseau would permanently mar his luster.

One of the greatest minds of his century, Diderot would have gone down in history as a second-rate thinker had his unpublished works not seen the light of day, some of them salvaged through incidents so improbable that he seems a figure of destiny. Those writings he dared publish after his imprisonment in 1749 were such as attested to his rectitude but were only moderately successful in his lifetime and have faded with the passage of time. In private Voltaire deemed *Le Père de famille* proof that "our century is a poor one compared with that of Louis XIV."[2] Though posterity agrees with Voltaire's negative verdict on Diderot's plays, it insists even more that Voltaire's own plays and poetry demonstrate the futility of trying to return artistically to the Grand Siècle.

Posterity always has the last laugh, and on Voltaire posterity has played the most dirty of tricks. He who in his age was at its pinnacle for so many years, he who treated all Rousseau's works with contempt and Diderot's with supercilious tolerance, has been demoted to a status far below that of the two great minds he refused to take seriously. Posterity has played a trick on Diderot and Rousseau as well. Each was prepared to be the darling of posterity or its refuse if the other triumphed; neither could comprehend that both might triumph, as has happened. When works such as *Rameau's Nephew* and *D'Alembert's Dream* finally found their way into print after coming perilously close to disappearing forever, it was only a matter of time before the full measure of Diderot's genius would be known. Rousseau's writings were already enormously successful in his lifetime, and if he has subsequently suffered more than his fair share of abuse at the hands of hostile readers, it is also true that exceptionally sensitive and discerning scholars have atoned for the injustices he has suffered.

Rousseau counted on posterity for absolution and redemption, Diderot for fame, and both for the victory of their respective definitions of Enlightenment. They also looked to ages to come because they agreed that even if their contemporary audience responded approvingly of their works, it did so only insofar as it felt amused, not because it was willing to be instructed. "Many have read me, some have even approved, and as I had foreseen, all have remained what they were before," Rousseau remarked in 1762.[3] Several years previously he had, in effect, commented on his own popularity when he explained why *Arlequin sauvage*, a play about a natural man, was a smashing success: "This play appeals to the turn of mind [of my contemporaries], which is to love and seek out new and singular ideas. Now there is nothing newer to them than what has to do with nature."[4] Diderot, too, and his sidekick Naigeon, believed the contemporary audience corrupt and starving for singularity, and in their fury cited the brisk sales of Rousseau's books as evidence that the French preferred amusement to instruction.[5] Wishful thinking took the form of a radically erroneous prediction when the philosophes declared that future ages would forget about Rousseau but remember the writings of the enlightened thinkers whose influence he decried.[6]

Even though both Rousseau and the philosophes have succeeded in rallying posterity to an appreciation, sometimes a deep and discriminating appreciation, of their thought, it is also true that posterity has been lost at the same time that it has been won—lost because the autocritique of Enlightenment Diderot articulated in *Rameau's Nephew* and Rousseau in all his writings has frequently been overlooked by the most outstanding students of eighteenth-century thought. How else can one explain why the finest studies of philosophical history often omit Rousseau altogether, or why a leading interpretation of the Enlightenment, cast in the mold of a philosophical history of the inheritance the Enlightenment received from earlier enlightenments, barely mentions Rousseau?[7]

Perhaps my attempt in the preceding chapters to re-create the autocritique of Enlightenment can now serve as a device for uncovering the reason why so vital a topic has suffered from relative neglect in studies of ideas in the eighteenth century. It is only to be expected that thinkers in the nineteenth century and beyond should carry the agendas of their period, romanticism, collectivism, and the like, back to the "century of philosophy." What is surprising and of the utmost consequence is that the protagonists themselves, Rousseau and the philosophes, should have buried the meaning of their conflict as their age approached the succeeding era. Fundamentally, as we have seen, the philosophes responded to Rousseau's brilliant challenge by denying he had said anything that merited their intellectual attention. All their efforts went to discrediting the message by denigrating the messenger, which led to Rousseau's unending quest to justify his life. Much may have been gained along the way, particularly within the realm of autobiography, but everything pertaining to Rousseau the figure of the Enlightenment was lost. The two parties to the battle, Rousseau and the philosophes, unconsciously worked together in obliterating the meaning of Rousseau's critique of the Enlightenment. During the final years of the *siècle des lumières,* the thinkers of that period unwittingly covered the footsteps that otherwise would have led posterity back to a reconsideration of one of the richest intellectual events of their time. Hence when the romantics set out to read themselves into Rousseau they met with little resistance from the historical record.

One other consequence follows from this singular turn of events, namely, that historians of our day who study French thought in the eighteenth century, rather than gaining from hindsight, frequently repeat the philosophical debate at its worst. All too often scholars hostile to Rousseau treat his thought as an irrational mishmash while praising his eloquence, failing to realize that they are merely repeating one of the standard ways through which the philosophes evaded Rousseau's powerful internal critique of their intellectual position. Likewise, the failure of historians of science to note Rousseau's efforts to tie his thought to the scientific debates of his day reinforces one of the less admirable strategies utilized by the philosophes to denigrate Rousseau. Even worse are the psychohistorians who use their Freud to dismiss the thinker by reducing his works to this or that quirk of personality, just as the philosophes called upon the psychology of their age to attack the man and to take comfort in his eventual madness.

The romantic interpretation of Rousseau, our foil throughout this study, need not be altogether rejected. Misreadings and unwarranted appropriations of an earlier thinker are an important part of the historical record and therefore merit serious study. The Aristotle of Aquinas may no longer be Greek or pagan, but we cannot afford to neglect what Aquinas made of Aristotle. Machiavelli's Livy is the Roman historian turned upside down, but this inversion of meanings may well be precisely the meaning the Florentine meant to convey.[8] Similarly, what the romantics read into Rousseau is of genuine significance to the study of romanticism, even if it amounts to a gratuitous and self-serving misreading. And by my own account the nineteenth-century chase after the ever-receding ideal of sincerity was itself born of the Enlightenment, particularly in Rousseau's grand and pitiful attempts to answer the philosophes by attempting to make his life conform to his thought. Finally, there is the sentence that appears near the end, fittingly, of both *La Nouvelle Héloïse* and *Emile:* "There is nothing beautiful except that which is not."[9] With those words Rousseau opened the way to a new aesthetic just as surely as he and the philosophes were unduly limited by the old in their insistence upon discussing music through the imitation of nature thesis.

My basic finding is that as Rousseau evolved from philosophe to ex-philosophe to antiphilosophe he never for a moment left the Enlightenment. Sometimes more radical, at other times more conservative than the philosophes, he remained staunchly loyal to the ideals of freedom, individual autonomy, and toleration that typified the "century of philosophy." At the very moment the philosophes were rejecting the third word in the expression "Liberty, Truth, Poverty," Rousseau made it his calling to live in accordance with d'Alembert's motto. By sacrificing material comfort he maintained his independence and earned his position as spokesperson for the cause of humanity. "Everyone has his vocation; mine is to tell the public hard truths, hard but useful."[10]

These hard truths Rousseau spoke through the "philosophy of the Enlightenment." In common with the philosophes, he made his arguments by having recourse to the epistemology of Locke, or by turning the genre of philosophical history to new uses, and again by conscientiously studying the findings and modes of thought of the natural sciences, paying special attention to whatever might lend itself to the development of a regenerative social science.

His political program was one of republicanism, a republicanism he would never share with even the most republican of the philosophes. Rousseau's republic was egalitarian, which set it apart from that of Helvétius, Diderot, or Holbach. Intellectuals, Rousseau was convinced, will always be the persons least willing to accept equality because they are the beings most consumed by *amour-propre*. Already in the philosophes one encounters the belief that was to be a commonplace of liberalism in the next century, that the quest for equality must take second place to the claims of freedom. Rousseau, in contrast, stressed the primacy of equality "because freedom cannot last without it";[11] our unfreedom is the consequence of the history of inequality he had taken great pains to record. From Rousseau's point of view it was not implausible that a republic might come to the rescue of the republic of letters, in fulfillment of the wishes of some of the philosophes. What was unthinkable was that such a republic would mean anything to the people, victims no less in the new world of talents than they had been in the old world of hereditary status.

More than any of the philosophes, Rousseau believed that light is precious because our candle may soon be snuffed out. Perhaps it is not too late for Poland to be divided into thirty-three republics, but Helvétius is surely wrong to think that overcivilized France can be saved if carved into thirty.[12] As Rousseau indicated in both *Julie* and *Emile,* the only hope for the French lay in building a familial fortress, walling out the world as long as possible before the march of progress crushes everything worthwhile. Before Rousseau, it was possible to believe that the choice was between light and darkness; after him, it was difficult to deny that some forms of light are as pernicious as darkness.

To say that Rousseau belongs to the Enlightenment is an understatement. His significance is best expressed by pointing out that his presence fundamentally altered the character of the *siècle des lumières.* Without him the Enlightenment would be a far poorer thing; with him the age of criticism contains a systematic self-criticism which gives the lie to the romantic interpretation of the eighteenth century that never seems to go out of style. Surely an age such as ours, in which critiques of Enlightenment are in constant demand, can benefit from a reconsideration of the first and perhaps the most telling critique of Enlightenment, the one it gave of itself. The autocritique is especially pertinent to those of us who cling to the world view of the Enlightenment despite its tarnished image and the obscurity of the path on which we walk into the future.

Notes

I have used the Pléiade edition of Rousseau's *Oeuvres complètes*. When it was necessary to look elsewhere, I have chosen editions both accessible and reliable: for instance, the Charles Porset edition of the *Essai sur l'origine des langues* (Paris: Nizet, 1970) and the Michel Launay edition of the *Lettre à d'Alembert* (Paris, 1967), published by Garnier-Flammarion. Many of the translations are my own but I have also used those of Judith and Roger Masters and Allan Bloom. For Diderot I have first called upon the readily available Classiques Garnier editions. Other citations are to Diderot's complete works; "A-T" designates citations to the old Assézat-Tourneux edition of Diderot's complete works, "H" to the new Hermann edition. For d'Alembert's *Discours préliminaire* I have used the Flammarion edition, *Encyclopédie* (Paris, 1986), vol. I. All other references to d'Alembert writings are to the *Oeuvres de d'Alembert*, 5 vols. (Paris: A. Belin, 1821–22). In the case of Condillac, references are to the *Oeuvres philosophiques de Condillac*, ed. G. Le Roy (Paris: Presses Universitaires de France, 1947–48). The very few citations to Montesquieu are to the Pléiade edition. For Helvétius I have called upon the Fayard edition; for Buffon, whenever possible, the *Oeuvres philosophiques de Buffon*, edited by Jean Piveteau (Paris: Presses Universitaires de France, 1954). Citations to the complete works of Buffon are to the version published by Eymery, Fruger et Cie (Paris, 1828–29), though unfortunately the volumes of this edition are not in chronological order. For Voltaire I have used the Moland edition (1877–1885) whenever it was necessary to consult the complete works. But insofar as possible I have referred to more accessible editions: for example, the Garnier Frères edition of the *Romans et contes*. My source for the complete works of Turgot is the edition edited by Gustave Schelle, 5 vols. (Paris: Félix Alcan, 1913–1922). References to Turgot's two lectures on progress are to R. Meek, ed., *Turgot on Progress, Sociology, and Economics* (Cambridge: Cambridge University Press, 1973); references to the *Mémoire sur les municipalités* are to K. Baker, ed., *The Old Regime and the French Revolution* (Chicago: University of Chicago Press, 1987). As for the other authors, Holbach, Duclos, La Mettrie, and so on, the sources are as indicated in the endnotes. I have employed standard abbreviations when citing articles in scholarly journals: *SVEC = Studies on Voltaire and the Eighteenth Century; JHI = Journal of the History of Ideas; AJJR = Annales de la Société Jean-Jacques Rousseau.* I wish to thank the Mazur Faculty Fund of Brandeis University for assistance in collecting the sources necessary to write this book.

Introduction

1. Jean Morel, "Recherches sur les sources du *Discours sur l'inégalité*," *AJJR*, 5 (1909), 119–198; René Hubert, *Rousseau et l'Encyclopédie* (Paris: J. Gamber, 1928); Jean Fabre, "Deux frères ennemis: Diderot et Jean-Jacques," *Diderot Studies*, 3 (1961), 155–213; Jacques Proust, *Diderot et l'Encyclopédie* (Paris: Armand Colin, 1962), pp. 359–398; Henri Gouhier, *Rousseau et Voltaire* (Paris: J. Vrin, 1983); Robert Wokler, *Rousseau on Society, Politics, Music, and Language* (London: Garland, 1987).

2. Paul Hazard, *La Pensée européenne au XVIIIème siècle* (Paris: Boivin, 1946); Peter Gay, *The Enlightenment*, 2 vols. (New York: Knopf, 1967, 1969).

3. Jean Starobinski, *Jean-Jacques Rousseau: La transparence et l'obstacle* (Paris: Gallimard, 1971); Roger Masters, *The Political Philosophy of Rousseau* (Princeton: Princeton University Press, 1968); Judith Shklar, *Men and Citizens: A Study of Rousseau's Social Theory* (Cambridge: Cambridge University Press, 1969). Subsequent notes will identify other studies of Rousseau to which I am indebted.

4. J. H. Brumfitt, *The French Enlightenment* (Cambridge, Mass.: Schenkman, 1972), pp. 7–8.

5. Norman Hampson, *The Enlightenment* (New York: Penguin, 1968), p. 9.

6. E.g., Daniel Mornet, *Les Sciences de la nature en France au XVIIIe siècle* (Paris: Armand Colin, 1911), pp. 223, 233; Thomas Hankins, *Jean d'Alembert* (Oxford: Oxford University Press, 1970), pp. 27, 133, 234; Hankins, *Science and the Enlightenment* (Cambridge: Cambridge University Press, 1985), p. 161. Jacques Roger omits Rousseau from his study *Les Sciences de la vie dans la pensée française du XVIIIe siècle* (Paris: Armand Colin, 1963).

7. Gay, *The Enlightenment*, vol. I, p. x.

8. Ibid., vol. II, pp. 529–552.

9. Ibid., vol. I, p. 4.

10. Fabre, "Deux frères ennemis."

11. Ernst Cassirer, *The Question of Jean-Jacques Rousseau* (Bloomington: Indiana University Press, 1963); Cassirer, *Rousseau, Kant, and Goethe* (New York: Harper, 1963).

12. The appendix of Robert Derathé's *Le Rationalisme de Jean-Jacques Rousseau* (Paris: Presses Universitaires de France, 1948) contains a valuable critique of neo-Kantian readings of Rousseau.

13. Rousseau, *Oeuvres complètes* (hereafter *O.C.*), vol. III, p. 101; Rousseau, *Confessions*, in *O.C.*, vol. I, pp. 223, 436, 492, 570; Rousseau, *Emile*, in *O.C.*, vol. IV, pp. 241, 348, 582, 632n.

14. *Confessions*, p. 436. See also Rousseau, *Correspondance complète*, ed. R. A. Leigh, vol. IX, p. 27. (Hereafter *Corr.* [Leigh].)

15. Rousseau, *Fragments politiques*, in *O.C.*, vol. III, p. 516. (Hereafter *Frag. Pol.*)

16. Carl Becker, *The Heavenly City of the Eighteenth-Century Philosophers* (New Haven: Yale University Press, 1932), p. 41. For correctives see Robert Mauzi, *L'Idée du bonheur au XVIIIe siècle* (Paris: Armand Colin, 1960), p. 12, and Jean Fabre, *Lumières et romantisme* (Paris: C. Klincksieck, 1963), p. ii.

17. Yvon Belavel, *L'Esthétique sans paradoxe de Diderot* (Paris: Gallimard, 1950), p. 240.

18. E.g., Peter Gay, *The Party of Humanity* (New York: Norton, 1971), p. 204.

19. Hume, *An Enquiry Concerning the Principles of Morals,* ed. Selby-Bigge, 156.
20. Bentham, "The Declaration of Rights," *Anarchical Fallacies.*
21. For an example of Pufendorf's use of the notion of self-interest in his writings on natural law, see *On the Law of Nature and Nations,* bk. II, ch. 3, sects. 15–17.
22. Ira Wade, *The Clandestine Organization and Diffusion of Philosophic Ideas in France from 1700 to 1750* (Princeton: Princeton University Press, 1938).
23. The current scholarly wisdom locates the seeds of radicalism in the low Enlightenment, e.g., Robert Darnton, *The Literary Underground of the Old Regime* (Cambridge, Mass.: Harvard University Press, 1982). The standard view of the high Enlightenment, e.g., Alan Kors, *D'Holbach's Coterie* (Princeton: Princeton University Press, 1976), is that the very success of the philosophes made them conservative. I hope to show that Kors is correct on the lesser figures (Marmontel, Morellet, and so on) but wrong on such central thinkers as Helvétius, Diderot, Holbach, and possibly Turgot.
24. Arthur Wilson, *Diderot* (Oxford: Oxford University Press, 1972), p. 310.
25. D'Alembert to Voltaire, 17 Jan. 1765, in *Oeuvres de d'Alembert,* vol. V, p. 136.
26. By Holbach but attributed to the deceased Nicolas-Antoine Boulanger.
27. On Rousseau and Geneva, see Gaspard Vallette, *Jean-Jacques Rousseau, Genevois* (Paris: Plon-Nourrit, 1911); J. S. Spink, *Jean-Jacques Rousseau et Genève* (Paris: Boivin, 1934); Michel Launay, *Jean-Jacques Rousseau, écrivain politique* (Grenoble: C.E.L., 1971); James Miller, *Rousseau: Dreamer of Democracy* (New Haven: Yale University Press, 1984).
28. Roy Porter and Mikulas Teich, eds., *The Enlightenment in National Context* (Cambridge: Cambridge University Press, 1981).
29. Franco Venturi, *Utopia and Reform in the Enlightenment* (Cambridge: Cambridge University Press, 1971), ch. 5, underscores the special role of France. So does Hankins, *Science and the Enlightenment,* p. vii.
30. Roger Picard, *Les Salons littéraires et la société française* (New York: Brentano's, 1943), p. 19, stresses the peculiarly French nature of salon society.
31. A. Smith, *The Theory of Moral Sentiments,* pt. III, ch. 2, sects. 18–23. Compare d'Alembert's position as stated in Chapter 3 of this book.
32. Hazard, *Pensée européenne,* ch. 1; Gay, *The Enlightenment,* vol. I, p. 130.

1. The Virtue of Selfishness

1. See Elie Halévy, *The Growth of Philosophic Radicalism* (Boston: Beacon, 1966), p. 33, on the need to reform the language of morals; Mauzi, *L'Idée du bonheur,* on having it both ways in French thought.
2. Holbach, *Système de la nature* (Hildesheim: G. Olms, 1966), vol. I, p. xxxii.
3. Augustine, *City of God,* XIV, 28.
4. J. S. Spink, *French Free-Thought from Gassendi to Voltaire* (London: University of London, Athlone Press, 1960), p. 312.
5. Mara Vamos, "Pascal's *Pensées* and the Enlightenment," *SVEC,* 97 (1972), 17–145.
6. Voltaire placed Pascal's vision of the human condition first, his theology second, thereby inviting the philosophes to read the *Pensées* as originally intended, not as

rewritten by the Port Royal editors who put the theology first. Since the philosophes were weaned on Voltaire's *Lettres philosophiques,* I infer that Vamos has overstated the case for a misunderstood Pascal. I do agree, however, that Pascal had no influence on the political thought of the encyclopedists.

7. Voltaire's *Lettres philosophiques,* letter 25.
8. Ernst Cassirer, *The Philosophy of the Enlightenment* (Boston: Beacon, 1964), p. 144.
9. See d'Alembert, *Discours préliminaire,* for an appreciation of Pascal the scientist, in *Encyclopédie* (Paris: Flammarion, 1986), vol. I, p. 147.
10. Pascal, *Pensées,* ed. Brunschvicg, 425, 465.
11. Ibid., 434.
12. Ibid., 425.
13. Ibid., 430.
14. Ibid., 131, 129.
15. Ibid., 109.
16. Ibid., 127.
17. Ibid., 377. On the misery of self-knowledge, 144.
18. Ibid., 164; also 139–143.
19. Ibid., 172.
20. Ibid., 553.
21. Ibid., 211.
22. Ibid., 123.
23. Ibid., 101.
24. Ibid., 100.
25. Ibid., 67.
26. Ibid., 206.
27. Ibid., 72.
28. Ibid., 91, 252.
29. Ibid., 346, 348, 434.
30. Ibid., 412.
31. Ibid., 274.
32. Ibid., 233.
33. Voltaire, *Lettres philosophiques,* letter 25, no. 23.
34. Ibid., no. 35.
35. Given Port Royal's rewrite of the *Pensées,* Voltaire may have mistakenly thought Pascal a Cartesian. Or he may have sensed Pascal's skepticism but decided to use the occasion to attack dualism. Certainly Voltaire knew the French had long used skepticism to defend Catholicism. See Richard Popkin, *The History of Scepticism from Erasmus to Descartes* (Berkeley: University of California Press, 1979), for a thorough account of this tradition.
36. Voltaire, *Lettres philosophiques,* letter 25, no. 37.
37. Ibid., no. 23.
38. Ibid., letter 13.
39. Ibid., letter 25, no. 56.
40. Locke, *Essay Concerning Human Understanding,* ed. A. C. Fraser, bk. II, ch. xx, no. 6; ch. xxi, no. 31.
41. Voltaire, *Lettres philosophiques,* letter 25, no. 26.

42. Ibid., no. 23.
43. Ibid., no. 11. Though unappreciative of Shakespeare, Voltaire should have enjoyed this line: "Self-love . . . is not so vile a sin as self-neglecting." *Henry V*, act II, scene 4.
44. Pascal, *Pensées*, 477.
45. Ibid., 420.
46. Ibid., 199.
47. Voltaire, *Lettres philosophiques*, letter 25, no. 6.
48. Diderot, *La Religieuse*, pp. 310–311; cf. *Les Bijoux indiscrets*, p. 21. Both works in Diderot, *Oeuvres romanesques* (hereafter *O.R.*).
49. Diderot, *Supplément au voyage de Bougainville*, pp. 495, 499, in Diderot, *Oeuvres philosophiques* (hereafter *O. Phil.*).
50. Diderot, *Pensées philosophiques*, no. i.
51. Ibid., no. iii; cf.: "Tout ce que la passion inspire, je le pardonne." 31 July 1762, *Lettres à Sophie Volland*, ed. André Babelon (Paris: Gallimard, 1938), vol. I, p. 258.
52. Diderot, *Pensées philosophiques*, no. xiv.
53. E.g., Bayle, *Pensées diverses sur la comète*, CXXXVI.
54. Hume, *A Treatise of Human Nature*, bk. II, pt. 3, sect. 3.
55. Diderot, *Introduction aux grands principes*, A-T, vol. II, p. 88n.
56. Duclos, *Considérations sur les moeurs* (Cambridge: Cambridge University Press, 1946), p. 51. (Hereafter Duclos, *Moeurs*.)
57. Cf. Albert Hirschman, *The Passions and the Interests* (Princeton: Princeton University Press, 1977).
58. Diderot, *De la Poésie dramatique*, p. 195, and *Entretiens sur Le Fils naturel*, p. 128, both in Diderot, *Oeuvres esthétiques* (hereafter *O.E.*); Diderot, *Introduction aux grands principes*, p. 77; Diderot, 6 Nov. 1760, in *Correspondance*, ed. Roth, vol. III, p. 226 (hereafter *Corr.* [Roth]).
59. R. R. Palmer, *Catholics and Unbelievers in Eighteenth-Century France* (New York: Cooper Square, 1961), p. 175. Originally published by Princeton University Press in 1939.
60. Montaigne, *Essais*, I, 1; III, 9.
61. Pierre Nicole, "De la Charité et de l'amour-propre," in *Oeuvres philosophiques de Nicole* (Paris: Hachette, 1845), p. 179.
62. Ibid.
63. Moreover, we do not know intentions. Helvétius, *De l'Esprit*, bk. II, ch. 2.
64. On the Jansenist preparation for the philosophes, see Marcel Raymond, "Du Jansénisme à la morale de l'intérêt," *Mercure de France* (June 1957), 238–255; on the persistence of the theme of self-love in French thought, see Nannerl Keohane, *Philosophy and the State in France* (Princeton: Princeton University Press, 1980).
65. Saint-Lambert [?], "Interêt (Morale)," *Encyclopédie*, vol. VIII, pp. 818–819.
66. Helvétius, *De l'Esprit*, bk. I, ch. 4.
67. Ibid., preface: "J'ai cru qu'on devait traiter la morale comme toutes les autres sciences, et faire une morale comme une physique expérimentale."
68. Mandeville, *The Fable of the Bees*, pt. I, "A Search into the Nature of Society."
69. Hume, "Of Refinement in the Arts," last page. See also Halévy, *Growth of Philosophical Radicalism*, p. 16.

70. Diderot, *Essai sur le mérite et la vertu,* A-T, vol. I, pp. 13, 30, 57.
71. Holbach, *La Morale universelle* (Tours, 1792), vol. I, p. 23.
72. Voltaire, "Amour-propre," in the *Dictionnaire philosophique.*
73. See Holbach, *La Morale universelle,* vol. I, p. xxi, for a repudiation of Mandeville. Jean Ehrard, *L'Idée de nature en France à l'aube des lumières* (Paris: Flammarion, 1970), p. 235.
74. Pope, *Essay on Man,* epistle III, 317–318; cf. epistle IV, 396.
75. Ibid., epistle I, 248.
76. Ibid., epistle IV. On Pope and Mandeville, see Isaac Kramnick, *Bolingbroke and His Circle* (Cambridge, Mass.: Harvard University Press, 1968), pp. 201–204, 217–223.
77. See Ira Wade, *The Philosophe in the French Drama of the Eighteenth Century* (Princeton: Princeton University Press, 1926), for a survey.
78. Holbach, *La Morale universelle,* vol. III, p. 330.
79. Holbach, *Système de la nature,* vol. I, p. 380; Holbach, *Système social* (Amsterdam, 1773), vol. I, p. 119.
80. Holbach, *Système de la nature,* vol. I, pp. 376, 380.
81. D'Alembert, *Essai sur les élémens de philosophie,* in *Oeuvres de d'Alembert,* vol. I, p. 137. (Hereafter *Élémens de philosophie.*)
82. Holbach, *Système de la nature,* vol. I, p. 181.
83. Holbach, *La Morale universelle,* vol. I, p. 40.
84. Holbach, *Système de la nature,* vol. I, pp. 161–162.
85. Ibid., vol. II, p. 250; vol. I, p. 379.
86. Diderot, *Introduction aux grands principes,* p. 85.
87. Robert Mauzi, "Les Rapports du bonheur et de la vertu dans l'oeuvre de Diderot," *Cahiers de l'Association Internationale des Études Françaises* (July 1960), 255–268.
88. E.g., Diderot, *Salon de 1765* (Paris: Hermann, 1984), p. 127; Diderot, *Salons de 1759, 1761, 1763* (Paris: Hermann, 1984), pp. 120–121, 162.
89. Diderot, *Salon de 1765,* p. 59. Cf. Diderot, *Salon de 1763,* p. 195.
90. Diderot, *Réfutation de l'ouvrage d'Helvétius intitulé De l'Homme,* A-T, vol. II, p. 304.
91. Helvétius, *De l'Esprit,* bk. II, ch. 19; Diderot, *Réfutation de L'Homme,* pp. 314–315.
92. Diderot to Voltaire, 29 Sept. 1762. Diderot, *Corr.* (Roth), vol. IV, pp. 176–177.
93. Diderot, *O. E.,* p. 31; Diderot, *Corr.* (Roth), vol. VII, p. 164.
94. Holbach, *La Morale universelle,* vol. I, p. 37.
95. D'Alembert, *Élémens de philosophie,* p. 213.
96. Diderot, *Le Fils naturel,* Act III, scene 9.
97. Ibid., act V, scene 3. See also Mauzi, "Les Rapports du bonheur et de la vertu."
98. Diderot, *Le Fils naturel,* act V, scene 3; act IV, scene 3. Diderot, *Essai sur le mérite et la vertu,* A-T, vol. I, pp. 89, 121.
99. Richard Tuck, *Natural Rights Theories* (Cambridge: Cambridge University Press, 1979).
100. Holbach, *La Morale universelle, ou les devoirs de l'homme fondés sur sa nature;* cf. *Éthocratie* and all Holbach's works.
101. D'Alembert, *Réflexions sur l'histoire,* in *Oeuvres de d'Alembert,* vol. II, p. 9.
102. Burke, *Reflections on the Revolution in France* (Indianapolis: Hackett, 1987), p. 41.
103. Diderot, *Entretiens sur Le Fils naturel,* p. 105; Diderot, *De la Poésie dramatique,* p. 196; Diderot, *Paradoxe sur le comédien,* p. 348, in *O.E.* See also Belavel, *L'Esthétique sans paradoxe de Diderot,* p. 212.

104. Diderot, *Entretiens sur Le Fils naturel*, p. 153.
105. Diderot, *Poésie dramatique*, p. 192.
106. Voltaire, "Vertu," in the *Dictionnaire philosophique*. See the *Traité de métaphysique*, ch. 8, for the notion of "une bienveillance naturelle."
107. Voltaire, *Traité de métaphysique*, ch. 9.
108. Mauzi, *L'Idée du bonheur*, pp. 216–218.
109. Holbach, *Contagion sacrée*.
110. Herbert Dieckmann, *Le Philosophe: Texts and Interpretation* (Saint Louis, Mo.: Washington University Series, 1948), p. 46.
111. Holbach, *La Morale universelle*, vol. I, p. 441.
112. At the beginning of the *Second Discourse* Rousseau treats pity and self-love as two givens of human nature; in *Emile* pity appears to be a development of self-love. Bk. IV.
113. Boulanger, "Œconomie politique," *Encyclopédie*, vol. XI, pp. 366–383.
114. It should be noted, however, that while monarchical in their political bearing, Boulanger's writings suggested a complicity between tyrants and priests that disturbed Voltaire but delighted Diderot and Holbach, whose political thought by the 1760s was growing more radical. John Pappas, *Voltaire and d'Alembert* (Bloomington: Indiana University Press, 1962), p. 92.
115. Hubert, *Rousseau et l'Encyclopédie*, was the first to show that Rousseau wrote to refute "Droit naturel."
116. Diderot, "Hobbisme, ou Philosophie de Hobbes," *Encyclopédie*, vol. VIII, pp. 232–241.
117. Diderot, "Droit Naturel," pp. 29–35 in *Oeuvres politiques* (hereafter *O. Pol.*).
118. Rousseau, *Du Contract social (première version)* (hereafter *Geneva MS*), in *O.C.*, vol. III, p. 282.
119. Ibid., pp. 283, 284.
120. Rousseau, *Lettre à d'Alembert*, ed. Launay, pp. 78–79. (Hereafter *L.A.*) Launay omits a passage that appeared in the edition of 1782; in it Rousseau commented wryly on "these weeping ladies in the boxes at the theatre, so proud of their tears."
121. Robert Derathé, *Jean-Jacques Rousseau et la science politique de son temps* (Paris: J. Vrin, 1974), p. 145.
122. Rousseau, *Discours sur l'origine et les fondemens de l'inégalité parmi les hommes* (hereafter *Second Discourse*), pp. 153–154; *Geneva MS*, p. 288; Rousseau, *Écrits sur Saint-Pierre*, pp. 601–602. All in *O.C.*, vol. III.
123. Hobbes, *Leviathan*, ch. 8.
124. *Geneva MS*, pp. 285, 286.
125. Rousseau, *Discours sur l'Économie Politique* (hereafter *Pol. Econ.*), in *O.C.*, vol. III, pp. 271–272.
126. Ibid., p. 252.
127. Ibid., p. 255.
128. Ibid., pp. 260, 262.
129. John Lough, "The Problem of the Unsigned Articles in the *Encyclopédie*," *SVEC*, 32 (1965), 327–390.
130. Helvétius, *De l'Esprit*, bk. II, ch. 15; bk. III, ch. 15.
131. Montesquieu, *De l'Esprit des lois*, bk. V, ch. 2.
132. Rousseau, *Emile*, p. 249.

133. Ibid., p. 468.
134. *L.A.*; Rousseau, *Projet de constitution pour la Corse* (hereafter *Corsica*), in *O.C.*, vol. III. This point will be developed in Chapter 4.
135. Rousseau, *Considérations sur le gouvernement de Pologne* (hereafter *Poland*), in *O.C.*, vol. III, p. 1019; see also p. 968.
136. *L.A.*, pp. 131, 237.
137. Rousseau, *La Nouvelle Héloïse* (hereafter *Julie*), in *O.C.*, vol. II, pp. 358–359.
138. Proust, *Diderot et l'Encyclopédie*, pp. 384–385.
139. *Du Contract social* (hereafter *Social Contract*), in *O.C.*, vol. III, p. 373; cf. p. 368.
140. Ibid., p. 371.
141. Judith Shklar, "General Will," in Philip Wiener, ed., *Dictionary of the History of Ideas* (New York: Scribner, 1973), vol. II, pp. 275–281.
142. Rousseau, *Corr.* (Leigh), vol. IX, p. 96.
143. *Emile*, p. 334; cf. p. 523n.
144. Ibid., p. 329.
145. Ibid., pp. 345, 358, 363.
146. Ibid., pp. 261, 286–288.
147. Ibid., p. 447.
148. Ibid., pp. 456–460.
149. *Pol. Econ.*, p. 256.
150. Helvétius, *De l'Esprit*, bk. II, chs. 23, 24.
151. Rousseau, "Notes sur *De l'Esprit*," in *O.C.*, vol. IV, p. 1126. Turgot shared Rousseau's fear that the utilitarianism of Helvétius was destructive of rights. Turgot, *Oeuvres*, ed. Schelle, vol. III, pp. 636–641.
152. The capacity to live in the present is the prerogative of natural man. *Second Discourse*, p. 144.
153. Ibid., pp. 174, 193; Rousseau, *Discours sur les sciences et les arts* (hereafter *First Discourse*), in *O.C.*, vol. III, pp. 7–8.
154. Pascal, *Pensées*, 477, 483.
155. *Poland*, p. 966.
156. On the general will in the thought of Pascal, see Patrick Riley, *The General Will before Rousseau* (Princeton: Princeton University Press, 1986), pp. 14–24; Keohane, *Philosophy and the State*, p. 280.
157. René Pomeau, *La Religion de Voltaire* (Paris: Nizet, 1956), pp. 193, 232–234, 418; Holbach, *Système de la nature*, vol. II, 332n–333n; Diderot, 3 August 1759, *Lettres à Sophie Volland*, vol. I, p. 38.
158. For my purposes it is important to stress that Rousseau's move to a position that parallels Pascal's was a development of the thought of the Enlightenment rather than a return to an Augustinian tradition. Ann Hartle's *The Modern Self in Rousseau's Confessions* (Notre Dame, Ind.: University of Notre Dame Press, 1983) shows that all relevant comparisons of the *Confessions* of Rousseau to those of Augustine take the form of strong contrasts. Riley, *The General Will before Rousseau*, has proved conclusively that Malebranche, not Augustine or Calvin, is the religious thinker who mattered to Rousseau and the philosophes, and that Rousseau vindicated Bossuet's fear that the *Treatise on Nature and Grace* of Malebranche would end by being all nature and no grace.

2. Philosophical History

1. Ruhlière, *Discours de réception à l'Académie française*, 4 June 1787. Quoted in Maurice Pellisson, *Les Hommes de lettres au XVIIIe siècle* (Paris: Armand Colin, 1911), p. 247.
2. Voltaire, *Essai sur le siècle de Louis XIV*. See also Voltaire, *Oeuvres complètes*, vol. XIV, p. ix, "Avertissement de Beuchot."
3. For the old history, see Orest Ranum, *Artisans of Glory: Writers and Historical Thought in Seventeenth-Century France* (Chapel Hill: University of North Carolina Press, 1980).
4. Frank Manuel, *The Eighteenth Century Confronts the Gods* (Cambridge, Mass.: Harvard University Press, 1959).
5. Voltaire, *Nouveau plan d'une histoire de l'esprit humain* (*Mercure de France*, April 1745), in the Garnier Frères edition of the *Essai sur les moeurs et l'esprit des nations*, ed. René Pomeau (Paris, 1963), vol. II, pp. 815–817. All citations to the *Essai sur les moeurs* will be to the Pomeau edition.
6. Voltaire, *Le Siècle de Louis XIV* (hereafter Voltaire, *Siècle*), ch. 1.
7. Ibid., ch. 11.
8. D'Alembert, preface to vol. III of the *Encyclopédie*, in *Oeuvres de d'Alembert*, vol. IV, p. 389.
9. Voltaire, *Siècle*, ch. 1. Voltaire celebrates the four great ages again in the *Essai sur les moeurs* and attacks Rousseau. Vol. II, p. 174. Though Voltaire made the notion of the four ages a commonplace, it may be found earlier in Dubos, *Réflexions critiques sur la poésie et sur la peinture* (Paris: Pissot, 1755), vol. II, p. 141.
10. Turgot, *A Philosophical Review of the Successive Advances of the Human Mind*, p. 51, in Ronald Meek, ed., *Turgot on Progress, Sociology, and Economics* (Cambridge: Cambridge University Press, 1973). Duclos, *Considérations sur les moeurs*, p. 136, was unusual in expressing concern for the decline of erudites. On Gibbon and the philosophes, see Jean Seznec, *Essais sur Diderot et l'antiquité* (Oxford: Clarendon Press, 1957), pp. 81–82.
11. D'Alembert, *Réflexions sur l'histoire*, in *Oeuvres de d'Alembert*, vol. II, p. 6.
12. Ibid., p. 2.
13. D'Alembert, *Mémoires et réflexions sur Christine*, in *Oeuvres de d'Alembert*, vol. II, p. 119.
14. D'Alembert, *Discours préliminaire*, p. 134.
15. D'Alembert, *Élémens de philosophie*, p. 122.
16. The philosophes were especially fond of the literary prowess evinced in Pascal's *Lettres écrites à un provincial*. E.g., Voltaire, *Siècle*, ch. 32; D'Alembert, *Oeuvres*, vol. II, p. 34, and vol. IV, p. 362.
17. Voltaire, *Siècle*, ch. 32.
18. Meek, ed., *Turgot on Progress*, pp. 59, 57.
19. Fontenelle, *Digression sur les Anciens et les Modernes*, in *Textes choisis* (Paris: Éditions sociales, 1966), pp. 253, 259, both cites the age of Augustus as that of artistic perfection and congratulates the moderns on creating new genres.
20. In part, as Charles Frankel has suggested in *The Faith of Reason* (New York: King's Crown Press, 1948), differing views of progress were based upon two opposing understandings of scientific research, one dogmatic, the other more skeptical but embold-

ened by the self-corrective nature of science. For Turgot on progress, see Frank Manuel, *The Prophets of Paris* (New York: Harper, 1965), ch. 1.

21. Norman Torrey, ed., *Voltaire and the Enlightenment* (New York: Crofts, 1931), p. 24.
22. Voltaire, *Siècle*, ch. 32.
23. See J. H. Brumfitt, *Voltaire Historian* (Oxford: Oxford University Press, 1958) for Voltaire's strategy. See John Lough, *Writer and Public in France* (Oxford: Oxford University Press, 1978), pp. 108–112, and Pellisson, *Les Hommes de lettres*, p. 55, for Voltaire's exaggerated account of Louis XIV's support of the arts.
24. Voltaire, *Siècle*, ch. 34.
25. Voltaire, *Lettres philosophiques*, letter 24.
26. Meek, ed., *Turgot on Progress*, pp. 52, 113.
27. For the history of science as written by the philosophes, see Georges Gusdorf, *De l'histoire des sciences à l'histoire de la pensée* (Paris: Payot, 1966), pp. 54–92.
28. D'Alembert, *Discours préliminaire*, p. 161.
29. Ibid., p. 154.
30. Hankins, *Jean d'Alembert*; Ronald Grimsley, *Jean D'Alembert* (Cardiff: University of Wales Press, 1963).
31. Meek, ed., *Turgot on Progress*, pp. 55–56, 115–116.
32. Henry Vyverberg, *Historical Pessimism in the French Enlightenment* (Cambridge, Mass.: Harvard University Press, 1958), includes some useful information, not all of which is well digested.
33. Brumfitt, *Voltaire Historian*, p. 108.
34. Fontenelle, *De l'Origine des fables*, in *Oeuvres complètes* (Paris: Fayard, 1989–1991), vol. III, pp. 187–202, and *Histoire des oracles*, vol. II, pp. 137–295. See also Manuel, *Eighteenth Century Confronts the Gods*, pp. 52–53.
35. Diderot, *Prospectus*, H, vol. V, pp. 98–99; D'Alembert, *Préface du troisième volume de l'Encyclopédie*, in *Oeuvres de d'Alembert*, vol. IV, p. 389.
36. Diderot, *Prospectus*, p. 96; Judith Shklar, "Jean d'Alembert and the Rehabilitation of History," *JHI*, 42 (1981), 643–664.
37. Diderot, *Prospectus*, p. 99; Diderot, "Encyclopédie," *Encyclopédie*, vol. V, pp. 635b, 637b. For more on the uses of history in the *Encyclopédie*, consult René Hubert, *Les Sciences sociales dans l'Encyclopédie* (Paris: Félix Alcan, 1923), and Nelly Schargo, *History in the Encyclopédie* (New York: Columbia University Press, 1947).
38. Diderot, "Encyclopédie," p. 647b; Diderot, "Art," *Encyclopédie*, vol. I, pp. 714b–715a.
39. Diderot, "Encyclopédie," p. 636b.
40. Diderot, "Art," p. 716a.
41. Diderot, *Prospectus*, pp. 99–100; Proust, *Diderot et l'Encyclopédie*, ch. 6.
42. Diderot, "Art," p. 716b.
43. Ibid., p. 714.
44. D'Alembert, "Caractère," *Encyclopédie*, vol. II, p. 666a.
45. Diderot, "Art," p. 715a. The same view may be found in d'Alembert, "Elémens des sciences," *Encyclopédie*, vol. V, p. 495a.
46. E.g., Brumfitt, *Voltaire Historian*, pp. 10, 34.
47. Diderot, *Interprétation de la nature*, no. xix.
48. Diderot, "Encyclopédie," p. 637b.
49. Diderot, *Interprétation*, nos. xviii, xix, xl.

50. George A. Kelly, "Eulogy: Celebrating the New Hero," ch. 3 of *Mortal Politics in Eighteenth-Century France* (Waterloo, Ontario: Historical Reflections Press, 1986); Charles B. Paul, *Science and Immortality: The Éloges of the Paris Academy of Sciences, 1699–1791* (Berkeley: University of California Press, 1980).

51. Voltaire, *Siècle*, ch. 1.

52. Fontenelle, *Sur l'histoire,* in *Oeuvres complètes,* vol. III, p. 179.

53. *First Discourse,* p. 20.

54. Ibid., pp. 12, 20.

55. Voltaire, *Siècle,* ch. 39; Voltaire, *Essai sur les moeurs,* vol. I, pp. 33, 66–71, 205–226; vol. II, pp. 394–399, 410, 785–793.

56. *First Discourse,* p. 11.

57. Wilson, *Diderot,* p. 93.

58. D'Alembert, *Sur la destruction des Jésuites en France* in *Oeuvres de d'Alembert,* vol. II, pp. 11–118. Voltaire deemed the expulsion of the Jesuits a problem, because they would no longer offset the Jansenists. Pappas, *Voltaire and d'Alembert,* p. 35n.

59. *Emile,* pp. 667n, 250; *Social Contract,* p. 361n.

60. *First Discourse,* p. 26.

61. Ibid., p. 7.

62. Ibid., p. 27.

63. Ibid., pp. 21, 25–26.

64. Ibid., p. 25.

65. Ibid., pp. 13–14, 30.

66. *Confessions,* p. 404.

67. Fontenelle, *Sur l'histoire* and *De l'Origine des fables,* in *Oeuvres complètes,* vol. III, pp. 169–185, 187–202.

68. Lafitau, *Moeurs des sauvages amériquains comparées aux moeurs des premiers temps* (1724).

69. *First Discourse,* p. 11n; Montaigne, "Of Cannibals," *Essais,* I, 31.

70. *First Discourse,* p. 9.

71. Ibid., p. 6.

72. Ibid., p. 28.

73. Diderot, "Encyclopédie," pp. 635b, 646a.

74. Rousseau, *Dernière réponse,* in *O.C.,* vol. III, p. 80n.

75. Diderot, "Cité," *Encyclopédie,* vol. III, p. 485b.

76. Rousseau, *Confessions,* p. 347.

77. Voltaire, "Histoire," *Dictionnaire philosophique,* in *Oeuvres complètes* (Paris: 1877–1885), vol. XIX, pp. 346–370; "Le Pyrrhonisme de l'histoire," vol. XXVII, pp. 235–299. See also Brumfitt, *Voltaire Historian,* p. 3.

78. D'Alembert, *Discours préliminaire,* p. 111.

79. Locke, *Essay Concerning Human Understanding,* bk. I, ch. ii, no. 23; Holbach, *Système de la nature,* vol. I, p. 201, and vol. II, p. 49; Condillac, *Traité des sensations,* in *Oeuvres philosophiques de Condillac,* vol. I, pp. 221, 244.

80. Helvétius, *De l'Homme,* sect. V, ch. 3; Holbach, *La Morale universelle,* vol. I, pp. xi, 77, and vol. III, p. 314; Holbach, *Système social,* vol. I, pp. 48–51, 102, 156; Holbach, *Système de la nature,* vol. I, p. 200; Diderot, *Salon de 1767,* H, vol. XVI, p. 87.

81. Diderot, 4 Oct. 1767, *Corr.* (Roth), vol. VII, pp. 163–164.

82. Diderot, *O.E.*, p. 428.
83. 2 Sept. 1762, *Lettres à Sophie Volland*, vol. I, pp. 281–282. See also Herbert Dieckmann, "Diderot's Conception of Genius," *JHI*, 2 (1941), 151–182.
84. Diderot, *Interprétation*, nos. xxx, xxxi.
85. "Encyclopédie," p. 647b.
86. Locke, *Essay Concerning Human Understanding*, intro., no. 2; cf. bk. II, ch. xi, no. 15.
87. Lancelot and Arnauld, *Grammaire de Port Royal* (1660).
88. *First Discourse*, p. 6.
89. E.g., Turgot's two lectures before the Sorbonne in 1750.
90. *Second Discourse*, p. 171; see also p. 162.
91. Ibid., pp. 133, 162.
92. Ibid., pp. 193, 127.
93. It is arguable that Turgot invented the word, but Rousseau put it into circulation. See the editorial comment in Rousseau's *Oeuvres complètes*, vol. III, pp. 1317–1318.
94. *Second Discourse*, p. 170; *First Discourse*, p. 28.
95. *Second Discourse*, pp. 123, 133.
96. Marmontel, "Critique," *Encyclopédie*, vol. IV, p. 491a–b.
97. Locke, *Essay Concerning Human Understanding*, bk. IV, ch. xvi, no. 12.
98. Fontenelle, *Sur l'histoire* and *De l'Origine des fables*.
99. Pomeau, *La Religion de Voltaire*, pp. 50, 155, 382; Voltaire was horrified when he discovered a primitive religion, p. 180.
100. Hume, *Enquiry Concerning Human Understanding*, ed. Selby-Bigge, 83. Diderot assisted in translating this work into French. Proust, *Diderot et l'Encyclopédie*, p. 270.
101. Palmer, *Catholics and Unbelievers in Eighteenth-Century France*, pp. 55–73.
102. Holbach, *La Morale universelle*, vol. I, p. 7.
103. *Second Discourse*, p. 132.
104. Ibid., p. 145.
105. Ibid., pp. 122–123.
106. Ibid., p. 162.
107. Ibid., p. 122.
108. Buffon, "Des sens en général," *Histoire naturelle de l'homme*, in *Oeuvres complètes de Buffon* (Paris, 1828), vol. X, pp. 308–315.
109. Diderot, *Lettre sur les sourds et muets*, H, vol. IV, p. 140.
110. Diderot, "Encyclopédie," p. 635b.
111. *First Discourse*, p. 7.
112. *Second Discourse*, p. 202.
113. Ibid., pp. 162–163.
114. Diderot, "Art," p. 715a.
115. *First Discourse*, p. 8.
116. Voltaire, *Lettres philosophiques*, letter 25, no. 11.
117. Helvétius, *De l'Esprit* bk. II, ch. 2; bk. III, ch. 6; bk. I, ch. 4; Holbach, *Système de la nature*, vol. I, p. 59.
118. *Second Discourse*, p. 193.
119. Ibid., pp. 169–170, 188–189.
120. Ibid., p. 122.
121. Ibid., p. 164.

122. Ibid., p. 169.
123. *Emile*, p. 493.
124. *Second Discourse*, p. 189.
125. Ibid., p. 171.
126. Ibid., p. 189.
127. Rousseau, *Preface to Narcisse* (hereafter *Pref. Narcisse*), in *O.C.*, vol. II, p. 966.
128. On spreading oneself: *Second Discourse*, p. 179; cf. *Emile*, p. 307. On natural man: *Second Discourse*, p. 136.
129. Peter Laslett, ed., *Patriarcha and Other Political Works of Sir Robert Filmer* (Oxford: Blackwell, 1949), p. 273. Primitive communism, an old notion in the Christian tradition, was suggested in natural rights thinking by Grotius, *The Law of War and Peace*, bk. II, ch. ii.
130. See Laslett's introduction to Locke's *Two Treatises of Government* (Cambridge: Cambridge University Press, 1988), pp. 101–102.
131. *Second Discourse*, pp. 176–177.
132. Ibid., p. 179; Rousseau, *Écrits sur l'Abbé de Saint-Pierre*, in *O.C.*, vol. III, pp. 563–682.
133. *Second Discourse*, p. 176.
134. Ibid., p. 177.
135. *Pol. Econ.*, p. 273.
136. Diderot, "Autorité Politique," in *O. Pol.*, pp. 9–20; Bossuet, *Politique tirée des propres paroles de l'Ecriture sainte*, bk. IV.
137. Diderot, *O. Pol.*, p. 33.
138. Montesquieu, *De l'Esprit des lois*, bk. X, ch. 3; Montesquieu, *Lettres persanes*, letter xciv: "mettre l'iniquité en système."
139. Grotius, *Law of War and Peace*, bk. III, ch. iv, sects. 6, 9, 10; ch. v, sect. 1; ch. vi, sect. 2; ch. vii, sects. 1–3. See also Garrett Mattingly, *Renaissance Diplomacy* (Boston: Houghton Mifflin, 1955), ch. 28.
140. *Social Contract*, p. 353.
141. *Emile*, p. 836.
142. *Second Discourse*, p. 182.
143. Ibid., p. 177.
144. Ibid., p. 141; freedom is our most noble faculty, p. 183.
145. *Social Contract*, p. 356.
146. Ibid., p. 370.
147. *Second Discourse*, p. 124.
148. Ibid., pp. 125–126.
149. Ibid., pp. 154–156.
150. Ibid., p. 176.
151. Ibid., p. 126; *Geneva MS*, pp. 288–289.
152. The subtitle of the *Social Contract*.
153. *Geneva MS*, pp. 328–329.
154. *Social Contract*, p. 360. Masters, *The Political Philosophy of Rousseau*, and Wokler, *Rousseau on Society, Politics, Music and Language*, have, in my judgment, decisively refuted Derathé on the question of natural right in Rousseau.
155. *Social Contract*, pp. 360–361.
156. *Second Discourse*, p. 188.

157. "L'esprit universel des Loix de tous les pays est de favoriser toujours le fort contre le foible." *Emile,* p. 524n.

158. *Social Contract,* p. 381.

159. Ibid., p. 394.

160. Meek, ed., *Turgot on Progress,* p. 41.

161. *Social Contract,* p. 425.

162. *Emile,* p. 415n.

163. *Second Discourse,* p. 191.

164. Victor Goldschmidt, *Anthropologie et politique: Les principes du système de Rousseau* (Paris: J. Vrin, 1974), p. 256.

165. *Second Discourse,* p. 171.

166. Rousseau, *Essai sur l'origine des langues* (hereafter *E.O.L.*), ch. 1. For the position of the philosophes, Diderot especially, on gesture and language, see Herbert Josephs, *Diderot's Dialogue of Language and Gesture* (Columbus, Ohio: Ohio State University Press, 1969).

167. *E.O.L.,* ch. 10.

168. Ibid., ch. 9, p. 123.

169. Ibid., ch. 12.

170. Ibid., ch. 3.

171. Ibid., ch. 4.

172. Ibid., ch. 7.

173. Alfred Oliver, *The Encyclopedists as Critics of Music* (New York: Columbia University Press, 1947).

174. "I conclude that the French nation neither has music nor can it have any." Rousseau, *Lettre sur la musique française,* final sentence.

175. D'Alembert, "Fondamental" and "Gamme," *Encyclopédie,* vol. VII, pp. 54–63, 457–465.

176. Wokler's discussion of Rousseau's response to Rameau is excellent. *Rousseau on Society,* ch. 4.

177. *E.O.L,* ch. 12; Condillac, *Essai sur l'origine des connoissances humaines* (hereafter Condillac, *E.O.C.H.*), in *Oeuvres philosophiques de Condillac* (Paris: 1947), pp. 68, 73ff.

178. *E.O.L.,* ch. 5.

179. "Opéra," *Dictionnaire de musique;* Starobinski, *Le remède dans le mal* (Paris: Gallimard, 1989), pp. 208–232.

180. *E.O.L.,* ch. 14; Condillac, *E.O.C.H.,* p. 81.

181. See notes 177, 180 of this chapter.

182. Wokler, *Rousseau on Society,* pp. 169–172.

183. *Second Discourse,* p. 144.

184. Condillac, *E.O.C.H.,* pp. 76–77; *E.O.L.,* chs. 10, 19.

185. *E.O.L.,* ch. 7.

186. Condillac, *E.O.C.H.,* p. 69.

187. Ibid., pp. 94, 102.

188. See, in general, René Wellek, "The Price of Progress in Eighteenth-Century Reflections on Literature," *AJJR,* 155 (1976), 2265–2284.

189. *Second Discourse,* p. 191.

190. *Emile,* p. 468n.

191. R. A. Leigh, "Manuscrits disparus de J.-J. Rousseau," *AJJR,* 34 (1956–1958), 62–77.

3. From Criticism to Self-Criticism

1. *Confessions*, p. 403.
2. D'Alembert, *Essai sur la société des gens de lettres et des grands* (hereafter D'Alembert, *Men of Letters*), in *Oeuvres de d'Alembert*, vol. IV, p. 367.
3. Marquis d'Argenson, *Journal et mémoires*, 9 vols. (Paris: Libraire de la société de l'histoire de France, 1859–1867), vol. 7, p. 457, 16 April 1753.
4. Ruhlière, *Discours de réception à l'Académie française*, 4 June 1787.
5. D'Alembert's *Essai sur les Élémens de Philosophie* is a superb example.
6. Lucien Brunel, *Les Philosophes et l'Académie Française au dix-huitième siècle* (Paris: Hachette, 1884).
7. Kors, *D'Holbach's Coterie*. Darnton, *The Literary Underground of the Old Regime*, p. 14, asks the question: "Was the establishment becoming enlightened or the Enlightenment established?"
8. Voltaire, *Lettres philosophiques*, letter 25, no. 23.
9. Rousseau agreed. *Lettres morales*, in *O.C.*, vol. IV, pp. 1092–1093.
10. Condillac, *E.O.C.H.*, p. 6.
11. E.g., Holbach, *Système de la nature*, vol. I, pp. 80, 139, 485; vol. II, pp. 4, 172, 187, 456. Cf. Hume, *The Natural History of Religion*. Fontenelle may be regarded as the French pioneer.
12. E.g., Montesquieu, *Mes pensées*, in *Oeuvres complètes* (Paris, 1949, 1951), vol. I, pp. 1537, 1546; Condillac, *Traité des systèmes*, ch. 6.
13. Montesquieu, *Mes Pensées*, p. 1546. Voltaire commented that Locke had written the history of the soul, unlike other philosophers who had written a novel on the same topic. *Lettres philosophiques*, letter 13.
14. Dieckmann, *Le Philosophe: Texts and Interpretation*.
15. Dumarsais [?], "Le Philosophe," *Encyclopédie*, vol. XII, pp. 509b–511a. Subsequent references are to the version of this essay that appeared in the *Encyclopédie*.
16. Diderot, "Jouissance," *Encyclopédie*, vol. VIII, p. 889.
17. Diderot, "Epicuréisme," *Encyclopédie*, vol. V, pp. 779–785.
18. Voltaire, *Lettres philosophiques*, letter 13.
19. Montesquieu, *Lettres persanes*, letter lxxxvii; Duclos, *Moeurs*, p. 98.
20. Aristotle, *Nicomachean Ethics*, bk. I, chs. 8, 10; Dumarsais [?], "Le Philosophe," p. 511a.
21. Madame du Deffand to Voltaire, 28 Oct. 1759. *Voltaire's Correspondence* (Besterman), vol. XXXVII, p. 167.
22. D'Alembert, *Men of Letters*, p. 368.
23. Diderot, *Lettre sur le commerce de la librairie*, A-T, vol. XVIII, p. 32.
24. Voltaire, "Gens de lettres," *Encyclopédie*, vol. VII, pp. 599b–600a.
25. Pellisson, *Les Hommes de lettres*, p. 222.
26. Voltaire, "Gens de lettres," p. 599b.
27. Duclos, *Moeurs*, pp. 135–136.
28. Horace, *The Art of Poetry*, 333ff.; Daniel Mornet, "L'Art de plaire" in *Histoire de la littérature française classique* (Paris: Armand Colin, 1947).
29. Picard, *Les Salons littéraires*, part I, ch. 6.
30. Ibid., pp. 138, 161.
31. Voltaire, *Micromégas*, ch. 2 in *Romans et contes* (Paris: Garnier Frères, 1960).

32. D'Alembert, *Élémens de philosophie*, pp. 174–175; also known as the "science de se conduire avec les hommes."

33. Even d'Alembert, so much more skeptical about the *grands* than Voltaire, believed that Louis XIV's concern for the arts had made the nobility less ignorant. D'Alembert, *Men of Letters*, pp. 338–339. Still, as we shall see, their education was largely a matter of mere show, or so d'Alembert believed.

34. Quoted in Pellisson, *Les Hommes de lettres*, p. 219.

35. Duclos, *Moeurs*, p. 136.

36. Ibid., pp. 135, 140–141.

37. Ibid., p. 138.

38. Ibid., p. 139.

39. Brunel, *Les Philosophes et l'Académie Française*, pp. 51–54; Pellisson, *Les Hommes de lettres*, p. 215.

40. Duclos, *Moeurs*, ch. 2, on education; pp. 10, 130, 170, 200 on the merger of interest and virtue; pp. 20–22, on civic concern.

41. Picard, *Les Salons littéraires*, p. 161.

42. Ibid., part II, ch. 6; Hankins, *Jean d'Alembert*, p. 11.

43. Diderot, *Mémoires pour Catherine II*, ed. Paul Vernière (Paris: Garnier Frères, 1966), p. 251.

44. Diderot, "Encyclopédie," *Encyclopédie*, vol. V, p. 636b.

45. Wilson, *Diderot*, p. 165.

46. Diderot, *Mémoires pour Catherine*, p. 265.

47. Duclos, *Moeurs*, p. 138.

48. Diderot, "Encyclopédie," p. 637b.

49. Montaigne, *Essais*, I, 20; III, 12.

50. La Rochefoucauld, *Maximes* (Paris: Garnier Flammarion, 1977), no. 54; for other hits at stoics: nos. 46, 504, 589.

51. D'Alembert, *Men of Letters*, p. 339.

52. La Rochefoucauld, *Maximes*, no. 22.

53. D'Alembert, *Men of Letters*, p. 340.

54. Ibid., p. 372.

55. Ibid., p. 349.

56. Ibid., pp. 359–360.

57. Ibid., p. 341.

58. Duclos, *Moeurs*, p. 135.

59. Ibid., p. 343; D'Alembert, "Collège," *Encyclopédie*, vol. III, pp. 634a-637b.

60. D'Alembert, *Men of Letters*, p. 344.

61. Ibid., p. 357.

62. Ibid., p. 342.

63. Ibid., p. 346.

64. Voltaire, "Lettres, gens de lettres ou lettrés," in *Dictionnaire philosophique*.

65. Duclos, *Moeurs*, p. 147.

66. D'Alembert, *Men of Letters*, p. 360.

67. Ibid., p. 355.

68. Ibid., p. 363.

69. Ibid., p. 367.

70. Dumarsais [?], "Le Philosophe," p. 510b.

71. D'Alembert, *Men of Letters*, p. 356.

72. Ibid., p. 360.

73. Ibid., p. 365.

74. Duclos, *Moeurs*, p. 139.

75. Brunel, *Les Philosophes et l'Académie Française*, p. 39.

76. Duclos, *Moeurs*, pp. 145–146.

77. D'Alembert, *Men of Letters*, p. 359.

78. Ibid., p. 372.

79. Ibid., p. 344.

80. Ibid., p. 361.

81. Ibid., p. 348.

82. Ibid., pp. 367–368.

83. Ibid., pp. 353–354.

84. Pascal, *Pensées*, 294, 299, 303, 312, 320, 335.

85. D'Alembert, *Men of Letters*, p. 357; D'Alembert, *Élémens de philosophie*, p. 119.

86. Darnton's *Literary Underground* is excellent on the plight of writers who did not succeed.

87. See Diderot's own account in a letter to Sophie Volland, 1 Aug. 1765, *Lettres à Sophie Volland*, vol. II, p. 58.

88. Diderot, *Le Neveu de Rameau*, in *O.R.*, p. 446.

89. Marie-Angélique de Vandeul, "Mémoires pour servir à l'histoire de la vie et des ouvrages de Diderot," in A-T, vol. I, p. xxxiii.

90. Diderot, *Les Bijoux indiscrets* (1748). This is one case in which the authorities were justified in confounding philosophical with pornographic books under the label of *livres philosophiques*.

91. Horace, *Satires*, II, vii, lines 79–82.

92. Diderot, *Neveu*, p. 476.

93. Diderot, *Salon de 1765* (Paris: Hermann, 1984), p. 24.

94. D'Alembert, *Réflexions sur l'état présent de la république des lettres*, no. ii. Printed as an appendix to Brunel, *Les Philosophes et l'Académie Française*.

95. Diderot, *Corr.* (Roth), vol. XIV, pp. 223–224, 227.

96. Diderot, *Neveu*, p. 424.

97. Ibid., p. 441.

98. Ibid., p. 457.

99. *Second Discourse*, p. 189.

100. Duclos, *Moeurs*, p. 128.

101. Diderot, *Neveu*, p. 503.

102. Ibid., p. 477.

103. Ibid., p. 473.

104. Ibid., p. 458.

105. Ibid., p. 473.

106. Lough, *Writer and Public in France*, ch. 4.

107. Diderot, *Neveu*, p. 499.

108. Diderot, *Corr.* (Roth), vol. II, p. 39.

109. Duclos, *Moeurs*, pp. 15–17.

110. "What Is Enlightenment?" in H. Reiss, ed., *Kant's Political Writings* (Cambridge: Cambridge University Press, 1977), p. 54. Holbach's works, in particular, abound with statements of our need to advance beyond childhood.
111. Diderot, *Neveu,* p. 510.
112. D'Alembert, *Men of Letters,* pp. 361–362.
113. Diderot, *Neveu,* pp. 482–483.
114. Ibid., p. 477; cf. p. 472.
115. Ibid., pp. 507, 455.
116. Ibid., p. 455.
117. Ibid., p. 460.
118. Diderot, *Réfutation de L'Homme,* A-T, vol. II, p. 345.
119. Diderot, *Neveu,* p. 457.
120. Ibid., p. 501.
121. Ibid., pp. 453–454.
122. Ibid., p. 490.
123. Ibid., p. 475.
124. Ibid., p. 476.
125. Ibid., p. 448.
126. Ibid., pp. 503–505.
127. Ibid., p. 507.
128. Ibid., p. 461.
129. Ibid., pp. 505–506.
130. Ibid., p. 456.
131. Diderot, *Prospectus,* H, vol. V, p. 103; Diderot, "Encyclopédie," p. 644b.
132. Diderot, *Le Pour et le contre, ou Lettres sur la postérité,* H, vol. XV, p. 33.
133. Diderot, *Neveu,* p. 510.
134. Ibid., p. 443.
135. Ibid., p. 433.
136. Ibid., pp. 513–514.
137. Montaigne, "Of Presumption," in *Essais* (Paris: Garnier-Flammarion, 1979), II, 17, p. 298.
138. Diderot, *Neveu,* p. 442 on defecation; hunger and eating are constants in the dialogue.
139. Diderot, *Neveu,* p. 514; Montaigne, *Essais* (Paris: Garnier-Flammarion, 1969), I, 31, p. 263.
140. Diderot, *Neveu,* pp. 483–484, 502.
141. Ibid., p. 515.
142. Ibid., p. 516.
143. Diderot, "Cynique," *Encyclopédie,* vol. IV, p. 599a.
144. Diderot, *Neveu,* p. 517.
145. Donal O'Gorman, *Diderot the Satirist* (Toronto: University of Toronto Press, 1971), effectively highlights this Stoic theme in the writings of the philosophes. I do not, however, accept his argument that the nephew is Rousseau in disguise.
146. Diderot, *Neveu,* pp. 424, 486.
147. Diderot, *Paradoxe sur le comédien* in *O.E.,* pp. 299–381.
148. Diderot, *Neveu,* p. 431. Voltaire wrote a poem entitled "Le Pauvre Diable," which Darnton uses well in *Literary Underground.*

149. Diderot, to Falconet, 15 May 1767, *Corr.* (Roth), vol. VII, p. 61.
150. Diderot, *Neveu*, p. 520.
151. Diderot told Sophie Volland of his worries about the day when "les yeux de ma petite fille s'ouvriront, où sa gorge s'arrondira." 2 Oct. 1761, *Lettres à Sophie Volland*, vol. I, p. 223.
152. Proust, *Diderot et l'Encyclopédie*, p. 108.
153. Diderot to the Duc de Praslin, 27 April 1765, *Corr.* (Roth), vol. V, p. 28.
154. Diderot, *Corr.* (Roth), vol. XII, pp. 62–63.
155. Quoted in Wilson, *Diderot*, p. 596.
156. Herbert Dieckmann, *Cinq leçons sur Diderot* (Geneva and Paris: Droz & Minard, 1959), "Diderot et son lecteur."
157. 20 May 1765 and 25 July 1765, *Lettres à Sophie Volland*, vol. II, pp. 42, 52–53.
158. See 2 Oct. 1761 and 26 Sept. 1762, *Lettres à Sophie Volland*, vol. I, p. 223, and vol. II, p. 8, for his continuing belief that he was sparking a "revolution in the minds of men," tempered by his frustration on having to wait for applause until after death.
159. Diderot, *Neveu*, p. 518.
160. Ibid., p. 455.
161. Diderot, *Salon de 1763*, "A Mon Ami Monsieur Grimm."
162. Diderot, *Lettre apologétique de l'Abbé Raynal à M. Grimm* in *O. Phil.*, pp. 629, 633, 640.

4. Three Enemies in One Person

1. *L.A.*, p. 190n.
2. Although the philosophes agreed on the autonomy of morals, some of their numbers, Voltaire most notably, insisted the *peuple* needed a religion to enforce the injunctions of morality. See Ronald Ian Boss, "Rousseau's Civil Religion and the Meaning of Belief: An Answer to Bayle's Paradox," *SVEC*, 84 (1971), 123–193.
3. *L.A.*, p. 166.
4. Tocqueville, *The Old Régime and the French Revolution* (New York: Doubleday Anchor, 1955), pt. 3, chs. 1, 3.
5. Voltaire, *Lettres philosophiques*, letter 23.
6. Grimm, *Correspondance littéraire, philosophique, et critique* (hereafter Grimm, *Corr. litt.*), vol. VII, p. 45.
7. Diderot, *Introduction aux grands principes*, A-T, vol. II, p. 80n.
8. Tocqueville, *Old Regime*, p. 158.
9. Voltaire, *Siècle*, ch. 39. See also Voltaire, *Essai sur les moeurs*, vol. I, pp. 33, 66–71, 205–226; vol. II, pp. 394–399, 410, 785–793.
10. Voltaire, *Lettres philosophiques*, letters 8–10.
11. Voltaire spoke of England as a "republic under a king." Peter Gay, *Voltaire's Politics* (New York: Norton, 1965), p. 54n.
12. Mark Hulliung, *Montesquieu and the Old Regime* (Berkeley: University of California Press, 1976); Thomas Pangle, *Montesquieu's Philosophy of Liberalism* (Chicago: University of Chicago Press, 1973). Keith Baker, *Inventing the French Revolution* (Cambridge: Cambridge University Press, 1990), pp. 177–178, now accepts this view but

fails to re-create the comparative analysis of regimes that explains Montesquieu's ambivalence about England's far too centralized government.

13. Montesquieu, *De l'Esprit des lois*, bk. II, ch. 4.

14. Ibid., bk. V, ch. 19.

15. Ibid., bk. XIII, ch. 12.

16. Kramnick, *Bolingbroke and His Circle.*

17. Diderot, *Réflexions sur le livre De l'Esprit*, A-T, vol. II, p. 274.

18. Helvétius, *De l'Esprit*, bk. II, ch. 7, on refraining from bickering; bk. II, ch. 20, on refusing to flatter the great. On the willingness of youths to credit a writer on his accomplishments, bk. IV, ch. 16; cf. d'Alembert, *Discours préliminaire*, p. 151.

19. Voltaire briefly connects the two in letter 20.

20. Montesquieu, *De l'Esprit des lois*, bk. XIX, ch. 27, p. 583.

21. Helvétius, *De l'Esprit*, bk. II, ch. 20.

22. Even when quoting the *Spirit of the Laws* on the absence of intermediary bodies in England, Voltaire completely misses Montesquieu's point. E.g., *L'A, B, C,* vol. XXVII of the *Oeuvres complètes*, premier entretien, p. 319. Unfortunately Voltaire's superficial reading of the *Spirit of the Laws* has proved highly influential, especially with historians seeking a ready-made link between social and intellectual history. Mark Hulliung, "Montesquieu's Interpreters: A Polemical Essay," in Harry Payne, ed., *Studies in Eighteenth-Century Culture* (Madison, Wis., 1981), vol. 10, pp. 327–345.

23. Helvétius, *De l'Esprit*, bk. II, ch. 20.

24. Ibid., bk. II, ch. 22.

25. Ibid., bk. II, ch. 5.

26. Ibid., bk. IV, ch. 14.

27. Ibid., bk. IV, ch. 2, the final paragraph, on how monarchy denies the strong passions; bk. IV, ch. 13, on the small and pliable characters who succeed under such a government.

28. Ibid., bk. II, ch. 20.

29. Ibid., bk. II, ch. 9.

30. Ibid., bk. IV, ch. 4.

31. Ibid., bk. III, ch. 29.

32. Ibid., bk. II, ch. 20; bk. III, ch. 29.

33. Ibid., bk. II, ch. 19.

34. Ibid., bk. II, ch. 19; bk. IV, ch. 2. For further reflections on love, see bk. II, ch. 20.

35. Ibid., bk. II, ch. 19.

36. Holbach, *Système social*, vol. III, ch. 5. Holbach's republicanism has been systematically missed by scholars. Virgil Topazio, *D'Holbach's Moral Philosophy* (Geneva: Institut et Musée Voltaire, 1956), omits the theme of civic humanism; Kors, *D'Holbach's Coterie*, does not address the baron's thought; Maurice Cranston's statement, *Jean-Jacques* (Chicago: University of Chicago Press, 1982), p. 272, that Holbach stood for a planned society under the direction of an enlightened despot is stunningly inaccurate; Pierre Naville, *D'Holbach et la philosophie scientifique au XVIIIe siècle* (Paris: Gallimard, 1967), is good on science but does not include the baron's politics.

37. Diderot to Sophie Volland, 12 Oct. 1760, *Corr.* (Roth), vol. III, p. 130.

38. Diderot, "A Mon Ami M. Grimm," *Salon de 1763.*

39. Diderot, *Essai sur les règnes de Claude et de Néron et sur la vie et les écrits de Sénèque* (hereafter Diderot, *Nero and Seneca*), H, vol. XXV, pp. 43, 50; Diderot, *Réfutation de*

L'Homme, A-T, vol. II, p. 385. It is the priests in France who are permitted to speak to the assembled people. Diderot, *Mémoires pour Catherine,* p. 182.

40. Brunel, *Les Philosophes et l'Académie Française,* p. 97.

41. Diderot, *Les Bijoux indiscrets* in *O.R.,* p. 44; Diderot, "Encyclopédie," *Encyclopédie,* vol. V, p. 636; Diderot, *Salon de 1765* (Paris: Hermann, 1984), p. 61; Diderot to Falconet, July 1767, *Corr.* (Roth), vol. VII, p. 89; Diderot to Sophie Volland, 10 Sept. 1768, *Corr.* (Roth), vol. VIII, pp. 151–162; Diderot, *Réfutation de L'Homme,* p. 327; Diderot, *Mémoires pour Catherine,* p. 251.

42. Especially important is Diderot's *Observations sur le Nakaz,* in *O. Pol.,* pp. 343–458, which outlines proposals for a constitutional order in Russia. For the argument denouncing the debilitating effects of enlightened despotism, see Diderot, *Réfutation de L'Homme,* p. 381, and *Observations sur le Nakaz,* pp. 354–355.

43. Duclos, *Moeurs,* pp. 102, 108.

44. Brunel, *Les Philosophes et l'Académie Française,* p. 31.

45. D'Alembert to Voltaire, 14 April 1760, *Oeuvres de d'Alembert,* vol. 5, p. 65; cf. d'Alembert to Turgot, 24 Sept. 1772, in Charles Henry, ed., *Correspondance inédite de d'Alembert* (Geneva: Slatkine, 1967).

46. Guicciardini, *Ricordi,* series C, no. 18. For Diderot's use of Tacitus to comprehend and repudiate the reign of Frederick the Great, see his *Principes de politique des souverains,* in *O. Pol.,* pp. 159–207.

47. Tacitus, *Dialogue on Oratory,* no. 38: Augustus "not only triumphed over party and faction but subdued eloquence itself."

48. Pappas, *Voltaire and D'Alembert.*

49. As Durand Echeverria has noted. *The Maupeou Revolution* (Baton Rouge: Louisiana State University Press, 1985), pp. 16, 134.

50. Jean Starobinski's essay "Eloquence and Liberty," though brief, is well worth consulting. *JHI,* 38 (1977), 195–210.

51. Quoted in Wilson, *Diderot,* p. 162. The pattern of Malesherbes' thought is discussed by George Kelly, "The Political Thought of Lamoignon de Malesherbes," *Political Theory,* 7 (1979), 485–508; Baker, *Inventing the French Revolution,* pp. 117–119.

52. E.g., the parlement of Paris had tried to use *De l'Esprit* as an opportunity to gain control of the censorship. Competing centers of censorship accounted for much of the freedom of writers. D. W. Smith, *Helvétius: A Study in Persecution* (Oxford: Oxford University Press, 1965).

53. Echevveria, *The Maupeou Revolution.* Peter Gay's inaccurate presentation of the political position of the philosophes as one of unrelenting opposition to the parlements indicates how much he sees the Enlightenment through Voltaire's eyes.

54. D'Argenson, *Considérations sur le gouvernement ancien et présent de la France* (Amsterdam, 1765), ch. VIII, art. ii, p. 303.

55. Hulliung, *Montesquieu and the Old Regime,* pp. 94–97.

56. D'Argenson, *Considérations sur le gouvernement,* ch. III, art. xx. In his boldest moments, Bodin had favored Turkey as the model of a monarchy governed democratically, on the grounds that offices were not permitted to become private property, i.e., hereditary fiefs. Bodin, *Six Books of the Commonwealth,* trans. J. M. Tooley (Oxford: Blackwell, n.d.), pp. 172–173. Participation was central to d'Argenson's notion of a democratic administration, but not to Bodin's.

57. D'Argenson, *Considérations sur le gouvernement,* ch. III, art. xi.

58. Ibid., ch. III, art. viii.
59. Ibid., ch. III, art. viii; ch. VIII, art. i, pp. 64, 270.
60. Ibid., ch. VIII, art. i, pp. 267–268.
61. Ibid., ch. II, p. 28.
62. Ibid., ch. V, art. iii, p. 148.
63. Ibid., ch. V, art. vii; ch. VII, art. li.
64. Ibid., ch. VII, arts. i, vi, xli.
65. Ibid., Avertissement; ch. V, art. x.
66. Ibid., Avertissement.
67. Ibid., ch. II, pp. 23–24, 30; ch. V, art. vi; ch. VI, p. 211, ch. VII, art. xlii, pp. 253–254.
68. Ibid., ch. VIII, art. ii, pp. 305–306.
69. Ibid., ch. VI, p. 212; ch. VIII, art. ii, pp. 306, 308.
70. Keohane, *Philosophy and the State in France,* p. 391.
71. D'Argenson, *Considérations sur le gouvernement,* ch. VIII, art. ii, p. 303.
72. Ibid., ch. II, p. 35.
73. Ibid., ch. I, p. 3; ch. III, art. ii.
74. Note Keith Baker's language in his *Condorcet: From Natural Philosophy to Social Mathematics* (Chicago: University of Chicago Press, 1975), p. 210: Turgot did not "initially" intend for the provincial assemblies to legislate. This helpful ambiguity disappears in Baker's later treatment of Turgot: *Inventing the French Revolution,* pp. 120–123, 127.
75. All citations are to the readily accessible translation of the *Mémoire sur les municipalités* in Keith Baker, ed., *The Old Regime and the French Revolution* (Chicago: University of Chicago Press, 1987), p. 111. (Hereafter *Municipalities.*)
76. Ibid., p. 117.
77. Turgot, "Fondation," *Encyclopédie,* vol. VII, p. 75a.
78. E.g., D'Alembert, "Collège," *Encyclopédie,* vol. III, pp. 632–638.
79. *Municipalities,* p. 118.
80. Ibid., p. 101; *First Discourse,* p. 26.
81. *Municipalities,* p. 101.
82. *Lettre de J. J. Rousseau à M. de Voltaire,* in *O.C.,* vol. IV, pp. 1059–1075. For the transition from a religious to a civic "general will," see Riley, *The General Will before Rousseau,* and Alberto Postigliola, "De Malebranche à Rousseau: Les Apories de la volonté générale et la revanche du 'raisonneur violent,'" *AJJR,* 39 (1972–1977), 123–138. The critical text for the distinction between "general" and "particular" will, as Riley has demonstrated, is Malebranche's *Treatise on Nature and Grace.*
83. *Municipalities,* p. 99. Given that Turgot, like Rousseau and many of the philosophes, was much enamored of Malebranche's notion of a rational and "general will," one may well object to Baker's insistence upon placing Turgot in a "discourse of reason" as opposed to a "discourse of will." *Inventing the French Revolution,* ch. 1. In general the purport of Riley's *The General Will before Rousseau,* I think, is that Baker's categories for getting at the language of the eighteenth century would be rejected by many of the writers of that age on the grounds that Baker has separated what they were frequently intent upon uniting. One consequence of this questionable separation is Baker's unwillingness to acknowledge Turgot's affinities with Rousseau and with republicanism.

84. Turgot to Dupont de Nemours, 10 May and 21 June 1771. *Oeuvres de Turgot,* vol. III, pp. 487–488.

85. Ibid., pp. 486–487, for a criticism of "legal despotism." See R. R. Palmer, *The Age of the Democratic Revolution* (Princeton: Princeton University Press, 1959), vol. I, ch. 9, on Turgot and Ben Franklin.

86. Turgot to Hume, 25 March 1767, *Oeuvres de Turgot,* vol. II, p. 660.

87. As Riley notes, one physiocrat, Mercier de la Rivière, employed Malebranche's notion of the deity to argue for legal despotism. *The General Will before Rousseau,* p. 108. Turgot, however, repudiated that form of government.

88. Rousseau, *O.C.,* vol. III, p. 83.

89. *L.A.,* p. 90.

90. Rousseau, *O.C.,* vol. III, p. 1727.

91. Montaigne, *Essais,* I, 51.

92. Rousseau, *O.C.,* vol. III, p. 83.

93. Ibid., vol. III, p. 81; *Emile,* p. 362.

94. *Pol. Econ.,* p. 246.

95. *Frag. pol.,* p. 558.

96. *L.A.,* pp. 130–131.

97. Ibid., p. 140; *Pref. Narcisse,* p. 972.

98. *L.A.,* pp. 217–218.

99. Ibid., p. 154.

100. Ibid., p. 66.

101. Ibid., p. 79.

102. Ibid., pp. 78–80. The comment on the weeping ladies appears in the edition of 1782; it is omitted by Launay.

103. Ibid., pp. 69–71.

104. Ibid., pp. 91, 161.

105. Ibid., p. 74.

106. Molière, *Le Misanthrope,* act I, scene 2; *L.A.,* pp. 103–104, 106.

107. *L.A.,* pp. 222–223.

108. *L.A.,* p. 122.

109. The love theme of *Zaïre* was a reluctant concession to the demands of the audience. Raymond Naves, *Le Goût de Voltaire* (Paris: Garnier Frères, 1938), p. 461.

110. Holbach, *Système social,* vol. III, p. 134.

111. *L.A.,* p. 83n.

112. Ibid., pp. 89, 219.

113. Ibid., pp. 143, 246.

114. Rousseau, *Lettres écrites de la montagne* (hereafter *Mountain*), in *O.C.,* vol. III, p. 881.

115. *L.A.,* p. 64n.

116. Ibid., p. 234.

117. Ibid., pp. 236–249, 207–209.

118. *Emile,* p. 837; *Social Contract,* p. 371; Rousseau, *Saint-Pierre,* in *O.C.,* vol. III, p. 609.

119. See Helvétius' outspoken preface to *De l'Homme.*

120. *Poland,* in *O.C.,* vol. III, p. 962.

121. Ibid., pp. 956, 959–960.

122. Ibid., p. 968.

123. Ibid., p. 1010.

124. *Pref. Narcisse*, p. 971.

125. *L.A.*, pp. 144ff.

126. Rousseau largely ignores religion when dealing with Poland, as has frequently been noted, but see his comment in *Corsica*, in *O.C.*, vol. III, p. 944.

127. Holbach, *Éthocratie*, p. 4; Diderot, *Observations sur le Nakaz*, in *O. Pol.*, p. 349. "Ce sont les souverains qui font le caractère et les moeurs des humains," wrote Voltaire. Quoted in Albert Lortholary, *Le Mirage russe en France au XVIIIe siècle* (Paris: Boivin, 1951), p. 150.

128. Lortholary, *Le Mirage russe*.

129. *Social Contract*, p. 386.

130. Ibid., p. 382.

131. Lortholary, *Le Mirage russe*, p. 105; Voltaire to Catherine, 26 Feb. 1769, *Voltaire's Correspondence* (Besterman), vol. LXXI, p. 110.

132. Diderot's *Observations sur le Nakaz* ask her, in effect, to abdicate her absolute authority.

133. *Social Contract*, p. 381.

134. Ibid., p. 391.

135. Ibid., p. 385.

136. *Corsica*, p. 948. The Corsicans, like the Swiss mountain dwellers, are still innocent and naturally good. Pp. 914–915.

137. Ibid., p. 950.

138. Ibid., p. 903.

139. Rousseau explicitly draws a parallel between Peter's labors and the education French tutors give their charges: in both cases a brief outward show leads to less than nothing. *Social Contract*, p. 386.

140. *Corsica*, pp. 931, 945.

141. Ibid., pp. 922, 924–925.

142. The Corsicans should be like the Swiss mountaineers. Ibid., pp. 914–915.

143. Ibid., pp. 926, 928.

144. Ibid., p. 945, on carriages; p. 911, on cities; p. 904, on academies.

145. Ibid., p. 936.

146. Ibid., pp. 950, 902.

147. *Pref. Narcisse*, p. 967n.

148. Diderot, "A Mon Ami M. Grimm," *Salon de 1763;* Diderot, *Observations sur le Nakaz*, pp. 366, 411; Diderot, *Réflexions sur L'Homme*, pp. 417–418; Diderot, *Mémoires pour Catherine*, pp. 127, 129, 155, 163; Diderot, *Nero and Seneca*, p. 56.

149. *Corsica*, p. 940.

150. Turgot, *Lettre à Mme de Graffigny sur les Lettres d'une péruvienne*, in *Oeuvres*, vol. I, pp. 241–255, and his two lectures on progress. For the philosophes on equality, see Harry Payne, *The Philosophes and the People* (New Haven: Yale University Press, 1976), ch. 8.

151. *Corsica*, p. 914; *L.A.*, p. 134; *Emile*, pp. 456, 459.

152. *Emile*, pp. 459–460.

153. *Pref. Narcisse*, p. 966.

154. *Social Contract*, p. 392.

155. *Corsica*, p. 946.
156. *First Discourse*, p. 19.
157. *L.A.*, p. 150n.
158. Michel Launay argues against Robert Derathé that Rousseau knew his Melon and Mandeville, and responded to them at a level that was more than moralistic. *Jean-Jacques Rousseau, écrivain politique*, p. 223.
159. *Confessions*, p. 404.
160. Holbach's "Représentants" is reprinted in the *Oeuvres Politiques* of Diderot, pp. 40–54.
161. *Poland*, p. 979.
162. *Social Contract*, p. 430. In his writings on Saint-Pierre, Rousseau predicted that England would be ruined in twenty years. *O.C.*, vol. III, p. 573n. Cf. Holbach, who did not like what he saw during his visit to England in 1765.
163. *Social Contract*, p. 429.
164. Ibid., p. 421; *Poland*, p. 977; *Mountain*, p. 808.
165. As James Miller notes, Rousseau inverted the classical cycle of governments. *Rousseau: Dreamer of Democracy*, ch. 5.
166. *Geneva MS*, p. 316; *Social Contract*, p. 424.
167. *Social Contract*, p. 436.
168. Ibid., p. 362.
169. Derathé, "Les Réfutations du *Contrat social* au XVIIIe siècle," *AJJR*, 32 (1950–1952), 7–54. The stand taken by the procureur-général Jean Robert Tronchin is especially pertinent.
170. The Germanist views of the Encyclopedists are described by René Hubert, *Les Sciences sociales dans l'Encyclopédie*, ch. 6. Daniel Mornet stresses how vague the fundamental laws of the philosophes were, how disconnected from history and based on reason and equity. *Les Origines intellectuelles de la Révolution* (Paris: Armand Colin, 1947), p. 80. One could easily show on the basis of more recent scholarly studies, I believe, that the list of thinkers who saw no point in appealing to an "ancient constitution" and its fundamental laws includes, at a minimum, d'Argenson, Diderot, Helvétius, Holbach, Mably, Malesherbes, Montesquieu, Rousseau, and Turgot.
171. Michèle Duchet, *Anthropologie et histoire au siècle des lumières* (Paris: François Maspero, 1971), p. 69.
172. *L.A.*, p. 85.
173. Diderot, to Sophie Volland, 14 July 1762, *Corr.* (Roth), vol. IV, p. 45.
174. Diderot, *Le Père de Famille*, act II, scene 6. (Hereafter *Père.*)
175. Ibid., act II, scene 9.
176. Diderot, *Le Fils naturel*, act IV, act 5. (Hereafter *Fils.*)
177. Ibid., act IV, scene 3.
178. *Père*, act II, scene 1.
179. *Fils*, act IV, scene 3.
180. "Nous devrions laisser aux femmes la fonction de l'apostolat." 25 July 1765, *Lettres à Sophie Volland*, vol. II, p. 52.
181. *Fils*, act IV, scene 3.
182. Ibid., scene 7.
183. *Père*, act I, scene 7.

184. Ibid.

185. Holbach, *Système social,* vol. III, the title of ch. 11.

186. Ibid., vol. III, pp. 51–52.

187. Ibid., vol. III, p. 134.

188. Ibid., vol. III, pp. 132–133.

189. Ibid., vol. III, p. 9.

190. Ibid., vol. III, p. 45.

191. Ibid., vol. III, pp. 99–100.

192. Ibid., vol. III, pp. 97, 102–103.

193. Ibid., vol. III, p. 62.

194. Helvétius, *De l'Homme,* sect. VI, chs. 3–5.

195. Saint-Lambert, "Luxe," *Encyclopédie,* vol. IX, the final lines. For Diderot on luxury: *Mémoires pour Catherine,* ch. xxvi; *Salon de 1767,* H, vol. XVI, pp. 165ff.

196. Holbach, *Système social,* vol. II, pp. 37n, 65–75; vol. III, pp. 72–86.

197. Helvétius, *De l'Homme,* sect. IX, chs. 2, 4. Like Montesquieu, Helvétius was concerned that the English republic was too centralized. Hence the representatives were apt to place their interests above those of the represented. Sect. VI, ch. 7.

198. Holbach, *Éthocratie,* ch. 8; Helvétius, *De l'Homme,* sect. VI, ch. 7; Diderot, *Réfutation de L'Homme,* pp. 419, 431.

199. Quoted by Duchet, *Anthropologie et histoire,* in her chapter on Diderot, p. 462.

200. Diderot, *Réfutation de L'Homme,* p. 431.

201. Helvétius, *De l'Homme,* sect. VIII, ch. 26; Diderot, in a letter to Falconet, referred to Russia as "une nation naissante," *Corr.* (Roth), vol. VII, p. 54; *Second Discourse,* p. 170.

202. D'Alembert, *Men of Letters,* p. 354.

203. D'Alembert to the king of Prussia, 29 Jan. 1770, *Oeuvres de d'Alembert,* vol. V, p. 289.

204. Turgot, "Fondation," p. 75b.

205. Holbach, *Système social,* vol. II, pp. 10–11.

206. Ibid., vol. III, p. 97.

207. Ibid., vol. III, pp. 137, 143; vol. I, p. 218.

208. Ibid., vol. III, p. 149.

209. E.g., Diderot, *Mémoires pour Catherine,* pp. 148–149.

210. Holbach, *Système social,* vol. III, p. 140.

211. Ibid., vol. III, p. 122.

212. Johan Huizinga, *Homo Ludens* (Boston: Beacon, 1967).

213. Holbach, *Système social,* vol. III, p. 135.

214. Duclos, *Moeurs,* p. 13.

215. *Emile,* p. 850; see also *Julie,* p. 242.

216. *Julie,* pp. 19ff.

217. *L.A.,* pp. 132–133.

218. *Julie,* p. 272.

219. Ibid., p. 554.

220. See the editorial commentary in Rousseau's *Oeuvres complètes,* vol. II, pp. 1387–1388.

221. *L.A.,* p. 135; *Julie,* pp. 79–83.

222. *Julie,* p. 124.

223. Ibid., p. 409.

224. Ibid., p. 374.
225. Shklar, *Men and Citizens*, pp. 150–151.
226. *Social Contract*, p. 381.
227. *Julie*, pp. 490–491.
228. Ibid., pp. 373–374.
229. At Clarens and even before it, Julie's power to transform souls is evident. *Julie*, pp. 204, 229, 559, 592.
230. Ibid., p. 79.
231. Ibid., p. 234.
232. *Emile*, p. 252.
233. Ibid., pp. 468, 478.
234. *Julie*, pp. 536–538.
235. Ibid., pp. 546–548, 529.
236. On luxury, see ibid. pp. 441, 531, 546; on nature as a brake, p. 547.
237. Ibid., p. 442.
238. *Emile*, p. 463.
239. This particular expression is from *Emile*, p. 515, but the same view can be found everywhere. E.g., *Julie*, p. 527.
240. *Julie*, p. 462.
241. Ibid., pp. 444–445, 447.
242. Ibid., p. 467.
243. Ibid., p. 460.
244. Ibid., pp. 462–463.
245. *Poland*, p. 955.
246. *L.A.*, pp. 236–238.
247. *Julie*, pp. 456–458.
248. Ibid., p. 607.
249. *L.A.*, p. 94.
250. *Julie*, pp. 603, 607–609.
251. Ibid., p. 453.
252. Ibid., p. 603; *Emile*, p. 859.
253. André Morize, *L'Apologie du luxe au XVIIIe siècle et "Le Mondain" de Voltaire* (Geneva: Slatkine, 1970; orig. pub. 1909); Naves, *Le Goût de Voltaire*.
254. Michael Moriarity, *Taste and Ideology in Seventeenth-Century France* (Cambridge: Cambridge University Press, 1988).
255. These three articles on taste appeared in volume VII of the *Encyclopédie*, pp. 761–770.
256. Payne, *Philosophes and the People*, pp. 7–8.
257. *L.A.*, p. 224.
258. *Emile*, p. 677.
259. Ibid., p. 690.
260. Ibid., p. 674; see also *Julie*, p. 274.
261. *Emile*, pp. 672–673.
262. Theodore Besterman, *Voltaire* (New York: Harcourt, Brace & World, 1969), ch. 26.
263. *Julie*, p. 606.
264. Ibid., pt. IV, letter 11.
265. Daniel Mornet, *Le Sentiment de la nature en France de J.-J. Rousseau à Bernardin de*

Saint-Pierre (Paris: Hachette, 1912), pt. II, bk. 2, ch. 2. Boileau, *L'Art poétique,* chant I, lines 101–102.

266. *Julie,* p. 441.

267. Ibid., pp. 541–543, 552; cf. Voltaire, *Romans et contes* (Paris: Garnier Frères, 1960), p. 620: "toujours du plaisir n'est pas du plaisir."

268. *Emile,* p. 865.

269. *Julie,* pp. 557–558.

270. Indeed, no distinction was made between politeness and the heart. Mornet, *Histoire de la littérature,* p. 106.

271. *Emile,* p. 764.

272. *Julie,* p. 278.

273. *Emile,* p. 258.

274. *Julie,* pp. 275–277, 532.

275. Ibid., p. 359.

276. *Emile,* pp. 632, 636.

277. Rousseau, *Lettres morales,* in *O.C.,* vol. IV, p. 1101; *Emile,* pp. 523n, 600. See also Derathé, *Le Rationalisme de J.-J. Rousseau.*

278. *Julie,* p. 592; *Emile,* p. 632.

279. Voltaire to Helvétius, 27 Oct. 1766. *Voltaire's Correspondence* (Besterman), vol. LXIII, p. 42.

280. Diderot, *Corr.* (Roth), vol. IV, pp. 176–177. Even the Nephew admires the trinity of the true, the good, and the beautiful. *O.R.,* p. 495.

5. Generation, Degeneration, Regeneration

1. Diderot, "Encyclopédie," *Encyclopédie,* vol. V, pp. 635b, 646a.

2. See note 6 to the Introduction.

3. See note 11 to the Introduction. It is true, however, as Judith Shklar noted, that Kant has a place for an ethics of character in *The Metaphysical Principles of Virtue.* See her *Ordinary Vices* (Cambridge, Mass.: Harvard University Press, 1984), p. 232.

4. Charles Coulston Gillispie, "The *Encyclopédie* and the Jacobin Philosophy of Science," in Marshall Clagett, ed., *Critical Problems in the History of Science* (Madison: University of Wisconsin Press, 1959), ch. 9.

5. Victor Goldschmidt, *Anthropologie et politique: Les Principes du système de Rousseau* (Paris: J. Vrin, 1974), p. 784.

6. Rousseau, *O.C.,* vol. III, p. 36. Like d'Alembert, Rousseau thought science far less a problem than the arts and literature. *O.C.,* vol. III, p. 52; vol. II, 965.

7. P. Sloan and J. Lyon, *From Natural History to the History of Nature* (Notre Dame, Ind.: University of Notre Dame Press, 1981); Jean Starobinski, "Rousseau et Buffon," in the expanded 1971 edition of his *J.-J. Rousseau;* Robert Wokler, "Perfectible Apes in Decadent Cultures," *Dædalus,* 107 (1978), 107–134. The pioneer in this realm of Rousseau studies is Roger Masters, *The Political Philosophy of Rousseau.*

8. E.g., Hankins, *Jean d'Alembert;* Arnold Thackray, *Atoms and Powers: An Essay on Newtonian Matter-Theory and the Development of Chemistry* (Cambridge, Mass.: Harvard University Press, 1970).

9. Roger, *Les Sciences de la vie;* Colm Kiernan, *Science and the Enlightenment in Eighteenth-Century France,* in *SVEC,* vol. 59 (1968).

10. Ignored by Cassirer, the materialists have been vindicated by Aram Vartanian, *Diderot and Descartes* (Princeton: Princeton University Press, 1953).

11. *Confessions,* p. 409.

12. Voltaire, *Traité de métaphysique,* ch. 3.

13. Cassirer, *The Philosophy of the Enlightenment,* ch. 1; Baker, *Condorcet,* pp. 110–118; Hankins, *Science and the Enlightenment,* pp. 17–23; Isabel Knight, *The Geometric Spirit* (New Haven: Yale University Press, 1968).

14. Brumfitt, *Voltaire Historian,* pp. 87–89. In the "Philosophie de l'histoire" Voltaire attempted, belatedly (1765), to grapple with the problem of origins. For an example of his resistance to the new science see *L'Homme aux quarante écus,* in H. Bénac, ed., *Romans et contes* (Paris: Garnier Frères, 1960), esp. pp. 307–316.

15. Jacques Roger, *Sciences de la vie,* pp. 733–748, and René Pomeau, *La Religion de Voltaire,* pp. 387–402, discuss Voltaire's resistance to the life sciences and his campaign against atheism.

16. As Maurice Cranston notes, Voltaire remained neutral in the debate on music. *Jean-Jacques* (Chicago: University of Chicago Press, 1982), p. 277n.

17. Fontenelle, "Préface sur l'Utilité des mathématiques et de la physique," in *Textes choisis* (Paris: Éditions sociales, 1966), pp. 261–279, esp. p. 273.

18. Naves, *Le Goût de Voltaire;* Voltaire, *Siècle,* ch. 8, on luxury and the size of the political unit.

19. D'Alembert, "Expérimental," *Encyclopédie,* vol. VI, pp. 298–301; on rational mechanics, see Hankins, *Jean d'Alembert.*

20. D'Alembert, "Expérimental," p. 298a; D'Alembert, *Élémens de philosophie,* p. 337.

21. D'Alembert, *Discours préliminaire,* p. 91.

22. D'Alembert, *Élémens de philosophie,* p. 336.

23. Ibid., p. 154.

24. Baker, *Condorcet,* pp. 180–189.

25. D'Alembert, *Élémens de philosophie,* p. 344.

26. D'Alembert, *Réflexions sur l'inoculation,* in *Oeuvres de d'Alembert,* vol. I, pp. 463–514. See Lorraine Daston, *Classical Probability in the Enlightenment* (Princeton: Princeton University Press, 1988), for historical context and critical assessment.

27. Diderot, "De L'Inoculation," H, vol. II, p. 360.

28. Cf. Judith Shklar, "D'Alembert and the Rehabilitation of History," *JHI,* 42 (1981), 643–664.

29. D'Alembert, *Discours préliminaire,* p. 156.

30. D'Alembert, *Réflexions sur l'usage et sur l'abus de la philosophie dans les matières de goût,* in *Oeuvres de d'Alembert,* vol. IV, p. 332.

31. D'Alembert, *Élémens de philosophie,* p. 346.

32. D'Alembert, *Discours préliminaire,* p. 104.

33. D'Alembert, *De la liberté de la musique,* in *Oeuvres de d'Alembert,* vol. I, p. 521.

34. D'Alembert, *Discours préliminaire,* p. 77.

35. Ibid., p. 78.

36. Ibid., pp. 115, 139.

37. Ibid., pp. 83–84.

38. Ibid., pp. 110–111.
39. Ibid., pp. 111, 123; see also Robert Darnton, *The Great Cat Massacre* (New York: Basic Books, 1984), ch. 5.
40. D'Alembert, *Discours préliminaire*, p. 76; Robert McRae, *The Problem of the Unity of the Sciences* (Toronto: University of Toronto Press, 1961).
41. Manuel, *The Prophets of Paris*, ch. 1.
42. Condillac, *E.O.C.H*, p. 102.
43. Condillac, *La Logique*, in *Oeuvres philosophiques*, vol. II, p. 377.
44. Ibid., p. 371.
45. Ibid., p. 407.
46. Condillac, *E.O.C.H.*, p. 102.
47. Ibid., p. 94.
48. Rousseau to Dom Léger-Marie Deschamps, 8 May 1761, *Corr.* (Leigh), vol. VIII, p. 321; Rousseau, *Institutions chymiques*, published in *AJJR*, 12 (1918–19), 2–4.
49. *Emile*, p. 355.
50. Ibid., p. 434.
51. Rousseau, *Ecrits sur Saint-Pierre*, in *O.C.*, vol. III, p. 612.
52. *Emile*, p. 836.
53. Holbach, *La Morale universelle*, vol. I, p. 7.
54. *Emile*, p. 836.
55. Rousseau, *O.C.*, vol. III, p. 53n.
56. Ibid., p. 76.
57. Ibid., pp. 49–50.
58. *Social Contract*, p. 359.
59. Ibid., p. 361.
60. Ibid., p. 364.
61. The members of academies are worth more alone than when assembled. *Emile*, p. 676. In a proper republics the citizens assembled are more than the sum of the parts. *Social Contract*, p. 382.
62. Condillac, *E.O.C.H.*, p. 69.
63. Ibid., p. 77.
64. *Emile*, p. 362.
65. *E.O.L.*, ch. 20; *Social Contract*, p. 431.
66. Frankel, *Faith of Reason*, p. 48; Knight, *Geometric Spirit*, p. 153.
67. The notes to the Pléiade edition provide an excellent account of the operatic nature of Rousseau's novel.
68. Georges May, *Le Dilemme du roman au XVIIIe siècle* (New Haven and Paris: Presses Universitaires de France, 1963), discusses the vicissitudes of the French novel.
69. *Emile*, p. 281.
70. Rousseau, *Rousseau juge de Jean-Jacques*, in *O.C.*, vol. I, p. 935. (Hereafter *Juge.*)
71. Diderot, *De l'interprétation de la nature*, nos. ii, iv.
72. Ibid., no. iii.
73. Diderot, *Lettre sur les sourds et muets*, H, IV, pp. 164–165.
74. Diderot, *Poésie dramatique*, in *O.E.*, p. 218.
75. Diderot, *Salon de 1767*, H, vol. XVI, p. 222.
76. Diderot, *Le Rêve de d'Alembert* (hereafter Diderot, *Dream*) in *O. Phil.*, p. 355.

77. Diderot, *Salon de 1767,* p. 215.

78. Condillac, *Traité des systèmes,* ch. 1.

79. Diderot, *Interprétation,* no. xxxi. When denouncing religion, the philosophes rarely missed an opportunity to attack imagination. That, however, did not prevent them from applauding the uses of imagination in other realms. Marc Eigeldinger, *Jean-Jacques Rousseau et la réalité de l'imaginaire* (Neuchâtel: Editions de la Baconnière, 1962), ch. 2.

80. Condillac, *Traité des systèmes,* ch. 8.

81. Diderot, *Dream,* p. 281.

82. Diderot, *Réfutation de l'Homme,* A-T, vol. II, pp. 351–352.

83. See Diderot, *Dream,* p. 312, on how wrong it is to speak of individuals in nature.

84. Locke, *Essay Concerning Human Understanding,* bk. III, ch. v, no. 9. Also bk. III, ch. iii, nos. 12, 20; ch. vi, no. 8; bk. IV, ch. vi, no. 4.

85. Manuel, *Prophets of Paris,* p. 25.

86. Diderot, *Dream,* p. 342.

87. Condillac, *Traité des systèmes,* chs. 17, 15.

88. C. H. Hendel, *Jean-Jacques Rousseau, Moralist* (Oxford: Oxford University Press, 1934), vol. I, pp. 104–108.

89. *Geneva MS,* pp. 283, 287.

90. E.g., Ernest Barker, *Social Contract* (New York: Oxford University Press, 1962), introduction. Derathé, *Jean-Jacques Rousseau,* effectively destroys this view. Precisely because Otto Gierke ardently yearned for group warmth, he noted at an early date that Rousseau's philosophy remained fundamentally individualistic. *Natural Law and the Theory of Society, 1500–1800* (Boston: Beacon, 1957), p. 129.

91. *Emile,* p. 777; *Second Discourse,* p. 133.

92. E.g., Goldschmidt, *Anthropologie et politique;* Wokler, "Perfectible Apes"; Duchet, *Anthropologie et histoire.*

93. *Second Discourse,* p. 122.

94. Buffon does not, however, abandon the traditional tasks of natural history: "L'Histoire Naturelle est la source des autres Sciences physiques & la mère de tous les Arts." *Premier discours,* in *Oeuvres philosophiques de Buffon,* ed. Jean Pivetau (Paris: Presses Universitaires de France, 1954), p. 16a. (Hereafter Buffon, *O.P.B.*)

95. Diderot, *Dream,* pp. 299–300; Diderot, *Interprétation,* no. lviii.

96. Buffon, *O.P.B.,* p. 373b.

97. Ibid., p. 374a.

98. Ibid., p. 375a.

99. Ibid., p. 389b.

100. Buffon, *Histoire naturelle de l'homme,* in *Oeuvres complètes,* vol. X, p. 438.

101. Buffon, *O.P.B.,* pp. 239–240.

102. Duchet, *Anthropologie et histoire,* pt. 2, ch. 1.

103. Buffon, *Histoire naturelle de l'homme,* p. 107; Buffon, *O.P.B.,* p. 351a.

104. *Second Discourse,* pp. 132–133.

105. Ibid., pp. 123–124.

106. *Emile,* p. 532.

107. *Second Discourse,* p. 170.

108. Buffon, *O.P.B.,* p. 351a; *Second Discourse,* p. 126.

109. Buffon, *O.P.B.*, p. 351a; *Second Discourse*, p. 166.
110. *Second Discourse*, p. 139.
111. Ibid., pp. 138, 203–204.
112. Buffon, *O.P.B.*, p. 330b.
113. *Second Discourse*, p. 192.
114. Buffon, *Histoire naturelle de l'homme*, "Variétés dans l'espèce humaine," p. 473.
115. *Emile*, p. 294.
116. Ibid., p. 274.
117. Ibid., pp. 283, 287, 293, 322, 369, on the freedom of peasants from fear of spiders, on how peasant children do not abuse their freedom or suffer from a spoiled will, on their strong stomachs, on the practical knowledge of peasants.
118. Ibid., p. 360.
119. Ibid., p. 277.
120. Buffon, *Histoire naturelle de l'homme*, p. 141.
121. *Lettre de J. J. Rousseau à M. de Voltaire*, in *O.C.*, vol. IV, p. 1063.
122. *Pref. Narcisse*, p. 966.
123. *Second Discourse*, p. 138.
124. Diderot, to Sophie Volland, 7 Nov. 1762, *Corr.* (Roth), vol. IV, pp. 212–213; Diderot, *Plan d'une université pour le gouvernement de Russie*, A-T, vol. III, p. 524; Gilbert Chinard, *L'Amérique et le rêve exotique dans la littérature française* (Paris: Droz, 1934), p. 395.
125. *Second Discourse*, pp. 162, 171.
126. *Second Discourse*, p. 208; note the explicit reference to the "varieties . . . of the human species."
127. Ibid., p. 134.
128. Ibid., p. 213.
129. Ibid., p. 212; see "Des Voyages" in *Emile*, pp. 826ff.
130. Wokler, "Perfectible Apes."
131. Buffon, *O.P.B.*, p. 389b.
132. Buffon, *O.P.B.*, pp. 374a, 390a; Buffon, *Histoire naturelle de l'homme*, pp. 10–12.
133. *Second Discourse*, p. 210.
134. Ibid., p. 212.
135. Buffon, *Histoire naturelle de l'homme*, p. 1; *Second Discourse*, pp. 195–196.
136. *Second Discourse*, p. 142.
137. Marmontel, "Critique," *Encyclopédie*, vol. IV, p. 491a; *Oeuvres complètes de Buffon*, vol. VIII, p. 205; vol. IX, p. 329.
138. Ernst Cassirer, *The Philosophy of the Enlightenment*, p. vii, called attention to the distinction between the *esprit de système* and the *esprit systématique*.
139. Diderot, *Réfutation de L'Homme*, p. 302.
140. Dieckmann, "The Influence of Francis Bacon on Diderot's *Interprétation de la Nature*," *Romanic Review*, 34 (1943), 303–331.
141. Diderot, *Interprétation*, no. lvi.
142. Ibid., no. xxxi.
143. Ibid., nos. xlii, xliii, l.
144. Rousseau, *O.C.*, vol. III, pp. 105–106.
145. Rousseau, *Lettre à C. de Beaumont*, in *O.C.*, vol. IV, p. 951; Rousseau, *Lettres à Malesherbes*, in *O.C.*, vol. I, p. 1136.

146. *Emile*, p. 582.
147. Rousseau, *Lettres morales*, in *O.C.*, vol. IV, p. 1099. See Jean Perkins, *The Concept of the Self in the French Enlightenment* (Geneva: Droz, 1969), p. 40, for "Je sens, donc je suis" in eighteenth-century thought.
148. *Emile*, pp. 529–530.
149. Condillac, *Traité des systèmes*, ch. 1.
150. *Emile*, pp. 575n, 579, 584n.
151. Buffon, *O.P.B.*, p. 249; Rousseau, *Lettres morales*, pp. 1096–1097.
152. Diderot, *Interprétation*, no. 1 (p. 230 in *O. Phil.*).
153. *Emile*, p. 580.
154. D'Alembert, "Expérimental," 298a; D'Alembert, *Élémens de philosophie*, pp. 163, 337.
155. *Emile*, p. 831.
156. *Second Discourse*, p. 181.
157. *Emile*, p. 550.
158. Some other examples: Rousseau, *Lettres morales*, pp. 1090–1091; *Julie*, p. 427.
159. Rousseau, *Mon portrait*, in *O.C.*, vol. I, p. 1120.
160. In *Emile*, p. 475, Rousseau called for a treatise on the art of observing children.
161. *Julie*, p. 370.
162. Ibid., pp. 491.
163. Ibid., p. 487.
164. *Confessions*, p. 439; *Juge*, p. 778.
165. *Emile*, p. 550; *Lettres morales*, p. 1102; *Julie*, pp. 491–492. Briefly, in the *Dialogues*, when Rousseau decided he was not good for much of anything, he stated that he had been wrong to think of himself as an able observer. *O.C.*, vol. I, pp. 808–809.
166. *Emile*, p. 536.
167. Ibid., p. 348; Rousseau to the Prince de Würtemberg, 15 April 1764, *Corr.* (Leigh), vol. XIX, p. 301.
168. *Julie*, pp. 246–247.
169. *Emile*, p. 733; woman observes, man reasons, p. 737.
170. Ibid., p. 426.
171. Ibid., p. 536.
172. "Observation," *Encyclopédie*, vol. XI, p. 313b.
173. *Emile*, p. 532.
174. *Julie*, pp. 246, 492.
175. Ibid., pp. 296–297.
176. Buffon, *Histoire naturelle de l'homme*, "De l'age viril," pp. 119–123.
177. Diderot, *Sourds et muets*, p. 148; Wilson, *Diderot*, pp. 522, 620.
178. *Emile*, pp. 511, 516, 718.
179. Ibid., pp. 324, 510.
180. Ibid., p. 290.
181. Ibid., pp. 285–286.
182. Ibid., p. 490.
183. Ibid., p. 734.
184. Ibid., pp. 461, 362.
185. *Julie*, pp. 496, 672.
186. *Second Discourse*, p. 133; *Julie*, p. 657.
187. *Emile*, p. 348.

188. Ibid., p. 524.
189. Shklar, *Men and Citizens*, ch. 4, is invaluable.
190. *Second Discourse*, p. 213.
191. *Lettre à d'Alembert*, pp. 166, 168; *Emile*, pp. 270, 463, 509–510, 568–569, 632n–633n, 731, 736.
192. *Emile*, p. 831.
193. Ibid., pp. 325, 640.
194. Ibid., pp. 246, 325.
195. Ibid., p. 426; *Second Discourse*, p. 135.
196. *Emile*, pp. 301–302. In Emile and natural man the senses arouse the imagination; in social man the imagination prematurely stirs the senses. Pp. 495, 657.
197. *Emile*, p. 277. Cf. Buffon, *Histoire naturelle de l'homme*, pp. 24–28, 47–48.
198. *Emile*, pp. 381, 389, 392, 396–397.
199. Ibid., pp. 316–317; cf. Buffon, *O.P.B.*, p. 338a.
200. *Emile*, p. 369.
201. Ibid., p. 483.
202. Ibid., p. 281.
203. Ibid., pp. 428–429.
204. Ibid., pp. 448–450.
205. Ibid., pp. 437–439, 537.
206. Ibid., p. 454.
207. *E.O.L.*, ch. 9, p. 95.
208. *Emile*, p. 503.
209. Ibid., p. 548.
210. *Julie*, p. 96.
211. See *Emile*, p. 246n, for Rousseau's complaint that laws are attentive to property but not to persons, and his recommendation that mothers be granted more authority. His view that women dominate men, sometimes for better, usually for worse, is a constant in his thought, beginning with the *First Discourse*, p. 21n.
212. *Emile*, pp. 742, 746.
213. Ibid., p. 251.
214. Much has been written on Rousseau and women in recent years, but very few such studies pay attention to the historical context or attempt to place Rousseau's position on this subject within his larger scheme of thought. A noteworthy exception is Joel Schwartz, *The Sexual Politics of Jean-Jacques Rousseau* (Chicago: University of Chicago Press, 1984). I disagree, however, with his effort to find an intellectual rationale for Rousseau's relationship with Thérèse, pp. 104–106.
215. *Emile*, p. 665.
216. *Confessions*, pp. 409, 516.
217. Ibid., pp. 408–409; *Julie*, pp. 78–79.
218. Diderot, *Landois*, 29 June 1756, A-T, vol. XIX, p. 435.
219. *Second Discourse*, p. 141.
220. On Lamy, see Hendel, *Rousseau, Moralist*, vol. I, pp. 2–8.
221. Malebranche, *The Search after Truth*, trans. Thomas Lennon (Columbus, Ohio: Ohio State University Press, 1980), pp. xxviii–xxix on the inner light; p. 308 for the vindication of pleasure.

222. On systems as vanity, see Malebranche, *The Search after Truth*, p. 152; cf. *Pref. Narcisse*, pp. 965–966. On women and taste, see *The Search after Truth*, p. 130; cf. *Emile*, pp. 736–737.

223. Malebranche, *The Search after Truth*, pp. 8–9.

224. Knight, *Geometric Spirit*, p. 203. Paul Bénichou, *Morales du Grand Siècle* (Paris: Gallimard, 1948), has much to say on the Jansenist repudiation of the notion of the autonomy of the will. See also Anthony Levi, S.J., *French Moralists* (Oxford: Oxford University Press, 1964). A. J. Krailsheimer, *Studies in Self-Interest* (Oxford: Oxford University Press, 1962), pp. 37–38, argues that the systematic doubt of Descartes is an act of will, not intellect. Two studies by Patrick Riley are vital: *Will and Political Legitimacy* (Cambridge, Mass.: Harvard University Press, 1982) and *The General Will before Rousseau.*

225. Malebranche, *The Search after Truth*, p. 69; *Emile*, p. 483.

226. *Emile*, pp. 285, 324, 361, 380, 392, 396, 421, 458, 483, 486, 654.

227. Rousseau, *Notes sur De l'Esprit*, in *O.C.*, vol. IV, p. 1123.

228. *Emile*, p. 586.

229. Judgment and reason are the same, and both come down to the capacity to compare sensations. *Emile*, p. 486.

230. The reason of the senses, in a good education, is developed before intellectual reason. *Emile*, pp. 370, 417.

231. *Emile*, pp. 317, 486; *Lettres morales*, p. 1090. Cf. Condillac, *E.O.C.H.*, p. 33.

232. Rousseau challenged the equation of virtue with knowledge on historical grounds before repudiating it philosophically. *First Discourse*, p. 16.

233. E.g., Diderot, *Landois*, p. 434; Holbach, *Système social*, vol. I, p. 99.

234. *Social Contract*, p. 371: "La volonté générale est toujours droite."

235. *Social Contract*, pp. 371–372.

236. On "sentiment intérieur," *Emile*, p. 579; Rousseau, *Lettre à M. de Franquières*, in *O.C.*, vol. IV, pp. 1139, 1145. On reason perfected by sentiment, *Emile*, p. 481.

237. *E.O.L.*, chs. 15, 17.

238. *Emile*, p. 286.

239. Ibid., p. 600; *Lettres morales*, p. 1111.

240. *Confessions*, pp. 408–409.

241. *Lettres morales*, pp. 1112–1114.

242. "Cured" is a word frequently used in *Julie*: pp. 415, 417, 495, 618, 740.

243. Diderot, *Supplément au Voyage de Bougainville*, p. 464.

244. *Julie*, p. 509.

245. Ibid., p. 496.

246. Ibid., pp. 354–355, 364.

247. Ibid., pp. 520–521.

248. On *Julie* as an example of the materialism of the sage, see Étienne Gilson, *Les Idées et les lettres* (Paris: J. Vrin, 1932), pp. 275–298, and Georges May, *Rousseau* (Paris: Seuil, 1985), pp. 76–86.

249. Diderot, *Supplément au Voyage de Bougainville*, p. 455.

250. Diderot to Damilaville, 3 Nov. 1760, *Corr.* (Roth), vol. III, p. 216.

251. Buffon, *O.P.B.*, p. 341a; *Second Discourse*, p. 158.

252. Diderot, *Landois*, p. 436.

253. *Emile*, p. 362; *Pol. Econ.*, p. 250; *Julie*, pp. 374, 409, 467.

254. *Mountain*, p. 841.

255. *Emile*, pp. 307–308, 321, 422.

256. *Emile*, p. 820.

257. *Social Contract*, p. 351.

258. Pomeau, *La Religion de Voltaire*, p. 237.

259. Voltaire, *Lettres philosophiques*, letter 25, no. 56; Rousseau found both idealism and materialism dogmatic, *Emile*, p. 571.

260. *Emile*, pp. 271–276.

261. Ibid., pp. 275, 452n.

262. Ibid., p. 411; La Mettrie, *L'Homme machine* (La Salle: Open Court, 1912), pp. 21–22.

263. *Emile*, pp. 414–415.

264. Ibid., pp. 274, 464.

265. Ibid., p. 480.

266. Quoted in Naville, *D'Holbach et la philosophie scientifique au XVIIIe siècle*, p. 111.

267. Holbach, *La Morale universelle*, vol. I, pp. xiii–xiv. Margaret Jacob, *The Radical Enlightenment* (London: Allen & Unwin, 1981), p. 262, is mistaken in saying that Holbach "should not be described as republican." Having decided that materialism and republicanism are linked, she looks for Holbach's politics in the *Système de la nature*, his most notoriously materialistic work, when she should be looking to the *Système social*. She also goes wrong because she fails to see what is missing in Kors' study (on which she relies), namely, an effort to deal seriously with the thought of Holbach or Diderot.

268. Malebranche, *Traité de morale*, pt. I, ch. 2; *Fils*, act IV, scene 3.

269. Holbach, *La Morale universelle*, vol. I, p. 121.

270. Helvétius, *De l'Esprit*, bk. II, chs. 14, 20; bk. III, ch. 15. Helvétius, *De l'Homme*, sect. I, ch. 10, note 25; sect. II, chs. 7, 9. Diderot, *Réfutation de L'Homme*, pp. 293–294, 308.

271. Diderot, *Essai sur les règnes de Claude et de Néron et sur la vie et les écrits de Sénèque*, H, vol. XXV, pp. 247–248, 371. (Hereafter Diderot, *Nero and Seneca*.)

272. Aram Vartanian, *La Mettrie's L'Homme Machine* (Princeton: Princeton University Press, 1960), p. 35.

273. Diderot, *Neveu*, p. 501.

274. La Mettrie, *L'Homme machine*, p. 27.

275. Venturi, *Utopia and Reform*, p. 112, draws attention to Diderot's forfeiture of the notion that criminals can be rehabilitated. But he does not make the connection with La Mettrie.

276. La Mettrie, *Anti-Sénèque, ou Discours sur le bonheur*, in *Oeuvres philosophiques* (Paris: Fayard, 1987), vol. II, p. 62 (hereafter La Mettrie, *Discours sur le bonheur*); cf. Diderot, *Neveu*, p. 433.

277. Diderot, *Nero and Seneca*, p. 248. Cf. Holbach, *Système de la nature*, II, p. 344.

278. La Mettrie, *Discours sur le bonheur*, p. 259.

279. Buffon, *Histoire naturelle de l'homme*, p. 166. The self-punishment argument was so ingrained that even the Nephew took it seriously. Diderot, *Neveu*, p. 484.

280. *Emile*, pp. 269–270, 306.

281. Ibid., p. 680.

6. Judging Jean-Jacques

1. Henri Peyre, *Literature and Sincerity* (New Haven: Yale University Press, 1963); Lionel Trilling, *Sincerity and Authenticity* (Cambridge, Mass.: Harvard University Press, 1972).
2. Max Horkheimer, *Dialectic of Enlightenment* (New York: Herder and Herder, 1972).
3. D'Alembert, *Discours préliminaire*, pp. 161–162.
4. Even quite late in the day Diderot could still view the *First Discourse* as a paradox and a *jeu d'esprit: Réfutation de L'Homme*, A-T, vol. II, pp. 285, 363.
5. Grimm, *Correspondance littéraire, philosophique et critique* (hereafter Grimm, *Corr. litt.*), vol. II, pp. 318–322.
6. *Pref. Narcisse*, p. 969.
7. D'Alembert, *Discours préliminaire*, p. 162.
8. D'Alembert, *Élémens de philosophie*, p. 230.
9. Ibid., pp. 216, 230–231.
10. *Pref. Narcisse*, p. 972.
11. Holbach, *Système social*, vol. III, ch. 5; Holbach, *La Morale universelle*, vol. II, pp. 317ff.
12. Hence some of the philosophes turned to foreigners, who were assigned the role of a "living posterity." E.g., Helvétius, *De l'Homme*, sect. IV, ch. 5, note 13. For d'Alembert's skepticism in this regard, see *Men of Letters*, p. 352.
13. Holbach, *La Morale universelle*, vol. I, p. 105.
14. Grimm, *Corr. litt.*, vol. III, p. 54.
15. Ibid., vol. II, pp. 320–321.
16. Ibid., vol. III, pp. 153–154.
17. Ibid., vol. II, p. 320; vol. III, p. 153; vol. V, pp. 122–123.
18. As Proust notes, there was a debate within the ranks of the philosophes from 1754 to 1759 on free will and the problem of evil. *Diderot et l'Encyclopédie*, pp. 316ff.
19. Voltaire to Rousseau, 30 Aug. 1755, *Corr.* (Leigh), vol. III, pp. 156–157.
20. *L.A.*, p. 77; *Julie*, pp. 358–359; *Emile*, pp. 523n, 636.
21. *Oeuvres de d'Alembert*, vol. V, p. 289; Diderot, *Réfutation de L'Homme*, p. 345.
22. Grimm, *Corr. litt.*, vol. V, p. 137.
23. Deleyre to Rousseau, 3 July 1756, *Corr.* (Leigh), vol. IV, pp. 20–21.
24. John Lough, *Essays on the Encyclopédie of Diderot and D'Alembert* (Oxford: Oxford University Press, 1968), ch. 7.
25. Roger Tisserand, *Les Concurrents de J.-J. Rousseau à l'Académie de Dijon pour le prix de 1754* (Paris: Vesoul, 1936), p. 15.
26. Diderot, *Supplément au Voyage de Bougainville*, pp. 462, 466–467, 503–504, 507, 509.
27. Diderot, *Nero and Seneca*, H, vol. XXV, pp. 119–131, 206, 214, 231, 288, 405.
28. Grimm, *Corr. litt.*, vol. VI, pp. 176–182.
29. Vallette, *Jean-Jacques Rousseau: Genevois*; Spink, *Rousseau et Genève*; Launay, *Jean-Jacques Rousseau*.
30. It is arguable, however, that the aging Diderot, in his contributions to Raynal's *Histoire des Deux Indes*, moved to a position that was more democratic and sympathetic to popular rebellion. E.g., bk. XI, ch. 4, and bk. XVIII, ch. 42, in the edition of 1783. See Anthony Strugnell, *Diderot's Politics: A Study of the Evolution of Diderot's Political Thought after the Encyclopédie* (The Hague: Martinus Nijhoff, 1973), pp. 208, 227–228.

31. See George Havens, *Voltaire's Marginalia on the Pages of Rousseau* (New York: Burt Franklin, 1971; orig. pub. 1933), and Gouhier, *Rousseau et Voltaire*.
32. Or, at the very least, Voltaire would discredit himself. Grimm, *Corr. litt.*, vol. IV, p. 347.
33. Helvétius, *De l'Homme*, sect. II, ch. 6; sect. IV, ch. 3; sect. V, chs. 2, 3.
34. I agree with Henri Gouhier that Rousseau is far more Cartesian in *Emile* than he had been in the *Lettres morales*. Gouhier, "Ce que le Vicaire doit à Descartes," *AJJR*, 35 (1962), 141.
35. Helvétius, *De l'Homme*, sect. I, ch. 8; Diderot to Sophie Volland, 4 Oct. 1767, *Corr.* (Roth), vol. VII, p. 159.
36. D'Alembert, *Lettre à J.-J. Rousseau*, in *Oeuvres de d'Alembert*, vol. IV, pp. 444, 449–450. Grimm, *Corr. litt.*, vol. IV, pp. 100–102; vol. V, pp. 148–154.
37. David Williams, "The Politics of Feminism in the French Enlightenment," in D. Williams and Peter Hughes, eds., *The Varied Pattern* (Toronto: A. M. Hakkert, 1971). Montesquieu was a pioneer in his *Lettres persanes* (1721); Hulliung, *Montesquieu*, ch. V, sect. 2.
38. Diderot to Madame de Maux, *Corr.* (Roth), vol. IX, p. 61, May[?] 1769.
39. Diderot, *Histoire de la Russie*, A-T, vol. XVII, pp. 495–496.
40. Diderot, *Réfutation de L'Homme*, p. 411; cf. p. 287.
41. Ibid., p. 431.
42. Ibid., p. 317; Diderot to Sophie Volland, 25 July 1762, *Corr.* (Roth), vol. IV, p. 72. Helvétius, *De l'Homme*, sect. VIII, ch. 17.
43. Grimm, *Corr. litt.*, vol. III, pp. 53–58; vol. IV, pp. 75–77; Diderot, *Réfutation de L'Homme*, p. 285.
44. E.g., Diderot, *Observations sur le Nakaz*, p. 446.
45. Diderot, *Réfutation de L'Homme*, p. 339.
46. Diderot, *Nero and Seneca*, pp. 266, 436–437. I find the title of Hendel's excellent study *Jean-Jacques Rousseau, Moralist*, to be problematic.
47. D'Alembert, *Discours préliminaire*, p. 143.
48. Grimm, *Corr. litt.*, vol. V, pp. 111–117.
49. Darnton, *Literary Underground*, pp. 199–208.
50. Cranston, *Jean-Jacques*, p. 310n.
51. Gouhier, *Rousseau et Voltaire*, esp. pp. 170, 174, 191–194, 304.
52. Ibid., p. 330.
53. *Second Discourse*, p. 126.
54. *Geneva MS*, pp. 288–289.
55. *Emile*, p. 436. Cranston, *Jean-Jacques*, pp. 248, 347, is wrong to downplay Rousseau's interest in the encyclopedic "chain" and to imply that Rousseau abandoned science.
56. *Confessions*, p. 362.
57. Rousseau to Ribotte, 24 Oct. 1761, *Corr.* (Leigh), vol. IX, p. 201. This formula appears frequently in his writings.
58. *Confessions*, p. 513; cf. pp. 402–403.
59. Well noted by Proust, *Diderot et l'Encyclopédie*, p. 114.
60. Palissot, *Les Originaux*.
61. E.g., Helvétius, *De l'Esprit*, bk. II, chs. 8, 10; bk. IV, ch. 15.
62. Quoted in Jean Guéhenno, *Jean-Jacques Rousseau* (New York: Columbia University Press, 1967), vol. I, p. 397.

63. Diderot, *La Religieuse* in *O.R.*, p. 342.
64. Dieckmann, ed., *Le Philosophe*, p. 46; Holbach, *La Morale universelle*, vol. I, p. 441.
65. Rousseau to Grimm, 26 Oct. 1757, *Corr.* (Leigh), vol. IV, p. 299.
66. Diderot, *Nero and Seneca*, pp. 120, 405, on ingratitude.
67. *Confessions*, p. 627.
68. *Les Contre-Confessions: Histoire de Madame de Montbrillant* (Paris: Mercure de France, 1989), pp. 1234–1235.
69. Diderot, *Nero and Seneca*, p. 206.
70. Diderot's fascination with monsters and the abnormal is already evident in his relatively early (1749) *Lettre sur les aveugles*, in *O. Phil.*, pp. 73–146.
71. Grimm, *Corr. litt.*, vol. IV, p. 345.
72. *Emile*, p. 535.
73. Ibid., p. 731.
74. Ibid., p. 249.
75. Ibid., p. 569.
76. Ibid., p. 510.
77. Ibid., pp. 632n–633n.
78. *Juge*, pp. 967–968.
79. Helvétius, *De l'Homme*, sect. VII, chs. 11–12.
80. See Pierre-Paul Plan, *J.-J. Rousseau raconté par les gazettes de son temps* (Paris: Mercure de France, 1912), p. 102, for evidence that the journalists took note of the significance of Rousseau's action.
81. Diderot, *Nero and Seneca*, p. 437; Grimm, *Corr. litt.*, vol. VIII, p. 463. Helvétius remarked that the priests looked forward to the conversion of Jean-Jacques, the enemy of science. *De l'Homme*, sect. V, ch. 9, note 28.
82. Diderot to Sophie Volland, 18, 25 July 1762. *Corr.* (Roth), vol. IV, pp. 55, 72. Voltaire consistently interpreted Rousseau's religious beliefs as nothing more than an occasion to attack the philosophes.
83. Raymond Trousson, *Rousseau et sa fortune littéraire* (Paris: Nizet, 1977), p. 45.
84. Voltaire to Thieriot, 17 Sept. 1758, *Voltaire's Correspondence* (Besterman), vol. XXXIV, p. 95.
85. *Les Philosophes*, act II, scene 5.
86. *Emile*, p. 509.
87. *L.A.*, p. 190n; *Emile*, p. 632; *Mountain*, p. 758.
88. *Social Contract*, p. 468.
89. The theme of *Rousseau juge de Jean-Jacques* is that there exists a universal conspiracy to defame Rousseau, for which the philosophes are mainly responsible.
90. Diderot, *Éloge de Richardson*, in *O.E.*, pp. 29–48; Diderot, *Nero and Seneca*, p. 125. Cf. Grimm, *Corr. litt.*, vol. IV, pp. 343–346.
91. Against Diderot, Rousseau wrote that Richardson "has the fault common to most insipid writers of romance, who make up for the sterility of their ideas by the aid of characters and incidents." His own novel Rousseau likened to the classically simple and emotionally powerful *Princesse de Clèves* of Madame de La Fayette. *Confessions*, pp. 546–547.
92. Grimm, *Corr. litt.*, vol. V, p. 102. An extract from the text of *Le Nouveau Dédale* may be found in the *AJJR*, 38 (1969–1971), 183–191.
93. Grimm, *Corr. litt.*, vol. VI, p. 181; Cranston, *Jean-Jacques*, pp. 153, 258.

94. Grimm, *Corr. litt.*, vol. V, p. 100; *Confessions*, p. 556.
95. Diderot, *Nero and Seneca*, p. 120.
96. Wilson's account in *Diderot* is judicious, pp. 609–611.
97. Plan, *Gazettes*, pp. 141, 145, 179, 184, 189, 198, 267.
98. *L.A.*, p. 163.
99. Marmontel, *Mémoires* (Clermont-Ferrand: G. de Bussac, 1972), vol. I, bk. 3, p. 63.
100. Voltaire, *Lettres philosophiques*, letter 23.
101. Condillac, *E.O.C.H.*, pt. II, sect. I, ch. 1, ch. 4, no. 34.
102. *E.O.L.*, ch. 1; *Emile*, p. 647.
103. Diderot, *Éloge de Richardson*, p. 35.
104. Rousseau, *Les Rêveries du promeneur solitaire*, in *O.C.*, vol. I, p. 1014.
105. *Confessions*, p. 377.
106. *Second Discourse*, p. 192; *Reveries*, p. 1078; *Juge*, p. 792.
107. Diderot, "Cynique," *Encyclopédie*, vol. IV, pp. 594–599.
108. D'Alembert, *Men of Letters*, pp. 359–360.
109. Rousseau to Voltaire, 30 Jan. 1750, *Corr.* (Leigh), vol. II, pp. 123–124.
110. *First Discourse*, p. 21.
111. Diderot, *Essai sur la peinture*, in *O.E.*, p. 695.
112. *First Discourse*, p. 14; Rousseau, *O.C.*, vol. III, p. 65.
113. *Second Discourse*, p. 192.
114. *Pol. Econ.*, p. 255; Claude Pichois and René Pintard, *Jean-Jacques entre Socrate et Caton* (Paris: José Corti, 1972); Rousseau, *Discours sur la vertu du Héros*, in *O.C.*, vol. II, pp. 1268, 1274.
115. Rousseau, *O.C.*, vol. III, pp. 87–88.
116. Diderot, A-T, vol. XIX, pp. 438–439.
117. *L.A.*, pp. 96–97.
118. "Rousseau the monster" is repeated incessantly in *Rousseau juge de Jean-Jacques*. E.g., in the first dialogue alone, pp. 671, 675, 701, 703, 705, 725, 738, 746, 753, 755, 757, 768–770.
119. *Mon portrait*, p. 1125; *Lettres à Malesherbes*, pp. 1130, 1132; 1144; *Reveries*, p. 1066.
120. *First Discourse*, p. 13. Roger Masters, "Introduction" to *The First and Second Discourses* (New York: St. Martin's, 1964), p. 8n.
121. Raymond Trousson, *Socrate devant Voltaire, Diderot, et Rousseau* (Paris: Minard, 1967), p. 68; Trousson, *Rousseau et sa fortune littéraire*, p. 47.
122. So reported in the gazettes. Plan, *Gazettes*, p. 20.
123. Trousson, *Rousseau et sa fortune littéraire*, p. 48.
124. Holbach, *La Morale universelle*, vol. II, p. 93.
125. Diderot to Madame de Maux[?], summer 1769[?], *Corr.* (Roth), vol. IX, pp. 113–116.
126. Grimm, *Corr. litt.*, vol. V, p. 134.
127. *Emile*, p. 626.
128. Ronald Grimsley, *Rousseau and the Religious Quest* (Oxford: Clarendon Press, 1968), p. 30.
129. Rousseau, *Fiction ou morceau allégorique sur la révélation*, in *O.C.*, vol. IV, pp. 1053–1054; Rousseau, *Lettre à M. de Franquières*, in *O.C.*, vol. IV, pp. 1145–1146.
130. Rousseau to Claude Aglancier de Saint-Germain, 26 Feb. 1770, *Corr.* (Leigh), vol. XXXVII, p. 294.

131. Plan, *Gazettes*, p. 41.
132. Madame d'Épinay, *Histoire de Madame de Montbrillant*, p. 1304; Diderot, Nov. 1768, *Corr.* (Roth), vol. VIII, p. 214.
133. Diderot, *Nero and Seneca*, p. 231.
134. Diderot, *Réfutation de L'Homme*, p. 316.
135. Grimm, *Corr. litt.*, vol. VI, p. 178.
136. *Mountain*, pp. 835, 881.
137. Grimm, *Corr. litt.*, vol. IV, p. 77.
138. Ibid., vol. VI, p. 181.
139. Ibid., vol. V, p. 104.
140. *Reveries*, p. 1082.
141. *L.A.*, p. 163.
142. *Emile*, p. 535.
143. Darnton, *The Great Cat Massacre*, ch. 6; Samuel Taylor, "Rousseau's Contemporary Reputation in France," *SVEC*, 27 (1963), 1557.
144. *Reveries*, p. 1000. The best studies on the relationship between Rousseau's thought and his person are Starobinski, *Jean-Jacques Rousseau*; Ronald Grimsley, *Jean-Jacques Rousseau: A Study in Self-Awareness* (Cardiff: University of Wales Press, 1961); Pierre Burgelin, *La Philosophie de l'existence de J. J. Rousseau* (Paris: Presses Universitaires de France, 1952).
145. Gouhier, *Rousseau et Voltaire*, p. 289.
146. D'Alembert, *Men of Letters*, p. 345.
147. *Pref. Narcisse*, p. 962n.
148. *Confessions*, p. 473.
149. John Pappas and Georges Roth, "Les 'Tablettes' de Diderot," *Diderot Studies*, 3 (1961), 314–315.
150. *Lettres morales*, p. 1106.
151. Rousseau, *O.C.*, vol. I, pp. 1148–1155.
152. *Confessions*, p. 5.
153. Rousseau, *O.C.*, vol. I, p. 1149.
154. *Confessions*, p. 547; *Reveries*, p. 1025.
155. *Confessions*, p. 128.
156. Ibid., pp. 128, 148; *Juge*, p. 829.
157. *Confessions*, p. 86 ("la méchanceté").
158. Ibid., pp. 358–359.
159. Ibid., p. 278.
160. Ibid., p. 357.
161. Ibid., p. 469.
162. Carol Blum, *Diderot* (New York: Viking, 1974), ch. 4.
163. Diderot to Sophie Volland, 20 Dec. 1765, *Corr.* (Roth), vol. V, p. 228.
164. *Est-il bon? Est-il méchant?*, the finale.
165. A-T, vol. XIX, p. 443. Quoted in the *Confessions*, p. 476.
166. *Juge*, p. 813.
167. *Maximes*, nos. 431, 563, 458. See Pierre Nicole, "De la connaissance de soi-même," for a powerful repudiation of the notion of privileged access. Nicole, *Oeuvres philosophiques et morales* (Paris: Hachette, 1845), pp. 11–69.

168. *Juge*, pp. 925, 968.
169. Ibid., p. 985.
170. *Emile*, p. 253.
171. Cf. *Juge*, p. 888.
172. *Reveries*, p. 1051.
173. *Juge*, p. 962.
174. Gouhier, *Rousseau et Voltaire*, p. 308.
175. On the desire to be imprisoned: *Confessions*, pp. 638, 646–647; *Juge*, p. 754; *Reveries*, p. 1041; Rousseau to the Marquise de Verdelin, 8 March 1765, *Corr.* (Leigh), vol. XXIV, p. 172; Plan, *Gazettes*, p. 143; Gouhier, *Rousseau et Voltaire*, p. 307. On remaining free while imprisoned: Rousseau to Moultou, 7 June 1762, *Corr.* (Leigh), vol. XI, p. 36; *Lettres à Malesherbes*, p. 1132; *Reveries*, p. 1048. Ronald Grimsley is wrong, I believe, to construe the statement about freedom in the Bastille as humorous exaggeration: *Jean-Jacques Rousseau*, p. 295. It is a recurring theme, the ground for which was laid in *Emile* with the comment that liberty is in "le coeur de l'homme libre," p. 857.
176. *Juge*, p. 935.
177. *Confessions*, p. 417.
178. E.g., *Juge*, p. 939.
179. *Juge*, p. 812.
180. Rousseau to Mademoiselle Henriette, 7 May 1764, *Corr.* (Leigh), vol. XX, p. 19.
181. *Emile*, p. 550.
182. *Juge*, p. 816.
183. *Reveries*, pp. 1047, 1063.
184. Ibid., p. 1046.
185. Ibid., pp. 1046–1047; 1062–1063.
186. *Juge*, p. 794.
187. *Reveries*, pp. 1000–1001.
188. Ibid., p. 995.
189. Rousseau claimed his was a life setting an example for others in the *Lettres à Malesherbes*, p. 1143. See Christopher Kelly, *Rousseau's Exemplary Life: The Confessions as Political Philosophy* (Ithaca: Cornell University Press, 1987).

Conclusion

1. Plan, *Gazettes*, p. 179.
2. Voltaire to Madame du Deffand, 27 Dec. 1758, *Voltaire's Correspondence* (Besterman), vol. XXXIV, p. 267.
3. Rousseau to Vincent-Bernard Tscharner, 29 April 1762, *Corr.* (Leigh), vol. X, p. 226.
4. *L.A.*, p. 71.
5. Diderot, *Nero and Seneca*, pp. 228, 437.
6. E.g., Grimm, *Corr. litt.*, vol. VIII, p. 463.
7. Frank Manuel never deals with Rousseau in his important studies of philosophical history. The first volume of Gay's *The Enlightenment* is a philosophical history that omits Rousseau. One study of philosophical history that does pay some attention to

Rousseau is Ronald Meek, *The Ignoble Savage* (Cambridge: Cambridge University Press, 1976), ch. 3. In general, however, Meek's focus is on the Scottish Enlightenment.

8. Mark Hulliung, *Citizen Machiavelli* (Princeton: Princeton University Press, 1983).

9. *Emile*, p. 821; *Julie*, p. 693.

10. Rousseau to Ribotte, 24 Oct. 1761, *Corr.* (Leigh), vol. IX, p. 201.

11. *Social Contract*, p. 391.

12. *Poland*, p. 1010; Helvétius, *De l'Homme*, sect. IX, chs. 2, 4.

Index

Addison, John, 114, 116
Alembert, Jean Le Rond d', 6, 7, 23–24, 38, 77, 82, 85, 88–94, 95, 98, 104, 106, 112, 126–127, 129, 160–163, 202–203, 209; conjectural history, 53, 163; cultural versus political history, 40–42, 44, 47–48; natural rights, 171; republicanism, 120, 204; rural life, 146; self-doubt, 88–94, 98; self-interest, 21, 89, 142, 206; "systems" in scientific thought, 161, 182; theater, 126
Alexander the Great, 41, 105, 140, 205
Aquinas, St. Thomas, 241
Argenson, René-Louis de Voyer, marquis d', 77, 121–123
Aristophanes, 226
Aristotle, 41, 51, 81, 141, 215, 241
Arnauld, Antoine, 10, 13, 42
Augustine, St., 10
Augustus, 41, 48, 120, 140, 205

Bacon, Francis, 46, 57, 181
Balzac, Jean-Louis Guez de, 82
Bayle, Pierre, 16, 78, 111
Beaumont, Christophe de, archbishop of Paris, 223
Beccaria, Cesare, 1, 6
Bentham, Jeremy, 5, 9, 19, 22, 35
Berthier, Father Guillaume-François, 218
Bodin, Jean, 121
Bolingbroke, Henry St. John, first viscount, 115

Bossuet, Jacques-Bénigne, bishop of Meaux, 10, 48, 66, 112
Boucher, François, 22
Boucher d'Argis, Antoine-Gaspard, 32
Boulanger, Nicolas-Antoine, 27
Brumfitt, J. H., 2
Bruni, Leonardo, 42
Buffier, Father Claude, 30–31
Buffon, Georges Louis Leclerc, comte de, 7, 53, 60, 116, 157, 159, 169, 172–179, 181, 182, 184, 195, 200, 205
Burke, Edmund, 24

Caesar, Julius, 41, 48, 224
Calvin, Jean, and Calvinism, 126, 129
Cassirer, Ernst, 2–3, 157
Catherine the Great, 106–109, 119, 129–131, 204, 207
Cato, 101, 223–226
Châtelet, Emilie du, 144
Chaumeix, Abraham-Joseph de, 218
Choiseul, Étienne-François, duc de, 92
Cicero, 41, 48, 78, 119, 120, 126, 205
Clermont, Louis de Bourbon-Condé, comte de, 84
Colbert, Jean-Baptiste, 87, 122
Condillac, Étienne Bonnot de, abbé, 53, 55–56, 60, 67, 73–74, 79, 158, 163–165, 167–172, 179, 182, 190, 192–193, 196, 202, 221
Condorcet, Antoine-Nicolas de, 36, 39, 47, 54, 161, 171
Confucius, 58